About Island Press

Island Press is the only nonprofit organization in the United States whose principal purpose is the publication of books on environmental issues and natural resource management. We provide solutions-oriented information to professionals, public officials, business and community leaders, and concerned citizens who are shaping responses to environmental problems.

In 1994, Island Press celebrated its tenth anniversary as the leading provider of timely and practical books that take a multidisciplinary approach to critical environmental concerns. Our growing list of titles reflects our commitment to bringing the best of an expanding body of literature to the environmental community throughout North America and the world.

Support for Island Press is provided by Apple Computer, Inc., The Bullitt Foundation, The Geraldine R. Dodge Foundation, The Energy Foundation, The Ford Foundation, The W. Alton Jones Foundation, The Lyndhurst Foundation, The John D. and Catherine T. MacArthur Foundation, The Andrew W. Mellon Foundation, The Joyce Mertz-Gilmore Foundation, The National Fish and Wildlife Foundation, The Pew Charitable Trusts, The Pew Global Stewardship Initiative, The Rockefeller Philanthropic Collaborative, Inc., and individual donors.

The
Environment
and
NAFTA

In the hope that the dropping of barriers to trade presages the continental recognition of a shared responsibility toward our seamless environment

The

Environment
and

NAFTA

Understanding and Implementing
the New Continental Law

Pierre Marc Johnson
André Beaulieu

ISLAND PRESS

Washington, D.C. ● Covelo, California

Published in Canada by Broadview Press, P.O. Box 1243, Peterborough, Ontario K9J 7H5.

Library of Congress Cataloging-in-Publication Data

Johnson, Pierre Marc
    The environment and NAFTA: understanding and implementing
the new continental law/ Pierre Marc Johnson, André Beaulieu.
        p.   cm.
    Includes bibliographical references and index.
    ISBN 1-55963-467-7 (cloth: acid-free paper). — ISBN
1-55963-468-5 (paper: acid-free paper)
    1. Environmental law—North America. 2. Environmental policy—
America. 3. Free trade—Environmental aspects—North
America. I. Beaulieu, André. II. Title.
KDZ670.J64   1996
341.7'62—dc20   95-46911
                                                      CIP

Canadian Cataloging-in-Publication Data

Johnson, Pierre Marc
    The environment and NAFTA: understanding and implementing
the new continental law
Includes bibliographical references and index.
ISBN: 1-55111-113-6

1. Environmental law—North America. 2. Environmental policy—North America.
3. Free Trade—Environmental aspects—North America. I. Beaulieu. André.

KDZ670.J64 1996   341.7'62   C95-933034-8

Printed on recycled, acid-free paper ✪
Manufactured in the United States of America
10 9 8 7 6 5 4 3 2 1

Contents

Foreword

The North American Agreement on Environmental Cooperation (NAAEC), concluded in August 1993, marked a major step in the legal, political, and institutional regimes affecting environmental protection and trade and environment processes in North America. This book is the first systematic attempt to understand the legal consequences for the environment of the NAFTA and its accompanying side agreement, the NAAEC.

The NAAEC represents the conclusion of a debate surrounding NAFTA about the proper balance between trade and the environment and future directions for North American environmental enhancement. It also offers a significant opportunity to build on the existing North American framework through its Commission for Environmental Cooperation. The Commission provides a forum to aid the NAFTA Parties in avoiding and resolving environment and trade disputes, and it sets up a mechanism for cooperation in the development of sound and viable environmental policies, the enforcement of environmental laws and regulations, the optimum use of environmental technology, and the reduction of pollution in North America.

The Agreement and the Commission are looked to with a great sense of expectation by a wide range of communities of stakeholders within, and beyond, North America. In practice, the extent to which these opportunities are realized and the particular directions they take will ultimately be defined by the specific elements of the legal agreement itself and the work of the Commission and their governments, in elaborating and implementing the mandate of the agreement. This is particularly the case as many of the legal elements embodied in the Agreement are novel and without precedent and will therefore be subject to ongoing interpretation in the context of evolving environmental concerns of North Americans.

It is thus vital that legal scholars with a deep understanding of, and practical experience in, the broader policy context within which the NAFTA and NAAEC's legal regime will take effect explore in detail, with sensitivity, and in a forward-looking way, the provisions and potential of the NAAEC. Pierre Marc Johnson and André Beaulieu are exceptionally well positioned to take up this task. It is a challenge that requires the legal and analytic talents of those with distinguished experience in government and working with international institutions on a regional and global scale. It draws on considerable years of experience working with the many communities that form the constituencies of both NAFTA and the Commission, and who all have a stake in the successful resolution of trade concerns with the environment. More broadly, this task calls for an understanding of the human dimensions of sustainable development and a broad concern for social justice and equity.

This book is particularly timely. It will have a growing relevance as the provisions in the agreement are tested in its implementation and as the governments, their publics, and perhaps the Commission itself take up the larger task of addressing how the innovative NAAEC regime might be relevant to new issues that arise. At a time when the three parties of the NAFTA are committed to geographically broader processes of trade liberalization and environmental dialogue, the innovative provisions and far-reaching potential of the NAAEC stand out as an intellectual model and an institutional platform on which to build.

This book will represent a major contribution to the literature for legal professionals, policy makers, teachers, and students. The Commission for Environmental Cooperation enthusiastically welcomes the efforts of the authors. This book represents an important contribution to the work that has been undertaken by North Americans in their attempt to develop a deeper understanding of the economic and environmental interdependencies among us, and to an intellectual assessment of their implications for the future and their relevance to the ongoing hemispheric and global experience.

VICTOR LICHTINGER
Executive Director
Commission for Environmental Cooperation
Montreal, August 1995

Preface

Globalization is not only about more trade and investment. Enhanced commercial relations between the United States and the rest of the world, including its major and immediate partners Canada and Mexico, also means more people moving, more ideas exchanged and confronted, as well as a sharing in all three countries of concerns among citizens, civil organizations, and governments about the impacts of trade. This is the social agenda of trade liberalization of which environmental concerns represents a major and enduring component. While the United States agreed with Canada and Mexico to increase trade between the three countries, it also wanted the partners to include environment-related provisions in the legally binding commercial agreement. To what extent can the United States, Mexico, or Canada implement on their territory international treaties to protect the ozone layer or save endangered species using measures that adversely affect trade? To what extent is the sovereignty of each country limited as it adopts environmental legislation, consumer protection regulations, or measures that are there to protect the health of humans, animals, or plants, when these measures affect the trading of goods between the three commercial partners? How does this new trade agreement address the concept of weakening one's environmental legislation to attract new industries?

These are all very practical questions, not only asked by the environmental community but also by those whose chief interest is trade policy or the efficient operation of their international business. This book analyzes those preoccupations that were at least partially addressed in the 1992 North American Free Trade agreement between the United States, Canada, and Mexico. It soon became obvious during that presidential election year that more would have to be done. The three countries, after having wound up their discussions on trade and *some* environmental issues, began negotiating a very broad-scoped agreement of environmental cooperation (science, education, training, implementation and enforcement of legislation, standard harmonization questions, and so on). By doing so, the United States, Canada, and Mexico set up an original and novel set of institutions designed to implement a new (and untried) set of continental law.

As the commercial and the environmental agreements are gradually implemented, at the very moment Chile's accession to NAFTA is contemplated, it seemed to the authors appropriate and timely that this book should be made available to trade experts, the environmental community, as well as to academics and students concerned about law, trade, environment, and the social agenda of trade in the Americas. This work purports to contribute to the understanding of the design and operation of new North American institutions.

The authors thus hope that this book will allow a broad, specialized, or concerned audience to better grasp, through the presentation of this new continental law regime, the fundamentals of economic and social integration in the hemisphere.

Acknowledgments

This book evolved in the context of four years of collaboration between the authors on international environmental policy issues. Invited to give the November 1993 Ambassador's lecture, held jointly with the Fulbright Foundation, at the Canadian Embassy in Washington, D.C., Pierre Marc Johnson collaborated with André Beaulieu, then his research assistant at McGill Law School, to prepare a 40-minute piece on the environmental aspects of NAFTA. As a result of this cooperative effort, and following the advice of Ken Thomas who has helped both authors on a number of occasions, the two jointly published a short article in the *Journal of Environmental Law and Practice* in the spring of 1994. By then, the authors had accumulated an important database on the subject and resolved to write a book.

Beyond the usual written legal and policy analysis materials, abundantly quoted in this work, they were able to build on related seminars, meetings, research, and conferences coordinated by Sarah Richardson for the Foreign Policy Committee of the National Round Table on Environment and the Economy of Canada, which Pierre Marc Johnson has had the honor of chairing for the past five years. The McGill Hydro-Québec Chair on Environment and Ethics provided support at a crucial time for the project.

The authors are particularly indebted to five students of the McGill Law School—foremost, to Colin Chang for his remarkable input on commercial law aspects essential to the quality of Part II, devoted to NAFTA. We were also well supported by the assistance of Jay Sinha, Murray Mincoff, and Jean-Philippe Brisson. Without Anick Morin's contribution, the tables and charts in Appendix I would not have been as instructive or useful.

We extend our deep appreciation to all those institutions or persons mentioned above, those persons we interviewed, and those who generously shared their thoughts or read through materials, and in particular personnel of negotiation teams from Mexico, Canada, and the United States, members of the North American Commission for Environmental Cooperation, its Joint Public Advisory Committee, or its Secretariat, particularly its Executive Director Victor Lichtinger, as well as colleagues from various universities and nongovernmental organizations.

Many others were incipient to this intellectual endeavor by making data available, commenting, sharing concepts, confirming facts, or simply supporting the effort. They are too numerous to name all. Yet, we wish to extend our appreciation in particular to David Angell, Frédéric Beauvais, Conrad Black, Fmr. Amb. Derek Burney, Steve Charnovitz, Fmr. Amb. Gen. John de Chastelain, Amb. Raymond Chrétien, Denis Comeau, Aaron Cosbey, Anne Cronin-Cossette, Ann Dale, Ron Doering, Anne Fouillard, Eric Frothingham, Sanford Gaines, Karl Grenier, Leonard Good, Robert Housman, Stuart Hudson, Terry Karl, John Kirton, Gilles Lamoureux, Roderick MacDonald, Armand de Mestral, Ian McDonald, Daniel McGraw, Yves-Marie Morrissette, Jacques Neatby, Gustavo Alanis Ortega, Robert Page, Marc Paquin, Andrès Rozenthal, Michelle Schwartz, Frederic Seppey, Nevin Shaw, Bill Shea, Mauricio Siciliano, Dick Smith, Stephen Toope, Sheila Tooze, David Von Hoogstraten, Konrad Von Moltke, The Hon. Peter Watson, John Weekes, Peter White, and John Wirth.

We wish to thank for their efficient and often good humored assistance Louise Généreux and Linda Hunt, our secretarial staff. Finally, we must underline the patience of our families and friends who have graciously tolerated the encroachment of this project on time normally spent with them.

In addition, Pierre Marc Johnson would like to thank his long-time friend and colleague, Jacques Laurent, senior Partner at the law firm of Guy & Gilbert in Montréal, for his active encouragement and support throughout this project. Above and foremost, Pierre Marc Johnson wishes to express his gratitude to his co-author and collaborator, André Beaulieu.

Introduction

This book deals with NAFTA's environmental implications. It is about the context in which such implications were brought to the negotiating table and the legal mechanism put in place to address them, as well as the original trilateral institution set up to maintain the focus on environmental cooperation at the continental level.

On 17 December 1992 Canada, Mexico, and the United States entered into a historic trade pact, the *North American Free Trade Agreement* (NAFTA).[1] Short of a common market, this agreement, which entered into force on 1 January 1994, is the most comprehensive framework regarding trade and investment ever signed between such large sovereign countries.

A number of major issues such as labor market disruptions or import surges surrounded the debate over the agreement and fueled the NAFTA controversy. No argument, however, received as much coverage as the impact of NAFTA on the environment. In the three countries, opponents as well as proponents of the trade treaty used the environ-

---

1. *North American Free Trade Agreement*, 8 December 1992, Canada–Mexico–United States, 32 I.L.M. 289 [hereinafter NAFTA]. See Appendix II. See also: *North American Free Trade Agreement Implementation Act*, S.C. 1993, c.44; *North American Free Trade Agreement Implementation Act*, Pub. L. No. 103–182, 107 Stat. 2057.

ment to support their positions. The intensity and the relevance of this debate prompted the American, Canadian, and Mexican governments to include unprecedented environmental provisions in NAFTA and to sign a supplemental *North American Agreement on Environmental Cooperation* (NAAEC)[2] in late summer of 1993, a few weeks before the ratification vote in the U.S. Congress. The NAAEC also entered into force on 1 January 1994.

This book is thus about the important and ground-breaking international environmental public policy-making that took place in the context of NAFTA. Special attention is devoted to the role and positions of nongovernmental organizations (NGOs), as their contribution to both the emergence of the NAFTA environmental debate and its resolution in trilateral arrangements is central to the short history of NAFTA. This book also seeks, at an early stage, to inform the reader's understanding of the environmental stakes in NAFTA and the context in which the three governments had to integrate environmental concerns in a large, complex, commercial negotiation. It dwells at length on the innovative strategies and techniques that were used to devise the final legal package, their inadequacies, and their great potential. International law is the main tool of analysis of this book because in the international context, the boundaries between law and policy remain very porous and each informs the other. International environmental cooperation between states is usually formalized in legal instruments, and such instruments often form the foundation upon which cooperation is then expanded further. The reader will find more than a descriptive attempt at stating the new law in the light of international precedents, or an illustrated narrative of how environmental issues came to be so prevalent in the NAFTA debate. Rather, the authors are commenting at length on the policy and strategic choices embedded in the agreements, while always trying to let the reader know when analysis becomes opinion. It is hoped that the balance struck between traditional legal analysis and policy commentary will provide the reader with useful insight.

This book is also a modest attempt at gauging the impact of globalization (and, in the case of North America, regionalization or conti-

---

2. *North American Agreement on Environmental Cooperation*, 8 September 1993, Canada–Mexico–United States, 32 I.L.M. 1480 [hereinafter NAAEC]. See Appendix III. See also: *An Act to Amend the Crown Liability and Proceedings Act;* S.C. 1994, c.11; *Federal Implementation of the North American Agreement on Environmental Cooperation,* Executive Order 12915 U.S.C.C.A.N. (108 Stat.) B42.

nentalization) on our efforts to protect the human environment. NAFTA is of course very important for the future of Canada, Mexico, and the United States, but it has a larger significance. The Caribbean countries, North, South, and Latin America seem to be moving swiftly toward tighter commercial relations and even a form of economic integration. Hardly a month goes by without the announcement of a new trade initiative in the region. While the debate on how such integration will proceed is far from over, it is plain to see that the so-called social agenda of trade, which includes environmental, labor, and broad human rights issues, will and should remain a pressing concern. NAFTA puts forth a particular (and largely untried) model of cooperation on labor and environmental issues between trade partners that will durably influence the process and the substance of economic integration in the Americas. Indeed, to know how NAFTA parties have chosen to address environmental issues may provide a glimpse at the future of regional environmental cooperation.

After the Miami Summit of the Americas in December 1994, one might say that the New World finds itself at a crossroad encountered by the Old European World half a century ago. Evidently, as the circumstances and the actors are very different, the way the economic area of the Americas will be built will be vastly different than that which led to the establishment of the current European Union. It is safe to say that NAFTA and its successor agreements will not yield an institutional harvest as abundant as that of Europe for a very long time, if ever. Nevertheless, the same fundamental principle seems to be at work: trade and investment liberalization forcing states into a much broader cooperative agenda on social issues. In and of itself, the environmental aspects are important and merit much inquiry and study. Because the environmental cooperative agenda is the most advanced, however, it might tell us a lot about the future of the rest of the social agenda of trade in the region.

There are at least three specific ways in which the environmental content of the NAFTA package will influence the broader geographic trade and investment liberalization efforts. First, it creates an institution, namely the Commission for Environmental Cooperation (CEC), that will have a legitimacy and an expertise of its own and that may in turn become an important actor in the unfolding integration process. As a small step toward the recognition of shared sovereignties in the environmental jurisdiction, it might become the focus of attention of would-be NAFTA partners. Second, the parallel environmental agreement, NAAEC, institutes an environmental dispute settlement process of a peculiar kind that could, in time, become a genuine rule-generating instrument. Such rules will often find a broader constituency in the region if they favor both environmental protection and smoother trade competition. Third, NAAEC sketches the outline of a new, more significant role for nongovernmental organizations in international environmental forums. Environmental groups and their allies will argue intensely for such new openings to be replicated in regional and global trade and environmental arrangements.

This broader context is a further reason why the significance of NAFTA's environmental choices can hardly be overestimated. This book will therefore attempt to explain how the functioning of NAFTA (and its interaction with the environmental parallel agreement) might take place and how they will impact on trade policy and practices, domestic and regional environmental protection efforts, and the relationships among Canada, Mexico, and the United States.

Part I of this book, devoted to the general context of NAFTA and the debate surrounding its environmental implications, will be divided in two chapters. The first will present cursorily the political and historical context of North American trade and political relations in the early 1990s. It will also consider the relatively new place that environmental concerns and their promoters, the nongovernmental organizations (NGOs), occupy in the political landscape of the continent, especially in the area of foreign and trade policy. The second chapter of Part I will provide some insight into the recent but heated debate over the relationships among international trade, the environment, and the elusive search for sustainable development. This backdrop of GATT negotiations and global questioning is essential in assessing the shortcomings and the progress achieved by NAFTA.

Part II will present and analyze, in the light of precedents, the provisions of NAFTA that refer to or may have an impact on environmental policies and measures taken to implement them. Close attention will be paid to the treatment of environmental measures by NAFTA's standards-related trade disciplines, including the relevant NAFTA sections on sanitary and phytosanitary measures, technical barriers to trade, and the special provisions on international environmental agreements. Part II will, moreover, examine the provisions of NAFTA that address the concern that pollution havens may act as investment magnets, as well as the treatment of environmental standards harmonization under NAFTA.

Part III is concerned specifically with the NAAEC and its potential for improving environmental cooperation in North America. The origins of this environmental side-agreement will be explained and possibilities for its relationship with NAFTA and NAFTA institutions will be examined. Part III will also describe the newly created Commission for Environmental Cooperation and its three component parts: the Council (of Ministers), the permanent Secretariat, and the Joint Public Advisory Committee (JPAC), as well as the broad mandates that were given to those three bodies by the NAFTA parties. Special attention will be paid to two aspects of the NAAEC: first, the special investigatory reporting functions of the CEC, and second, its relationship with NGOs.

Part IV will focus on the formal procedures for the settlement of disputes that relate to the effectiveness of domestic environmental enforcement practices. Particular attention will be given to the issues of what constitutes sanctionable ineffective environmental enforcement, the definition of environmental laws and regulations, the possible consequences for noncompliance by parties with environmental enforcement obligations, as well as a special set of rules that apply only to Canada.

Part V will present the authors' preliminary conclusions on the environmental record of the NAFTA/NAAEC package and offer some suggestions on how to ensure that the new institutions and procedures set forth in both trilateral agreements translate into concrete gains for the environment. Finally, recalling the broader regional and global context, the authors will attempt to assess the meaning of NAFTA and NAAEC for the next stages of Pan-American economic integration and environmental cooperation.

Part I

The Context of
NAFTA and NAAEC

A thorough assessment of NAFTA's environmental impact this early in its implementation would be difficult to complete, especially because the NAAEC, at the time of writing, is still in its very early implementation stages.[1] After all, as one commentator remarked, "almost all the environmental aspects of the NAFTA package are unprecedented, par-

---

1. Only the United States has conducted an environmental review (though not a full-fledged environmental impact assessment study) of the whole NAFTA/NAAEC package, under the title *Report of Environmental Issues,* in addendum to the *Message from the President of the United States Transmitting North American Free Trade Agreement Supplemental Agreements,* 103rd Cong., 1st Sess., 4 November 1993, H. Doc. 103–160. Canada has conducted an environmental review of NAFTA, before the NAAEC was concluded. See Government of Canada, *North American Free Trade Agreement: Canadian Environmental Review* (Queen's Printer: Ottawa, October 1992). Mexico has not released publicly any environmental review of NAFTA that it may have conducted.

ticularly in the context of a trade agreement."[2] In fact the overall impact of trade liberalization regimes on the environment is still a hotly debated issue. By putting the NAFTA package, including the NAAEC, in a broader intellectual and factual context, it is possible to arrive at some preliminary conclusions on the effects of these international arrangements on domestic environmental policies. Part I is devoted to providing such a context. First, the historical and regional context of NAFTA will be presented along four axes: the evolution of the complex and ambivalent relationships Canada and Mexico have established with the United States over the years in the pre-NAFTA era; the nature of trade liberalization initiatives; the rise of environmental issues in the public consciousness of North Americans; and the central role of NGOs, particularly U.S. NGOs, on the negotiation process that resulted in NAFTA and NAAEC. Then, the five main arguments against trade and trade liberalization rules developed by environmentalists and repeatedly invoked in the NAFTA debate will be presented. They are: (1) trade is the engine of unsustainable economic growth; (2) trade disciplines are a threat to domestic environmental regulations; (3) trade is a vehicle for downward competitive pressures on environmental norms; (4) trade rules are a bar on environmentally inspired trade measures; and (5) the secrecy and lack of access that surround the international trade process and institutions prevents citizens from bringing forth their environmental concerns. All five will be cursorily outlined to provide necessary background. This survey will also touch on the problem of the contamination of the environmental arguments by other policy agendas that appear during trade negotiations and often weaken and threaten the coherence of otherwise legitimate environmental concerns. The NAFTA debate and the trade and environment controversy are essential to our understanding as both are still enduring well after the ratification of NAFTA.

---

2. D. Magraw, "NAFTA's Repercussions: Is Green Trade Possible?" (March 1994) 35 Environment 14 at 14.

Chapter 1

Historical and Regional Context

Historical Developments

There are remarkable similarities between both Canada's and Mexico's ambivalent relationship with their powerful American neighbor. The need to manage physical and economic proximity with the American behemoth has led both to develop various forms of defensive nationalism and fear of U.S. political influence. Both have tried to keep a safe distance from the United States by anchoring themselves in international groupings. Mexico has become an important leader in the developing world and maintains independent policies despite significant influence from the United States. Canada has used its membership first in the British Empire, then in the Commonwealth, the *Francophonie,* and UN institutions as a counterweight to the American gravitational pull—even though it has long ago become a trusted ally of the United States. The relationships have remained uneasy for both Canada and Mexico. For example, the 20th century has seen both countries erect tariff walls and adopt investment screening procedures to slow American economic and corporate penetration, with varying degrees of failure. Yet, in Canada the debate over "reciprocity," or free trade with the United States, was already a major electoral issue at the turn of the century, while Mexico negotiated two never-implemented trade agreements with the United States in the 19th century.[3]

It is worth mentioning that environmental issues, with the notable exception of water management around border areas, particularly in the Great Lakes Basin and along the Rio Grande, did not become prominent in North American bilateral relationships until the 1970s and early 1980s.[4] By the time NAFTA negotiations started, however, there already had existed a rich history of bilateral environmental cooperation and many treaties existed between the United States, Mexico, and Canada.[5]

In the 1980s, America's relationship with its two neighbors underwent profound change. In Mexico, after the 1982 debt crisis, liberal economic reformers in that country took charge and proposed a radi-

---

3. See William R. Manning, *Early Diplomatic Relations Between the United States and Mexico* (Baltimore: Johns Hopkins University Press, 1916) at 229–51; Christian L. Wiktor, ed., *Unperfected Treaties of the United States of America* (Dobbs Ferry: Oceana, 1976); Alfred Ecks, "U.S.–Mexican Trade, 1880's Style" *Journal of Commerce* (10 September 1992) at 8A.

4. The seminal treaty of the earlier part of the 20th century is the *Treaty Relating to Boundary Waters and Questions Arising Along the Boundary Between the U.S. and Canada,* 11 January 1909, United States–United Kingdom, 36 Stat. 2448, U.S.T. 548 [hereinafter *Canada–U.S. Water Boundary Treaty*].

5. To name a few important ones: the *North American Plant Protection Agreement,* 28 October 1976, Canada–Mexico–United States, 28 U.S.T. 6223 T.I.A.S. No. 8680; the *Canada–United States Air Quality Agreement,* 13 March 1991, 30 I.L.M. 676; the *Mexico–United States Agreement to Cooperate in the Solution of Environmental Problems in the Border Area,* 14 August 1983, 22 I.L.M. 1025 (commonly referred to as the *La Paz Agreement);* the *Mexico–United States Agreement on Cooperation for the Protection and the Improvement of the Environment of the Metropolitan Area of Mexico City,* 3 October 1989, 29 I.L.M. 25; the *United States–Mexico Convention Touching the Boundary Line Between the Two Countries Where It Follows the Bed of the Rio Grande and the Rio Colorado,* 12 November 1884, 24 Stat. 1011, 9 Bevans 865, T.S. 226; the *Great Lakes Water Quality Agreement,* 22 November 1978, United States–Canada, Can. T.S. 1978 No. 20, 30 U.S.T. 1384, T.I.A.S. No. 9257. There were also international conventions to which all three countries were party, the best known being *Convention on Nature Protection and Wild Life Preservation in the Western Hemisphere,* 12 October 1940, 565 Stat 1354, 1368. For further reading see Don Munton and John Kirton, "North American Cooperation: Bilateral, Trilateral, Multilateral" (March 1994) 4 North American Outlook 59 at 60–68 [hereinafter "Bilateral"]; Don Munton, "Great Lakes Water Quality: A Study in Environmental Politics and Diplomacy" in O.P. Dwivedi, ed., *Resources and the Environment: Policy Perspectives for Canada* (Toronto: McClelland and Stewart, 1980). See also: Steve Charnovitz, "NAFTA's Social Dimension: Lessons From the Past and Framework for the Future" (1994) 8 *Int'l Trade J.* 39 at 41–4 [hereinafter "NAFTA's Social Dimension"].

cal program of deregulation, privatization, and the rationalization of public finances. Establishing trade arrangements to better integrate Mexico into the economic network of the region and the hemisphere and to improve market access represents an almost necessary corollary of these policies. In Canada, the Progressive Conservative government of Prime Minister Brian Mulroney, elected in 1984, declared Canada "open for business" and adopted an approach to bilateral discussions with the United States that was more conciliatory than that of the previous Liberal administration. The same year, the United States signed its first major bilateral free trade agreement with the state of Israel, an agreement that influenced the text of later U.S. trade treaties.[6] In 1986, the government of Canada followed up by asking for formal free trade negotiations with the Reagan administration.

By the end of 1988, the *Canada–United States Free Trade Agreement*[7] was signed and ratified, and came into force on 1 January 1989 without any sustained public discussion or even vague assessment of its environmental impacts and despite the fact that Canada–U.S. FTA would become a pivotal issue in the Canadian federal elections that year. The Canada–U.S. FTA provided the basis and substance for most chapters of NAFTA, with two notable exceptions: new language on intellectual property and, most important for our purposes, a clearer link between trade rules and environmental protection. Then Vice President George Bush was the first to publicly call for a NAFTA-type agreement with Mexico.[8] In the spring of 1990, Mexico's President Carlos Salinas de Gortari, seeking to complement his market-oriented reforms by obtaining better access to American markets, officially requested that negotiations for a free trade agreement with the United States be undertaken. The United States obliged the Mexican government because it saw a significant opportunity to solidify its relationship with a major trade partner and create the foundation for a continental or even hemispheric trade bloc. Shortly after, in June of that year, Canada asked to be included in what then became full-blown North American trade liberalization negotiations. It is important to note that Canada reacted to the Mexican–American initiative. It did not have, at least in the beginning of 1990, North American free trade

---

6. *United States–Israel Free Trade Agreement*, 22 April 1985, 24 I.L.M. 653.

7, 22 December 1987, Can. T.S. 1989 No. 3, 27 I.L.M. 281 [hereinafter Canada–U.S. FTA].

8. See "Candidate's Trade Policy Statements Show There May Be Substance After All," (1988) 59 Metals Week 3.

as an element of its own trade and foreign policy agenda. The Canadian government felt there was a risk it would be left out of a larger trade area revolving around the United States if it did not join the discussions. The objective of the Canadian government was thus to avoid the emergence of a "hub and spoke" architecture for trade relations in the Americas, a mode of trade liberalization where it feared it would be subjected to the economic and political consequences without having a proper say. This time, it became clear early on to those involved that the resolution of certain environmental issues would be critical to the conclusion of an agreement.

Environmental issues achieved such a high profile in the NAFTA discussions largely because NAFTA is a true North–South comprehensive trade agreement. Two of the world's richest countries and a fast developing country sat down to negotiate and lay out rules that would govern their commercial relationship, thereby gradually opening up their economies to near-full competition with each other. The difference in wealth and in social and economic development between the partners made the social agenda of trade immensely more relevant than in the Canada–United States FTA negotiations.

Trade Liberalization: Multilateralism and Regional Initiatives

NAFTA is the most systematic effort yet by governments to address the wave of change coming with economic integration of the three countries of North America. The agreement, as it is implemented, will provide extensive rules on trade in goods and services, some guidelines for competition policy, and a common framework for investments and the protection of intellectual property for an economic zone where 360 million consumers partake in an annual three-way trade partnership representing $300 billion.

NAFTA is a regional trade agreement; its focus remains economic rather than environmental. It erects a framework for commerce, not for environmental cooperation. The reader will discover in the following pages that the authors do not believe that traditional trade agreements like NAFTA and the 1994 GATT can go very far beyond adequate sensitivity toward positive actions in favor of the environment. Other instruments are needed.

In recent years, the fortunes of trade liberalization have varied a great deal. Overall, regional trade initiatives, whether in Europe, Asia, or the Americas, have been more successfully and swiftly negotiated than global multilateral liberalization efforts under the auspices of the

General Agreement on Tariffs and Trade (GATT).[9] That the GATT parties could agree, in the end, to establish the World Trade Organization (WTO) in the last days of 1993 cannot diminish the fact that the negotiations of the Uruguay Round, the latest attempt to broaden and deepen the multilateral trading rules system, remained stalled for years.[10] The 125 negotiating partners were left exhausted and wary with barely enough time to regroup before the entry into force of the multilateral agreement in 1995. While a systematic comparison between the WTO agreements and the NAFTA/NAAEC package with regard to their respective environmental sensitivity would require much more space than would be allowed here, it must be noted that the North American agreements are relatively more accommodating of environmental concerns and that the positive recognition of the importance of environmental cooperation embodied in the NAAEC knows no equivalent in the WTO founding instruments.

It is important to note that NAFTA's impact will not be confined to North America. Many experts expect that NAFTA will expand to other Latin and South American countries like Chile, and possibly Argentina or Venezuela, before the end of the 1990s, while others have even proposed offering membership to some Asian countries like South Korea. At the time of writing, Canadian, Mexican and U.S. commentators in media, academic, and government circles were openly discussing the adequate modes of accession to NAFTA and the chances of future

---

9. *General Agreement on Tariffs and Trade (GATT)*, 30 October 1947, Can. T.S. 1947 No. 27, 61 Stat. A11, 55 U.N.T.S. 187, T.I.A.S. No. 1700, 1st Supp. B.I.S.D. (1953) 6. Of particular interest is the network of regional free trade agreements that sprung out or were revived in the Americas in recent years: the Central American Common Market, the Andean Pact, Mercosur, and the Group of Three. On the other hand, observers have noted that the actual, practical implementation of some of these treaties has lagged behind the rhetoric.

10. The new GATT was signed by the parties in Marrakech on 15 April 1994. The Marrakech Agreements do include a ministerial declaration on the environment. This declaration provided for the convening of a working group on trade and the environment. "Trade and Environment," *Inside U.S. Trade* (14 December 1993). See "GATT Trade and Environment Subcommittee Sets Workplan for Fall" *Inside U.S. Trade*, 15 July 1994 at 22; "GATT Argues Over Response to Earth Summit on Trade and Environment," *Inside U.S. Trade*, 30 October 1992, at 1, 16. See also: *Final Act Embodying the Results of the Uruguay Round of Multilateral Trade Negotiations: Agreement Establishing the World Trade Organization*, GATT Doc. MTN/FA II, art. V.2 (15 December 1993) [hereinafter *WTO Agreement* or *Uruguay Round Agreement*]; GATT, *Trade and the Environment*, Sub-Committee on Trade and Environment Begins Work Programme, 26 July 1994.

applicants. In that sense, the architecture and the solutions put forward in NAFTA have an undeniable precedent value. Both mistaken choices and enlightened policies written in NAFTA and the NAAEC will weigh heavily on future efforts aimed at economic integration in the Americas.

One of the main factors that has sustained a discussion of the impact of trade liberalization on the environment is the changing nature of the undertaking: trade liberalizing activism has been migrating from the realm of tariff barriers into the area of nontariff barriers to trade (of which environmental policy emerges as a sizable part). Through the Kennedy and Tokyo rounds of the GATT and regional agreements, most of the tariff barriers between the big trading nations have been abolished or significantly lowered. Now the major obstacles to improved market access appear to be in the form of technical regulations and government policies that have a much less direct connection with international trade, such as official procurement procedures, health and safety measures, intellectual property protection regimes, and various certification and licensing mechanisms. Conventional trade law calls for the disciplining of such domestic policies if they impede international trade. When the negotiations are almost exclusively aimed at concluding an intergovernmental transaction on tariff concessions, the two fundamental principles underlying international trade law, national sovereignty and the principle of comparative advantage, are somewhat easier to apply.[11] States are freely consenting to reciprocally lower tariffs, a policy area where infringements on national sovereignty have fewer direct impacts and far less symbolic value. The *quid pro quo* for a tariff reduction is another tariff reduction in a contract between sovereign states. National sovereignty in almost all domestic policy areas is preserved—even though the impact on private enterprises of modifying tariff schedules can be quite severe. This arrangement allows, in principle, the play of comparative advantage to benefit both consumers and the more competitive industries, since each party is to concentrate development efforts on sectors where it has a particularly rich endowment of resources or expertise.

Neither national sovereignty nor comparative advantages are as sim-

---

11. Some commentators think that the principle of comparative advantage, as first outlined by David Ricardo, *Principles of Political Economy and Taxation* (London: Dent, 1965; New York: Dutton, 1965) is altogether irreconcilable with sustainable development. Others think that there is no such opposition. For the classic debate, see Jagdish Bagwathi, "The Case for Free Trade"(November, 1993) 269 *Scientific American* 42; Herman Daly, "The Perils of Free Trade"(November, 1993) 269 *Scientific American* 50.

ply understood nowadays. Sovereignty may not be sufficient to protect social and environmental policies if they restrict the market access of trade partners who invoke the rules of GATT or NAFTA. Indeed, international jurists and diplomats are not quite sure what happens to national sovereignty when guaranteeing market access requires policy harmonization and possibly the disciplining of domestic statutes, particularly environmental laws. The principle of comparative advantages is even more difficult to reconcile with environmental protection policies. The reason is that unlike access to a pool of productive workers or proximity to important markets, low or high environmental compliance costs of doing business are almost entirely a function of domestic policy and legislation. When the environmental laws of a country are relatively permissive or when enforcement is predictably spotty, the production costs related to such laws for exporting firms are lower. At the moment, the evidence is simply insufficient to determine the impact of these lower costs on the competitive position of the firms. Among those who believe that the ultimate consequence of low environmental standards is to improve the competitive position of exporting firms, there are two groups. Members of the first group claim that this is a sovereign national policy choice that provides a legitimate advantage to exporting firms, not unlike lax minimum wage laws or maintaining low corporate taxes. Representatives of the second group claim that the missing environmental cost is evidence that the exporting country is engaging in "environmental dumping" by providing industry with a "subsidy" and ought to be sanctioned.

To answer the fear that inadequately low standards might allow a country to trade the health of its environment for an unacceptable competitive advantage gained by reducing production costs related to standards compliance, many are suggesting the convergence and eventual uniformization of environmental legislation across borders. Others will ask how national sovereignty can be preserved should international law mandate the convergence toward some form of global standards. Indeed, if competitive advantages purportedly gained at the expense of the environment can be denounced and challenged in the name of harmonized standards, what becomes of sovereignty?[12] In fact, before NAFTA the question was already squarely put: How can the

---

12. Indeed, Pakistan's Commerce Minister Chaudhry Ahmad Mukhtar, speaking at the WTO negotiations final meeting, expressed fears of what he called "a new brand of protectionism under the garb of protection of the environment or the promotion of the rights of workers in developing countries." Alan Riding, "Gore Insists Environment is a Trade Issue," *The New York Times* (15 April 1994) D2.

comparative advantages (on which all benefits from international trade are based) be allowed to work in a world of diverse levels of wealth, social programs, workers' rights, wages, and environmental protection policies?[13] When the rules on nontariff barriers are adopted in trade agreements and enforced on member states, is what is at stake the negotiation of a *transaction* between states (such as was the case with tariff negotiations) or rather a broader exchange between states striving toward *economic integration*? It is remarkable that now echoed in North America are the same arguments heard for more than a generation in Western Europe as the European Union gradually leaves behind the Community that built a free trade area to enter into a seemingly more integrative phase.[14]

NAFTA came at a time when aggressive trade activism clashed head-on with the new fundamental questions raised by the refocusing of trade law from discrete barriers like tariffs to the amorphous but vital matters included in the so-called social agenda, of which environmental policy is a central element. The challenge to the negotiators and the institutions was nothing short of formidable. Parts II and III will focus on how the NAFTA/NAAEC package measures up against this challenge. On the issue of market access, one of the conclusions will be that the threat posed by trade disciplines to domestic environmental laws is at once less potent than many authors have made it out to be and addressed relatively satisfactorily by the mechanisms put in place by the NAFTA. On the issue of competitiveness and harmonization, it will be demonstrated that the NAFTA/NAAEC package lays only a fragile foundation for the awesome but obligatory task of reconciling the environmental imperative of true cost internalization with the essential principles of cost competitiveness and "fair" competitive advantages. It is clear, however, that the national sovereignty and comparative advantage definitions, as well as the interplay between them, are becoming increasingly complex and that much work remains to be done.

One thing is certain: Whether the context be discussions of regional agreements like NAFTA and its future enlargement or multilateral

---

13. For a survey of earlier attempts to deal with the social agenda of trade see "NAFTA's Social Dimension," supra note 5, Part I at 44–47; Steve Charnovitz, "Exploring the Environmental Exceptions in GATT Article XX" (1991) 25 Journal of World Trade 37 [hereinafter "Environmental Exceptions"].

14. For example, complaints about the secrecy of the negotiations and the democratic shortcomings of NAFTA abound as they do about the European Commission. Robert F. Housman, "Democratizing International Decision-Making" (1994) 27 Cornell Int'l L.J 99 [hereinafter "Democratizing International Decision-Making"].

negotiations through the WTO, the social agenda, including environmental issues, is now front and center in the public debate over the effects of trade liberalization.[15] In addition to the conceptual challenges presented in the preceding paragraphs, the potency of the environmental issue in the NAFTA area will remain for three reasons: (1) Domestic concern with environmental issues has come of age in the hemisphere; (2) such environmental consciousness is quickly coming to terms with our improving knowledge of global economic and ecological interdependence; and (3) environmental interdependence is most vividly manifested in bilateral relationships between close neighbors who trade and invest a lot with each other.

Environmental Issues in Canada, Mexico, and the United States

The legal and economic linkages between trade and environment arguments are rather arcane. These issues might have remained more scholarly and technical than popular and politically potent. The 1990s, however, saw international trade and environmental protection very much brought together in the public mind. In hindsight, it is not a surprising outcome.

In all three North American countries, environmental issues have acquired a very high profile in the areas of public policy and private sector decision-making. The emergence of highly effective and influential environmental interest groups dedicated to fighting pollution and protecting nature, particularly in the United States and Canada, is well documented, as is their importance in defining and contributing to the solution of environmental controversies.[16]

An issue less well known is the extent to which Mexicans have become increasingly concerned by the amount of environmental degradation in their country. Pressed into action as much by international public opinion as by domestic demands, the Mexican government adopted the *General Law for Ecological Equilibrium and Environmental Protection (Ley General del Equilibrium Ecologico y la Proteccion*

---

15. This should not surprise the reader following European affairs where formal economic integration has been underway since the 1950s and discussions of *l'Europe sociale* predate the North American debate by a good decade.

16. See Doug MacDonald, *The Politics of Pollution* (Toronto: McClelland and Stewart, 1991).

al Ambiente) in 1988, its first general environmental law.[17] The newly elected Salinas Administration gave a number of signals that the environment had climbed up the priority ladder. Mexico City, several river basins, and the border area were identified as the regions where action was most urgently needed. Inspection rates of industrial plants increased. The government pledged 1 percent of the national budget to the environment. It declared that Mexico would implement and respect CITES.[18] The Salinas administration also quadrupled the size of its environmental inspection corps.[19] In 1992, the Secretariat of Social Development (*Secretario de Desarrollo Social*—SEDESOL) was created to better coordinate environmental measures within general government activity. SEDESOL succeeded the Secretariat for Urban Development (SEDUE). Two semi-autonomous environmental agencies were created under the aegis of SEDESOL: the National Institute of Ecology (INE), which is to formulate policy, and the Federal Attorney General for Environmental Protection (PFMA), which is entrusted with enforcement.[20] It must be remembered that the issue of enforcement, as opposed to the adequacy of the environmental legislation, was a main concern throughout the NAFTA negotiations and deeply influenced the formulation of the NAAEC. The new law and the new agency signaled a strong Mexican desire to improve its environmental reputation on the eve of the NAFTA negotiations. Such genuine efforts as the posting of performance bonds and surprise inspections, as well

---

17. D.O., 28 January 1988, reprinted in 4 Inter-American Legal Materials (ABA) 664 (1988) [hereinafter The Ecology Law]. In 1982, the creation of the first Cabinet-rank environmental agency did not improve either the remediation or the enforcement record. There was a *Ley Federal de Proteccion al Ambiente* on the books since 1971 which led to spotty enforcement of some pollution control provisions.

18. *Convention on International Trade in Endangered Species of Wild Fauna and Flora,* 3 March 1973, 27 U.S.T. 1087, T.I.A.S. No. 8349, 993 U.N.T.S. 243 [hereinafter CITES].

19. Stephen P. Mumme, "Mexican Environmental Reform and NAFTA," (1994) 4 North American Outlook 87 at 88–90 [hereinafter "Mexican Environmental Reform"]; Stephen P. Mumme, "Clearing the Air: Environmental Reform in Mexico," (1991) 16 Environment at 7–8. For a general survey, see Nicolas Kublicki, "The Greening of Free Trade: NAFTA, Mexican Environmental Law and Debt Exchanges for Mexican Environmental Infrastructure Development," (1994) 19 Columbia Journal of Environmental Law 59 at 80–100 [hereinafter "Greening Free Trade"]. See also: Edward M. Ranger, "Mexican Environmental Regulations," (1992) Bus. Mex., Special Ed. at 20.

20. U.S. General Accounting Office, *U.S.–Mexico Trade: Assessment of Mexico's Environmental Controls for New Companies,* GAO/GGD-92-113 (Washington, D.C.: August, 1992).

as environmental impact assessments, started in the 1991–1992 period.[21]

At the same time, many would say that these efforts were too little too late considering the impact of the industrial development *maquiladora* program. Under this Mexican–U.S. program, industries mostly concentrated along the U.S.–Mexico border are allowed to import duty-free components from the United States for further manufacturing and processing, before sending the finished products, again without paying duties, back to the United States. The concentration of industry and populations in small areas devoid of adequate infrastructure caused environmental degradation and serious health problems that sometimes spilled over on American territory.[22] Indeed, it seems foreign corporations operating in the border area do not care to apply the same environmental standards they do in the United States, Canada, Germany, or Japan.[23] Nevertheless, by the standards of developing countries, even by rapidly industrializing country standards,

---

21. C. Ford Runge, François Ortalo-Magne and Philip Wade Kamp, *Freer Trade, Protected Environment: Balancing Trade Liberalization and Environmental Interests* (New York: Council on Foreign Relations, 1994); Jan Gilbreath and J. Ben Tonra, *Environment: Unwelcome Guest at the Free Trade Party,* Center for Strategic and International Studies Policy Paper on the Americas, vol. 3, no. 10 (Washington, D.C.: 1992) at 24. As well, in 1992, 220 of Mexico's worst polluters were ordered by the Mexican government to lower their emissions by 70% over the next 18 months. Ibid., p. 37.

22. See, generally, J. Ward and G.T. Prickett, "Prospects for a Green Trade Agreement" (1992) 33 Environment 3. The American border area, particularly in the state of Texas, is not without serious environmental problems of its own. Alberto Szekely, "Emerging Boundary Environmental Challenges and Institutional Issues: Mexico and the United States" (1993) 33 Natural Resources Journal 33; Stephen P. Mumme, "State and Local Influence in Transboundary Environmental Policy-Making Along the U.S.–Mexico Border: The Case of Air Quality Management" 2 Journal of Borderlands Studies 1; Malissa H. McKeith, "The Environment and Free Trade: Meeting Halfway at the Mexican Border," (1991) 10 Pacific Basin Law Journal 183.

23. John Maggs, "G.M. to Treat Sewage at 35 Mexican Factories," *Austin American-Statesman,* (15 May 1991); Gaynell Terrell, "Tragic Puzzle Grips Families on the Border: Plant Pollution May Cause Brain Not to Develop," *Houston Post,* 17 May 1991, A1; Peter Emerson and Elizabeth Wallace Bourbon, "The Border Environment and Free Trade" (Prepared for the North American Institute, 8 November 1991) at 11; David Voigt, "The Maquiladora Problem in the Age of NAFTA: Where Will We Find Solutions?" (1993) 2 Minnesota Journal of Global Trade at 300–336 [hereinafter "The Maquiladora Problem"]. For a discussion of improvements in the border area see Gary Clyde Hufbauer and Jeffrey L. Schott, *North American Free Trade: Issues and Recommendations* (Washington: Institute for International Economics, 1992).

Mexico has made great strides in a short period of time.[24] The gamble
of NAFTA is that trade-induced growth in Mexico as well as a new
focus on environmental issues will translate into bigger environmental
budgets that will more than compensate for the environmental degradation brought by industrialization. In many ways, the NAAEC is a further attempt to tip the odds in favor of that outcome.

A key aspect of NAFTA is that Mexico has teamed up with rich industrialized countries having some of the world's most stringent environmental norms. NAFTA is arguably the first genuine North–South trade
arrangement that does not evolve out of a colonial past. During the
NAFTA debate the high standards of the United States and Canada
were often used to assess Mexico's environmental record, sometimes
without regard to the general social and economic context. In fact, the
issue of standards differentiation between rich and developing countries remains at the center of the debate on NAFTA and the environment. Are differing standards between countries inevitable given
resource discrepancies and varying ecological context? Should there
be uniformity in common trading areas if competition is to be preserved? Does justice lie, on the contrary, in a diversity of levels of protection that respects national differences? Is a middle ground between
harmonization and diversity possible through convergence within a
predefined range? None of these policy and principles issues were def-
initely resolved by NAFTA.[25]

Whereas in the 1960s and 1970s environmental activists and concerned citizens were almost exclusively preoccupied with local
instances of pollution, in the 1980s increasingly large numbers became
aware of the global nature of many environmental threats. The multi-
ple alarms sounded by the scientific community on the effects of CFCs
on stratospheric ozone depletion, of energy use patterns on climate
disturbances, of waste and emissions on oceans, soil and air contami-

---

24. Mexico's current status defies the usual categorizations. It remains a developing
country where per capita income and wealth does not really compare with most rich
countries. Yet Mexico has industrialized rapidly; its large economy has steadily out-
paced that of Canada and the United States in the last decade and it has become, in
1994, a member of the official club of the developed world, the Organization for Economic Cooperation and Development (OECD).

25. For a discussion of the advantages and disadvantages of different obligations for
rich and poor parties in international environmental agreements, see Günther Handl,
"Environmental Security and Global Change: The Challenge to an International Law"
in W. Lang, H. Newhold, and K. Zemanek, eds., *Environmental Protection and International Law* (London: Graham & Trotman, 1990).

nation, and of resources exploitation on species loss and deforestation created a shared international awareness of the interdependence of peoples and countries from the North and the South in facing these urgent challenges. This new awareness culminated in the 1992 Earth Summit in Rio.[26]

Furthermore, with the Brundtland Report[27] and the new paradigm of sustainable development, economic and environmental decisions came to be seen as two sides of the same coin. Increasingly, North American environmental groups began focusing on the impact of economic policy, including tax, subsidy, energy, and transport policies, research and development priorities, as well as international trade and investment policy, on the environment and efforts to protect it. Thus, starting in the late 1980s, lobbying in favor of the environment meant monitoring a country's economic decisions and international activities and attempting to influence them. In that light, the Earth Summit can be seen as the beginning of a new insight, as much as it marked the climax of an international process.

It has now become clear that a nation's international economic activity is as relevant to its environmental record as is its participation in international environmental treaty negotiations. In fact, one of the most striking features of the environmental movement worldwide in the last few years (especially in the United States and Canada) is the migration of international environmental concerns and activity from UN and social forums toward economic institutions or processes like the World Bank, the GATT, NAFTA, the OECD, and even the G-7 summits. Certainly, the effectiveness of international environmental treaties and declarations signed under the auspices of the UN has been hampered by a lack of resources, the particularly cumbersome nature of the UN political culture, and a sometimes inordinate tendency for formal displays. In the economic institutions, the intellectual universe is altogether different. In these forums, the influence of the top decision makers on global and domestic governance is undeniable, but so

---

26. The connection between international trade and the environment was largely disregarded at the Earth Summit, even though some individual participants raised the issue. See UN GA, Preparatory Committee for the United Nations Conference on Environment and Development, *International Cooperation to Accelerate Sustainable Development in Developing Countries, and Related Domestic Policies*, A/Conf.151/PC/L.71 (31 March 1992).

27. *Report of the World Commission on Environment and Development: Our Common Future* (New York: United Nations, 1987).

is, unfortunately, the skepticism of many of them—or their advisors—toward environmental issues. These economic forums, when they address environmental issues, can be very efficient and engage key decision makers who may not always be exposed to adequate discussions of environmental issues. Yet such forums are also deeply political and the struggle to get on the agenda can be fierce, leaving important environmental issues as a minor part of the debates at any given meeting. Indeed, while greater political efficacy can be achieved in economic institutions, environmental concerns remain extremely susceptible to their varying fortunes in public opinion.[28]

Moreover, a few fundamental cleavages are carried over from the discussions of the 1970s and early 1980s into the new debate, many as acutely divisive as ever, like the arduous North–South relationship or the communication breakdown between environmental specialists and traditional economic experts.[29] Nevertheless, one cannot deny a significant emerging phenomenon: The task of sorting out muddled questions of national sovereignty, trade rules, competitiveness concerns, and environmental protection policy has fallen to international economic law and its institutions. This shift in forum is likely to endure for many years. As a consequence, the level of environmental scrutiny of NAFTA and its works will probably go undiminished for a long time to come.

This new linkage of economic policy to the environment parallels another relatively recent phenomenon born out of the powerful idea of global interdependence—that of the legitimacy (even the necessity) of transboundary environmental intervention. With increasing regularity,

---

28. For example, at the G-7 Summit in Houston in 1990, the environment was a major item on the agenda. Since 1992, the annual summits have addressed the global environmental issues with greatly varying depth. Between 1990 and 1994, the OECD has been an effective forum for an in-depth investigation of trade and environment linkages. Even though consensus was difficult to build on in the end, many advances were made in OECD studies on the issue. U.S. Congressional Office of Technology Assessment, *Trade and Environment: Conflicts and Opportunities,* OTA-BP-ITE-94 (Washington: U.S. Government Printing Office, 1992), at 10, 25–27 [hereinafter *Conflicts and Opportunities*]; OECD, *The Polluter Pays Principle: Definition, Analysis, Implementation* (Paris: OECD, 1975); OECD, *Note to Members of the Joint Session on Trade and Environment,* COM/TD/ENV/(94) 39, 6–7 February 1994; OECD, Chairman's Report, *Environmental Perspectives on Trade–Environment Issues,* 7–8 December 1993; Pollution Probe, "Process-Related Trade Measures: Lessons From NAFTA" (Presentation at the OECD Workshop on Trade and Environment, 6–7 April 1994).

29. See "Environment and Trade: Talking Across Culture," box in Magraw, supra note 2, Part I.

citizens or the government of one country will publicly criticize the environmental mismanagements of the government or even the citizenry of another country out of fear of the global or transboundary effects of the behaviors they denounce, much to the dismay of public authorities. No country in the world is shielded from well-organized NGOs or foreign governments lashing out at unsustainable forestry policies, inadequate conservation measures, wasteful consumption patterns, or polluting enterprises. In this context, the widely publicized ecological problems of the United States–Mexico border area made it inevitable that NAFTA's environmental impact would be scrutinized and criticized by American environmental groups (the most articulate and resourceful in the world) and other policy analysts.[30] Past trade negotiations did not take place in a climate so conducive to transboundary environmental intervention. As is the case in the areas of fundamental human rights or international trade, the case for the old paradigm of noninterference in the affairs of other nation-states is almost impossible to make in the fields of environmental protection and sustainable development. Quite the contrary, a faltering but sometimes quite intrusive international consensus is slowly emerging on acceptable behavior toward the environment.[31]

The newness of the NAFTA project fed several fears for many Canadians, Mexicans, and Americans. Indeed, the diversity in the political, economic, and social realities of the three partners and the genuine uncertainty about the consequences of this new *rapprochement* of the three North American countries created several anxieties. Among these fears is a crippling sense of loss of sovereignty—which, for different

---

30. The fact that Canada and the United States have a long history of border environmental controversies should not be discarded; but clearly, the American NGOs that so influenced the NAFTA negotiations were obviously more focused on Mexico's environmental record.

31. The fledging consensus on environmental interventionism will by no means always translate into a willingness to act on the part of people, especially if such action entails a sacrifice, economic or otherwise. That will depend on other factors like the agenda, set in large part by the global media, and a sustained level of commitment that can be channeled in the political, governmental, or nongovernmental processes. A consensus may take root in the moral sphere but flounder in politics and economics. Moreover, the effect of the acknowledgment of global interdependence is not always to build bridges between North and South but also sometimes to deepen the cultural faults on environmental issues developing among powerful Western nations, fast-growing Asian and Latin-American states, recovering former communist countries, and large destitute regions of Africa and Asia.

reasons, is a particularly sensitive issue in all three countries. After all, unlike the European Union members, the NAFTA partners do not share close to 40 years of gradual integration through institutional collaboration between a larger number of states more comparable in size or where all sorts of alliances are possible. Furthermore, some Canadians and Americans have expressed a fear that economic integration will mean that all standards, including environmental standards, will converge toward the lowest common denominator and that the border areas would suffer accelerated environmental degradation brought about by increased industrial activity.

NGOs, U.S. Politics, the Fate of NAFTA, and the Genesis of NAAEC

This book is not devoted to the negotiation proper. Nevertheless, to fully understand NAFTA's provisions dealing with the environment, as well as the rationale for a NAAEC, the role of NGOs, in particular U.S. NGOs, in the debate must be explained. The political process that unfolded during the negotiations and culminated in the national ratification votes was indeed a determinant factor in the future of the NAFTA package, its implementation and management. Two aspects of the preratification process are central to its history. First, as expressed abundantly in the media coverage, the importance of the U.S. process dwarfed whatever events were unfolding in the two other countries because there was a real possibility Congress would reject NAFTA, while the governments' control of the domestic parliamentary institutions virtually ensured ratification in Canada and Mexico.[32] Second, environmental concerns and the powerful U.S. NGOs that promoted them played a very important role in the public debate over NAFTA ratification.

In fact, NAFTA met with a hostile reception in the U.S. Congress. Indeed, the hard sell put the ratification in jeopardy until the last days

---

32. As two commentators bluntly asserted: "[d]espite its important innovations, the NAFTA environmental regime is the product not of any fundamental, enduring commitment to environmental values on the part of governments in North America, but of a temporary need on the part of a Republican and then a Democratic President to secure sufficient domestic support to ensure legislative passage of a historic free trade agreement." This assessment may be overly categorical, but it underlies the fundamental importance of the U.S. political process in the development of NAFTA. See "Bilateral," supra note 5, Part I at 82.

before the final successful votes were held on 17 November (234 to 200 in the House) and 20 November (61 to 38 in the Senate). To be fair, in the final days, the political showdown on NAFTA was fought more with economic and labor market arguments related to industry dislocation and Mexico's alleged lack of readiness than environmental ones. Probably for the first time, the larger public, suffering from a severe recession and more pessimistic than before, no longer took for granted the crucial link between trade, prosperity, and employment opportunities. Nevertheless, the environmental community managed to forcefully present its agenda on trade and environment using two advantages: (1) the NGOs were on the ground early in 1991—surprising many trade experts and diplomats who never saw the issue coming, thanks to the combination of the awareness-raising 1987 Brundtland Report, the mobilizing process of the 1992 Rio Earth Summit, the headline-gathering GATT 1991 Tuna–Dolphin ruling,[33] and sometimes shocking environmental degradation in the U.S.–Mexico border area brought about by 20 years of unregulated and anarchic trade-induced growth; and (2) they deftly used their resources and skills to maintain a close proximity with some key political players, both in the House and in the Senate, as well as in the Executive branch.

As the NAFTA debate raced toward its conclusion, the importance of environmental issues diminished, particularly after the labor side-agreement and the NAAEC were negotiated in September 1993. In absolute terms, the NAFTA discussion on trade and environment had much more depth and profile than anything ever before. In relative terms, however, not all the issues were satisfactorily resolved and many questions remained unanswered. The decrease in interest in the environmental consequences of NAFTA at the end of 1993 is probably related to the fact that after two years of heated exchanges, the environmental NGOs were profoundly divided about the acceptability of the NAFTA package and remained thus, in the end less able to reach a wide public and political audience with a unified message.[34]

---

33. *United States-Restrictions on Imports of Tuna (Mexico v. United States)* (1991), GATT Doc. DS21/R, 39th Supp. B.I.S.D. (1992) 155; 30 I.L.M. 1594 [hereinafter Tuna Dolphin Case]. See infra notes 94–115, Part I and accompanying text.

34. Steve Charnovitz has accurately described the three stages in the U.S. of the environmental aspects of NAFTA during the 1990–1992 period as a "denial" of the problem, "adaptation" to the need to address environmental issues, and "hyperbole" in the government's assessment of NAFTA's environmental achievement. See "NAFTA's Social Dimension," supra note 5, Part I at 47–55.

Before the Signing of NAFTA

The NAFTA environmental agenda was more concrete than the abstract world of GATT for one principal reason: the disastrous environmental record of the Maquiladoras. The issue was raised as soon as the possibility of trade talks between the U.S. and Mexico appeared in early 1990, well before Canada had entered the picture.[35] Moreover, the Canada–U.S. FTA had given rise to at least one trade disciplines controversy related to natural resource conservation.[36] As well, a fear was expressed that trade institutions (and their often denounced "culture of secrecy") would prevent environmental NGOs from convincing legislators to act on behalf of the environment.[37] Nevertheless, the NGOs' ticket to the forefront of the trade negotiation was undoubtedly the border issue.

While NGOs were asking that trade talks address the border pollution issue, the governments of Mexico and the United States were quite reluctant to do so. Meeting in Monterrey in the Fall of 1990, Presidents Salinas and Bush announced a new environmental border initiative, but neither they nor their officials, in particular the Office of the U.S. Trade Representative (USTR) Carla Hills, were willing to link this initiative with eventual trade negotiations. The NGOs kept trying to use

---

35. The initial objectives of the negotiators were to "eliminate barriers to trade, promote conditions of fair competition, increase investment opportunities, provide adequate protection for intellectual property rights, establish effective procedures for the implementation and application of the Agreement and for the resolution of disputes and to further trilateral, regional and multilateral cooperation." Runge, supra note 21, Part I at 55; *Description of the Proposed North American Free Trade Agreement,* prepared by the governments of Canada, Mexico and the United States of America, 12 August 1992, at 1.

36. "Canada's Landing Requirement for Pacific Coast Salmon and Herring" (Panel Report, October 16, 1989); and "Lobsters from Canada" (Panel Report, May 25, 1990); Daniel C. Esty, "Making Trade and Environment Policies Work Together: Lessons From NAFTA," (1992) 49 Aussenwirtschaft 1 at 4 [hereinafter "Making Trade"]; See "Binational Statement on Environmental Safeguards that Should be Included in the North American Free Trade Agreement," Canadian Nature Federation, Canadian Environmental Law Association, Sierra Club—Canada, Rawson Academy of Aquatic Sciences—Canada, Friends of the Earth—Canada, Cultural Survival—Canada, Pollution Probe—Canada, National Audubon Society, National Wildlife Federation, Community Nutrition Institute, Environment Defense Fund, 28 May 1992. See also: *Inside U.S. Trade,* 29 May 1992; "Environmentalists Assessment of NAFTA Green Language," *Inside U.S. Trade,* 17 July 1992.

37. Even though many in the NGO community were proposing the very kind of supranational environmental arrangements that could have the effect of reducing domestic legislators' freedom of action.

border issues to pry the NAFTA negotiations open both before and after the "fast track" authorization debate in the Spring of 1991.[38] Their message was relatively simple: If NAFTA did not properly address environmental concerns, the environmental degradation of the border area would spread to the rest of the planned free trade zone. One of the first congressional briefings was organized by the National Wildlife Federation (NWF) and the Border Ecology Group in January 1991. This effort and other lobbying attempts were successful enough for such congressional leaders as Lloyd Bentsen, the chair of the Senate Finance Committee, Dan Rostenkowski, the chair of the House Ways and Means Committee, and Richard Gephart, House Majority leader, to make their support for "fast track" conditional on a proper action plan on environmental issues.[39]

When President Bush obtained fast track authority to negotiate NAFTA, on May 24, 1991, he thus had to promise Congress to include environmental specialists on important advisory committees and, crucially, "not to do anything to hurt existing environmental and worker safety laws."[40] On the other hand, the President steadfastly refused to make the signing of NAFTA conditional on the successful treatment of environmental issues, nor did he agree, as was requested by most NGOs, to form a special working group to work on these issues.[41] Environmental groups were critical of the parallel track approach because

---

38. The fast-track procedure authorizes the U.S. President, after a 90-day period of consultation with Congress, to submit wholesale and as a package, before an agreed date, a trade agreement for ratification by the House and the Senate. This prevents congressmen and senators from modifying or amending it as they could for ordinary legislation.

39. Letter from House Majority Leader Richard Gephart to President George Bush, March 17, 1991.

40. U.S. Government, The White House, *May 1 Action Plan in Response to Concerns Raised by Congress Regarding A North American Free Trade Agreement,* May 1, 1991. See also: *Trade Act* of 1974, §§101–102, 151, Pub. L. No. 93-618, 88 Stat. 1978, 1982, 2001 (codified at U.S.C. §§2101, 2111–2112, 2191) (1988); *Omnibus Trade and Competitiveness Act* of 1988, Pub. L. No. 100-418, 102 Stat. 1107, 1102–03 (codified at 19 U.S.C. §§ 2902–2903). See also: U.S. House of Representatives, Committee on Ways and Means, *Exchange of Letters on Issues Concerning the Negotiation of a North American Free Trade Agreement,* WMCP 102–110, 1 May 1991.

41. A number of observers in favor of both NAFTA and strong environmental provisions believe that the parallel track process has made both more difficult. As Housman asserts: "Although the parallel track approach was intended to ease the NAFTA process, ultimately it had the opposite effect. The failure to integrate trade and environmental issues from the outset created obstacles to a final agreement both during negotiation

they believed that only cross-track compromises and tradeoffs would produce a truly environmentally sensitive NAFTA.[42] The presidential action plan, nevertheless, was the first permanent anchor for environmental NGO involvement in the NAFTA process.

In 1991–1992, the NGOs published a number of position papers and joint or single statements enumerating a list of concerns or conditions for eventual support of NAFTA. Among the most significant were the joint statement of the National Wildlife Federation and Pollution Probe Canada as well as the position paper of the Natural Resources Defense Council.[43] While there were some differences in emphasis and priorities, the most important of those demands can be summarized as: (1) Guarantees for upward harmonization of environmental standards in the NAFTA area; (2) more transparency and NGO participation in the administration and dispute settlement mechanism of NAFTA;[44] (3) better enforcement of environmental regulations as well as some built-in procedure to make violations of this principle actionable under NAFTA (thus raising the possibility of trade sanctions); (4) elaborated protection of environmental laws and regulations against preemption and NAFTA trade discipline challenges; and (5) a major and well-financed effort to clean up the Mexico–U.S. border area. As soon as the negoti-

---

and Congressional consideration. During the negotiations it became clear that environmental issues would have to be dealt with to some degree in the agreement itself, and new and unanticipated issues had to be added to an already extensive negotiating docket. Had these emerging issues been on the negotiation docket from the outset they could have been handled more effectively and deliberately. Instead, their late addition caused difficult eleventh-hour negotiations that delayed and threatened passage of the agreement as a whole." See Robert F. Housman, "The North American Free Trade Agreement's Lessons for Reconciling Trade and the Environment" (1994) 30 Stanf. J. Int'l L. 379 at 383 [hereinafter "Reconciling Trade and the Environment"].

42. Robert F. Housman and Paul M. Orbuch, "Integrating Labor and Environmental Concerns Into the North American Free Trade Agreement: A Look Back and a Look Ahead" (1993) 8 Am. U.J. Int'l L. & Pol'y 719 at 768 [hereinafter "Integrating Labor"].

43. National Wildlife Federation and Pollution Probe Canada, "Environmental Issues Related to the North American Free Trade Agreement," March 7, 1992; Natural Resources Defense Council et al., "Review of Environmental Concerns Arising from a North American Free Trade Agreement," April 7, 1992.

44. According to the Canadian Environmental Law Association, under NAFTA, "[a] secretive, unelected international commission that favors industry over the environment will rule on trade disputes and give a voice to corporations that is denied to environment protection organizations and the general public." Moreover, "the panel will meet behind closed doors, and the public will hear only its final decision. This is a shocking departure from the public access to regulatory hearings Canadians are accustomed to." "NAFTA and Democratic Process," Canadian Environmental Law Association—NAFTA Facts (Toronto, 1992) at 1.

ations started in August 1991, the NGOs directed most of their efforts at USTR and the negotiating team, thus often bypassing the U.S. Environmental Protection Agency (EPA), which had little formal trade policy role.[45] In Canada, under the leadership of Pollution Probe, trade officials were also presented with similar demands, even though the leverage of Canadian NGOs, in the Canadian domestic context, was much less than that of U.S. NGOs.[46] Of the 20 working groups that were formed in the United States at that point, five included environmental representatives.[47] In Canada, environmentalists were appointed to the International Trade Advisory Committee (ITAC) and to some of the Sectoral Advisory Groups on International Trade (SAG-ITS).[48] It is generally agreed that the Mexican government was not as forthcoming in engaging NGOs and the general public in the NAFTA debate. While this allowed the government of Mexico a freer hand in negotiating the deal, it has raised serious questions about the reaction of the Mexican people and of the NAFTA process as a model for future North–South negotiations.[49]

---

45. J.J. Audley and E.M. Uslaner, "NAFTA, the Environment, and American Domestic Politics" (1994) 4 North American Outlook at 30 [hereinafter "American Domestic Politics"]. On the other hand, the involvement of the EPA was larger than in previous trade negotiations, and its representatives, as well as those of the Food and Drug Administration, served as co-chairs of two of the three standards negotiation subgroups. See Peter L. Lallas, "NAFTA and Evolving Approaches to Identify and Address 'Indirect' Environmental Impacts of International Trade" (1993) 5 Geo. Int'l Envt'l L. Rev. at 519, 543. See generally: Jan McAlpine and Pat LeDonne, "The United States Government, Public Participation and Trade and Environment" in D. Zaelke, ed., Trade and Environment: Law, Economics and Policy (Washington: Island Press, 1993).

46. For an account of the mobilization in Mexico, see Regina Barba, "NAFTA and NACE: A Mexican Perspective" in Sarah Richardson, ed., Shaping Consensus: The North American Commission on the Environment and NAFTA (Ottawa: National Round Table on the Environment and the Economy, 1993) at 10–12.

47. On an expanded role for the EPA see Esty, "Making Trade," supra note 36, Part I at 10–11. See also: Michael Gregory, "Environment, Sustainable Development, Public Participation and the NAFTA: A Retrospective" (1992) 7 Journal of Environmental Law and Litigation at 99, 106–107.

48. Government of Canada, North American Free Trade Agreement: Canadian Environmental Review, supra note 1, Part I at 1.

49. Housman, "Reconciling Trade," supra note 41, Part I at 389–390; Regina Barba, "NAFTA and NACE: A Mexican Perspective" in Sarah Richardson, ed., supra note 46, Part I; Adolfo Aguilar Zinser, "Authoritarianism and North American Free Trade" in R. Grinspun and M. Cameron, eds., The Political Economy of North American Free Trade (Ottawa: Canadian Center for Policy Alternatives; Montreal: McGill-Queen's University Press, 1993); Jorge G. Castañeda, "Can NAFTA Change Mexico?" Foreign Affairs, (September-October, 1993) 66.

The intensity of NGO activism had the effect of partially erasing the parallel track scheme. Many environmental issues migrated into the trade discussions and were in turn integrated into the NAFTA text itself. Quite simply, environmental concerns were too politically potent to be marginalized in a remote corner of the negotiations.[50]

When NAFTA was completed in August 1992, no U.S. environmental NGO formally supported it, presumably because the minimal conditions for their acceptance were not met. On September 16, 1992 Canada, the United States, and Mexico agreed to negotiate a parallel environmental agreement. This allowed the National Wildlife Federation, two weeks later, to break ranks and express qualified support for "the environmental provisions" of NAFTA.[51] Generally, other NGOs were still asking for the reopening of NAFTA to include more environmental provisions, while some were demanding the completion of a very strong environmental side-agreement before considering the whole package.

On the Way to the NAAEC

The position of the three governments never wavered during the negotiations leading to the NAAEC: NAFTA was not going to be reopened and the NAAEC would have to stand on its own. Within that framework, the NGOs continued to press for essentially the same concerns as during the NAFTA negotiations, with, for most, a pragmatically diminished emphasis on modifying trade disciplines. The last stretch of the presidential campaign provided for a dramatic shift in context. Presidential candidate Clinton, who until then had made only rather ambiguous statements about NAFTA, declared on October 4, 1992 that he could support NAFTA only if it were accompanied by two supplemental agreements on environmental protection and labor issues. The

---

50. "Reconciling Trade," supra note 41, Part I at 382.

51. National Wildlife Federation, Press Release, September 27, 1992. According to Stewart Hudson of the National Wildlife Federation, "NAFTA is, most assuredly, the greenest trade agreement that has yet been negotiated, and it represents a positive step toward unifying economic and environmental concerns in pursuit of sustainable development throughout North America." Will Dunham, "Wildlife Group Backs Free Trade," *Houston Chronicle* (17 September 1992) at 2; Jay D. Hair, President of the National Wildlife Federation, contends that NAFTA marks the "first time in international trade agreements the environment is incorporated as a significant factor." See Jay D. Hair, "Turning a Perceived Threat Into a Positive Step," (Mar.-Apr. 1993) International Wildlife.

purpose of the supplemental agreements, according to Governor Clinton, would be to "require each country to enforce *its own* environmental and worker standards."[52] The consequence was unmistakable: Should the Democratic candidate be elected President, not an unlikely turn of events, the survival of NAFTA would be conditional on the successful negotiation of the NAAEC.[53]

That caused some realignment in the NGO community. The NGO landscape, largely made up of organizations that were supportive of Governor Clinton's candidacy, became further split.[54] The NWF and World Wildlife Fund (WWF) urged the candidate not to make NAFTA conditional on NAAEC—in large part because their most pressing concern was poverty alleviation in Mexico through trade and growth—while Friends of the Earth and the Sierra Club were asking for a complete reopening of NAFTA, a fresh start for the whole trade treaty because its content was so far below the original NGO demands.[55] Most business organizations that supported Mr. Clinton were pressuring him to endorse NAFTA before the election. After his election on November 4, President Clinton eventually sided with those who did not want to reopen the NAFTA text, making such a promise to President Salinas in January 1993, but left all options open for a "greening" of NAFTA through a strong NAAEC. In a letter drafted by the Sierra Club in February 1993, 13 NGOs expressed their hope that the NAAEC would ensure that their outstanding concerns were adequately answered.[56]

At the same time, those were dire days for NAFTA: Public support (in all three countries) was low, the transition paralyzed the parallel accord negotiations for months, and many new legislators had campaigned on an explicitly anti-NAFTA platform. Concurrently, the new administration seemed more open than the previous government had

---

52. Bill Clinton, "Expanding Trade and Creating American Jobs," reprinted in (1993) 23 Environmental Law at 683–684.

53. Ibid. See also: Presidential candidate Gov. Bill Clinton, Address, University of North Carolina, October 4, 1992. A mechanism to control import surges from Mexico was also mentioned as one of three conditions but dropped out of the picture some months later.

54. This endorsement was not formal in the case of most NGOs because it would have meant endangering their tax-exempt status.

55. "American Domestic Politics," supra note 45, Part I at 34.

56. The Sierra Club et al., Letter to Ambassador Mickey Kantor, 27 February 1993.

been to the environmental agenda of NAFTA.[57] Both U.S. Trade Representative Mickey Kantor and negotiator Rufus Yerxa had met with NGO representatives and, in March 1993, regular briefings were held to keep nongovernment actors abreast of new developments. A number of similar briefings were also held in Canada.

On March 6, 1993, 25 organizations sent a letter to Mr. Kantor outlining their hopes and objectives for the NAAEC.[58] While important organizations such as the Sierra Club, Friends of the Earth, and Defenders of Wildlife signed this document, there was a central difficulty that prevented others such as NWF, WWF, and the NRDC from joining: The letter was emphasizing problems with the NAFTA text itself, not just demanding a strong NAAEC. Increasingly, the rift seemed to widen between NGOs that appeared to have no difficulty with (or even a preference for) NAFTA failing, like Public Citizen, the Sierra Club, and Greenpeace, and those that had some degree of commitment toward the NAFTA package, such as NWF, WWF, the Environmental Defense Fund, or the Nature Conservancy. Without oversimplifying complex circumstances, it seemed that the NGOs were divided in relation to the first issue we present in Part I: whether environmental protection and economic growth can be at all reconciled. The groups more supportive of the agreement were hopeful that more trade would mean more growth—particularly in Mexico where poverty remains endemic—and political decisions allowing more resources to be devoted to environmental protection. In general, the NGOs that opposed NAFTA on any terms had come to the conclusion that more trade meant more environmentally harmful economic activity, as exemplified by the maquiladoras, and that growth would only benefit corporate interests and Mexican business elites.

On May 7, the members of the U.S. private governmental advisory team (NWF, WWF, the Audubon Society, NRDC, Nature Conservancy,

---

57. Or, as one seasoned observer commented: "[t]he U.S. Administration recognized that it could not get NAFTA accepted against the environmental lobby. So, it set about buying the opposition off." In February 1993, EPA and Environment Canada funded a colloquium hosted in Santa Fe by the North American Institute. This meeting produced the framework document on cooperation: "The North American Environment: Opportunities for Trinational Cooperation by Canada, the United States and Mexico." This report helped build a foundation for NGO support for the institutional cooperation aspects of the side agreement and diminish somewhat the focus on enforcement and sanctions.

58. Defenders of Wildlife, Center for International Environmental Law et al., Letter to Ambassador Mickey Kantor, March 6, 1993.

and the Environmental Defense Fund) in addition to the Center for International Environmental Law (CIEL) and Defenders of Wildlife published a letter supporting a NAFTA/NAAEC package that reduced the pressure on USTR and therefore lowered the threshold of what the government was expected to accomplish at the negotiating table. Even though many environmental groups, and even House Majority Leader Gephart, criticized this conciliatory position, the "March 7 letter became the standard by which the NAFTA package would be judged" by U.S. NGOs.[59] The perception in the wider public was that credible environmental organizations supported NAFTA on the condition that the parallel agreement be substantive enough. At that point, it became clear that the environmental NGO community had expended a significant amount of its political leverage to push for a strong parallel agreement. At the same time, this accomplishment undoubtedly was attained at the cost of a diminished influence in the rest of the debate.

Environmental groups did however continue to make their presence felt. The initiative of organizations such as the Sierra Club, Public Citizen, and Friends of the Earth, in urging for an environmental impact statement (EIS) of NAFTA did produce dividends: On June 30, 1993 the U.S. District Court ruled in their favor against the U.S. Trade Representative. The latter, in expressing its intention to appeal the decision, maintained that NAFTA was not subject to the National Environmental Policy Act, which calls for an EIS for those federal actions "significantly affecting the quality of the human environment." It was the view of the Clinton administration that, while NAFTA did require implementing legislation, presidential actions, of which NAFTA is one, do not require EIS review.[60] Other environmental groups suggested a quicker EIS process, where existing data could be compiled within a time period of several months.[61] With the legal issue still unresolved, in August 1993, the debate shifted again to substantive questions as the NAAEC negotiations entered their final phase.

The final text of the NAAEC was completed in August 1993, and an elaborate signing ceremony was conducted at the White House on September 14. The day before, the division in the environmental commu-

59. "American Domestic Politics," supra note 45, Part I at 34.

60. Keith Bradsher, "U.S. Appeals Trade-Accord Requirement," *The New York Times,* 25 August 1993, C1.

61. "Brief of *Amici Curiae* Natural Resources Defense Council et al.," U.S. Court of Appeals for the District of Columbia Circuit, No. 93-5212, *Public Citizen et al. v. U.S. Trade Representative,* 14 August 1993.

nity was made irrevocable when the president of the Sierra Club, speaking on behalf more than 300 mostly smaller grassroots organizations, announced its formal opposition to the NAFTA package.[62] The day after, six larger environmental organizations announced their formal support for the NAFTA package at a press conference organized by Senator Max Baucus and attended by Vice President Gore and EPA administrator Carol Browner: NWF, WWF, Audubon, NDRC, EDF, and Conservation International. While the environmental issues became less important in the following weeks leading to the final votes, this alignment of environmental forces against one another persisted. In the fall, more grassroots and activist-led organizations like Public Citizen and Greenpeace relied on public advocacy to criticize NAFTA's environmental provisions, while organizations more sympathetic to trade, such as NWF and WWF, remained close to the inside political process gathering support for the NAFTA package, which was eventually ratified on November 17, 1993 and signed by President Clinton on December 8, 1993.

In the end, division in the U.S. NGO community was a factor contributing to the steadily diminishing profile of the environmental agenda during the negotiations leading to NAFTA and NAAEC. And indeed, by the end, many, including leading environmentalists, had come to the conclusion that the improvements to the NAFTA package were, if not ideal, certainly significant enough to consider the package in a new light, especially given the environmental efforts demonstrated by the Mexican government in the preceding three years. While in mid-1992 it appeared the environmental issue might prove to be the "linchpin" determining the fate of the agreement, by the Summer of 1993 the perception in the wider public was that NAAEC was going to satisfactorily address the environmental consequences of NAFTA.

---

62. For its part, the Canadian Environmental Law Association, an Ontario-based NGO, considered that "[n]othing in the so-called NAFTA 'side-agreements' or proposed North American Environmental Commission can fix the environmental problems that will flow from NAFTA." See "NAFTA and Democratic Process," Canadian Environmental Law Association—NAFTA Facts (Toronto, 1992).

Chapter 2

Trade and Environment: Issues for the 1990s

While the historical and political context forced environmental issues onto the NAFTA stage, the ongoing debate on the relationship between international trade and the global environment provided many elements of the script.[63] Free trade and environmental issues were not always closely associated in the minds of trade specialists and environmental activists.[64] In 1988, the Canadian opponents of free trade predominately focused their attention on the issues of protecting distinctive Canadian social programs and a rather ill-defined notion of

---

63. For some references to the trade and environmental issues that predate the current debate, see Williams Commission, *United States Economic Policy in an Interdependent World* (1971) at 777–779; Charles S. Pearson, "The Trade and Environment Nexus: What Is New Since '72" in D. Zaelke et al. eds., supra note 45, Part I; Seymour J. Rubin and Thomas R, Graham, eds., *Environment and Trade: The Relation of International Trade and Environmental Policy* (Totowa, New Jersey: Allan Held, Osmun, 1982). "Environment and Development: The Founex Report" (1972) 586 International Conciliation 28; Robert Boardman, *International Organization and the Conservation of Nature* (Bloomington: Indiana University Press, 1981) 89–92.

64. For a discussion of the cultural gap between environmentalists and trade experts, see "Environment and Trade; Talking Across Culture," box in Magraw, supra note 2, Part I at 19. Furthermore, as C. Ford Runge noted: "[o]verall, the *environmental* com-

national sovereignty. As has been suggested, with NAFTA all that had changed. Apart from transboundary and border issues, the environmental concerns of NAFTA opponents mirror quite closely the main arguments that have been used by environmentalists against trade liberalization in the context of the GATT and other international trade negotiations.

Generally, there are five main arguments. The first is that promoting economic growth through trade liberalization is intrinsically incompatible with environmental protection and sustainable resource management. The second argument is that specific trade liberalizing rules (such as the so-called disciplines against technical barriers to trade) threaten the ability of national governments to legislate in favor of the environment. Third, it is argued that the mobility of capital would also put downward pressure on environmental norms because investors would systematically seek to improve their competitiveness by locating in the least regulated areas (so-called pollution havens), an argument that raises the complex and politically tricky matter of international environmental harmonization. The fourth argument against current international trade law principles is that they appear to prevent, as we shall see, an importing country from making access to its markets contingent on the exporter's ensuring sound domestic environmental practices and adherence to international environmental agreements.[65] This question has especially mobilized American NGOs who feel a powerful pressure instrument is threatened by international economic law. The fifth and final argument against free trade is a recurrent criticism of trade regimes as to their lack of transparency and access, undermining their environmental credibility and political legitimacy. Literature on these issues has multiplied in recent years. The following is intended

---

munity generally sees risks in more open trade, while the *trade* community sees threats to economic growth and integration if environmental concerns lead to barriers to trade. Advocates of more open trade and environmentalists alike share concerns over how global environmental and trade agreements are to be linked, whether one or the other should take precedence, and the methods by which conflicts should be resolved." Runge, supra note 21, Part I at 5–6. See also "Making Trade," supra note 36, Part I at 2–3.

65. In fact there is increasing pressure to incorporate trade measures as an enforcement mechanism in international environmental agreements to provide discipline on signatories and nonsignatories alike. See generally Department of Foreign Affairs and International Trade, *Stacking the Deck: Compliance and Dispute Settlement in International Environmental Agreements,* (Policy Staff Paper No. 93/15) by K. H. Christie (Ottawa: Queen's Printer, December 1993).

simply as a cursory examination of these interlocking arguments to serve as a background to a more thorough analysis of NAFTA's environment-related provisions and the significance of the NAAEC. The reader will have to refer to some of the works mentioned in the footnotes for a more comprehensive review.

Trade, Growth, and the Environment

The argument that international trade promotes economic growth and that such economic growth intrinsically threatens the environment is at once true, incomplete, and misleading.[66] It is formally true that, in the absence of environmental regulations, expanded economic activity puts more pressure on natural renewable and nonrenewable resources. For this reason, 150 years of industrialization have left the developed countries with a legacy of environmental degradation and resource depletion that governments are only now beginning to understand and redress. Moreover, rapid new industrialization threatens to inflict the same environmental destruction on many developing countries. If more and easier trade means more growth, it is necessary to ask ourselves what kind of growth it will be. It cannot be growth of the kind seen throughout the Industrial Revolution of the West.

However, the unqualified assertion that economic growth by definition always threatens the environment is simplistic and misleading.[67] Environmental pollution and resource depletion can be mitigated and counteracted. The extent to which economic growth is managed in an environmentally sustainable way depends most of all on the political leadership, at both the national and international level.[68] Thus while no one expects industrial capitalistic civilization to wither away, some

---

66. For examples of this view see Michael McClosky, "NRDC Urges Environmental Protection Within North American Free Trade Agreement," Testimony Before the Senate Committee on Foreign Relations, 22 March 1991; Sierra Club, Press Release, "Administration Mexican Free Trade Proposal Sierra Club Charges a Lack of Assured Environmental Performance Measures" (2 May 1991).

67. Jagdish Bhagwati, "Trade and the Environment: The False Conflict" in Durwood Zaelke et al. eds., supra note 45, Part I.

68. For a recent and articulate exposition of this view see: *Freer Trade*, supra note 21, Part I. See also Robert Repetto, *Trade and Environmental Policies: Achieving Complementarities and Avoiding Conflicts* (Washington, D.C.: World Resources Institute, 1993). For a different perspective, see also Herman E. Daly and John B. Cobb Jr., *For the Common Good: Redirecting the Economy Toward Continuity, the Environment and a Sustainable Future* (Boston: Beacon Press, 1989).

of the wealth created by economic growth will have to be directed toward environmental protection. If, however, adequate environmental spending is to be assured through fiscal transfers and reallocations or regulatory schemes designed to increase private spending on pollution control and sustainable resource management (that is, the polluter pays principle), then steady wealth creation becomes a necessity.[69] In essence, environmental protection and economic growth may go hand-in-hand; the significant environmental progress achieved in developed countries over the last two decades, albeit insufficient, squarely attests to this.[70]

Our societies and the global community they form will determine whether or not economic growth degrades the environment we share. Overall, the evidence shows that as per capita income rises in a country, the level of pollution generated per unit of GNP tends to level off and eventually decline.[71] Of course, there is nothing inevitable about this phenomenon, but there is also some evidence that the share of GDP dedicated to the environment rises sharply when the US$ 5,000 per capita income mark is reached.[72]

---

69. On the application of that principle, see "The Maquiladora Problem," supra note 23, Part I at 329. For other examples of this view, see generally: "National Wildlife Federation Endorses Green Provisions in Trade Pact with Mexico," (Jan.-Feb. 1993) International Wildlife; Peter Emerson, "NAFTA Passage Can Protect the Environment," (8 January 1993) Austin American Statesman; William K. Reilly, "Pollution Won't Be a Byproduct," L.A. Times (2 August 1992) at M5; Sen. Phil Gramm, "Leaving Mexico at the Altar," The Washington Post (1 June 1993) at A17.

70. As Runge asserts:" [t]rade and environmental interests can often be pursued jointly, in a manner that protects the benefits that expanded trade can bring, while ensuring that these benefits do not come at the expense of the environment. Finding areas of complementarity is a difficult balancing act. Different circumstances will imply different priorities attached to trade and environmental interests. If a new doctrine is expressed in this study, it is the doctrine of balance between trade and the environment." Runge, supra note 21, Part I at 7.

71. Gene M. Grossman and Alan B. Krueger, "Environmental Impacts of a North American Free Trade Agreement" (Paper presented to Mexican Secretaria de Comercio y Fomento Industrial, 8 October 1991).

72. See G.M. Grossman and A.B. Krueger, "Environmental Impacts of the North American Free Trade Agreement" (Paper presented to the Woodrow Wilson School, Princeton University, February 1992) Discussion Paper No. 158 at 8–20. The authors acknowledge, however, that the mechanics of the relationship they appear to have discovered remain unexplored. See also: Keith Bradsher, "Impasse Ends on Sanctions for American Trade Pact," International Herald Tribune (14–15 August 1993) at 1. It was only with President Salinas' commitment to incorporate minimum wage standards into NAFTA that deadlock to side agreement negotiations was broken. The fact that these

As well, increased trade and investment may have some positive environmental implications for North America. The point is not often made in the trade and environment debate, but trade competition does favor more efficient resource allocation and may prevent resource degradation and depletion in important areas like agriculture, forestry, and wood products. Concretely, improved market access for environmentally friendly products and services can provide better instruments for pollution prevention and cleanup. Increased international exchange and communication means that the best environmental management techniques will travel more freely in the NAFTA area.[73] Some empirical evidence suggests that in Latin America, economies that can be classified as relatively open ones are more likely to adopt cleaner production technologies than are those that are more closed.[74]

Moreover, economic growth is essential to respond to demographic growth and legitimate material aspirations, particularly south of the American border. To say that decision makers are unable to devote some of the economic benefit brought by freer trade to making economic development more environmentally sustainable is misleading. It is like arguing in 1900 that higher national income was useless because the government would refuse to spend new revenues on health, education, and assistance to the neediest—a lack of faith in the power of institutions to evolve, improve, and ultimately reform themselves.

Finally, the argument that economic growth inherently threatens the environment is also misleading because its proponents, like the least enlightened industrialists, pit development against the environment in a zero-sum game. Since the Brundtland Report, we should know better. With direction and perseverance and great efforts, it is possible to

---

findings are "based on a narrow empirical base (sulfur dioxide emissions in the seventies), from a time when environmental policies were manifestly inadequate" has, however, attracted criticism of the conclusions reached.

73. Including, in the NAFTA, special provisions for accelerated tariff reductions and removal of barriers to specialized environmental products and services would have been as much of a gain for the environment as making the trade disciplines more sensitive or including the provision on pollution havens. Arguably, such inclusion was also easier. In 1992, the Mexican market for environmental technology and services was estimated at $1 billion. See Andrew Lowry, "North American Free Trade and the Environment," *Bus. Am.* (19 October 1992) at 22.

74. Nancy Birdsall and David Wheeler, "Openness Reduces Industrial Pollution in Latin America: The Missing Pollution Haven Effect" (Paper presented to the World Bank Symposium on International Trade and the Environment, 21–22 November, 1991).

feed billions and preserve the stock and quality of the world's culti-
vated lands. It is possible for industry to operate in the northeastern
part of the continent without destroying the Great Lakes water system.
It is possible to consume substantial amounts of energy for human welfare and production without destabilizing global ecosystems. It is possible to industrialize Mexico further without proportionally increasing
pollution. To believe that environmentally sensitive growth is possible
is really to believe in human possibilities. In short, the optimistic and
humanistic wager of sustainable development is that trade-supported
economic growth and environmental protection can be pursued simul-
taneously without systematically undermining each other.[75]

Ultimately, an argument that trade must be curtailed to slow economic growth and environmental degradation has to rest on the dubi-
ous foundation that all modern economic activity is *by definition* a
threat to the environment. The challenge against trade then becomes
a small element of a vast agenda designed to change not only business
practices, government regulations, or even the definition of economic
growth, but also the very essence of our relationship with the natural
world. While this agenda may be promoted by a minority, it often borders on misanthropy, and it falls well beyond the scope of this work.

Downward Pressures on Environmental Standards

While the case for the reconciliation of trade, growth, and sound environmental practices can be made strongly, opponents of free trade
have rightly pointed at two phenomena that accompany trade liberalization that may put downward pressure on environmental standards:
the legal mechanisms designed to allow the challenge of environmental technical barriers to trade, and the market phenomenon of capital
gravitating to areas where environmental costs related to production
are the lowest because they are not properly internalized. The unacceptable environmental impacts of increased trade and economic
growth are better treated as a classic market failure. They are the consequence of administrative practices and a regulatory system that prevent proper internalization of environmental compliance costs.[76]

---

75. As Runge maintains: "[s]triking a balance between trade and the environment
requires a careful assessment of these impacts and the cost of minimizing damages, and
recognition of the fact that additional environmental regulations may be necessary.
Fundamentally, this is a matter of offsetting damages linked to trade by imposing some
type of regulation, including changes in economic incentives through taxes, subsidies,
or fees." Runge, supra note 21, Part I at 12.

76. Ibid. at 24.

International Legal Disciplines

Simply stated, free trade agreements like NAFTA liberalize trade in one or both of two ways: They provide for the phasing out of tariffs, and, additionally, they provide legal instruments to remove unnecessary nontariff barriers to trade (the so-called trade disciplines). It is this latter mechanism that may threaten environmental norms.[77] For example, an exporting country can file a complaint under GATT or NAFTA rules alleging that a Canadian or a Mexican norm on pesticides in produce, on car emissions, or on an appliance's energy efficiency, is either an unnecessary measure, a disguised way to keep imports out, or a measure that impedes trade more than is truly "necessary" to protect the environment. The arbitration of that complaint (and the inevitable counterclaim of the party complained against) is undertaken by an international panel that will qualify the domestic measure and the norms embodied thereby. Such environmental standards may be imperiled even if they are not targeting trade activity, even if they are not singling out imported goods as such, or even if they are taken pursuant to international environmental agreements. In fact, the claim that trade disciplines immediately threaten the environmental policies of states has gained such currency among NGOs that it often seems to go unchallenged.[78] That being said, trade rules will always raise at least two questions: Is the environmental measure imposing a burden

---

77. For example, a full-page ad in *The Washington Post* and *The New York Times* purchased by a group of NGOs in 1992 claimed that: "the only thing free about free trade is the freedom it gives the world's largest corporations to circumvent democracy and kill those local and national laws that protect people and the planet.. . .In the present GATT talks called the *Uruguay Round,* new trade rules may soon give foreign governments the ability to challenge U.S. (and other democracies') laws as 'barriers' to free trade . . . these new sets of trade rules. . .could be used against *thousands* of laws. . .that give priority to clean food and clean water, protect sea mammals and wildlife, preserve trees or other resources, restrict poisonous pesticide sprays, save rain forests, and safeguard small farmers from being overpowered by agribusiness."

78. As the Canadian Environmental Law Association was typically claiming in 1993, "[u]nder NAFTA, existing Canadian regulations on occupational health, worker safety, pollution levels and protection of the environment will be 'harmonized' with lower standards in the U.S. and Mexico. This is worrisome enough. But provincial, state and federal governments will also lose much of their power to adopt new laws in these areas. And for the first time, Canadian health and safety regulations will have to balance risks to human health with economic factors—a losing proposition." See "NAFTA and Standards," Canadian Environmental Law Association—NAFTA Facts (Toronto, 1993). In fact, since modifications to domestic environmental protection legislation, arising out of closed international trade negotiations, are carried out by agencies exercising their discretion over the implementation of legislation, such changes are rarely subject to Congressional or Parliamentary scrutiny. One can consider, for example, the

on trade? Can that burden be justified by the necessity of and the benefits from the application of that environmental measure?[79]

In 1993–1994, there was a dispute between the province of Ontario and the United States regarding an Ontario government measure designed to promote the reuse of glass beer bottles by means of a tax on metal aluminum cans. U.S. beer producers claim that such a measure is protectionist because American beer, available predominantly in cans, and thus subject to the extra tax, is at a disadvantage against Canadian beer, which comes mostly in bottles, the container favored by the policy. The Ontario government has responded that bottled beer is promoted because reusable containers reduce waste. The United States could take Canada to dispute settlement and gain the right to take trade sanctions against Canada if a panel finds that the provincial recycling policy violates trade law. This illustrates how the legal discipline against technical barriers to trade could undermine environmental regulation.[80] Opponents of NAFTA worry that its prohibitions on unnecessary technical barriers to trade are too demanding to give governments enough room to adopt needed and appropriate environmental protection legislation, which often by definition constrains trade activities.

It must be noted at the outset that the seminal example of environmentally hostile trade disciplines was the 1991 GATT Tuna–Dolphin case.[81] In this instance, the main grounds for the successful arbitral commercial challenge of an environmentally related provision of law (banning tuna imports based on the damage inflicted upon dolphin populations by the fishing methods used) were its arbitrary character and the violation of sovereignty by the extraterritorial application of conservation measures; it was not the discrimination or unnecessariness of U.S. restrictions. Of course, the panel's decision may not be a reliable guide for predicting the future interpretation of trade disciplines with regard to environmental laws, and there have been only a

---

1990 *Clean Air Act* Amendments. For a discussion of this, see "Democratizing International Decision-Making," supra note 14, Part I at 737. See also: *Regulation of Fuels and Fuel Additives; Standards for Reformulated and Conventional Gasoline,* 57 Fed. Reg. 13,416 (1992); Michael Bergsman, "EPA to Change Clean Air Rule to Ward Off Threatened GATT Challenge," *Inside U.S. Trade,* 25 March 1994, at 1, 13–14.

79. Robert Hudec and Daniel Farber, "Distinguishing Environmental Measures from Trade Barriers." (Prepared for Workshop on International Economic Policy, University of Minnesota, 17 November 1992).

80. On this issue, see the similar European dispute described in the "Danish bottle case," *Commission v. Denmark (Beverage Containers)* Case 302-86, 1988, E.C.R. 4607.

81. Supra note 33, Part I.

few more cases where such disciplines were used to challenge environmental legislation. Moreover, one of the motivating principles underlying the decision in the Tuna–Dolphin affair is precisely the national sovereignty of Mexico over conservation and fisheries policy. This decision undercut American sovereignty only to the extent that its unilateral actions seemed intent on regulating activities lying outside its jurisdiction. Indeed, under current international law, the principle of national sovereignty will tend to favor the upholding of domestic environmental measures, whatever their merits, over trade law challenges. The reader will find a more extended discussion of both this panel ruling and a further decision in the following pages.

Investment Flow Distortion, Pollution Havens, and the Competitiveness Issue

Even if NAFTA's legal disciplines could be tailored to completely protect existing and future environmental norms in the three countries, another threat to environmental regulations is often invoked: that of the natural functioning of a free market economy when the regulatory landscape is uneven. In other words, the applicability of the principle of comparative advantage in the environmental arena would put pressure on governments to loosen environmental standards. According to that argument, the least environmentally regulated areas would be magnets for investment and, as hosts to the most competitive enterprises, would put downward pressure on environmental standards in neighboring countries and economic partners.[82] In such a situation, three sets of circumstances can lead to environmental degradation: (1) Absent regulations, business enterprises are not adopting adequate internal environmental measures that would allow them to properly internalize environmental costs that are then borne by the natural world and society at large; (2) the norms adopted by regulatory authorities are too low and do not make companies adopt such measures and standards; or (3) the authorities are not adequately enforcing environmental norms that would otherwise provide for an accept-

---

82. See H. Leonard, *Are Environmental Regulations Driving U.S. Industry Overseas?* (Washington, D.C.: The Conservation Foundation, 1984); P. Low and A. Yeats, "Do 'Dirty' Industries Migrate?" (Discussion paper presented at the World Bank Symposium on International Trade and the Environment, 21–22 November 1991). For a further exposition of this view, see Daly and Cobb supra note 68, Part I at 209; U.S. Congress, General Accounting Office, *U.S.–Mexico Trade: Some U.S. Wood Furniture Firms Relocated from Los Angeles Area to Mexico,* GAO/NSIAD-91-191 (Gaithersburg, MD.: U.S. General Accounting Office, 1991).

able level of cost internalization. From an environmental point of view, such failure to internalize environmental costs prevents proper conservation and pollution control because it costs too little to waste, degrade, and pollute. Many claim liberalized trade unleashes market forces that end up preventing proper cost internalization. From a trade point of view, some specialists and politicians carry the argument further and contend that these three situations are different versions of the same evil: both an unfair "subsidy" to enterprises that export to jurisdictions where environmental costs are better internalized and an unfair magnet for international investment. This is the ground on which some environmentalists and trade lobbyists sometimes meet.

The argument that market forces threaten high environmental standards rests on three assumptions: (1) Countries want to attract investments and prevent capital from leaving; (2) increasingly footloose investment capital will go to the regions that present business with a competitive advantage; and (3) low or unenforced environmental standards represent an often decisive competitive advantage because they allow meaningful savings on production costs.

The first proposition is obviously true. The second one is defendable, even if the mobility of capital is always restricted by the costs of moving and adapting (not *every* kind of business can relocate to *any* region.) The third proposition is the weakest argument in an unresolved debate. That debate centers on the fear that parties, especially Mexico, would be able to attract investment by lowering their environmental standards or by not applying them, thereby putting pressure on Canada and the United States to do the same if they wanted to keep and attract business investment. This is the area where environmental concerns become most intelligible to trade specialists. It can be argued that if appropriate environmental policies are uniformly in place, the principle of comparative advantage retains its original force, since national competition is now based on appropriately internalized environmental costs. The difficulty lies in finding instruments to measure and compare the environmental cost internalization effected by each trading partners' domestic policies.

With regard to the environment as a competitiveness issue, it must be said at the outset that the drafters of NAFTA and NAAEC seem to accept that argument. Consider NAFTA's declaration that parties should not lower environmental standards with the goal of attracting investment.[83] Consider also a NAAEC dispute settlement procedure

---

83. See infra notes 144–146, Part II and accompanying text.

that clearly indicates, as will be shown, that the drafters thought lax environmental law enforcement confers on a country an unfair competitive advantage.[84] These two concrete, deliberate choices indeed betray a clear apprehension that some parties might lower standards or pay no attention to enforcement in order to attract investment or improve the competitiveness of their exports. This admission of sorts that competitive pressures threaten environmental norms might in time be proven to be a needed precaution, but it is not yet supported by a wealth of evidence.[85]

For most industries, the cost of complying with environmental regulations represents a small portion of the cost of doing business as compared with the costs of capital equipment, inputs, or the costs associated with workforce productivity, political stability, wages, communication and transportation infrastructures, or tax rules.[86] But for other industries, such as, for example, the mining, chemical, and pulp and paper industries, environmental compliance costs tend to be more significant, are generally on the rise, and may influence investment decisions more directly.[87] As well, substantive regulatory constraints, thresholds, and standards, as they evolve, will affect the relative com-

---

84. See infra notes 12–18, Part IV and accompanying text.

85. A review by the U.S. Congressional Office of Technology Assessment found that the studies that examined the relative competitive impacts of environmental regulation for manufacturing did not offer a clear conclusion on such impacts. See *Conflicts and Opportunities*, supra note 28, Part I at 59, 97–104; See Judith L. Ugelow, "A Survey of Recent Studies on Costs of Pollution Control and the Effects of Trade," in Rubin and Graham, eds., supra note 63, Part I; Judith M. Dean, "Trade and the Environment: A Survey of the Literature," in Patrick Low, ed., *International Trade and the Environment*, World Bank Discussion Papers, no. 159 (Washington, D.C., 1992); "Reconciling Trade and the Environment," supra note 41, Part I; Carl Pasurka, "Environmental Control Costs and U.S. Effective Rates of Protection," (1985) 13 Public Finance Quarterly 161.

86. A 1990 study showed that the environmental costs of 24 pollution intensive agricultural and manufacturing industries averaged between 1.9 and 2.9% of total production costs. See James A. Tobey, "The Effects of Domestic Environmental Policies on Patterns of World Trade: An Empirical Test," (1990) 43 *Kyklos* at 193–194.

87. In a study carried out by Patrick Low, entitled "Trade Measures and Environmental Quality: Implications for Mexico's Exports," presented at the World Bank Symposium on International Trade and the Environment in November 1991, it was found that the cement industry is the heaviest polluter. Pollution control activities incurred by this industry represent only 3% of the total output of production. Moreover, only 18 of 123 Standard Industrial Classification (SIC) Code industries face environmental costs of greater than 1% of total production output, a figure above the average of 0.54% of production output for all SIC Code industries. These seemingly small figures are nevertheless not insignificant since the average tariff on nonprimary products is often at

pliance costs faced by each sector of economic activity. Some sectors will face higher and swifter compliance cost increases than others. Given the general trend of increasingly stringent environmental norms, the relative weight of environmental compliance costs will tend to rise for many industries.

In assessing the impact of differing standards on investment flows, it must be remembered that regulatory decisions at the national, provincial, or state levels are influenced by many factors other than the desire to attract investment. Public opinion, scientific expertise, the state of public finances, the corporate culture of environmental agencies, the political concerns of decision makers, negotiations with relevant jurisdictions, as well as wider resources management schemes all play a role. While a worry about competitiveness and its implications for growth and employment increasingly influences legislators and public servants, it is not always the dominant factor in choosing among alternative environmental policies. Empirical studies on the issues of relocation and investment flow pattern nullification do not, for the moment, support the hypothesis that environmental regulation is an important factor in the decision.[88]

While the debate has not yet been concluded and may not be for a long time, investment relocation based on the attractiveness of environmentally deregulated areas remains at least *perceived* by many as a major threat to the North American environment because of the downward pressure on standards it could cause. Indeed, the popularity of the canon of competitiveness among politicians the world over is an indication that a small environmental influence on competitiveness might, at times, be enough to put some environmental policies in jeopardy. At the same time, the purpose of a trade agreement like NAFTA

3–4%. See John H. Jackson, *The World Trading System: Law and Policy of International Economic Relations* (Cambridge: M.I.T. Press, 1989) at 53; Ingo Walter, "International Economic Repercussions of Environmental Policy: An Economist's Perspective," in Rubin and Graham, eds., supra note 63, Part I. On the other hand, a study of U.S. "maquiladoras" plants (plants located in Mexico near the U.S. border by virtue of a Border Industrialization Program) found no link between the low level of Mexican regulations and U.S. investment. Roberto Sanchez, "Health and Environmental Risks of the Maquiladora in Mexicali," (1990) 30 Natural Resources Journal.

88. "Trade and the Environment: A Survey of the Literature," supra note 85, Part I at 27. According to the Congressional Office for Technology Assessment, "in general, there is little evidence that large-scale shifts in industrial investment and relocation to pollution havens have occurred." See *Conflicts and Opportunities*, supra note 28, Part I at 40.

is to promote a freer flow of investment and to allow the mechanism of comparative advantage to bring about maximum efficiency in production. There is only so much that such an agreement can do to slow financial migrations that are motivated by environmental permissiveness. Therefore, an intervention to prevent investment flows from unduly influencing environmental policies may ultimately have to lie mostly outside trade treaties.[89] For this reason, most of the safeguards against the impact of capital mobility on environmental policies are really found in the NAAEC. Within these constraints both official texts do address, even if in an incomplete fashion, the issue of competitiveness and investment flows.

Harmonization of Environmental Standards

Having recognized that trade legal disciplines and capital relocation could, particularly in the uneven North American environmental protection terrain, impose downward pressures on environmental norms, many, both inside and outside the environmental community, have proposed harmonization of standards as a solution to this danger. Indeed, experience seems to indicate that some degree of harmonization of laws and policies, including environmental regulatory schemes, is the natural companion of economic integration and intensified trade. The objective must be, of course, to harmonize upward to a greater level of protection for the environment in all NAFTA countries. However, harmonization in North America and elsewhere remains a lengthy and difficult task for at least two reasons.

First, the harmonization of North American environmental standards amounts to harmonization between a developing country and two of the richest, most environmentally regulated countries in the world. This type of harmonization is the most difficult because developing countries, even fast developing ones like Mexico, often do not have access to the necessary technical and financial resources to par-

---

89. Which is not to say that trade regimes should not be sensitive to the impact of investment flows on environmental policies and respectful of eventual international legal instruments designed to address that issue. Runge argues: "[e]nvironmental targets, in other words, are generally best met by environmental policies; trade targets by trade policies. Whereas environmental problems may be *reinforced* by trade policies, they are unlikely to be best resolved through trade measures alone. Instead, some *combination* of trade and environmental policies will be most efficient." Runge, supra note 21, Part I at 28. See also Kerry Kruntila, "Environmental Regulation in an Open Economy," (1991) 20 Journal of Environmental Economics and Management 127.

ticipate on an equal footing with richer countries in upward harmonization.[90] Moreover, if formal harmonization of laws and regulations does take place, the means to implement the policies and enforce the higher norms might still be missing. Developing countries are wrestling with urgent problems of poverty, social cohesion, health, and unruly demographics. Social and environmental progress, as badly needed as it may be, even if it is the key to long-term sustainable prosperity, often remains relatively more taxing on the economies of poorer countries. Harmonization is difficult to effect without interfering to some extent with the decisions and the priorities chosen by the governments of the harmonizing countries. The difficulties that European countries continue to have in harmonizing environmental and other standards, despite their relatively similar incomes and converging economies, must give pause.[91] The practical and ethical challenges involved in environmental harmonization are not to be underestimated.

Second, environmental harmonization between NAFTA countries in areas such as impact assessment or pollution control would likely mean that Mexico would have to do most of the harmonizing and change many of its norms and practices to align them with often

---

90. Some commentators have suggested that legislation be adopted in Canada and the United States to make Canadian and American companies operating in Mexico subject to Canadian and American environmental regulations, respectively, and liable for violations of such regulations before their home tribunals. See "The Vital Treaty That Must Not Die: Dealing with Legitimate Criticism of NAFTA," *L.A. Times* (25 March 1993) at B6.

91. For a discussion of trade and environment issues in the European context, see generally Commission of the EU, *European Community, Environmental Legislation,* vol. I: *General Policy* (Luxembourg: Office of Official Publications, 1992); Stanley P. Johnson and Guy Corcelle, *The Environmental Policy of the European Communities,* International Environmental Law and Policy Series (London: Graham and Trotman, 1989); Amelia Porges, "Harmonization in the EU" (Geneva: Office of Legal Affairs, GATT Secretariat, 1993); Commission of the European Communities, Task Force on Environment and the Internal Market, *1992: The Environmental Dimension* (Bonn: Economica, Verlag, 1990); Runge, supra note 21, Part I at 35–53. It must be noted that Europe has the advantage of supranational institutions, which in principle facilitate harmonization. See also: F. Burrows, *Free Movement in European Community Law* (Oxford: Clarendon Press, 1987); *Conflicts and Opportunities,* supra note 28, Part I at 20; Cameron Keyes, *The European Community and Environmental Policy: An Introduction for Americans* (Baltimore: World Wildlife Fund Publications, 1991); Nigel Haigh and Konrad von Moltke, "The European Community: An Environmental Force" (July/August 1990) 16 EPA Journal.

higher American and Canadian standards. This uneven burden would not go unnoticed in Mexico where national affirmation is still tinged with anti-Americanism and an acute sense of the North/South divide. Indeed most developing countries are leery of what they see as a touch of imperialism and paternalism in the way wealthy Western countries regularly call for the upward harmonization of environmental norms toward protection levels they have only recently achieved themselves. Yet, the calls for tying improved trade access to promises of environmental action remain numerous in those Western countries.[92] Facing these calls, the feelings of unfairness remain palpable in countries of the developing world.

Another difficult question, aside from the relative scarcity of resources and the usual North–South political pitfalls, is whether *all* countries, rich and poor, big and small, should, in principle, from a scientific point of view, adopt the same level of environmental protection in *all* the fields of industry and human activity, even if they could. Different states and their ecosystems may present different ecological carrying capacity for certain types of contamination and different vulnerabilities to resource depletion. The acknowledgment of this reality, let alone the carrying out of its consequences in international environmental instruments, remains a politically explosive but legitimate question.[93] That question in turn reveals both the limits of our scientific knowledge on the relationship between human activity and the

---

92. While developing countries often resent "conditionality" (as when the International Monetary Fund demands anti-inflationary policies in return for loans), it may be a necessary prod in promoting them to raise environmental standards. In many respects, the environmental side agreement to NAFTA provides the clearest constructive example of the benefits of tying market access to a joint commitment to raise environmental standards. Presumably, these environmental improvements can be paid for in part out of the economic benefits of market access.

93. Larry Summers, then Chief Economist at the World Bank, created an international controversy on the eve of the Earth Summit of 1992 when he suggested that the World Bank should *encourage* the migration of dirty industries to developing countries. The justification was that much of the southern world was underpolluted and that its inhabitants should be willing to accept more toxic waste and pollution because the "costs" related to air pollution, aesthetic degradation, health problems, and even death were much lower than in wealthier countries. See "Let them eat pollution," *The Economist* (8 February 1992) 66. Can a developing country that is free from the contaminations befalling most developed countries really be characterized as "underpolluted"and present "such ecological" space as a simple resource that market forces can best allocate? Under that logic—if the word is not too strong—permissive environmental laws that allow developing countries to become pollution havens bring about the optimal allocation of resources. This crass, disembodied economic analysis gave liberalized trade

planet's health, and the complexity of the maze of interlocking and competing ethical concerns that form the social agenda of international trade and economic integration.

Trade Measures with Environmental Objectives and the Issue of Process and Production Methods (PPMs)

To the extent that harmonization is necessary and desirable to prevent distortions in competition as well as global environmental degradation, it cannot be limited to the *environmental product standards* targeted by the legal disciplines evoked earlier (that is, those standards that regulate the intrinsic characteristics of a product, like car emissions or a chemical's hazardous nature). Environmental damage often comes more from the *way* a product comes into existence than from the *use or the presence* of the product itself. Harmonization hence should extend to the environmental standards governing the *production* of goods and the manner in which natural resources are extracted or harvested. Harmonization, therefore, should extend to the regulation of environmental *process and production methods* (or so-called PPMs) relating to such things as air emissions, toxic releases, waste management, fishing methods, or even recycling regulations. In the trade and environment debate, the regulation of foreign PPMs is a recurring theme because it can directly affect international trade as it is meant to apply to all goods, wherever they are made or harvested. While meaningful harmonization must include these most important of environmental norms, the best way to undertake that harmonization is a hotly debated issue. In principle, international agreements providing for the harmonization of PPMs could contribute to the stability of the current trade regime because environmental costs would be the same for all producers. Trade-restricting measures could be used to enforce the international standards, even if, as was shown, there are potent political, ethical, and scientific arguments supporting the claim that environmental costs should *not* be uniform everywhere. On the other hand, if multilateral harmonization of PPMs proceeds too slowly, this could mean the unilateral raising of environmental non-

---

a bad name in environmental circles. It ought to be possible to discuss differentiated environmental policy without speaking of the "vastly inefficient air quality" of Africa, or that the "logic of dumping a load of toxic waste" in developing countries is "impeccable." See reply by Larry Summers, "Summers on sustainable growth," *The Economist* (30 May 1992) 65.

tariff barriers purportedly to restore the competitiveness balance, provide an incentive for compliance with harmonized standards, or punish environmental villains. In GATT law, the current interpretation is that PPMs are violations of GATT principles.[94]

Whether multilateral or unilateral in origin, a trade-restricting measure is always implemented in the end by individual countries. In other words, trade-restricting measures with environmental objectives can evolve out of a desire to enforce an international consensus, or they can reflect the opinion of a state that such consensus is not forming quickly enough in the international community.

Multilateral Trade-Affecting Measures

There thus are two main ways to deal with the harmonization of PPMs. The first is for countries to engage in multilateral discussions that may lead to banning or restricting certain practices by creating a minimum standard that all the parties promise to respect. The quintessential example of the multilateral approach is the *Montreal Protocol on Substances that Deplete the Ozone Layer*.[95] In this Protocol, *processes* as well as products involving certain banned substances are restricted and prohibited according to a schedule agreed to by a large number of countries. Funding instruments as well as provisions for the use of trade sanctions against violators are also included in this agreement. Other international agreements that contain provisions for trade sanctions and trade-affecting measures include most notably the *Convention on International Trade in Endangered Species of Wild Fauna and Flora* (CITES)[96] and the *Basel Convention on the Control of Transboundary Movement of Hazardous Waste and Their Disposal*.[97]

In each of these instances there is an international constituency that supports the objectives of the conventions and, presumably, accepts the infringement of the principle of the free movement of goods and the inefficiencies such derogation might entail. This is the major dif-

---

94. In *Tuna–Dolphin I* case, supra note 33, Part I, the panel concluded that Article III requires a comparison between the relative treatment of products coming from the complaining party and the party complained against (i.e., the importer), rather than a comparison between the two nations' differing production methods when the latter have no effect on the products themselves.

95. 16 September 1987, 26 I.L.M. 1541.

96. Supra note 18, Part I.

97. 22 March 1989, Doc. UNEP/WG. 190/4 (1989), Can. T.S. 1992 No. 19, 28 I.L.M. 649.

ference between multilateral trade-affecting measures and unilateral trade measures.

Unilateral Trade Measures

Alternatively, to achieve compliance with its PPM standards a country may try to exert influence over others unilaterally by threatening or resorting to sanctions. The weapon of choice in this respect appears to be trade sanctions: Trade-restricting PPM standards in domestic trade laws that deny market access and benefits normally granted to trading partners on environmental grounds. For example, on 10 April 1995 the United States decided to impose trade sanctions on Taiwan for refusing to halt the sale of tiger bones and rhinoceros horns. The sanction involves a ban on all Taiwan wildlife product exports to the United States, a value estimated at $25 million per year. President Clinton said in a statement that "the world must know that the U.S. will take strong actions to protect the Earth's natural heritage."[98] This may be an extreme example, since the trade sanctions have only a faint connection to the subject matter and that no attempt was made to pretend that they were GATT-legal. However, it is a good indication that the issue of unilateral trade measures used for environmental objectives may have moved a bit higher on the trade agenda of the United States.

This approach remains problematic. The mainstream of international trade law, as expressed in the WTO agreements and NAFTA, increasingly considers trade access more like a *right* that must be respected rather than a revocable *privilege* granted at the discretion of the importer. Unimpeded market access is derived from reciprocal obligations imposed by each contracting party upon itself in the form of tariff reductions and trade disciplines. In effect, imposing restrictions (such as duties, special rights, quotas) on the imports of a trading partner in excess of what a trade agreement allows is the denial of a right granted by that agreement. This remains true even if the motivation of the importing country is a dislike of the exporting country's environmental practices. As long as the trade agreement does not allow restrictions on imports based on environmental mismanagement in the exporting countries (the way it does for restrictions based on the harmfulness of the imports), unilateral environmental trade measures would generally imply a breach of contract by the importing country.

The unilateral approach involves putting pressure on other countries

---

98. Thomas L. Friedman, "U.S. Puts Sanctions on Taiwan" *The New York Times* (11 April 1995) B1.

by barring imports of products that are not produced in accordance with specific minimum PPMs. In effect, this signifies the extraterritorial application of internal environmental decisions and, if necessary, the enforcement of such decisions through trade sanctions. The best example and, in many ways, the catalyst for the current trade and environment debate is the aforementioned Tuna–Dolphin case.[99] In 1991, the GATT provoked the wrath of environmentalists by ruling that a U.S. statute, the *Marine Mammal Protection Act*,[100] was inconsistent with GATT rules in its prohibition of the importation of Mexican tuna.[101] This U.S. Act stipulated that where foreign fishing activities killed more than 1.25 times as many dolphins as the average number killed by American fishermen, the product of such fishing could not be "imported" into the United States.[102] The MMPA mandated trade embargoes on yellowfin tuna from any exporter to the United States, whose average killing of dolphin related to tuna harvesting in the Eastern Tropical Pacific exceeded this limit. The Act also required secondary embargoes on nations that did not ban imports from the nations targeted by the primary embargo declared by the

---

99. For a detailed account of the Tuna–Dolphin international legal saga see S. Charnovitz, "Dolphins and Tuna: An Analysis of the Second GATT Panel Report" (1994) 24 Environmental Law Reporter at 1967 [hereinafter "Dolphins and Tuna"]. See also: Jeffrey L. Dunoff, "Reconciling International Trade and Preservation of the Global Commons: Can We Prosper and Protect?" (1992) 49 Wash. & Lee L. Rev. 1407 at 1409–1422 [hereinafter "Can We Prosper?"]. Thomas E Skilton, Note, "GATT and the Environment in Conflict: The Tuna–Dolphin Dispute and the Quest for an International Conservation Strategy" (1993) 26 Cornell Int'l L.J. at 455; Robert F. Housman and Durwood J. Zaelke, "The Collision of the Environment and Trade: The GATT Tuna/Dolphin Decision" (1992) 22 Envtl. L. Rep. at 10268; Ted L. McDorman, "The 1991 U.S.–Mexico GATT Panel Report on Tuna and Dolphin" (1992) 17 N.C J. Int'l. L. & Com. Reg. 461 at 461–466. See also: Public Law 92-522, as amended by Public laws 100-711 and 101-627. Codified at 16 U.S.C. §1371. Implementing regulations are at 50 C.F.R. Part 216, and for commercial fleets at 50 C.F.R. 216.24.

100. 22 U.S.C. §1978 (1971) and 16 U.S.C. §1821 (1979).

101. Venezuela was also targeted by the MMPA. Between 1988 and May 1992, it is estimated that its tuna fishing fleet shrunk from 118 boats to just 34. James Brooke, "America—Environmental Dictator?" *The New York Times* (3 May 1992).

102. Tuna–Dolphin case, supra note 33, Part I at 1598. In June 1994, the MMPA was amended to include all tuna that is "sold" in the U.S., not only that which is imported, possibly in the hope of making it more acceptable under GATT rules. On the other hand, the amendments also include more severe penalties for offenders and prohibit all tuna that is not "dolphin-safe" under its own definition. It has been argued that such changes do not really represent an accommodation to GATT standards.

United States.[103] The GATT panel ruled on a number of issues. It declared that because the conditions imposed by U.S. law on foreign fishing were essentially unpredictable and unknowable, they could not be considered to be primarily aimed at the conservation of dolphins and thus could not avail themselves of the protection of GATT Article XX (b) and (g) environmental exceptions.[104] Most controversially, the panel ruled further that measures adopted by a country discriminating against the exports of a trading partner on the basis of the method of production or harvesting, for the purpose of applying its conservation policies extraterritorially, were not saved by the exception of GATT Article XX(g), which allows measures restricting trade when they relate "to the conservation of exhaustible natural resources."[105] It did so by introducing the concept of "extrajurisdictionality," which is an apparent attempt to prevent parties from trying to regulate activities that lie outside their domestic jurisdiction.[106] The reaction of U.S. NGOs was immediate and forceful. They quickly embarked on a quest

---

103. The GATT panel ruling did not, in fact, prevent a San Francisco judge in January 1992, a few months after the ruling, from issuing a secondary embargo on no less than 20 nations thought to be engaged in "tuna laundering." "America—Environmental Dictator?" supra note 101, Part I.

104. On the other hand, the panel did not rule out requiring green labeling using "Dolphin Friendly" labels on tuna products as a legitimate method of promoting both environmentally sound products and fishing methods. This possibility is important because eco-labels allow consumers in the most environmentally sophisticated markets to show manufacturers or producers that they expect them to adhere to the environmental standards of such markets. Indeed, in the year that followed the panel report, most major U.S. canners switched to exclusively dolphin-safe tuna, and many chose to advertise that decision on their labels.

105. The panel also ruled that the MMPA provisions were not covered by the Article III rule on "national treatment" because the embargo was not imposed in conjunction with a similar internal restrictive measure and was in violation of Article XI, which prohibits quantitative restrictions on imports.

106. Many U.S. NGOs feared this ruling would doom other provisions of U.S. law that sought to use trade-affecting measures for environmental objectives, such as the Packwood and Pelly Amendments (The Packwood Amendments to the Magnuson *Fishery Conservation and Management Act,* 16 U.S.C. §1821(e)(2); and the Pelly Amendment to the *Fishermen's Protective Act* of 1967, 22 U.S.C. §1978) designed to further the goals of the *International Convention for the Regulation of Whaling,* 2 December 1946, 1 U.S.T. 506, 161 U.N.T.S. 72, the *Endangered Species Act* 16 U.S.C. §1531, which prohibits trade in endangered species, and the *African Elephant Conservation Act,* 16 U.S.C. § 420, which bans ivory imports from countries that do not have adequate elephant conservation programs. See Steve Charnovitz, "Environmental Trade Sanctions and the GATT: An Analysis of the Pelly Amendment on Foreign Environmental Practices,"

to change GATT rules so as to prevent more rulings against environmentally motivated unilateral trade measures.[107]

A few points are worth noting on this affair.[108] First, the *ratio decidendi* is far from clear: There were many reasons for the partial Mexican victory. Second, dolphins were not—and are still not—an endangered species as such.[109] Third, the panel decision is neither GATT law nor NAFTA law, nor the received interpretation of international law.[110] Indeed, a second GATT panel report was prepared at the instigation of the European Union, and it appears to contradict the first panel report on the issue of whether Articles XX(b) and XX(g) forbid "extrajurisdictionality."[111] Fourth and last, the important role played by various U.S. lobbies who wanted to exclude Mexican exports underlines a funda-

---

(1994) 9 Am. U.J. Int'l, L. and Pol'y 751 [hereinafter "Environmental Trade Sanctions"]; Steve Charnovitz, "Encouraging Environmental Cooperation Through the Pelly Amendment" (1994) J. Env. & Dev 3.

107. *Impacts of Trade Agreements on U.S. Environmental Protection and Natural Resource Conservation Efforts: Hearing Before the Subcommittee on Environment and Natural Resources of the House Committee on Merchant Marine and Fisheries*, 103d Cong., 1st Sess., 23–24 (1993) (statement of John Audley, Trade Analyst, Sierra Club); *The Environmental Implications of the Uruguay Round of GATT: Hearing Before the Subcommittee on Economic Policy, Trade and the Environment, of the House Committee on Foreign Affairs*, 103d Cong., 2d Sess. (1994).

108. There is also an interesting debate around the historical interpretation of Article XX as it relates to extraterritoriality. See "Can We Prosper?" supra note 99, Part I; "Environmental Exceptions" supra note 13, Part I at 37; John H. Jackson, "World Trade Rules: Congruence or Conflict?" (1992) 49 Wash. and Lee L. Rev. 1227 at 1241–1242 [hereinafter "World Trade Rules"]; Steve Charnovitz, "GATT and the Environment: Examining the Issues" (1992) 4 International Environmental Affairs 203 at 209; Runge, supra note 21, Part I at 77–78; Steve Charnovitz "Green Roots, Bad Pruning: GATT Rules and their Application to Environmental Trade Measures" (1994) 7 Tulane Environmental L.J. 299 at 323–343 [hereinafter "Green Roots, Bad Pruning"].

109. "[I]t is sometimes argued that an animal has to be endangered to be covered by Article XX(b)." "Green Roots, Bad Pruning." Ibid. at 336; Tuna–Dolphin I, supra note 33, Part I at para. 4.29, 30 I.L.M. 1594 at 1645–1646.

110. The Panel decision has not been adopted by the GATT Council where all parties are represented: Mexico did not push for such an adoption because it did not want to jeopardize the NAFTA negotiations and GATT was severely criticized by the world environmental community for the panel decision. The Uruguay Round equivalent provisions might be interpreted differently. As well, there is no clear rule of precedent or *stare decisis* in international arbitration; a future panel might decide a similar issue in a different fashion.

111. *United States—Restrictions on Imports of Tuna*, 16 June 1994, 33 I.L.M. 839. Most important, the panel noted that the text of Article XX(g) does not specify or other-

mental fact: Trade politics and the various economic interests associated with it will often play a larger role in future trade and environment controversies than sound environmental science or fairness and equity. Indeed, there will rarely be clear-cut cases where essential environmental measures come under attack from a NAFTA partner brandishing trade disciplines when there is no domestic industry to protect.[112]

Given the often repeated official objective of upward harmonization of environmental norms, the NAFTA negotiators were presented with a number of options in the area of harmonization and extraterritoriality. They could have set up processes in NAFTA that sought to promote standardization and harmonization. As will be shown, to a certain extent they did.[113] They could have included substantive provisions in the NAAEC. They did not, even though the CEC might over time, develop recommendations on specific environmental norms that all NAFTA partners should share.[114] They could also have elaborated some rules allowing PPM-based unilateral trade sanctions on a circumscribed basis or in limited circumstances. The policing of the extraterritorial regulation of PPMs by the parties could have been envisaged using environmental criteria based either on immediate urgency or the

---

wise delimit the location of the resources to be conserved. This clearly illustrates that there is no *stare decisis* rule in international arbitration and thus no binding GATT precedents. See "World Trade Rules" supra note 108, Part I at 1273.

112. While preoccupations of space do not allow us to give them a fair treatment, there are other complaints about the lack of environmental sensitivity of international trade law, beyond the trade disciplines of Article XX. Chief among them are the effect of old GATT Article XI, which prohibits quantitative restrictions on imports, and Article III, which forces equal treatment for "like" foreign products as compared to the domestic equivalent. See "Green Roots, Bad Pruning," supra note 109, Part I at 305–308, 316–323, 332–335.

113. See infra notes 143–159, Part II and accompanying text.

114. The reason is very simple: NAFTA is not a very thorough economic integration package. It only creates a freer trading area where disputes are settled by an intergovernmental process. While three NAFTA commissions on trade, labor, and the environment are created, there is practically no formal delegation of sovereignty toward central institutions, including judicial institutions. In the European Union, formerly the European Community, the issues of environmental protection and standards harmonization are enormously complex and have not always been dealt with effectively. Nevertheless, a central institution, the European Court of Justice, was able to rule in 1989 that Denmark was free to require the reuse of drink containers, even if it conflicted with the application of the free movement of goods provisions of the Treaty of Rome, using legal tests of nondiscrimination and proportionality, balancing free trade with the protection of the environment as a mandatory requirement of Community law. See: *RE Disposable Beer Cans* (1989) 1 C.M.L.R. 619.

standards of international environmental agreements, as well as trade-based criteria and norms of behavior (like the avoidance of compliance costs or injury to domestic producers). The NAFTA negotiators did no such thing, thereby making it more likely that the Tuna–Dolphin interpretation hostile to such unilateral action will ultimately prevail in the NAFTA arena, although the authors will explore some arguments against this restrictive interpretation in Part II. Instead, the NAAEC provides for the upward harmonization of environmental *enforcement* (not protection) levels if need be through the use of panel-sanctioned trade measures.

On trade-affecting measures, NAFTA provides a fairly clear direction. The principle of market access is given precedence over the freedom to use unilateral trade action to attempt to protect the environment outside one's territory.[115] Trade measures designed to further the implementation of multilateral environmental agreements are, however, generally acceptable under innovative exemption rules. Harmonization of environmental standards as envisioned in NAFTA will not be a coerced affair.

On the whole, the NAFTA/NAAEC package might represent a rejection of resorting to unilateral trade action.[116] NAFTA parties, however, have fully retained their ability to use or modify their trade legislation purportedly to achieve environmental objectives. Some pregnant silences in the legal text on this very issue will allow, in the United States particularly, the claim to be made once again that such unilateral actions are necessary.

The Lack of Transparency of Traditional Trade Institutions

The last argument that environmental NGOs have been invoking against the current trade regimes is a recurrent criticism of their lack of transparency and access to the process, thus undermining their environmental credibility and political legitimacy.[117] Either through trade discipline arbitration or through their impact on regulators, trade disputes will affect the administration and the very existence of environ-

---

115. Unless these trade sanctions are taken in accordance with an international environmental agreement listed under NAFTA Article 104.2. See infra notes 128–142, Part II and accompanying text.

116. This is the position that the GATT Secretariat forcefully took in 1992. See GATT, *International Trade 90–91*, vol. I (Geneva, 1992) at 19–39.

117. Housman writes: "[i]n this era of economic belt tightening, international trade agreements hold considerable sway over the domestic policies of nations. The strength

mental regulation. Yet trade dispute settlement whether formal or informal remains for the most part opaque. Interested parties are neither apprised of the progress of a particular dispute nor allowed to make representations of any kind. Indeed, in July 1994, in a little-known epilogue to the Tuna–Dolphin dispute, Mexico and Canada, along with a majority of countries, voted down a U.S. proposal to allow NGOs to participate in a debate on the ruling at GATT headquarters.[118] In the same fashion, the negotiations leading to trade treaties are largely conducted by governments without allowing the kind of input and consultations with major groups that would satisfy environmental NGOs. Indeed, it is not only environmental organizations that are unsatisfied with the lack of access to trade institutions and trade talks but essentially the entire spectrum of NGOs promoting social objectives such as human rights and international development. Such lack of access is contrasted with the seemingly close relationship business and corporate interests share with governments on trade issues.

In the case of NAFTA, such complaints were voiced throughout the period 1991–1993. Environmental NGOs were quite vocal about the issue of transparency. They were mostly unsuccessful with NAFTA: They remained on the periphery of the negotiation and the main trade treaty does not include provisions to increase public participation and input. As for the NAAEC, events unfolded quite differently: Building on their momentum, NGOs became major actors in the crafting of the parallel agreement (and ultimately in the U.S. congressional ratification process) and ensured that the NAAEC included unprecedented provisions, opening up the Commission for Environmental Cooperation to public input.

---

of these agreements can be an important tool to encourage the growth of democracy internationally. However, in their current form, the institutions and agreements of international trade not only fail to export democracy around the globe, but also undercut the exercise of democratic governance in nations that are currently democratic in nature. These threats to democracy must be corrected. The rules of international trade decision-making must be changed to incorporate basic elements of democratic governance, namely the rights of citizens to have access to these decision-making forums and to participate in decisions that affect their interests. "Democratizing International Trade Decision-Making," supra note 14, Part I at 746.

118. John Zarocostas, "GATT Snubs U.S. Request to Open Tuna–Dolphin Debate to Public," *Journal of Commerce,* 21 July 1994. See also: "U.S. to Call for NGO Observers in WTO Environment Committee" *Inside U.S. Trade* (16 September 1994) 13–15.

Parallel Agendas: Protectionism and Nationalism

Some details of the Mexican tuna and Ontario beer disputes highlight the fact that, beyond the five arguments that have been outlined, two "outside" forces play a central and disturbing role in environmental international trade debates: protectionism and nationalism. Indeed, protectionist and nationalistic agendas have sometimes clouded some of the main issues in the trade and environment controversy. The confusion has neither helped the credibility of the environmental claims nor enriched the public debate. The discussion that took place in 1992 and 1993 over the environmental record of the NAFTA/NAAEC package has been scattered with this intrusion of sometimes worthwhile but altogether different concerns.

Protectionism

The importance of protectionism and internal trade politics in the trade and environment discussion can hardly be overestimated. When an industry perceives a threat to its market share from more competitive imports whose market access is or would be enhanced by lower tariff barriers, such industry can respond in two ways. Where the tariffs are actually lowered, the industry can seek to have new ones imposed or some other form of barrier to imports erected. Or, where such tariff reductions are only threatened, the industry can (and often does) fight the agreement before its adoption.

In both instances, environmental concerns can be easily and sometimes quite effectively enlisted. Environmental protection is a popular social issue and, as demonstrated earlier, environmental regulation, particularly in respect of PPM standards, can be portrayed as a reasonable motive for keeping certain imports out. For this reason, the NAFTA debate has led lobbyists with a protectionist agenda, particularly in the United States, to make use of environmental arguments that suited their purposes.[119] Of course, mere association with protectionist lobbies creates an aura of cynicism around the most thoughtful environmental argument on free trade—not to mention that protec-

---

119. Vice President Gore, at the WTO signing meeting in 1994, went out of his way to reassure the United States' trading partners that Washington opposed "Green Protectionism." See Alan Riding, "Gore Insists Environment Is a Trade Issue," *The New York Times* (15 April 1994) at D1.

tion-seeking trade-wary industries are often the least modern and the most polluting of all.[120]

Since 1989, the United States and the European Union have been waging a fierce battle over E.U. regulations banning the sale of beef treated with supplementary growth hormones. The United States alleges a disguised restriction on trade, while the E.U. claims that the measure is a legitimate action to counter a perceived risk to human health and safety. It is indeed very difficult to disentangle the environmental and economic motivations of the disputants in this conflict, which was still, at the time of writing, unresolved.[121]

At the time of writing, Germany was considering asking automobile makers to recuperate and recycle their old cars. German car manufacturers are seen as leaders in car recycling technology and techniques. Even if they were not, it is plainly easier for BMW or Volkswagen to recuperate one of their old models in Dusseldorf than it is for Chrysler or Toyota. Thus a legitimate environmental initiative might also be characterized as protectionist because it favors local producers. In such a case, the relative weight of the principle of free trade and the principle of environmental protection is difficult to assess.[122]

Nationalism and Environmental Sovereignty

The influence of nationalism is less blunt but it may be even more pervasive. The defense of national sovereignty is a permanent fixture in most international trade debates because trade liberalization, with its corollary of economic integration and its legal lists of do's and don'ts, inevitably entails encroachments and restrictions on national sover-

---

120. In particular, U.S. and E.U. agricultural policies protect domestic industries that thrive, while generating substantial environmental degradation. For example, special access to E.U. producers for tapioca-based animal feed translates into expanded polluting livestock facilities in the Netherlands. Runge, supra note 21, Part I at 11. Also, protected and subsidized agricultural production in the U.S. Midwest and Western Canada accounts for a substantial share of water pollution in these regions.

121. See *Conflicts and Opportunities*, supra note 28, Part I at 86; "The U.S.–EC Hormone Beef Controversy and the Standards Code: Implications for the Application of Health Regulations to Agricultural Trade" (1989) 14 North Carolina Journal of International Law 135; Holly Hammonds, "A U.S. Perspective on the EC Hormones Directive," (1990) 11 Michigan Journal of International Law 840; Werner P. Meng, "The Hormone Conflict Between the EEC and the United States Within the Context of GATT," (1990) 11 Michigan Journal of International Law 818.

122. "Un nouveau spectre hante le tiers-monde: L'Éco-colonialisme," *Courier international* (11 mars 1993) at 7–10.

eignty. In the case of NAFTA's impact on the environment, nationalist arguments against the obligation for domestic governments to submit themselves to trade disciplines have been used a great deal in all three countries—although one is never quite sure how much defense of sovereignty and how much concern for environmental impact underpins the arguments.[123] The problem with some environmentalists' defense of sovereignty in the context of NAFTA is that it is not consistent with their attacks on sovereignty in other forums.

Often, a limitation on Ottawa's or Washington's ability to adopt some kind of environmental regulation is denounced with a vigor that would lead one believe that these governments were about to adopt far-reaching progressive environmental protection schemes. This vigor is best explained by the environmentalists' well-founded concern for NAFTA's environmental impact and the necessity to preserve avenues for improved environmental protection. Their concern, however, often becomes aggressive opposition because of a deep, legitimate, but completely different discomfort with the curtailment of their government's legislative sovereignty. As Charnovitz himself asks: "Should nations be able to set the environmental standards they want? Yes, of course. Should countries establish supranational organizations to review and dictate changes in domestic laws when such laws impede international trade? Only to a limited extent. The aim should be to expose commercial measures disguised as environmental ones. The GATT should not aim to harmonize national environmental policies or to prevent environmental extremism."[124] The confusion lies in the fact that, away from the NAFTA trade and environment debate, most North American environmentalists remain committed internationalists, eager to support international environmental treaties that will bind and restrict governmental autonomy, be it Malaysia's forestry practices, China's

---

123. For example, the Canadian Environmental Law Association posited that "[t]he only democratic alternative to NAFTA is to ensure that all three national governments retain their powers to adopt laws and programs that protect the environment." See "NAFTA and Democratic Process," Canadian Environmental Law Association—NAFTA Facts (Toronto, 1992). During the NAFTA debate, Mexico also argued that environmental policy, enforcement practices, community right-to-know procedures, and environmental agencies' budget were strictly domestic matters. Attempts to include such elements in the NAAEC were formally deemed as infringements on national sovereignty. "Mexican Environmental Reform," supra note 19, Part I at 91, 96.

124. "Green Roots, Bad Pruning," supra note 108, Part I at 350. See generally, pp. 347–352.

energy policies, Japan's nuclear waste disposal, Norway's whaling, or Canada's car air emissions standards.

The muddled link between environmentalism and nationalism can lead activists to adopt other seemingly contradictory positions. On the one hand, many will criticize the legal disciplines of NAFTA because they allegedly restrict the signatories' "environmental sovereignty," their ability to freely choose the kind of environmental protection schemes they want. On the other hand, many of the same individuals will attack both the GATT Tuna–Dolphin decision and the fact that the NAAEC targets only ineffective environmental *enforcement,* not ineffective *norms* even though both approaches are rooted precisely in the recognition of the sovereign right of each country to chose its own environmental norms and level of protection.

Some conceptual disentanglement is in order here. In an increasingly interdependent world where both ecosystems and economic zones straddle and disregard national borders, the erosion of national sovereignties is now a permanent feature of the international landscape. Sometimes justification for such erosion will be made in the name of freer trade, sometimes in the name of protecting the global environment—but it will continue. Interdependence cannot be used in the morning to call on global coordination for sustainable development and shelved in the afternoon when it is time to defend as a matter of principle the sovereignty of one's own government in environmental matters as a fundamental principle.

Until more thought is devoted to sorting out the nationalist and environmentalist agendas in the NAFTA debate, this type of contradiction will persist. It is disingenuous to suggest that the same governments are environmental heroes when international environmental instruments are negotiated and environmental villains when free trade arrangements are contemplated (or indeed the reverse). What is worth campaigning against is the apparent double standard in international negotiations where sovereignties are sometimes more easily curtailed in the name of liberalizing trade, a beneficial undertaking, than in the name of protecting the environment, an absolute necessity.

Legitimate and Relevant Concerns

Despite exaggerations by a few, and some confusing parallel issues, the environmental impacts of NAFTA could not, have not, and should never be ignored. There are legitimate concerns respecting the potential effects of environmentally unsound legal trade disciplines and the consequences of environmental compliance costs on investment decisions. Indeed, the effects of expanded economic activity brought about by a successful NAFTA underscores the need to couple North American economic integration with a healthy measure of trinational collaboration on social issues and the environment. The NGO community and the public would not have accepted government pretense that those are not significant and sometimes urgent issues to attend to on this continent.

Faced with this challenge, the NAFTA negotiators have had two opportunities to address the issue of the impacts of North American free trade on environmental priorities and policies. The first one was in the text of the main treaty where the management of some environmental aspects of the trading relationship was integrated. The extent to which environmental issues may be addressed in a trade liberalizing agreement is limited. It does not necessarily mean, however, that the drafters actually achieved all that was possible and desirable in NAFTA. Part II of this discussion will inquire as to whether or not they did and will consider the implications of the main NAFTA treaty for environmental protection. The second opportunity was the NAAEC, the supplemental environmental agreement, where further environmental aspects of trade were tackled and a wide measure of non-trade-related environmental cooperation was formalized. Part III will be devoted to the implications of the NAAEC. The NAAEC is innovative and groundbreaking in many ways but, considering that the drafters had by then moved out of trade negotiations proper, some opportunities to further the harmonious integration of trade and environment concerns may have been missed. Part IV will investigate the nature and the eventual development of the NAAEC Dispute Settlement process. The next part will therefore be dedicated to NAFTA's environment-related provisions.

Part II

Environmental Content in the Main Treaty Text

The representatives of Canada, Mexico, and the United States who negotiated the NAFTA text were confronted with a difficult problem. Their political masters, sensitive to the public's perception that North American free trade would threaten environmental policies and the environment itself, had given them a mandate to address the environmental issue in the accord. Though most of the negotiators were trade specialists, many understood that the environmental impact of trade and the trade impact of environmental initiatives were real and needed to be taken into account in the treaty.[1] To do so, however,

---

1. To be fair, we must recall that representatives of environmental agencies and ministries were also integrated, with more or less significance, in all three NAFTA negotiating teams. See supra notes 47 and 48, Part I and accompanying text.

would require caution. After all, NAFTA would substantially reconfigure North American economic relations for decades to come. Moreover, since few trade agreements contain environmental provisions (and since such provisions have rarely been tested in adjudication), reliable precedents are scarce.[2]

The political concerns outlined above translated into a trade agreement containing an unprecedented number of environment-related provisions. Indeed, NAFTA, its proponents claim, goes "further than any previous trade agreement in addressing environmental concerns and actively promoting environmental protection."[3] Of course, this is hyperbole since the NAFTA trade agreement itself is designed to promote trade, not environmental protection. The fact that one can point out the absence of many conceivable anti-environmental provisions from the NAFTA text does not make it a pro-environment document. NAFTA does not benefit the environment directly. It mitigates the threat posed to domestic environmental laws and regulations by trade disciplines and it promotes economic growth that may result in additional resources being directed to the environment.[4]

Setting the tone in this respect is NAFTA's preamble, which grants to environment-related concerns a degree of recognition unheard of in trade agreements. Out of 15 preambular statements, three relate to the environment or sustainable development. The governments of Canada,

---

2. It is equally worth noting that some of the negotiators of NAFTA feared that environmental provisions would inevitably encroach upon the free trade principles embedded in the agreement. These negotiators were, after all, specialists in trade rather than environmental matters.

3. Carla Hills, then U.S. Trade Representative, Presentation to Senate Finance Committee Hearing, 8 September 1992. As Charnovitz writes: "President Bush boasted that the 'NAFTA contains unprecedented provisions *to benefit* the environment.' Ambassador Hills claimed that the NAFTA is the first such accord to include provisions to protect and improve the environment.'" Cited in "NAFTA's Social Dimension,", supra note 5, Part I, at 50. See *Weekly Compilation of Presidential Documents,* 1992 at 1620; Carla Hills, "America's Free Trade 'Firsts,'" *Journal of Commerce* (14 August 1992) at 8A. An extreme example of this view is the letter sent to President Bush in April 1993 by Republican Senators which states that "[p]erhaps the most significant action that can be taken to improve enforcement of environmental and labor laws throughout North America is the implementation of the NAFTA." *Inside U.S. Trade,* 7 May 1993 at 22.

4. As Charnovitz asserts, "[t]he bottom line is that the NAFTA has no positive provisions (i.e. telling governments what to do) on the environment. What it has is one negative exhortation. More significant is what is largely absent from the NAFTA, i.e. negative disciplines (telling governments what not to do) on environmental standards." "NAFTA's Social Dimensions," supra note 5, Part I at 53.

Mexico, and the United States resolve, in the preamble, to "undertake each of the proceedings in a manner consistent with environmental protection and conservation," "promote sustainable development," and "strengthen the development and enforcement of environmental laws and regulations." Neither the Canada–U.S. FTA[5] nor the final Uruguay Round Agreement[6] of the GATT afford similarly unequivocal recognition to environmental concerns. One must remember, however, that the general provisions of the preamble are not enforceable and that experience with previous trade agreements has shown that they will rarely be used by dispute settlement panels to interpret other provisions of NAFTA.[7] Furthermore, as critics readily point out, the protection of the environment goes unmentioned in the enumeration of NAFTA's basic objectives.[8] (The same critics denounce the environmental references in the preamble as amounting to no more than a public relations exercise.) Nonetheless, NAFTA's unusually "environmental" preamble may bespeak a new willingness on the part of the signatories to recognize the impact of trade liberalization on the environment and the need to mitigate that impact.[9]

In addition to the preamble, environment-related stipulations can be found in the provisions on the recognition of international environ-

---

5. Supra note 7, Part I.

6. Supra note 10, Part I.

7. However, the *Vienna Convention on the Law of Treaties,* 23 May 1969, U.N. Doc. A/CONF.39/27 (1969), 8 I.L.M. 679 specifically recognizes at Article 31 the preambles of international treaties as a legitimate basis of interpretation.

8. NAFTA's objectives, listed in art. 102, include *inter alia* eliminating trade barriers, promoting fair competition, increasing substantially investment opportunities in the parties' territories, establishing a framework for further trilateral cooperation, and creating procedures for the resolution of disputes. On the "missing language" see Michelle Swenarchuk, "The Environmental Implications of NAFTA: A Legal Analysis" in Canadian Environmental Law Association, ed. *The Environmental Implications of Trade Agreements* (Toronto: Queen's Printer, 1993) 101 at 102, (report prepared by the Canadian Environmental Law Association for the Ontario Ministry of Environment and Energy, August 1993).

9. Additionally, since the objective of NAFTA is to liberalize trade, it may be more appropriate to put environmental concerns in the preamble rather than suggest that NAFTA is a genuine environmental instrument by including environmental language in Article 102. The Canadian implementing Act follows the same model by including "environmental protection" and "sustainable development" in the preamble, but leaving those concerns out of Section IV, which outlines the purpose of NAFTA. See Section IV of the *North American Free Trade Agreement Implementation Act,* supra note 1, Introduction.

mental agreements,[10] the two chapters on standards,[11] the "pollution havens investment" clause (hereinafter the "pollution havens clause"),[12] and the chapter on formal dispute settlement.[13] The ensuing discussion will assess the extent to which these provisions address each of two principal environmental objections raised by opponents of NAFTA and introduced earlier in Chapter 2 of this book: Namely (1) that trade liberalization rules, particularly those restricting technical barriers to trade, threaten the ability of governments to legislate in favor of the environment; and (2) that trade liberalization puts downward pressure on environmental norms since investors systematically seek to improve their competitiveness by locating in the least regulated territory.[14]

---

10. NAFTA, supra note 1, Introduction, art. 104. See Appendix II.

11. Ibid., Chapter Seven (Section B) regarding sanitary and phytosanitary measures and Chapter Nine governing standards-related measures generally.

12. Ibid., art. 1114.

13. Ibid., Chapter Twenty, Section B [hereinafter referred to as "Chapter Twenty"].

14. This includes the related concern that trade liberalization discourages upward harmonization of environmental norms adopted by individual governments.

Chapter 3

NAFTA and the Ability of Governments to Legislate in Favor of the Environment

NAFTA's impact on a party's ability to legislate in favor of the environment is principally a function of two factors: (1) the extent to which that party's environment-related measures can survive a challenge under NAFTA's dispute settlement procedures and (2) the readiness of each NAFTA party to invoke dispute settlement procedures against another's measures. The second factor is largely a political question and therefore difficult to assess by anticipation.[15] Gauging the first, however, entails a more concrete, two-step analysis: One must first identify the kinds of environmental measures that are specifically susceptible to a challenge and, second, assess the likelihood that such measures could be sustained once challenged. This latter task itself implies an appreciation of not only the applicable substantive legal

---

15. At the moment, because of the very intensity of the debate surrounding NAFTA's environmental impact, it does not seem likely that politicians would risk facing the wrath of NGO-led public opinion by challenging another party's environmental standards. However, NAFTA will probably be around a very long time, and the environmentally accommodating political climate may change.

rules and disciplines prescribed in NAFTA but also the dispute settlement procedures (and, in particular, the degree to which these procedures accommodate particular environment-related concerns).

Environment-Related Measures Susceptible of Being Challenged Under NAFTA's Dispute Settlement Procedures

Under NAFTA, two types of domestic environment-related measures are susceptible to dispute settlement review. The first are trade-affecting standards and regulations governing products sold in the territory of the adopting party. These may be impugned as barriers to trade on the basis of two legal disciplines: Section B of Chapter Seven (hereinafter referred to as "Chapter Seven"), which sets forth the criteria for domestic sanitary and phytosanitary measures (hereinafter "S&P measures"), and Chapter Nine, which outlines the general test for all other standards-related measures including environmental norms.[16] In essence, the parties will apply these disciplines with a view to distinguishing between legitimate technical environmental measures and measures unjustifiably restricting trade—not necessarily an easy line to draw. Beauty is usually in the eyes of the beholder. Just as trade lawyers might fail to appreciate the legitimacy and the need for environmental protection statutes given the impediments to trade they sometimes create, environmentalists may have trouble appreciating where the adequate balance is struck between measures they consider essential and their negative impacts on trade and its benefits.

The second type of measures subjectible to dispute settlement are those that implement listed international environmental treaties. The general rule is that these named agreements take precedence over NAFTA so that measures *implementing* such treaties and affecting trade are not subjected to NAFTA's trade disciplines. A party's implementing provisions may still be challenged, however, on grounds that implementing measures more consistent with NAFTA could have been adopted—likewise a nebulous test, given the paucity of precedents.[17] This restriction on a party's right to adopt treaty-implementing measures will likely gain in importance in the event that the parties set out

---

16. S&P measures are defined as measures to protect animal, plant, or human life in the party's territory from the risks associated with a pest or disease released into the environment or with the presence of an additive, contaminant, toxin, or disease-causing organism in a food, beverage, or feedstuff. NAFTA, supra note 1, Introduction, art. 724.

17. See infra notes 128–142, Part II and accompanying text.

to supplement the list with other international environmental and conservation agreements (as they can and as the authors think they should).

The Overall Dispute Settlement Context and Environment-Related Concerns

The degree to which the above environment-related measures may yield to a successful trade law challenge is not simply a function of the applicable disciplines; much depends on the dynamics of NAFTA's dispute settlement procedures.[18] Generally, disputes arising under both NAFTA and the equivalent provisions of GATT may be settled in either forum at the discretion of the complaining party.[19] Where the dispute concerns sanitary or phytosanitary measures, standards-related measures to protect the environment, or measures for implementing the named international environmental treaties, however, the party complained against may require that recourse be taken solely under NAFTA.[20] This is particularly important since, as will be discussed below, NAFTA's environment-related disciplines as well as its dispute settlement procedures appear on the whole to be less hostile to environmental concerns than their GATT counterparts.

Under the dispute settlement procedure, there are two principal grounds for a challenge. First, a party may claim that an actual or a proposed measure of another party is or would be inconsistent with its obligations under NAFTA.[21] Second, even if the measure is or proves to be consistent with NAFTA, a party may still complain that the application of the measure would deny that party a benefit it reasonably expected to obtain under NAFTA (this concept of nullification and impairment was articulated under GATT).[22] Interestingly, nothing in NAFTA requires that a party seeking to invoke both grounds should do so in the same instance,[23] though of course confining all recourses to

---

18. The right to recourse to dispute settlement is articulated principally in NAFTA, supra note 1, Introduction, art. 2004.

19. Ibid., art. 2005(1).

20. Ibid., arts. 2005(3) in respect of measures implementing international environmental treaties and 2005(4) in respect of S&P and standards-related measures.

21. Ibid., art. 2004.

22. Ibid. and Annex 2004 regarding Nullification and Impairment. On GATT rules see infra discussion at notes 104–115, Part II.

23. A complaining party may perceive a two-step challenge as tactically advantageous. Should a panel rule that the defending party's measure is consistent with

a single instance will likely be preferable for reasons of convenience and practicality.

Whatever strategy is chosen, it is clear that the complaining party may get two swipes at a particular measure. Yet certain dispute settlement provisions may improve the chances for survival of environment-related measures contemplated in Chapter Seven and Chapter Nine. For example, the burden of proof in these matters lies with the complaining party.[24] This can be viewed as a departure from dispute settlement under GATT, where many contend that once a *prima facie* case is established against a standard-related measure the burden shifts to the defending party to justify its measure under GATT Article XX exceptions.[25] Also, upon request of the disputing party or on its own initiative, provided the disputing parties agree, the panel may seek the advice of a technical expert[26] or a scientific review board.[27] Finally, the roster of individuals from which the dispute settlement panels are selected may include experts on environmental law, science, or policy—though there is no requirement that such specialists be named to panels settling environment-related disputes.[28] The possibility remains

---

NAFTA, the complaining party could then raise the issue of nullification and impairment before a separate panel perhaps more suitably constituted to its liking and less influenced by the findings in the first instance.

24. NAFTA, supra note 1, Introduction, arts. 723(6) and 914(4).

25. *General Agreements on Tariffs and Trade,* supra note 9, Part I. However, the practical significance of NAFTA's placing the burden on the complaining party (and, for that matter, the practical significance of the approach under GATT law) may be limited since the dispute settlement process takes place before a panel, not a court. As one commentator aptly concludes in respect of NAFTA, "the lack of both established evidentiary procedures and a settlement panel with legal experience may cloud the question of which side bears what burden of proof at any particular point in the proceedings. As a result, precisely how Article 723(6) will operate in the context of Chapter Seven's other provisions remains unclear." See James E. Bailey, "Free Trade and the Environment—Can NAFTA Reconcile the Irreconcilable?" (1993) Westlaw at 6. Moreover, the rigorously judicial process suggested by NAFTA's provisions regarding the burden of proof may be ill-adapted to adjudication of complex policy issues. However the burden of proof is distributed, each party will feel compelled to put forward the most complete case it can. The panelists will in turn weigh all the evidence and the arguments with, as the case may be, little regard to burden of proof considerations.

26. NAFTA, supra note 1, Introduction, art. 2014.

27. Ibid., art. 2015.

28. Interestingly, however, NAFTA does require that disputes concerning financial services legislation be adjudicated by persons "who have expertise or experience in financial services, law or practice"—presumably in recognition of the highly specialized

however that under the NAAEC, the CEC will be consulted when experts are chosen in the case of environmentally related trade disputes. It must be noted that the parties are under no obligation to render public their briefs and the arguments included therein. Without public scrutiny it will remain difficult to judge whether environmental concerns will be given due consideration during trade arbitration proceedings.[29]

Environment-Related Standards and NAFTA Legal Trade Disciplines

As briefly mentioned above, NAFTA features two trade disciplines applying to domestic environmental standards: one for sanitary and phytosanitary (S&P) standards (Chapter Seven) and one for all other environment-related standards (Chapter Nine). These disciplines dictate the legal criteria to which a party's trade-affecting domestic environmental standards must adhere to be considered valid under NAFTA challenge. Domestic standards that would be vulnerable to a formal challenge under NAFTA's dispute settlement procedure are those that either relate too imprecisely to their stated environmental policy objectives (e.g., promote what is really a protectionist rather than an environmental goal), effect varying degrees of discrimination against imported products, or, in some cases, pose unnecessary obstacles to trade. Because the language of NAFTA's trade disciplines borrows conspicuously from GATT texts and panel decisions, critics understandably worry that GATT's often alleged insensitivity to environmental concerns may have found its way into NAFTA's trade disciplines. Whether or not this fear has any legal basis is the subject of the ensuing discussion.

---

nature of this industry. [NAFTA, supra note 1, Introduction, art. 1414(3)(a)] Environment-related disputes are sufficiently specialized, it would seem, to merit similar consideration. Compounding this shortcoming is NAFTA's failure to guarantee even a supporting role for technical experts or scientific review boards in environment-related dispute settlement. The lack of assured environmental representation in the adjudication of environment-related disputes is all the more significant since NAFTA hearings are (as was explained) not public, and the dispute resolution process does not allow for amicus briefs or friendly intervention by recognized public interest groups.

29. In GATT arbitration, the only party that makes its briefs partially public is the United States. See *Trade and the Environment: Hearing Before the Subcommittee on Foreign Commerce and Tourism of the Senate Committee on Commerce, Science and Transportation*, 103d Cong., 2d Sess. 49, 51, 52–62 (1994).

Sanitary and Phytosanitary Measures

Generally speaking, S&P measures are defined as measures "to protect animal, plant or human life in the adopting party's territory" from the risks associated with "a pest or disease released into the environment or with the presence of an additive, contaminant, toxin or disease-causing organism in a food, beverage or foodstuff."[30] This is very relevant in the case of NAFTA because of the significant gap between U.S. and Mexican standards for pesticide use and levels of pesticide application and residue on crops.[31] Under Chapter Seven, two aspects of a party's S&P control offer legitimate targets for a dispute settlement challenge: the overall *level* of protection chosen by the public authorities and the *measures* adopted by those authorities to achieve that chosen level of protection.

With regard to the level of environmental protection, Chapter Seven gives each party the right, "notwithstanding any other provision of this Section," to establish "its appropriate levels of protection."[32] A level of protection is a general objective of environmental protection such, for example, as a maximum quantity of contaminants to be found in a given setting, or a goal to prevent the release of certain substances in the environment. A specific rule designed to prevent contamination such as an import ban or special packaging regulations are not a level of protection but measures taken to achieve it. The choice of a level of environmental protection is to be done by way of a risk assessment[33] obliging the parties only to "take into account" such vague criteria as "relevant scientific evidence," "relevant ecological and other environmental conditions," and "the relative cost-effectiveness of alternative approaches to limiting risks."[34] Apparently, given the chosen formulation, the risk assessment requirement does not seriously restrict the right of the NAFTA parties to establish appropriate levels of environmental protection.

Indeed, a foremost characteristic of Chapter Seven (and of Chapter

---

30. See definition of S&P measure at NAFTA, supra note 1, Introduction, art. 724.

31. See Runge, supra note 21, Part I at 66.

32. NAFTA, supra note 1, Introduction, art. 712(2). It is unclear from the text what exactly a "level of protection" is. Article 724 which, somewhat redundantly, defines "appropriate level of protection" as "the level of protection of human, animal, or plant life or health in the territory of a Party that the Party considers appropriate" provides no clues in this respect.

33. Ibid., art. 712(2).

34. Ibid., arts. 715(1) and (2).

Nine) is the considerable leeway that each party is afforded in order to establish the level of protection it desires and the level of risk it deems acceptable. Of all the limitations on the right to establish appropriate levels of protection, only one may have any teeth: In establishing its appropriate levels of protection, a party "shall . . . avoid arbitrary or unjustifiable distinctions in such levels in different circumstances, where such distinctions result in arbitrary or unjustifiable discrimination against a good of another Party or constitute a disguised restriction on trade between the Parties."[35] Yet even this provision is of little value to the complaining party. Though the meaning of the language is not entirely clear, the test appears to set a forbiddingly high threshold for the party challenging levels of protection established by another party. Successfully making the case for an arbitrary or unjustifiable *distinction* in levels of protection between two NAFTA parties would be insufficient. Indeed, the complaining party would have to show that such distinction, in turn, brings about arbitrary or unjustifiable *discrimination* against a good of the complaining party or amounts to a disguised restriction on trade between the parties. Moreover, as will be shown, GATT panels have proven singularly reluctant to find that a particular measure effects arbitrary or unjustifiable discrimination or constitutes a disguised restriction on trade.

Because of these obvious difficulties facing the complaining party, the *levels* of protection established by a party pursuant to Chapter Seven are not likely to provide the main focus of any challenge. Rather, the real battleground will be the S&P *measures* adopted by a party to achieve its chosen level of protection. Such measures may include, among other things, testing and inspection procedures and criteria, regulated risk assessment methods, packaging and labeling requirements, and even quarantine treatment.[36] The basic NAFTA rule is that each Party may "adopt, maintain or apply any sanitary or phytosanitary measure *necessary* for the protection of human, animal or plant life or health in its territory, including a measure more stringent than an international standard."[37] Such measures must use "as a basis" rel-

---

35. Ibid., art. 715(3)(b). The other limitations are the reliance "as appropriate to the circumstances" on risk assessment under Article 715(1) and (2), and an admonishment to "take into account the objective of minimizing negative trade effects under 715(3)(c).

36. Ibid.

37. NAFTA, supra note 1, Introduction, art. 712(1). Once the inclusion of this provision in NAFTA was confirmed, the United States, during the Uruguay Round negotia-

evant "international standards, guidelines or recommendations"[38] and, where they conform to these, they are presumptively valid—that is, presumed to satisfy the assortment of exacting criteria set forth in Chapter Seven and detailed below.[39] Where the stringency of an S&P measure exceeds that of "a relevant international standard, guideline or recommendation," however, no such presumption avails.

NECESSARY MEASURES

Chapter Seven requires that a party's S&P measures be *necessary* for the protection of human, animal, or plant life or health.[40] Critics argue that the use of the term "necessary" would inevitably recall the environmentally insensitive narrow GATT panel interpretations of the

---

tions, was able to have changes made to the S&P provisions of the Final Agreement that are more consistent with the main principles of the NAFTA S&P text. See "GATT TBT Agreement Reveals Failure of U.S. to Secure Changes," *Inside U.S. Trade*, 24 December 1993, at 11.

38. Ibid., art. 713(1). The same provision stipulates that a party need not base its S&P measures on the relevant international standards, guidelines, or recommendations where to do so would reduce the level of S&P protection. However, even if a party were to argue that it did not base its S&P measures on international standards because to do so would have lowered the level of protection, the measures would likely still have to meet the principal criteria set forth at NAFTA art. 712. International standards include those set by the following organizations: the *Codex Alimentarius, the International Office of Epizootics, the International Plant Protection Convention, the North American Plant Protection Organization.* NAFTA art. 724(5) requires the parties to participate in these standardizing organizations "to the greatest extent practicable."

39. Ibid., art. 713(2). Chapter Seven offers no guidance as to how rebuttable this presumption is. Moreover, one commentator argues that this presumption renders illusory the advantages gained from charging the complaining party with the burden of proving that an S&P measure is inconsistent with Chapter Seven. If an S&P measure's consistency with the relevant rules can be presumed from their conformity with international standards, then, the authors suggest, inconsistency can be established simply by demonstrating that the S&P measure in question is more stringent than its international counterpart. A *prima facie* case would be established thereby shifting the burden to the party complained against to establish compliance. See Bailey, supra note 25, Part II, at 5–6. This argument is ultimately unpersuasive. After all, to demonstrate that a domestic S&P measure is more stringent than the relevant international standard would in most cases be easy. Could this really be all that is required for a complaining party to discharge the legal burden contemplated by NAFTA art. 723(6)? Moreover, art. 713(2) adds that "A measure that results in a level of S&P protection different from that which would be achieved by a measure based on relevant international standard, guideline or recommendation shall not for that reason alone be presumed to be inconsistent with this Section."

40. See Ibid., art. 712(2).

same term used in old GATT Articles XX(b) and (d).[41] These two last provisions respectively refer to (and allow) trade-restricting measures "necessary to protect human, animal or plant life or health" (GATT's S&P exception) and those "necessary to secure compliance with laws or regulations which are not inconsistent with provisions of GATT." GATT panels have ruled regularly that a measure otherwise inconsistent with GATT could not be considered "necessary" under either Articles XX(b) or (d) "if an alternative measure which [the Contracting Party] could reasonably be expected to employ and which is not inconsistent with other GATT provisions is available to it." If, however, there is no reasonably available GATT-consistent measure, a GATT Contracting Party must adopt the measure that "entails the least degree of inconsistency with GATT provisions."[42] For example, in the Dolphin I case, the panel ruled that Article XX(b) did not apply because the United States had not "exhausted all options reasonably available to it . . . in particular through the negotiations of international cooperative arrangements."[43] In other words, if this interpretation were applied by a NAFTA panel, a measure would be judged necessary only if it entails either no inconsistency or the least inconsistency with other NAFTA provisions. No measure scrutinized under GATT adjudication has ever survived this test.[44] More controversial still is the suspect reasoning GATT panels have employed in concluding that a particular measure

---

41. See, for example, Steve Charnovitz, "NAFTA: An Analysis of Its Environmental Provisions" (1993) 23 Environmental Law Reporter 10067 at 10068 [hereinafter "Environmental Provisions"] and Swenarchuk, supra note 8, Part II, at 115–118.

42. See *United States-Section 337 of the Tariff Act of 1930 (European Economic Community v. United States)* (1989), GATT Doc. L/6439, para 5.26, 36th supp. B.I.S.D. (1990) 345 at 392–393; *Thailand-Restrictions on Importation of and Internal Taxes on Cigarettes (U.S. v. Thailand)* (1990), GATT Doc. DS10/R, paras. 74–75, 37th supp. B.I.S.D. (1991) 200 at 223; and *United States-Measures Affecting Alcohol and Malt Beverages (Canada v. U.S.)* (1992), GATT Doc. DS23/R, para. 5.43, 39th Supp. B.I.S.D. (1992) 206 at 283.

43. See Tuna Dolphin I, supra note 33, Part I at para 5.28. This was the ruling in spite of the fact that the U.S. unilateral action had been preceded by attempts to promote an international agreement on dolphin protection since the early 1970s under the auspices of the *International Convention for the Regulation of Whaling,* supra note 106, Part I; and the *United States–Costa Rica Convention for the Establishment of an Inter-American Tropical Tuna Commission,* 31 May 1949, 1 U.S.T. 230, T.I.A.S. No. 2044. See "Dolphin and Tuna," supra note 99, Part I, at 10571.

44. See *Conflicts and Opportunities,* supra note 28, Part I at 82–87; Pierre Pescatore et al., *Handbook of GATT Dispute Settlement* (Ardsley-on-Hudson, N.Y.: Transnational Juris Publications, 1991). This is not surprising given the particularly exacting nature

did not entail the least degree of inconsistency with other GATT provi-sions.[45] Even if this test is transformed into a "least-restrictive" test, the party complained against is almost in the position of having to prove a negative proposition: There are no other alternatives less disturbing to trade. This is getting close to a logical impossibility. In general, GATT documentation has more to say about why environmental exceptions do not apply or should not be granted than about how such exceptions

---

of this test. The term "necessary" has been interpreted to rule out any environmental measure that adversely affects trade if there is any possibility of achieving the environ-mental objective without affecting trade in a manner inconsistent with GATT rules. Such a test largely bypasses the realities of lawmaking. Since the art of governing mainly involves making political choices between options, there are always alternatives to any particular measure. Hence, the complaining party would have little difficulty suggesting to a NAFTA panel measures that are less GATT-inconsistent than the chal-lenged measure. A negative proposition such as "there are no alternatives" is practically impossible to sustain from a strictly logical standpoint. As a matter of fact, no GATT panel has ever attempted to justify so restrictive an approach involving such a high bur-den on the party adopting a trade-restricting measure. The general language of GATT, in Articles XX(b) and (d), could just as readily have supported other choices: a propor-tionality test, a balancing of inconvenients, or even a weighing of the importance of the legislative objective (to name just a few). Moreover, GATT panels appear to have side-stepped any serious evaluation of the effectiveness of the alternative measure deemed less GATT-inconsistent.

45. In *United States-Measures Affecting Alcoholic and Malt Beverages*, supra note 42, Part II at para 5.43, a GATT panel found that the discriminatory wholesaler require-ments imposed by some states were not necessary in terms of Article XX(d) to enforce liquor tax laws. According to the panel, "[t]he fact that not all fifty states maintain dis-criminatory distribution systems indicates that alternative measures for enforcement of state excise tax laws do indeed exist." In effect, the mere unevenness of the subnational legislative terrain may be fatal to a particular measure. Insofar as this position ignores the all-too-obvious—that legislative differences between states may arise from differ-ences in what individual states perceive to be their needs—it is a marked assault on the idea of subnational legislative competence. Indeed, one need only imagine the conse-quences of applying the same kind of comparison not between states or provinces but between nations. In the 1989 case *United States-Section 337 of the Tariff Act of 1937*, supra note 42, Part II (where the necessity test was first articulated), the U.S. invoked GATT Article XX(d) in defense of its enforcement of patent laws. While a GATT panel concluded that such measures were not necessary in terms of Article XX(d) and thus not allowable under GATT, it was silent as to what legitimate alternative measures could have been implemented instead. Reassuringly, it did allow that the contracting party would not be obliged to change its substantive patent law or its desired level of enforcement. This report is nonetheless disturbing because the GATT panel glibly as-serted that alternative measures were available but never suggested any. If a panel could be so easily convinced as to the availability of alternative measures, then one must wonder whether any measure (including environmental measures) could ever pass the necessity test.

can be invoked and what situations they cover. In summary, a necessity test imported into a NAFTA dispute settlement context could prove crippling to challenged S&P measures—particularly those more stringent than corresponding international standards.

While it is plausible that a NAFTA panel would resort to GATT's exacting treatment of the term "necessary" in a dispute concerning S&P measures, an equally plausible argument can be advanced against this approach. Under NAFTA Article 2101(1), GATT Article XX and its interpretative notes (and any equivalent provision of a successor agreement[46] to which all the NAFTA parties are party) are incorporated into NAFTA, for the purposes of most of Part Two (Trade in Goods) and Part Three (Technical Barriers to Trade) of NAFTA.[47] Although Chapter Seven falls into Part Two of NAFTA, Article 710 explicitly provides that "the provisions of Article XX(b) of the GATT as incorporated into Article 2101(1) . . . do not apply to any sanitary or phytosanitary measure." This arguably constitutes an express rejection of GATT interpretations (including the stringent criteria for necessity as articulated by GATT panels) from eventual NAFTA dispute settlement in relation to S&P measures. This would be consistent with the Uruguay Round Agreement, which also distances itself from the old GATT texts on S&P measures.

Some commentators point to NAFTA Article 103, whereby the parties affirm their existing rights and obligations under GATT, as an incorporation of GATT by reference.[48] But here too the case for the applicability of traditional GATT interpretations to S&P measures is wobbly. If the parties truly intended that Article 103 constitute an

---

46. A "successor agreement" presumably includes the *Uruguay Round Agreement,* supra note 10, Part I.

47. NAFTA, supra note 1, Introduction, art. 2101(1). The parties go even further in affirming "that the measures referred to in GATT art. XX(b) include environmental measures necessary to protect human, animal or plant life or health." The term "environment" never appears in GATT XX(b) or anywhere else in the original GATT text. Whether GATT art. XX(b) was ever intended to cover environmental measures could thus be a point of contention in any Article XX dispute before a GATT panel, even though this question was not directly addressed in either the Dolphin I or II decisions. Before a NAFTA panel, on the other hand, there would be no such controversy because of this important clarification in NAFTA art. 2101(1).

48. These commentators include Charnovitz, in "Environmental Provisions," supra note 41, Part II at 10068. Interestingly, that the parties affirm only their *existing* rights and obligations appears to exclude rights and obligations under the *Uruguay Round Agreement,* supra note 10, Part I, since, at the time of NAFTA signing and ratification, this Agreement had yet to be ratified by any of the NAFTA parties.

incorporation by reference of all GATT rules concerning trade disciplines, the provision would have said so explicitly. The fact that specific language on incorporation of GATT Article XX is found in the special clause at NAFTA Article 2101(1) diminishes the importance of Article 103. If Article 103 was really meant to be a general incorporation of GATT, it would have rendered superfluous NAFTA Article 2101(1)'s incorporation of a specific GATT provision. The better view is that, by affirming existing rights and obligations under GATT and its successor agreement, the parties merely preserve their GATT-sponsored legal recourses. NAFTA's explicit recognition of the parties' right to challenge measures by way of GATT dispute settlement procedures lends added credence to this interpretation.[49]

It can thus be persuasively argued that the necessity test articulated by a succession of GATT panels should have no bearing on a NAFTA panel's disposition of a matter involving S&P measures. It is a more difficult task, however, to determine, in the absence of any other relevant precedent, what NAFTA's own necessity test will be. Moreover, the S&P discipline features other conspicuous restrictions on the right of a party to adopt S&P measures affecting trade. These strictures may altogether obviate the need for the stringency of a GATT-type necessity test if a panel is set to decide against a domestic measure. For instance, each party must ensure that its S&P measures are applied *only to the extent necessary*" to achieve its appropriate levels of protection, "taking into account technical and economic feasibility."[50] Since this test appears to be more explicit (i.e., necessity entails an appreciation of technical and economic feasibility), it conceivably should prevail, during NAFTA dispute settlement, over any GATT-inspired general necessity standard.

In the Adopting Party's Territory

NAFTA imposes other significant restrictions on a party's right to adopt S&P measures. For instance, each party may adopt such measures to protect only that human, animal, or plant life located "in its territory" (and not its neighbor's).[51] In respect of S&P measures, therefore, NAFTA fully embraces the interpretation that some extrajurisdictional effects (and intents) of domestic environmental standards are incompatible with trade law, a principle that underlies the report of the panel

---

49. NAFTA, supra note 1, Introduction, art. 2005(1).

50. Ibid., art. 712(5).

51. Ibid., art. 712(2).

in the Dolphin I case (even though the MMPA was not an S&P measure).[52] A party therefore cannot enact standards with a view to sanction their nonenforcement in another party's jurisdiction with trade-affecting measures. Accordingly, an S&P regulation limiting pesticide residue on imported fruits and vegetables would be allowable. In contrast, an S&P regulation banning imports that are produced in a way that overly exposes agricultural workers to pesticides would likely allow a successful challenge under Chapter Seven.[53] A similar measure limiting the level of pesticide contamination in the soil in which imported fruits and vegetables are grown would be challengeable unless the importing country could show that there is a connection between the contamination levels in the soil and the presence of the contaminant in the imported produce itself. In other words, Chapter Seven appears to represent a complete bar on extrajurisdictional S&P PPM measures.

SCIENTIFIC BASIS AND RISK ASSESSMENT

Moreover, a party's S&P measures must be "based on scientific principles"[54] and "risk assessment, as appropriate to the circumstances"[55] and may not be "maintained where they no longer have a scientific basis"[56] (defined as "a reason based on data or information derived using scientific methods"[57]) for them. NAFTA's requirement of a scientific basis is more permissive than its counterpart in the final *Uruguay Round Agreement,* wherein S&P measures may not be maintained in the absence of "sufficient scientific evidence" (in other words, a thresh-

---

52. Supra notes 102–112, Part I, and accompanying text.

53. Under NAFTA, supra note 1, Introduction, art. 724, the S&P measure must target processing or production methods that are "product-related" to be a legitimate S&P measure.

54. Ibid., art. 712(3)(a).

55. Ibid., art. 712(3)(c). The "risk assessment" called for here is identical to that required in respect of the establishment of appropriate levels of protection. Though one cannot be entirely sure as to the meaning of "as appropriate to the circumstances," the term could tip the scales in favor of an even greater variability in respect of risk assessment than the already permissive language of NAFTA Article 715 would suggest. Also, it must be noted that the term "risk assessment" does not in any way imply what the conclusion of that assessment should be. This may suggest that for any risk a degree of acceptability exists.

56. Ibid., art. 712(3)(b).

57. See definition at Ibid., art. 724.

old of advanced scientific proof).[58] While environmentalists may take some comfort in NAFTA's markedly less stringent criterion, they still worry that even the requirement of a scientific basis (particularly when accompanied by the requirement of risk assessment) may compromise a party's ability to provide for margins of safety substantially greater than scientifically justifiable. In other words, S&P measures that attempt to take into account unknown or imponderable risks or heightened public fears may be at risk under NAFTA.[59] NAFTA's wording, though looser than that of the *Uruguay Round Agreement,* is no less hostile to the precautionary principle, the idea that scientific uncertainty arising from insufficient, inconclusive, or contradictory data should *not* justify inaction in the face of certain types of environmental risks. Like the *Uruguay Round Agreement,* Chapter Seven, it seems, confers some legal recognition to what is an increasingly discredited view that public policy should be based on so-called definitive or conclusive scientific evidence rather than on a prudent assessment of the risks and opportunities uncovered by scientific inquiry.[60]

ARBITRARY AND UNJUSTIFIABLE DISCRIMINATION

Another NAFTA obligation is that each party must ensure that its S&P measures do not effect "arbitrary and unjustifiable" discrimination against a good or a service of a party "where identical or similar conditions prevail."[61] Former GATT Article XX likewise forbade arbitrary and unjustifiable discrimination[62]—but only "where the *same* condi-

---

58. Article 6 of the *Agreement on the Application of Sanitary and Phytosanitary Measures,* a part of the Uruguay Round Agreements. See supra note 10, Part I.

59. For instance, in the United States, the so-called Delaney Clauses in the Federal *Food, Drug, and Cosmetic Act* impose a zero-tolerance standard for carcinogenic substances in foods. Since the scientific basis of these measures is insubstantial and since zero tolerance means zero risk assessment, the Delaney Clauses may be susceptible to challenge under NAFTA. See Robert F. Housman and Paul Orbuch, "Integrating Labor and Environmental Concerns into the North American Free Trade Agreement: A Look Back and A Look Ahead" (1993) 8 Am. U. J. Int'l L. & Pol'y. On the other hand, a NAFTA panel could determine that risk assessment is not "appropriate" in these specific circumstances.

60. On the "precautionary principle" see infra note 80, Part IV.

61. NAFTA, supra note 1, Introduction, art. 712(4).

62. Strangely, no GATT panel decision has ever concluded that a particular domestic measure was "applied in a manner which would constitute a means of arbitrary or unjustifiable discrimination." See "Environmental Exceptions," supra note 13, Part I at 47.

tions prevail." By contrast, the NAFTA threshold, virtually duplicated in the final *Uruguay Round Agreement*,[63] gives the nod to an obvious reality: Given the cultural, geographic, and economic dissimilarities between, say, the United States and Mexico, it would often be impossible for the complaining party to demonstrate that the *same* conditions prevail between the two parties.[64] NAFTA's acknowledgment that arbitrary or unjustifiable discrimination may occur even where *similar* conditions prevail between the disputing parties appears to establish a more realistic test. Because "similar" conditions are more common than "identical" ones, however, Chapter Seven conceivably widens the range of S&P measures vulnerable to a complaint based on claims of arbitrary and unjustifiable discrimination against imports. For example, an American manufacturer of pesticides could claim that Alberta's banning of a pesticide widely used in Montana and North Dakota creates an unjustifiable discrimination where undoubtedly similar conditions prevail between these states and this province. In this example, Canada could thus not defend the measure on the ground that the conditions are not exactly identical.

ONLY TO THE EXTENT NECESSARY

Chapter Seven also requires that S&P measures be applied "only to the extent necessary" to achieve the desired or chosen level of protection, "taking into account technical and economic feasibility."[65] Critics contend that the term "only to the extent necessary" echoes the restrictive requirement, first formulated by a GATT panel, that S&P measures be the "least restrictive to trade."[66] Significantly however, the negotiators did not employ the actual expression "least restrictive to trade" in

---

63. Article 7 of the *Agreement on the Application of Sanitary and Phytosanitary Measures*, supra note 10, Part I.

64. For an interesting discussion of the meaning of the term "the same" in the U.S. context, see *International Trade Reporter*, 27 May 1992 *Mississippi Poultry Association Inc. v. Madigan*, No. J91-0086 [W], DC SMiss 4/23/92.

65. Supra note 39, Part II.

66. This test was articulated in *United States-Measures Affecting Alcoholic and Malt Beverages*, supra note 42, Part II, with regards to Article XX(d). It is not out of the question that the panel perceived this test as interchangeable with the test for the least GATT-inconsistency. The "least restrictive to trade" test is on sounder juridical footing. While determining the extent to which a measure restricts trade is generally a straightforward test, assessing inconsistency with the plethora of provisions stipulated in GATT or NAFTA may prove unrealistic. After all, as Steve Charnovitz asks pithily at supra note 13, Part I at 49, "how should one weigh an action inconsistent with Article XI, for ex-

Chapter Seven (even though such language does appear in the corresponding provision of the *Uruguay Round Agreement*).[67] Furthermore, as discussed above, NAFTA appears to preclude the automatic application of traditional interpretations of GATT Article XX and of subsequent related agreements to its S&P discipline.[68] It therefore follows that a NAFTA panel may choose to apply the GATT "least trade-restrictive" test. NAFTA's language may also, however, constitute a license for a less stringent approach than the latter test (though it is difficult to determine exactly what that approach may be).[69]

DISGUISED RESTRICTION ON TRADE

Under Chapter Seven, a party may not apply S&P measures "with a view to, or with the effect of, creating a disguised restriction on trade between the Parties."[70] Under GATT Article XX, by comparison, S&P measures may not be applied in a manner that would "constitute a dis-

---

ample, against an alternative inconsistent with Article XIII?" He further adds that "if the 'nothing in this Agreement' clause in Article XX means what it says, then why are *any* conditions outside the Preamble relevant?"

67. Despite reliance on the least-trade-restrictive criterion, the *Uruguay Round Agreement* spells out a much clearer approach. According to Article 21 of the *Uruguay Round Agreement on the Application of Sanitary and Phytosanitary Measures,* supra note 10, Part I, each party must ensure that its measures are "not more trade restrictive than required . . . taking into account technical and economic feasibility." A footnote to this provision states that a particular measure would not pass this test if there is another measure that (1) is "reasonably available taking into account technical and economic feasibility," (2) "achieves the appropriate level of protection," and (3) "is *significantly* less restrictive to trade." The third criterion offers a measure of reprieve to endangered sanitary and phytosanitary measures because any reasonably available alternative would have to be not simply less trade-restrictive but significantly less so. This compares favorably with the old GATT test it replaces whereby the existence of any measure that does entail a lesser "degree of inconsistency with other GATT provisions" would be fatal to the challenged measure.

68. See infra note 142, Part II and accompanying text.

69. One possible interpretation proposed by Schott and Hufbauer, supra note 23, Part I at 94: "a country's environmental measures should be sustained by a dispute panel, even if they are not in a theoretical sense the 'least trade-restrictive,' if no less trade-restrictive measure is both 'equally available' and 'equally effective.'" This approach is less stringent than the relevant GATT panel interpretations but does not stray too far from the "least-trade-restrictive" orthodoxy. It is to be hoped that a plain language interpretation will prevail: An S&P measure is acceptable if does not impede trade more than is necessary for the achievement of its environmental and health objectives.

70. NAFTA, supra note 1, Introduction, art. 712(6).

guised restriction on international trade." On the rare occasions that GATT panels addressed this restriction their interpretation stripped it of any real significance: In effect, a measure would not constitute a disguised restriction on trade as long as it is publicly announced as a trade-restricting measure (for example, an import restriction or exclusion order adopted to enforce domestic law).[71] Were NAFTA panels to apply such a test to trade-restricting S&P measures, it would be difficult to imagine that any publicly announced S&P measure operating to restrict imports from a NAFTA party could ever be imperiled. However, that NAFTA prohibits S&P measures adopted "with a view to" or "with the effect of" creating a disguised trade restriction hints at a more rigorous test involving a determination of either the underlying intent of the adopting party or the real or potential consequences of the challenged measure on market access. In this light, the fact that an import prohibition flowing from an S&P measure is legally prescribed and thus visible might not by itself suffice to meet the NAFTA criterion of validity (even though it would meet GATT's) and defeat a challenge against such import prohibition. Rather, in order to rule against the challenger, a panel would perhaps have to be satisfied that the import prohibition is not a mere trade restriction *disguised* as a legitimate environmental measure. Of course it remains to be seen whether NAFTA's nuanced wording will translate into a perceptible departure from GATT law and practice.

Assessment of NAFTA's Chapter Seven S&P Measures

Though NAFTA's S&P discipline could prove corrosive to a party's ability to adopt environment-related measures to which the discipline applies, it is, on balance, no more menacing to domestic environmental measures than existing international law. In some ways, Chapter Seven may appreciably narrow the window established under GATT

---

71. In *United States-Prohibition of Imports of Tuna and Tuna Products from Canada (Canada v. U.S.)*, (1982), GATT Doc. L/5198, para. 4.8, 29th supp. B.I.S.D. (1983) 91 at 108, a GATT panel ruled that a U.S. prohibition on imports of Canadian tuna did not constitute a disguised restriction on international trade since the prohibition "had been taken as a trade measure and publicly announced as such." In *United States-Imports of Certain Automotive Spring Assemblies (Canada v. U.S.)* (1983), GATT Doc. L/5333, para. 56, 30th supp. B.I.S.D. (1984) 107 at 125, the GATT panel decided that a U.S. order excluding from importation certain automotive spring assemblies for reasons of patent infringement did not create a disguised restriction on trade partly because "[n]otice of the exclusion order was published in the Federal Register and the order was enforced by the United States Customs at the border."

allowing trade-affecting environmental measures. Consider, for instance, the importing of the word "necessary" from GATT and the replacement of the GATT rule against discrimination "where the same conditions prevail" with a similar rule applying "where identical or similar conditions prevail." In addition, the GATT Article XX restriction against measures applied in a manner that would constitute a disguised trade restriction gives way in NAFTA to language targeting measures adopted "with a view to" or "with the effect of" creating such a restriction. This language expands the scope of Panel inquiries by allowing both a teleological analysis of the regulators' motives, or possibly even an assessment of the publicized but seemingly ill-motivated trade-affecting environmental measure.

On the other hand, certain provisions in Chapter Seven conceivably pry the environmental window open. Of particular note is the fact that the applicability of GATT panel interpretations of GATT Article XX to Chapter Seven is in doubt. Whereas the *Uruguay Round Sanitary and Phytosanitary Agreement* requires S&P measures to be the "least restrictive to trade," NAFTA demands only that they be applied "to the extent necessary" to achieve the appropriate level of protection (and levels of protection are largely invulnerable to challenge). Moreover, such measures need not be premised on "sufficient scientific evidence" (the Uruguay Round standard); a mere "scientific basis" will do (though the conspicuous failure to accommodate the precautionary principle is disappointing). In addition, NAFTA's dispute settlement procedures easily outdo their GATT counterparts in hospitality to environment-related concerns. In short, there is ground for concern that Chapter Seven could give way to challenges undermining environmental legislation, but outright pessimism about such use would be premature.

Technical Barriers to Trade

NAFTA's Chapter Nine, entitled "Technical Barriers to Trade," prescribes the legal discipline governing all standards-related measures that are not S&P measures. Standards-related measures include standards (generally, voluntary rules and guidelines approved by a recognized body[72]) and technical regulations (mandatory product-related rules implemented by governments[73]) and are adopted to secure a legitimate objective. Protection of the environment and sustainable development are both recognized as legitimate objectives by Chapter

---

72. See definition of "standards" at NAFTA, supra note 1, Introduction, art. 915.

73. The definition of "technical regulation" is also found at ibid., art. 915.

Nine.[74] In light of this and the fact that the applicable scope of Chapter Seven is narrowly circumscribed, it is clear that most environmental measures affecting trade between the parties would be covered by Chapter Nine rather than Chapter Seven. This is particularly important because, as will be discussed below, Chapter Nine involves a demonstrably less stringent test for domestic environmental regulation than is Chapter Seven.

On its face, the distinction between standards-related measures and S&P measures may seem less than watertight. Pesticide regulation, some may argue, could fall into either category, thereby posing a problem since applying each discipline could quite plausibly lead to a different outcome. In reality, there is less overlap than meets the eye. Chapter Seven defines a sanitary or phytosanitary measure as inter alia a measure aimed at protecting human and animal life or health from risks caused by "the presence of an additive, contaminant, toxin or disease-causing organism in a food, beverage or feedstuff."[75] The term "contaminant" includes "pesticide residue."[76] It follows that measures which restrict the presence of pesticide residue (or for that matter additives or toxins) in imported foodstuff or beverages would be classified as S&P measures whereas environmental regulations aimed at controlling pesticide or other toxic content in soil, water, or air, insofar as they restrict trade, would rightly be reviewable under Chapter Nine.

Chapter Nine is architecturally similar to Chapter Seven. In an obvious parallel to the latter, Chapter Nine permits each party, "notwithstanding anything else in this Chapter" and "in pursuing its legitimate objectives of safety or the protection of human, animal or plant life or health, the environment or consumers" to "establish the levels of protection that it considers appropriate."[77] In establishing such levels, a party "should [not shall] avoid arbitrary and unjustifiable distinctions between similar goods and services where such distinctions (a) "result in arbitrary or unjustifiable discrimination,"[78] (b) "constitute a disguised restriction on trade,"[79] or (c) "discriminate between similar goods or services."[80] Given the use of the term "should," the provision

---

74. See definition of "legitimate objective" at ibid., art. 915.
75. See definition at ibid., art. 724.
76. Ibid.
77. Ibid., art. 904(2).
78. Ibid., art. 907(2)(a).
79. Ibid., art. 907(2)(b).
80. Ibid., art. 907(2)(c).

is undeniably hortatory. Moreover, in Chapter Nine, risk assessment with a view to determining the appropriate level of protection remains optional.[81] Taking into account the apparent absence of enforceable restrictions on the right to establish appropriate levels of protection, NAFTA in effect assures each party a free hand in this respect; as in Chapter Seven, overall levels of protection are not likely ever to be successfully challenged.

Again as in Chapter Seven, the grist for the dispute settlement mill will lie in the standards-related *measures* adopted to secure appropriate levels of protection. Under Chapter Nine, each party may adopt any standards-related measure "relating to safety, the protection of human, animal or plant life or health, the environment or consumers, and any measure to ensure its enforcement or implementation."[82] Such measures may even include "those to prohibit the importation of a good of another Party . . . that fails to comply with the applicable requirements of those measures or to complete the Party's approval procedures."[83] Standards-related measures generally must be based on international standards,[84] and such measures that conform to these are presumed not to violate certain restrictions on a party's right to adopt trade-

---

81. According to ibid., art. 907(1), "[a] Party *may,* in pursuing its legitimate objectives, conduct an assessment of risk." Even the criteria for such an assessment are optional: a party *may* take into account (a) available scientific evidence or technical information, (b) intended end uses, (c) processes or production, operating, inspection, sampling or testing methods, or (d) environmental conditions. In Chapter Seven, by contrast, risk assessment with a view to setting appropriate levels of protection is not presented as optional for domestic regulators.

82. Ibid., art. 904(1).

83. Ibid.

84. Ibid., art. 905(1). The provision further explains that a party need not base its standards-related measures on international standards where such standards would be "an ineffective or inappropriate means to fulfill its legitimate objectives, for example because of fundamental climatic, geographical, technological or infrastructural factors, scientific justification or the level of protection that the parties consider appropriate." The regulatory maneuvering room implied by this provision appears to be enhanced by Article 905(3), which stipulates that nothing in [Article 905(1)] prevents a party, in pursuing its legitimate objectives, from enacting measures which would result in a higher level of protection than would be achieved if the measure were based on the relevant international standard. However, an overly generous interpretation of Article 905 would render meaningless other Chapter Nine restrictions on the right to enact standards-related measures found elsewhere. An "international standard" is defined as a standard adopted by an international standardizing body. Such organizations include the *International Organization for Standardization* (ISO), the *Codex Alimentarius Commission,* the *World Health Organization,* and the *Food and Agriculture Organization.* (NAFTA Article 915).

affecting measures in furtherance of legitimate objectives relating to the environment or sustainable development.[85] As we shall see, in comparison with Chapter Seven, Chapter Nine contains fewer such restrictions. What is more, these restrictions are markedly more environmentally sensitive, so that in principle challenged environmental measures have a better chance of being upheld during dispute settlement.

The four key elements that will shape the interpretation of Chapter Nine are the obligation that the measures be "related to" the protection of the environment, the absence of a reference to "the adopting party's territory," the requirement for "nondiscriminatory treatment," and the bar on "unnecessary obstacles to trade."

"RELATING TO"

Chapter Seven's "necessity" requirement, however interpreted, gives way to an appreciably more lax test in Chapter Nine: To be acceptable standards-related measures need only be "relating to" (rather than "necessary for") safety, the protection of human, animal or plant life or health, the environment or consumers.[86] It is worth remembering that GATT Article XX is incorporated into Chapter Nine by way of NAFTA Article 2101(1). The term "relating to" is all the more conspicuous since a GATT panel has had occasion to interpret it for the purposes of GATT Article XX(g) allowing governments to adopt certain measures "relating to" the conservation of exhaustible natural resources: In *Canada-Measures Affecting Exports of Unprocessed Herring and Salmon*,[87] the panel concluded that, for a measure to be considered as "relating to" the conservation of an exhaustible natural resource, it has to be "primarily aimed at" such conservation.[88] In short, it must do what it purports to do. In *Canada–U.S. Salmon and Herring* prohibitions on exports of Canadian salmon and herring *not yet processed* were not considered to be "primarily aimed at" the conservation of salmon and herring stocks because the measures did not limit access to salmon and herring supplies in general but only to certain salmon and herring supplies in unprocessed form. Furthermore, Canada limited purchases of these unprocessed fish only by foreign processors and consumers

---

85. NAFTA, supra note 1, Introduction, art. 905(2).

86. Ibid., art. 915.

87. See *Canada—Measures Affecting Exports of Unprocessed Herring and Salmon (United States v. Canada)* (1988), GATT Doc. L/6268, para. 4.6, 35th supp. B.I.S.D. (1989) 98 at 114.

88. Ibid., at para. 4.7.

and not by domestic processors and consumers. The Canada–United States FTA (at Article 1201) also incorporates GATT Article XX, subject to FTA Articles 409 and 904. It is interesting to note that in *In the Matter of Canada's Landing Requirement for Pacific Coast Salmon and Herring,*[89] the Canada–U.S. Free Trade Commission Panel interpreted GATT Article XX(g) (as incorporated in the FTA) more restrictively than did the GATT Panel. At issue were Canadian regulations requiring that certain species of salmon and herring caught on the West Coast be landed in Canada for biological sampling—ostensibly for monitoring and conservation purposes. The United States argued that the Canadian landing requirement was a disguised restriction on international trade—in other words, environmental policy-pretend. Canada maintained that the landing requirement was squarely and primarily aimed at the conservation of salmon and herring stocks. The panel sought to determine not whether the measure was "primarily aimed at conservation" but whether the measure "would have been adopted for conservation reasons alone." Since a sampling of only 10 to 20 percent rather than the entire catch (as required by the regulation) would have been sufficient for biological sampling, the panel ruled that the landing requirement could not have been adopted for conservations reasons alone. Thus, a U.S. government requirement that all cars sold in the United States meet certain emission standards would likely be considered as "primarily aimed at" protecting the American environment (notwithstanding the measure's incidental impact on trade) and survive a challenge. By contrast, the same American requirement imposed only on certain types of car (types that happen to be mostly imported cars) would not, because cars manufactured in the United States account for most of the domestic market and hence most of the exhaust pollution. Furthermore, whether or not the challenged measure is the least inconsistent with other provisions of NAFTA (or the "least trade-restrictive") is immaterial to this primary purpose test.

In general, both panel rulings involved in the *Salmon and Herring* affair showed greater sensitivity to environmental concerns than did the Tuna–Dolphin reports—particularly, the first one. The environmental exceptions to trade rules were given a less narrow interpretation. Even if the FTA panel rulings were more severe, it nevertheless points in the direction of a clearer understanding of proper comparisons between the burden put on trade by environmental measures and the burden put on environmental protection policies by the need

---

89. (1989), 2 T.C.T. 7162 (Chapter 18 Panel), 1 T.T.R. 237.

to respect international trade and the cost-benefit therein.[90] The use of the term "relating to" in NAFTA's Chapter Nine is thus encouraging, since it increases the likelihood that future dispute settlement interpretation will diverge from the classic GATT necessity test.

IN THE ADOPTING PARTY'S TERRITORY

In contrast to Chapter Seven, nowhere in Chapter Nine does NAFTA explicitly state that a party's standards-related measures may protect only the environment or consumers located "in its territory." Traditional legal interpretation would suggest that this omission is not meaningless—for example, that Chapter Nine's stance toward the extraterritorial targeting of domestic environmental measures environmental protection differs from Chapter Seven's. Does the absence of such language from Chapter Nine legitimize a party's standards-related measures that purport to protect the environment in the territory of another party or even the global environment (standard-related measures governing so-called process and production methods or PPMs)? In the United States, such process-related measures, despite their repugnance to GATT, have met with considerable political support[91] (as discussed in Part I). It is not out of the question that the United States or another party would attempt to defend as valid and justifiable under Chapter Nine standards-related measures aimed at extrajurisdictional environmental protection, if such measures were challenged under NAFTA.

In reality, the case for mandatory standards in respect of PPMs has probably made no more headway under Chapter Nine than under Chapter Seven. Considering the extent to which international law has

---

90. "How genuine the conservation purpose of a measure is, must be determined by whether the government would have been prepared to adopt that measure *if its own nationals had to bear the actual cost of the measure.*" U.S.–Canada Binational Panel Final Report, para. 7.08– 7.09, ibid.

91. As a matter of fact, in the wake of the Tuna–Dolphin Report, the U.S. House of Representatives passed a nonbinding resolution calling upon the President ". . . to initiate and complete negotiations, as part of the current Uruguay Round GATT talks *to make the GATT compatible with* the Marine Mammal Protection Act and other U.S. health, safety, labor, and environmental laws, including those laws that are designed to protect the environment *outside the geographic borders of the United States* .. . ." House Congressional Resolution 246, Congressional Record, 6 August, 1992, at 117699. Not surprisingly, the government of the United States is unlikely to adopt the GATT report in the foreseeable future.

consecrated the principle of national sovereignty,[92] the mere omission of the words "in its territory" could hardly suffice to license a major derogation to this principle. Indeed, had NAFTA's drafters truly intended to allow domestic environmental measures to target extra-jurisdictional environmental practices, a muscular affirmation to that effect would doubtless have been made. Moreover, what reason would the drafters have had for disallowing the domestic sanctioning of the extraterritorial effects enforcement of foreign S&P measures under Chapter Seven but not that of all other environmental standards-related measures under Chapter Nine? This outcome would be difficult to justify. The more defensible view is that Chapter Nine does not sanction compulsory standards-related measures aimed at protecting the environment beyond the adopting party's borders. *Technical regulations,* which under NAFTA are by definition always mandatory,[93] would therefore be suspect were they to include attepts to police exterritorially the foreign PPMs of imported goods. The same cannot be said, however, for simple *standards* that would target foreign environmental practices in such a way because *standards* are defined under NAFTA as voluntary "guidelines,"[94] not strictly enforceable by law. What is enforceable are the measures taken to implement them. Consequently declarations that the application of the standards (not the measures) should extend beyond the adopting party's territory would not really infringe upon national sovereignty.[95]

---

92. Indeed, the GATT Tuna Dolphin Report amply illustrates the tenacity of conceptions of national sovereignty under international law. See supra notes 104 and 105, Part I and accompanying text.

93. The term "technical regulation," as defined at NAFTA, supra note 1, Introduction art. 915, denotes a document which sets forth "goods' characteristics or their related processes and production methods." Compliance with these is always mandatory.

94. Standards, according to ibid., art. 915, include rules, guidelines, or characteristics for "goods or related processes and production methods." Standards are set by a recognized body, and compliance with them is always voluntary.

95. This is precisely the position adopted by the Canadian government. Standards may apply in such a manner as to afford extraterritorial protection. Since compliance with standards is voluntary, the Canadian government does not perceive such measures as a threat to national sovereignty. However, "(t)he extraterritorial verification of the enforcement of technical standards would require the setting aside of the principal (sic) of sovereignty, including the sovereignty of Canada's federal, provincial, and local governments." See Government of Canada, *North American Free Trade Agreement: Canadian Environmental Review,* note 1, Part I, at 20.

NONDISCRIMINATORY TREATMENT

The other limitations on the right to adopt environmental standards-related measures do not significantly diminish a party's legislative or regulatory reach. Chapter Nine features two strictures against discriminatory treatment: (1) Each party must, in adopting standards-related measures, accord to goods of another party national treatment;[96] and (2) such goods must be accorded treatment no less favorable than the treatment accorded to like goods of any other country.[97] Neither of these measures signals any divergence from usual international trade rules.

UNNECESSARY OBSTACLES TO TRADE

Moreover, standards-related measures may not be adopted "with a view to creating an unnecessary obstacle to trade."[98] However, an unnecessary obstacle to trade would not be inferred where (1) "the measure's demonstrable purpose is to achieve a legitimate objective"[99] and (2) "the measure does not operate to exclude another party's goods which meet that legitimate objective."[100] One would have difficulty imagining any thoughtfully drafted and duly enforced environmental standards-related measure that this exonerating clause could

---

96. NAFTA, supra note 1, Introduction, art. 904(3)(a).

97. Ibid., art. 904(3)(b). For a discussion of the "like" product requirement in the context of the environment see "Green Roots, Bad Pruning," supra note 108, Part I at 316–322; R. E. Hudec, *The GATT Legal System and World Trade Diplomacy*, 2nd ed., (Salem: Butterworth, 1990) [hereinafter "The Gatt Legal System"]; Jackson, *The World Trading System,* supra note 87, Part I; *Spain-Tariff Treatment of Unroasted Coffee* (1981), GATT B.I.S.D. 28S/102, at para. 4.6. The conventional interpretation is that the old GATT Article III, which embodies the rule, does not allow product standards to differentiate between "like" products coming from another country and one's own equivalent with regards to PPMs. It seems that the MFN requirement was the consequence of restricting the use of trade-affecting PPM measures because differences in production methods do not stop two products from being classified as "like" products, unless the different production methods result in different product characteristics. See Tuna–Dolphin I, supra note 33, Part I, at 1617–1618. For example, a requirement by country X that all newsprint sold contain at least one-third recycled paper may be held invalid as per Article 904(b)(6) if country Y wants to export virgin paper in country X and challenges the requirement. Country Y will be successful if it can show that partially recycled paper constitutes a "live" product. See Christopher Thomas, "The Future: The Impact of Environmental Regulations on Trade" (1992) 18 Can.–U.S. L.J. 383.

98. Ibid., art. 904(4).

99. Ibid., art. 904(4)(a).

100. Ibid., art. 904(4)(b).

not save. The restriction appears all the more ineffectual when compared to the corresponding provision in the *Uruguay Round Agreement*, visibly more onerous for the adopting party in three important respects.[101] First, the Uruguay Round prohibition encompasses not only technical regulations "with a view to" but also those "with the effect of" creating unnecessary obstacles to international trade. Coupled to this restriction is the requirement that technical regulations "not be more restrictive than necessary to fulfill a legitimate objective, taking account of the risks nonfulfillment would create." Finally, the *Uruguay Round Agreement* makes no mention of exonerating conditions similar to those described above.

RESTRICTIONS UNMENTIONED IN CHAPTER NINE

The comparatively benign restrictions on the right to adopt standards-related measures tell only half the story. Equally suggestive of Chapter Nine's unprecedented permissiveness to most environmental standards-related measures is the omission of the more biting restrictions found in NAFTA's S&P discipline. Indeed, Chapter Nine establishes no requirement that standards-related measures be based on scientific principles or risk assessment. Nor is each party required to ensure that its standards-related measures are applied only to the extent necessary to achieve its appropriate level of protection—a restriction that some commentators, as has been demonstrated, liken (perhaps inappropriately) to the GATT panel-sponsored least-trade-restrictive test. Moreover, the right to adopt such measures is unfettered by either an "arbitrary or unjustifiable discrimination" clause or a "disguised restriction on trade" clause. Rather, such restrictions apply only to the right to set appropriate levels of protection, and their impact is further diluted by their hortatory character.

ASSESSMENT OF NAFTA's CHAPTER NINE ON TECHNICAL BARRIERS TO TRADE

What emerges from the foregoing analysis is a regime that, contrary to many recent claims, does not threaten many domestic environment-related measures. Most tellingly, to survive a NAFTA trade challenge, standards-related measures need not be "necessary" for environmental protection, but only "primarily aimed at" such protection—a much more forgiving test. In addition, Chapter Nine drops all direct and indi-

---

101. Article 2.2 of the *Agreement on Technical Barriers to Trade* in the *Uruguay Round Agreement,* supra note 10, Part I.

rect references to a "least trade restrictive" test. And while both Chapter Nine and the *Uruguay Round Agreements* target "unnecessary obstacles to trade," such obstacles would not be found under the NAFTA regime where "the demonstrable purpose [not effect] of the measure is to achieve a legitimate objective" and "the measure does not operate to exclude goods of another Party that meet that legitimate objective." It must be remembered, too, that the burden of proving that a disputed measure does not pass Chapter Nine's undemanding conditions would lie squarely with the complaining party. The upshot of all this is that, with the exception of mandatory process and production standards, any trade-restricting measure rationally connected to the objective of environmental protection will likely survive a challenge under Chapter Nine. Since Chapter Nine applies only to those standards-related measures not covered by the S&P discipline, the party complained against would do well to ensure that a challenged law or regulation is not classified as an S&P measure. And, as discussed above, to do so would not prove unduly problematic, given that S&P measures—not to mention their policy objectives—are precisely defined.

Nullification and Impairment

Even if a disputed environment-related measure is found not to violate any provisions in Chapter Seven or Chapter Nine, the complaining party may have one more card to play: nullification and impairment. This ground avails when a party considers "that any benefit it could reasonably have expected to accrue" from certain parts of NAFTA (including most of Part Two dealing with trade in goods[102]) "is being nullified or impaired as a result of the application of any measure that is not inconsistent with [NAFTA]."[103] In other words, in the event that an environmental standards-related trade-affecting measure passes muster under Chapter Nine (as is likely), it would still be open to the complaining party to argue that the application of that measure would deny it a benefit that it reasonably expected to flow from certain provisions of NAFTA. This begs a critical question: to what extent would so-called nonviolation nullification and impairment counteract the permissiveness of NAFTA's standards-related disciplines, particularly

---

102. NAFTA, supra note 1, Introduction, Annex 2004(1)(a). Some important omissions relate to Annex 300-A (Automotive Sector) and Chapter Six (Energy) relating to investment.

103. Ibid., Annex 2004(1).

the rules found in Chapter Nine? The answer depends in large measure on (1) what a benefit is and (2) when it could reasonably be expected. Since GATT Article XXIII does assert so-called nonviolation nullification and impairment as a basis for contesting a trade-restrictive measure and since NAFTA's more explicit language draws directly from a GATT Working Party report,[104] one could reasonably look to GATT practice for guidance.[105]

What Is a Benefit?

The above-mentioned Working Party perceived the "benefit" as "the value of a concession granted [by one party to another party]."[106] GATT establishes a mechanism for reciprocal tariff concessions between parties. In this contractual context, the value of a particular concession is the price the benefiting party is willing to pay—that is, the concession it offers in return for the same. A benefit is nullified or impaired, therefore, when a party is not getting what it paid for—when a tariff concession it received in return for its own concession is being undermined by the unforeseeable decision of the granting party. Regarding nullification and impairment as a *contractual inequity* preempts an argument that general GATT obligations could legitimately be considered a benefit. Given the numerous waivers and wholesale reservations from GATT obligations, one could hardly view the GATT text as a contractual exchange of legal compliance between the parties.[107] Moreover, this narrow conception of "benefit" as the *quid pro quo* of a contract augurs badly for claims based on nonviolation nulli-

---

104. *The Australian Subsidy on Ammonium Sulfate, (Chile v. Australia)* (1950), GATT Doc. C.P.4/39, 2 B.I.S.D. (1952) 188. The case involved the Australian government's withdrawal of a Chilean product from a list of closely related subsidized products. This action effectively nullified the anticipated "benefit" of a tariff concession which Australia had granted Chile while the subsidy was still in force. A GATT Working Party concluded that, though no GATT rules were violated, there was nonetheless nullification and impairment since Australia's action "*could not reasonably have been anticipated* by the Chilean Government, taking into consideration all pertinent circumstances and the provisions of the General Agreement, at the time it negotiated for the duty-free binding on sodium nitrate [the Chilean product]." (para. 12)

105. For an in-depth history and analysis of nonviolation nullification and impairment under GATT, see Robert E. Hudec, "Retaliation Against 'Unreasonable' Foreign Trade Practices: The New Section 301" (1975) 59 Minnesota Law Review 461 at 481–505 [hereinafter "Retaliation"] and also Hudec, *The GATT Legal System,* supra note 97, Part II at 159–179.

106. Supra note 104, Part II at para. 13.

107. See "Retaliation," supra note 105, Part II at 503–504.

fication and impairment of wider, more speculative, and less measurable "benefits."[108] In essence, international law has, perhaps by necessity, construed "benefit" in the narrowest possible terms.

At least with respect to benefits accruing under Part Two (Trade in Goods), the same constrained interpretation of a "benefit" may arguably be distilled from key NAFTA provisions. NAFTA prescribes a sanction for nonimplementation of the findings of a dispute settlement panel: If in its final report, a panel has concluded that a measure is inconsistent with NAFTA rules or causes nullification and impairment and no satisfactory agreement is reached on the implementation of the panel's findings, the complaining party "may suspend the application to the Party complained against of benefits of equivalent effect."[109] The contractual perspective informs the requirement that the benefits to be suspended be of equivalent effect to the ostensibly nullified benefits (even where the two do not fall into the same sector[110]). If the latter benefit is not discrete and ascertainable, then one could not determine whether another benefit is "of equivalent effect."[111] This suggests that, as in GATT dispute settlement practice, a nullified benefit under NAFTA is rightly viewed as something that a party paid for but whose value was subsequently denied. Only reciprocal tariff concessions neatly fit this contractual mold. After all, what reflects the value of a tariff concession more reliably than an equivalent benefit of equivalent effect? Clearly, the GATT panel-sponsored view of what constitutes a benefit survives unproblematically in a NAFTA context.

---

108. Such a claim was made unsuccessfully in the *Uruguayan Recourse* (1961), 11th supp. B.I.S.D. (1962) 97–98. In this case, Uruguay argued that the totality of trade-restricting measures adopted by 15 countries against Uruguayan exports upset the overall balance between Uruguay's GATT obligations and benefits. The GATT panel was unwilling to recognize the relevance of nonviolation nullification and impairment to situations falling outside the immediate contractual inequity context. To be fair, as Robert Hudec notes, Uruguay never really developed the argument beyond mere assertion. See supra note 105, Part II at 497–500.

109. NAFTA, supra note 1, Introduction, art. 2019(1)

110. Ibid., art. 2019(2)(a) stipulates that, in considering what benefits to suspend, the complaining party "*should* first seek to suspend benefits in the same sector as that affected by the measure or other matter that the panel has found to be inconsistent with [NAFTA] or to have caused nullification or impairment. . . .." Only if such tailoring is "not practical or effective" may the complaining party suspend benefits in other sectors— though the requirement of equivalent effect still applies.

111. Under NAFTA Article 2019(4), the challenged party may request the establishment of a panel to determine whether the level of benefits suspended by the complaining party is "manifestly excessive."

When Is the Benefit Reasonably Expected?

Under GATT practice (and perhaps under NAFTA's as well), each party may reasonably expect that a tariff concession it bargained for will be given effect.[112] The question of reasonable expectations for the purposes of nonviolation nullification and impairment was addressed by a GATT Review Session in the context of a discussion on domestic subsidies (those benefiting only domestic producers or manufacturers). The Contracting Parties agreed that "a contracting party which has negotiated a concession . . . may be assumed to have a reasonable expectation, failing evidence to the contrary, that the value of the concession will not be nullified or impaired . . . by the subsequent introduction or increase of domestic subsidy on the product concerned."[113] Whether the benefit is denied through a subsidy or a technical regulation, the reasoning remains the same: Some measure of intent or bad faith

---

112. Under GATT practice, reasonable expectations may also arise from reliance-inducing conduct at the time of the tariff negotiations. This is exemplified by conduct by a party which leads another party reasonably to expect, as consideration for the tariff concessions it grants, that the former would maintain an existing market-access-enhancing measure. Precisely this situation arose in *The Australian Subsidy on Ammonium Sulfate,* supra note 104, Part II. In this case, it was found that Chile, in negotiating for a tariff concession on its sodium nitrate fertilizers, could reasonably expect that Australia would continue to subsidize sodium nitrate fertilizers to the same extent as Australian ammonium sulfate fertilizers (the two being closely related products). The Working Party noted, in support of this conclusion, that (1) both products had been distributed in Australia through the same agency and sold at the same price, and (2) the system was still maintained in respect of both fertilizers at the time the tariff concession in respect of sodium nitrate was negotiated. In essence, Chile's reliance on these and other circumstances was entirely valid. Reliance-inducing conduct was also found to give rise to nullification and impairment in *Treatment by Germany of Imports of Sardines (Norway v. West Germany)* (1952), GATT Doc. G/26, 1st supp. B.I.S.D. (1953) 53. While there is no reason to think that reliance-inducing behavior could not underpin reasonable expectations in respect of NAFTA benefits as well as GATT benefits, the more likely scenario where environmental disputes are concerned involves violation of the general obligation to give effect to a tariff concession by enacting or modifying legislation in a way that effectively denies expected and just-granted market access for regulated products.

113. See GATT, *Other Barriers to Trade,* (Report Adopted 3 March 1955), GATT Doc. L/334 & Addendum, para. 13, 3rd supp. B.I.S.D. (1955) 222 at 224. A subsequent Review Session concluded that the qualifying expression "failing evidence to the contrary" elevates the rule to the status of a virtual "presumption" in favor of reasonable expectations "unless such pertinent facts were available at the time the tariff concession was granted." See GATT, *Subsidies: Operation of the Provisions of Article XVI,* (Report Adopted 21 November 1961), GATT Doc. L/1442 & Addendum 1–2, paras. 27–28, 10th supp. B.I.S.D. (1962) 201 at 209. The concept of reasonable expectations was also dealt

would have to be shown in support of a contention that reasonable expectations are being thwarted.[114] In other words, a party that bargained for a tariff concession may reasonably expect that the granting party would not subsequently adopt a purportedly environment-related measure whose *real purpose* or underlying intent is to defeat the purpose of such concession. Divining the real purpose or underlying intent would normally involve such considerations as the reach and effect of the suspect measure and the availability of less trade-restrictive alternatives fulfilling the same legitimate objective. Where, for instance, an environment-related technical regulation's trade-restricting impact is too precisely targeted at a particular imported product upon which a tariff concession has been granted, a degree of bad faith may conceivably be ascribed to the adopting party—thereby allowing a NAFTA claim in nullification and impairment.

Environmental Standards in Light of Nullification and Impairment

In this light, the interrelationship between NAFTA's nullification and impairment clause and, say, Chapter Nine becomes more decipherable. Suppose that, for ostensibly environmental purposes, a party adopts a mandatory standard that, suspiciously, serves only to prevent the importing of a product upon which a tariff concession has been recently negotiated. Even though it collides with a tariff concession, it may still have all the trappings of a perfectly legitimate measure under

---

with in the FTA Report *In the Matter of Puerto Rico Regulations on the Import Distribution and Sale of U.H.T. Milk from Quebec,* USA 92-1807-02-1992-though the reasoning therein is of little help in the context of NAFTA's environmental standards-related disciplines.

114. This narrow reading is called for since the language of the Review Session's conclusion suggests, on its face, that virtually any measure whose effect is to undermine a tariff concession would be at odds with the reasonable expectations of the party that bargained for that concession. Under the auspices of GATT and NAFTA, tariff concessions have been negotiated in respect of thousands of products in practically every market sector. A trade-restricting environmental measure would have to steer clear of all of these if a claim in nullification and impairment is to be forestalled. Most absurdly, a standards-related measure that effectively prevents the sale of both domestically produced goods and the identical imported goods subject to a negotiated tariff reduction could, based on this logic, be found to nullify the value of a tariff concession, despite the measure's certifiably nondiscriminatory character. To require a degree of intentional wrongdoing, then, realistically acknowledges that some standards-related measures will inevitably encroach upon tariff concession terrain but explicitly deters parties from actively and purposely pursuing this objective.

NAFTA.[115] However, insofar as the complaining party in this instance reasonably expected that the value of the tariff concession would not be negated by a subsequently adopted measure, a solid claim may lie in nonviolation nullification and impairment. For example, a panel, looking for evidence of bad faith, could perhaps infer it from the near-surgical precision with which the measure attacks a particular imported product. It is quite plausibly this kind of conduct by a party that the concept of nonviolation nullification and impairment was designed to address.

On the other hand, where a standards-related measure serves to restrict the sale of both a domestically produced good and the identical imported product upon which a tariff has been reduced, the circumvention of the negotiated concession is more likely to be seen as an incidental consequence of a legitimate environmental measure. If a dispute settlement panel accepts the argument that bad faith must be demonstrated in order for a claim based on nullification and impairment to succeed, then the door would likely be shut on a party's recourse based on nullification and impairment. After all, the point of nullifying the value of a tariff concession is to restore the preconcession competitive advantage of a domestic good. Since the environmental measure affects domestic goods in the same manner as it affects like imported goods, the competitive position of the former is not enhanced. Thus, the real purpose or underlying intent of the measure must be something other than to defeat the purpose of a tariff concession, and there would be no case for bad faith. In summary, it seems that any standards-related measure enacted in good faith for the purposes of environmental protection will likely withstand a claim premised on nonviolation nullification and impairment.

Sanitary and Phytosanitary Measures and Standards-Related Measures

The above discussion contemplated the extent to which S&P or standards-related measures could be sustained in the face of a substantive legal challenge under NAFTA. It is, however, predicated on a hereto-

---

115. The complaining party would have difficulty making the case that the standard is not "primarily aimed" at a legitimate objective—in this case, environmental protection. The measure would be consistent with national treatment since the same product manufactured in the territory of the adopting party would have to meet this standard. Moreover, there would be no question of unnecessary obstacles to trade because, had the product met the standard, its access to the adopting party's market would not be impeded.

fore unspoken assumption that all S&P and standards-related measures could be challenged under the disciplines set out in Chapter Seven and Chapter Nine. While the assumption is true for most such measures, it may be inaccurate with respect to (1) measures that do not affect trade between the parties and (2) measures adopted by the subnational governments of the parties. In the case of the former, Chapter Seven and Chapter Nine do not apply. In the latter case, the disciplines do apply, but, since states and provinces are not, in a strict sense, "parties" to NAFTA, subnational compliance is secured only indirectly.

The Applicability of S&P and Standards-Related Disciplines to Measures That May Directly or Indirectly Affect Trade

Chapter Seven and Chapter Nine apply respectively to all S&P measures and standards-related measures that "may, directly or indirectly affect trade between the Parties."[116] The expression "directly or indirectly" signifies that the two disciplines apply not just to S&P and standards-related measures that govern products exported from one party to another but to any such measures that have an effect, however incidental, on trade between the parties. Therefore, the fact that a party's standards-related measure applies only to products that are neither imported nor exported does not by itself render that measure immune to a challenge. Indeed, the measure may still be found to affect trade insofar as the components from which those products are manufactured were imported from the territory of another party. Moreover, S&P and standards-related measures would be actionable not only where they do affect trade between the parties but also where they "may" affect such trade. In other words, the mere fact that such a measure threatens to restrict trade (even if only indirectly) could suffice to ensure the applicability of either of the two NAFTA disciplines.

The importance of such jurisdictional sweep cannot be overstated. Indeed, it appears that the negotiators of NAFTA intended to expand as much as was conceptually possible the scope of applicability of the two disciplines. And so, a party may find its S&P and standards-related measures open to dispute settlement challenge even though their effects on trade were marginal or wholly unanticipated. Moreover, with the promised exponential growth of trade between parties under NAFTA, it becomes unlikely that any domestic S&P or technical standard-related measure will be found *not* to have some indirect effect on North American trade. As small as the domain of unexposed domestic

---

116. NAFTA, supra note 1, Introduction, arts. 709 and 901, respectively.

S&P and technical standards-related measures may be, it will probably be getting smaller with time.

Compliance by Provinces and States

All three NAFTA signatories are federations. Whereas in Mexico the division of powers appears to spawn little controversy,[117] the debate over states' rights is a recurring political and legal issue in the United States-with jurisdiction over environmental law a growing point of contention. In Canada, too, federal—provincial jurisdictional disputes over the constitutional division of power are central to political life. Despite a number of controversial areas such as environmental impact assessment, natural resources protection, the protection of larger rivers, most Canadian domestic environmental law falls into provincial rather than federal jurisdiction.[118] The question hence arises as to the vulnerability of state and provincial environmental laws and regulations to challenges brought under NAFTA's trade disciplines.

It is to be noted that provinces and states were informed and, to a certain degree, consulted during the NAFTA negotiations. For example, Canada's Federal–Provincial Committee on NAFTA held regular meetings during the course of the NAFTA process and even after, during the NAAEC discussions.

While provincial and state governments are not signatories of NAFTA, they are not insulated from NAFTA's jurisdictional reach since the parties are subject to obligations to secure subnational compliance. In theory, the stringency of these obligations varies depending on whether one is dealing with measures contemplated under Chapter Seven or those subject to Chapter Nine. Where subnational S&P measures are involved, the parties have an obligation to take "all necessary measures" to ensure that such subnational laws and regulations are consistent with Chapter Seven.[119] The corresponding GATT provision requires only that each contracting party take "such reasonable measures as may be available to it" to ensure subnational compliance with GATT provisions.[120] Though the GATT wording is, on its face, less strin-

---

117. The recent rebellion in the Chiapas region and other regional tensions on the occasion of the presidential election of 1994 will, however, likely cast the political spotlight on hitherto lesser known jurisdictional issues and controversies.

118. The unwieldy nature of Canadian federalism will be a particularly important constraint on the implementation of the NAAEC in Canada. For a detailed discussion, see infra notes 147 to 180, Part IV, and accompanying text.

119. NAFTA, supra note 1, Introduction, art. 105

120. GATT, supra note 9, Part I, art. XXIV(12)

gent than that found in NAFTA, a pivotal GATT panel report construed the provision as an absolute requirement that each party take every measure constitutionally available to it to secure subnational observance of GATT provisions.[121] If the expression "all reasonable measures" could translate into so exacting an obligation, then a NAFTA panel is all the more likely to ascribe the same meaning to the expression "all necessary measures." Thus, in principle, where the national government of a party is empowered to override subnational S&P legislation found to be inconsistent with Chapter Seven, it could be obligated to resort to such power, should other avenues such as negotiations with the offending subnational government fail following a successful challenge against such legislation. Usually, however, a party will try, when it is involved in a dispute over market access with a federation like Canada, the United States, or Germany, to avoid embarrassing one another by pressing federal authorities to take action, without due regard for domestic political sensitivities.

The general obligation of the parties to take all necessary measures to ensure subnational compliance gives way to a seemingly less stringent requirement in the case of standards-related measures governed by the rules of Chapter Nine. The parties are obliged merely to seek "through appropriate measures" observance by subnational governments of the NAFTA provisions limiting the right of parties to adopt standards-related measures.[122] The term "appropriate measures" in NAFTA is used instead of the expression "all necessary measures," found in GATT. It means, *in theory,* that the parties do not have to go as far in enforcing subnational compliance with the standards-related

---

121. *United States-Measures on Alcoholic and Malt Beverages,* supra note 42, Part II at para. 5.79–5.80. For a discussion of this case as well as the history of the treatment of subnational compliance issues under GATT and American law, see Steve Charnovitz, "The Environment vs. Trade Rules: Defogging the Debate" (1993) 23 Environmental Law 475 at 501–510 [hereinafter "Defogging the Debate"]. See also: In *Re: Ultra-High Temperature Milk from Quebec,* supra note 113, Part II. At issue in this case was the testing and certification standards imposed upon U.H.T. milk processed for sale in Puerto Rico. Canada maintained that the laboratory testing of milk by certified inspectors and the periodic certification of manufacturing facilities represented an unnecessary and discriminatory barrier to trade.

122. NAFTA, supra note 1, Introduction, art. 902(1) stipulates that NAFTA Article 105, which sets forth the general obligation by the parties to take all necessary steps to secure subnational compliance, does not apply to Chapter Nine. In its place is substituted, by way of NAFTA art. 902(2), the requirement that each party merely "seek, through appropriate measures, to ensure observance of [NAFTA] Articles 904 to 908 by state or provincial governments and by nongovernmental standardizing bodies in its territory."

discipline as they must in respect of the S&P discipline.[123] In other words, it seems that subnational regulatory nonconformity with NAFTA disciplines is more tolerable for most environmental regulations (covered by Chapter Nine) and less tolerable in the specific case of S&P measures (covered by Chapter Seven).

However, one cannot be sure that lowering the threshold from "necessary measures" to "appropriate measures" will have any practical significance. Under the general rules of international law, a country may not invoke its constitutional law in defense of its noncompliance with international obligations.[124] Thus, where a state or provincial environmental measure is inconsistent with NAFTA, one may cogently argue that it is the NAFTA party that would be in breach—even though the measure falls outside the central government's legislative competence. This means that the party would be answerable for NAFTA-inconsistent subnational environmental legislation whether or not the breach could be rectified by way of "appropriate measures."[125] As well, it is difficult to see how requiring the taking of "appropriate measures" instead of "all necessary measures" to ensure state or provincial compliance would make any difference where a party has a history of securing subnational compliance by way of informal negotiations.[126] It would, after

---

123. It may be plausible for a party to argue, for example, that, insofar as its power to override subnational legislation is an extraordinary recourse fraught with incalculable long-term political risks, it would not constitute an appropriate measure.

124. *Vienna Convention on the Law of Treaties,* supra note 7, Part II at Article 27. See Kenneth J. Cooper, "To Compel or Encourage: Seeking Compliance with International Trade Agreements at the State Level" (1993) 2 Minn. J. Global Trade 143.

125. Recall that since states and provinces are not "parties" under NAFTA, they have no standing in dispute settlement. Even though nothing in NAFTA directly compels a party to defend allegedly inconsistent state or provincial legislation, Article 27 of the *Vienna Convention* would likely leave a party little choice but to do so. In practice, this is what is done in North America under the Canada–U.S. FTA (see Article 103). If a central government fails to defend the consistency of a measure taken by a subnational government with NAFTA, it exposes itself to an adverse ruling and the possibility of trade sanctions.

126. Both the U.S. and Canadian governments are constitutionally equipped to override state and provincial legislation, respectively. In Canada, however, given the political and legal culture's hostility to federal preemption of provincial jurisdiction, Canadian governments have been painfully reluctant to exercise so-called power of disallowance. Indeed, they have not done so since 1943. In a country where federal–provincial jurisdictional disputes are the mainstay of political life, the use of the powers of disallowance would meet with vehement condemnation and provoke a severe constitutional crisis. Realistically, enforcing compliance of provincial S&P mea-

all, be absurd to suggest that the former obligation would permit a party to negotiate less vigorously with state or provincial authorities in order to meet international obligations or that abortive negotiations would satisfy the former obligation if not the latter. All told, the change in language from "necessary measures" to "appropriate measures" should not translate into a lesser obligation for federations (and their federated states and provinces) to enact standards-related environmental measures that comply with NAFTA's Chapter Nine discipline.[127]

Assessment of NAFTA's Standards-Related Disciplines

While one can engage in a detailed analysis of the relative environmental merits of different provisions, it is important first to remember that trade disciplines remain an inherent threat to domestic environmental legislation because they enable one country to challenge another country's laws under the auspices of trade dispute settlement. The real questions therefore pertain to (1) the immediacy and (2) the nature and potency of this threat. NAFTA involves no direct pre-emption: Trade disciplines do not spontaneously undermine domestic environmental legislation. The immediacy of the threat posed by Chapters Seven and Nine is hence directly a function of the willingness of NAFTA parties to resort to these disciplines to challenge each other's environmental laws. In the current political climate, it is likely that public opinion, informed by a heightened concern for environmental protection, would weigh heavily against one party's systematic challenges to the domestic environmental legislation of a neighbor. Instantaneous communications and activist NGOs would probably transform a complaining party's attempt into a controversy. For the moment, therefore, the threat of repeated attempts by any NAFTA party to dis-

---

sures with Chapter Seven would involve extensive negotiations between the federal government and its provincial counterpart. See *Constitution Act, 1867* (U.K.), 30 & 31 Vict., c.3, § 56, 90; Peter W. Hogg, *Constitutional Law of Canada*, 3rd ed. (Toronto: Carswell, 1992) at 112.

127. On the other hand, the *Vienna Convention on the Law of Treaties,* supra note 7, Part II, also stipulates at Article 31 that the entire text of a treaty must be interpreted so as to give effect to its object and purpose. Implicit in this provision is the idea that a treaty cannot be interpreted in such a manner as to render a particular stipulation superfluous. The lowering of the threshold from "all necessary measures" to "appropriate measures" must therefore have *some* significance—and much will be left to creative argument to flesh it out.

mantle the environmental standards regimes of its partners can hardly be said to be immediate.

As to the legal nature and potency of the threat, authoritative conclusions would be premature absent an established "NAFTA practice." Nonetheless, five key points are worth noting. First, NAFTA's drafters have fashioned the environment-related disciplines into a jurisdictionally intrusive regime. Indeed, most if not all S&P and standards-related measures adopted by a party or by its subnational governments will fall within NAFTA's reach. Second, while Chapter Seven is a potent weapon in the hands of a party challenging S&P measures adopted by another party, the threat posed by this discipline does not discernibly exceed that posed by the *Canada–United States FTA,* old GATT rules, or the *Uruguay Round Agreements.* In fact, environmentally responsive dispute settlement procedures and other provisions casting doubt on the applicability of GATT interpretations may measurably enhance an S&P measure's chances of being upheld by a NAFTA panel. Third, Chapter Nine, by comparison, promises the parties unprecedented freedom to enact environmental standards-related measures, since only those overtly discriminatory measures would not survive scrutiny. In effect, it appears that the parties may undertake any good faith effort to regulate products or their characteristics in the interests of *domestic* environmental protection—a real advance over old GATT law and the results of the Uruguay Round. Fourth, these gains are not likely to be substantially undercut by NAFTA's nullification and impairment clause. Fifth, where a dispute over an environmental standard arises under both GATT and NAFTA rules, the fact that the party complained against has the option of choosing the applicable regime virtually guarantees that the generally less restrictive NAFTA rules will be applied.

There is room for one last consideration. What is often forgotten in the sometimes overheated debate over the environmental implications of trade disciplines is that there is no international leviathan armed with a mandate to crush environmental laws that collide with international trade disciplines. Rather, the initiative to contest environmental legislation lies with the individual NAFTA parties, and the course of action that NAFTA prescribes in this respect is procedurally unwieldy and politically perilous. Should NAAEC deliver on its promise to establish institutional channels for collaboration on the environment—particularly in the setting of harmonized and mutually compatible environmental norms—it is quite possible that trade disciplines will over time lapse into irrelevance in the face of more significant developments.

NAFTA's Treatment of Domestic Measures to Implement International Environmental Treaties

International environmental agreements have been proliferating in recent years, particularly since 1970.[128] The use or potential use of trade restrictions is an increasingly common feature of international environmental agreements.[129] For example, the *Convention on International Trade in Endangered Species of Wild Fauna and Flora* (hereinafter "CITES")[130] prohibits the trade of certain threatened plants and animals; the *Montreal Protocol on Substances That Deplete the Ozone Layer*[131] features rules against trade in CFCs and products made using CFCs, and even provides for trade sanctions against violators. Domestic measures enacting trade restrictions pursuant to these and other international environmental treaties could be suspect under the GATT regime. The *Montreal Protocol,* for example, may in the future enable signatories to ban imports from nonsignatories of products made using certain substances that, when released, deplete the ozone layer. Such import restrictions constitute measures governing process and production methods (PPMs). As discussed above, they run afoul of Tuna–Dolphin doctrine.[132] This is why environmentalists, and indeed some trade

---

128. By 1990, the number of multilateral international environmental agreements already exceeded 150, about half of which were dedicated to the protection of marine life and the prevention of marine pollution. See U.S. Congress, General Accounting Office, *International Environment: International Agreements Are Not Well Monitored,* GAO/RCED-92-43 (Gaithersburg, MD.: U.S. General Accounting Office, 1992). P.W. Birnie and A.L. Boyle, *International Law and the Environment,* 2nd ed. (Oxford: Clarendon, 1992); Charnovitz, "Defogging the Debate," supra note 121, Part II at 481–482.

129. As has been explained, trade-affecting measures and outright trade sanctions are increasingly perceived as a principal recourse to induce urgently needed international environmental cooperation. See "Environmental Trade Sanctions," supra note 106, Part I at 756–757. See notes 94–116, Part I and accompanying text.

130. Supra note 18, Part I

131. 16 September 1987, 26 I.L.M. 1541, 30 I.L.M. 537 (amended in 1990) [hereinafter *Montreal Protocol*].

132. For a short discussion of the legality of the GATT-consistency of trade measures enacted to implement international environmental treaties, see U.S. Congress, Office of Technology Assessment, *Trade and the Environment: Conflicts and Opportunities,* OTA-BP-ITE-94 (Washington, D.C.: U.S. Government Printing Office, May 1992) at 46–52; Rodrigo J. Prudencio & Stewart J. Hudson, *The Road to Marrakech: An Interim Report on Environmental Reform of the GATT and International Trade System* (Washington, D.C.: National Wildlife Federation, 1994) at 16–17; and Alan Charles Raul & Paul E. Hagen, "The Convergence of Trade and Environmental Law" (1993) 8 Natural Resources and Environment 3 at 6.

specialists, have argued that trade agreements like NAFTA should be subordinated to trade-affecting environmental treaties, at least when the latter command broad international support (as evidenced by, among other things, the number and diversity of signatories).[133]

NAFTA explicitly defers to five international environmental treaties, three of which undoubtedly meet these criteria: CITES,[134] the *Montreal Protocol*,[135] and the *Basel Convention on the Control of Transboundary Movements or Hazardous Waste and Their Disposal*.[136] Where NAFTA rules clash with the obligations undertaken by Mexico, Canada, and the United States pursuant to these agreements, "[these] obligations shall prevail . . . provided that where a Party has a choice among equally effective and reasonably available means of complying with such obligations, the Party chooses the alternative that is *least inconsistent* [with NAFTA]."[137] This rule breaks new ground: Though it is increasingly commonplace for nations to subordinate their internal law to certain international obligations, one would be hard-pressed to find so explicit a "hierarchization" of international obligations where environmental treaties are perched at the top.[138] The subordination of

---

133. The *Vienna Convention* provides that treaties "later in time" prevail. However, that rule applies only when the treaties address the same subject matter. Supra note 7, Part II. In principle, this will mean that the more recent environmental treaties supersede GATT, but are superseded by the WTO agreements when the subject matter overlaps. There are, however, differing interpretations of that rule. See Robert F. Housman and Durwood Zaelke, "Trade, Environment and Sustainable Development: A Primer" (1992), 15 Hastings International and Comparative Law Review 535; Robert Housman, *The Interaction of International Trade and Environmental Agreements* (Washington, D.C.: Center for International Environmental Law, 1992); Jackson, "World Trade Rules," supra note 108, Part I at 1227–1228; J.O. Cameron, T. Mjolo-Thamage, and J.C. Robinson, UN Conference on Environment and Development, *In Our Hands: Earth Summit '92: Relationship Between Environmental Agreements and Instruments Related to Trade and Development,* Research Paper No. 35 (February, 1992).

134. Supra note 18, Part I.

135. Supra note 131, Part II.

136. Supra note 97, Part I. The other two named treaties are *The Agreement Between the Government of Canada and the Government of the United States of America Concerning the Transboundary Movement of Hazardous Waste,* 28 October 1986, Can. T.S. 1986 No. 39, T.I.A.S. No. 11099; and the *Mexico–United States Agreement to Cooperate in the Solution of Environmental Problems in the Border Area,* 14 August 1983, 22 I.L.M. 1025 (better known as the "La Paz Agreement").

137. NAFTA, supra note 1, Introduction, art. 104(1).

138. Leading authors, such as John Jackson of the University of Michigan Law School, suggested a "waiver" under GATT for international environmental agreements. "World Trade Rules," supra note 108, Part I at 1271.

NAFTA to domestic measures that implement international environmental treaties goes much further than other NAFTA provisions whereby the parties merely "reaffirm with respect to each other their existing rights and obligations" under other agreements (like GATT).[139] How these latter general provisions affect the relationship between NAFTA and the named international treaties is at best unclear. No such uncertainty exists, on the other hand, in respect of a stipulation that domestic measures implementing named international environmental agreements would *prevail* over NAFTA. This rule of paramountcy, or supremacy, of named environmental treaties is without precedent.[140]

This immunity, however, is only partial. A party's measures to control imports and exports of hazardous wastes or wild animals could still be challenged on grounds that, as means of performing the relevant international environmental obligations, they are not the "least inconsistent" with NAFTA. As amply discussed above, the expression "least inconsistent" has a worrying history in GATT practice and hence may, in a NAFTA context, set an insuperably high acceptability threshold for the validity of certain challenged trade-affecting environmental measures. Compounding this potential difficulty is the fact that the burden of showing that the implementation measure is the least inconsistent with NAFTA appears to fall to the party complained against, since the assignment of the burden of proof to the complaining party found in Chapters Seven and Nine is not replicated in Article 104.[141]

The concern that the "least inconsistency" test may derail domestic measures implementing international environmental treaties is tempered, however, by an important qualification: For a challenge to succeed, a panel must be satisfied not only that there is at least one measure that is more NAFTA-consistent than the challenged measure but also that this more NAFTA-consistent measure is both "equally effective" and "reasonably available." As discussed earlier, given the

---

139. For example, NAFTA, supra note 1, Introduction art. 103(1) and 903.

140. The wording of Article 104(1), however, could raise a delicate issue. It could be argued that trade-affecting measures required by the named environmental treaties are protected, but that trade-affecting measures explicitly allowed but ultimately discretionary (or optional) under the environmental treaties are not "specific trade obligations set out" in such treaties. Nevertheless, since NAFTA speaks of a "choice" between alternatives to implement these obligations, it could also be claimed that discretion is recognized and protected by the provision.

141. Supra note 24, Part II and accompanying text. The burden of proof falls to the challenging party only in disputes concerning domestic measures subject to Chapters Seven and Nine.

absence from the GATT "least inconsistency" test of such language, it is not surprising that GATT panels have not ever seriously assessed the effectiveness of alternative measures found to be less GATT-inconsistent than the challenged measures. A NAFTA panel, by contrast, would be required to engage in such an exercise—a genuine reprieve for domestic measures enacted in compliance with international environmental obligations. While it remains to be seen how well domestic measures enacted to perform international environmental treaty obligations would fare under NAFTA dispute settlement, the status of these measures under NAFTA is measurably more secure than their status under GATT.

The interpretation of the "least inconsistent" test will gain in importance if the parties use NAFTA Article 104(2) to add eventual amendments and protocols as well as new environmental and conservation agreements to the treaties listed at Article 104(1). While they are not obligated to do so, the parties should at least add the two Rio Conventions on Biodiversity and Climate Change and any protocols that may follow, as well as other important agreements such as the one against the commercial exploitation of Antarctica.[142] There have been preliminary discussions between the parties on supplementing the international treaty list but no official commitment has been made so far. There is no question for the authors that the NAFTA Free Trade Commission and the CEC should work hand-in-hand to enlarge the list of named international environmental agreements given partial priority over NAFTA rules. Given the increasing frequency with which countries will adopt domestic environmental and resource management legislation (whether in relation to forestry, fisheries, or carbon dioxide emissions) to implement international agreements, an aggressive drive to keep the NAFTA list of environmental agreements up-to-date is critical.

---

142. See the *Antarctic Treaty*, 1 December 1959, 402 U.N.T.S. 71.

Chapter 4

NAFTA's Downward Pressure on Environmental Norms and Upward Harmonization

As discussed above, one of the principal objections raised by environmentalists against trade liberalization (and, in particular, NAFTA) is that it exerts downward pressure on environmental norms since investors systematically seek to improve their competitiveness by locating in the least regulated country.[143] While evidence of this trend is more anecdotal than empirical, the fear has been keenly expressed, and the consequent political pressure to address this issue in NAFTA has proven irresistible. At the very least, NAFTA's pollution havens clause and the upward harmonization principle embedded in its standards-related disciplines signal unprecedented recognition that unshackling trade may trigger a continental slide in levels of environ-

---

143. For example, some have claimed that the implementation of NAFTA has led the United States to lower its food inspection and Corporate Average Fuel Economy Standards (CAFE). "Democratizing International Trade Decision-Making," supra note 14, Part I at 736–737. See also, *NAFTA Implementation Act,* Pub. L. No. 103-182, §361 (b), (e), (f), 107 Stat. 2057, 2122-24 (1993); "USTR Draft Reveals Intention to Implement GATT Dispute Panels," *Inside U.S. Trade* 4 March 1994, at S1, S2.

mental protection. However, as legal instruments for preventing downward regulatory movement and promoting upward harmonization of environmental standards, both the pollution havens clause and the upward harmonization principle will likely prove disappointing. At best, they offer a framework—rather than a compelling incentive—for the parties to enhance overall levels of environmental protection. Also, they provide poor protection against a relaxation of environmental laws and regulations brought about by a domestic political climate hostile to environmental protection.

Downward Regulatory Pressure and the Pollution Havens Clause

Formally recognizing that "it is inappropriate to encourage investment by relaxing domestic health, safety or environmental measures," NAFTA merely admonishes each party not to "waive or otherwise derogate from, or offer to waive or otherwise derogate from, such measures as an encouragement for the establishment, acquisition, expansion or retention in its territory of an investment of an investor."[144] The purely hortatory character of this provision confirms the absence of any enforceable sanction for breach. Where a party considers that another party has relaxed its environmental measures so as to attract or retain investment, the former would have recourse to consultations with the latter—not formal dispute settlement.[145]

Though critics understandably lament the feebleness of NAFTA's pollution havens investment clause, it is arguable that the negotiators went as far as they realistically could to forestall the relaxing of domes-

---

144. NAFTA, supra note 1, Introduction, art. 1114(2). It is interesting to note the absence of any language qualifying the terms "investment" and "investor." This suggests that the drafters of Article 1114(2) may have had in mind the relaxing of environmental measures to attract investment not simply from other NAFTA parties but from anywhere in the world.

145. Another environment-related provision can be found at ibid., art. 1114(1), which stipulates that "[n]othing in [Chapter Eleven] shall be construed to prevent a Party from adopting, maintaining or enforcing any measure . . . that it considers appropriate to ensure that investment activity in its territory is undertaken in a manner sensitive to environmental concerns." Though all domestic measures designed to ensure that investment activity is sensitive to environmental protection will be therefore consistent with Chapter Eleven, the possibility that they may be inconsistent with Chapters Seven and Eleven is not precluded by NAFTA. Nonetheless, Article 1114(1) may afford considerable protection for increasingly common environmental impact assessment legislation.

tic environmental measures as a means of attracting investment. Indeed, their decision to rule out dispute settlement may owe much to three conceptual problems that would necessarily accompany meaningful enforcement of the pollution havens clause. First, what constitutes a violation is difficult to define, especially since the provision clearly refers to the enacting government's intent. Given the knotty, convoluted nature of the legislative process, it would be immensely difficult to prove that a party's decision to dilute environmental protection legislation was *intended* as an inducement to foreign investors. Countless other justifications for such a legislative or regulatory adjustment could be advanced.[146] Second, how would an enforceable prohibition against lowering levels of environmental protection affect an environmental race to the bottom between the subnational governments of one party? This question seems all the more poignant when one considers that state and provincial measures account for a sizable chunk of environmental legislation in North America. Third, it is quite possible that a mandatory and enforceable pollution havens clause would have an unintended freezing effect on environmental norms. A party may calculate that it would be better not to enact a particular environmental measure than to risk enacting one that would be difficult to revoke without incurring trade sanctions under NAFTA. All told, NAFTA's negotiators, in response to fears of downward pressure on environmental norms, may have fashioned the worst possible pollution havens clause—except, to paraphrase Winston Churchill, for all the others.

This is not to say that NAFTA's pollution havens clause is devoid of all legal significance. On the contrary, the very existence of the clause signals unmistakable recognition by the NAFTA parties that the rigor of environmental protection in a jurisdiction influences its allure to investors and the competitiveness of the businesses established in that jurisdiction (or so it is said). Most strikingly, environmental protection is framed, albeit gingerly, as a competitiveness issue. Insofar as this perspective on environmental protection buttresses the actionable obligation under NAAEC to effectively enforce environmental laws, the pollution havens clause could legitimately be viewed as the embryonic origin of much of that agreement.

---

146. At least the trade disciplines of Chapters Seven and Nine articulate detailed rules by which a panel may second-guess a party's domestic measures. NAFTA, supra note 1, Introduction, art. 1114 is not similarly equipped to enable this kind of analytical exercise.

Upward Harmonization in Chapters Seven and Nine

NAFTA attempts to deal directly, if not problematically, with the related concern that liberalized trade may bring about downward harmonization of environmental norms. Both Chapters Seven and Nine deftly include provisions related to the upward harmonization of the parties' S&P and standards-related measures. In Chapter Seven, the parties undertake, "to the greatest extent practicable," to pursue equivalence of their respective sanitary and phytosanitary measures "[w]ithout reducing the level of protection of human, animal or plant life or health."[147] Similarly, in Chapter Nine, the parties are to pursue, also "to the greatest extent practicable," compatibility of their standards-related measures "[w]ithout reducing the level of safety or of protection of human, animal or plant life or health, the environment or consumers."[148] Each party is called upon to harmonize its S&P and standards-related measures with those of the other parties. However, since one party is precluded from lowering its domestic levels of protection (that is, relaxing the stringency of its S&P and standards-related measures) as a means of effecting such harmonization, the other parties with the lower standards would have to raise theirs to meet the higher standards.[149] And it is the party with the more stringent S&P or standards-related measures that would have the final say as to whether or not harmonization has actually occurred in respect of products imported from the territories of the harmonizing parties.[150] Thus, NAFTA could prompt, the parties' will allowing, a dynamic of upward harmonization between the parties' S&P and standards measures.

---

147. NAFTA, supra note 1, Introduction, art. 714(1).

148. Ibid., art. 906(2).

149. Although the Uruguay Round *Agreement on the Application of Sanitary and Phytosanitary Measures,* supra note 10, Part I and the *Agreement on Technical Barriers to Trade,* supra note 10, Part I, call for the use of international standards, neither agreement insists that this be done without reducing levels of protection.

150. This conclusion follows from NAFTA, supra note 1, Introduction, arts. 714(2) and 906(4). The latter provision stipulates that the importing party is obliged to treat the exporting party's technical regulation as equivalent to its own only "where the exporting Party . . . demonstrates to the satisfaction of the importing Party that its technical regulation adequately fulfills the importing Party's legitimate objective. Under Article 714(2)(b), the importing party "may, where it has a scientific basis, determine that the exporting Party's measure does not achieve the importing Party's appropriate level of protection." See Government of Canada, supra note 1, Part I at 19.

Yet two factors may counteract this dynamic. First, that the parties need only pursue harmonization "to the greatest extent practicable" points to the existence of circumstances under which a party may be excused from doing so. And while it is unclear what these circumstances may be, it appears unlikely that dispute settlement would ever be invoked on grounds that a party is not pursuing harmonization to the limits of practicability.[151] Second (and more ominously), a party facing the prospect of having to harmonize its own particular S&P or standards-related measure with another party's more stringent measure may prefer to challenge the latter measure before a dispute settlement panel. Indeed, insofar as antagonism to raising standards for the purpose of swift harmonization may foster assaults on the highest standards, the harmonization provisions may conceivably have an effect contrary to what the drafters had in mind if the drive toward harmonization becomes too aggressive. One thing is worth recalling in this respect: Though the requirement that S&P and standards-related measures be based on international standards (with a view to harmonization) does not preclude more stringent measures, these would still be subject to NAFTA disciplines respecting the general right to adopt such measures. Even so, where parties opt to challenge more often than harmonize, the upward harmonization principle ensconced in Chapters Seven and Nine may, at the very least, lend an interpretive hand to efforts to defend a challenged domestic measure. Given the clear intent of NAFTA's negotiators to promote upward harmonization of environmental standards (and given that NAAEC was largely created to promote those same objectives), the panelists may take a dim view of challenges that appear to be motivated more by efforts to stall the upward harmonization dynamic than by legitimate worries about trade protection and trade distortion.

Though the legal obligation to pursue upward harmonization of environmental norms is largely unenforceable, it could nonetheless provide a context for an energetic consultative and cooperative process aimed at harmonization. The success of such a process inevitably turns on two factors. The first is the presence of stable institutional venues and mechanisms for bringing together the various governmental actors. At least on paper, NAFTA scores in this respect. Chapter Seven

---

151. Nonetheless, one may think of economic scarcity, higher public health priorities, and genuine differences between the carrying capacity of the ecosystems of different NAFTA parties and regions as circumstances that could be invoked by a party refusing to harmonize upward.

provides for a Committee on Sanitary and Phytosanitary Measures, comprising representatives of each party.[152] The Committee's functions include facilitating (1) the enhancement of food safety and improvement of S&P conditions in the territories of the Parties;[153] (2) activities of the Parties relating to international standard-setting and the pursuit of equivalence between the norms of each party;[154] and (3) technical cooperation in the development, application, and enforcement of S&P measures.[155] Similarly, Chapter Nine provides for a Committee on Standards-related Measures charged with, among other things, (1) "facilitating the process by which the Parties make compatible their standards-related measures"[156] and (2) "enhancing cooperation on the development, application and enforcement of standards-related measures."[157] Both committees are empowered (though, regrettably, not required) to consult with experts and even nongovernmental organizations[158]—thereby inviting greater openness and political sensitivity in respect of harmonization activities. Moreover, that both committees may be convened by a single party increases the likelihood of sustained contact between the parties.[159] In theory, at least, NAFTA sets the stage for continuing dialogue and cooperation between the parties on harmonization of environmental norms. The real practice may come when this standards dialogue is joined with the cooperative agenda of the NAAEC.

Whether the governmental actors take to this stage with vigor (if at all) depends on the second factor: the political will of the parties. To be sure, the parties will inevitably resort to these committees as a means of heading off potentially serious conflicts arising from environmental measures. It would, however, take more than a sense of expediency or a passing political interest to convince all three parties to sit down and jointly revisit their environmental legislation with a view to upward harmonization, especially given the differences in levels of protection and policies outlined in Part I. This requires vision and perseverance, and it remains to be seen whether the parties will have

---

152. NAFTA, supra note 1, Introduction, art. 722.

153. Ibid., art. 722(2)(a).

154. Ibid., art. 722(2)(b).

155. Ibid., art. 722(2)(c).

156. Ibid., art. 913(2)(b).

157. Ibid., art. 913(2)(d).

158. Ibid., arts. 722(3)(b) and 913(4)(a).

159. Ibid., arts. 722(3)(d) and 913(3)(a).

enough of either. To date, unfortunately, the record for trade agreement-sanctioned environmental activism is not encouraging. Canada–U.S. FTA working groups and committees have often met only episodically, when they began their work at all.

The ever-present risk of political lethargy, however, pales against the threat that the committees outlined in Chapters Seven and Nine would succumb to active misuse. Indeed the committees were conceived as (among other things) forums for active consultation on harmonization, but they in fact may facilitate a party's doing behind closed doors what it wishes not to do publicly. If experience under the Canada–U.S. FTA is any indication, it would be difficult for a party under NAFTA to conceal a formal challenge to another's environmental legislation. And the consequent public controversy, exacting a potent price, would only compound the procedural and substantive legal complexity already inherent in NAFTA bilateral dispute settlement. Is it any wonder, therefore, that a party seeking to undo the environmental measures of its neighbor would be tempted to resort to exerting pressure in the relative privacy of the NAFTA standards harmonization committees? After all, these committees are under no obligation of either public consultation or disclosure. Moreover, their agendas are underdeveloped and their procedures virtually nonexistent (at least in comparison with NAAEC procedures for discussing harmonization, which will be discussed at length in the next part). Set against the backdrop of an unenforceable harmonization obligation, these committees may be simply inadequate to secure real upward harmonization of environmental standards, and NAFTA itself remains primarily designed to promote the removal of obstacles to trade, including, if need be, environmental regulation. It is thus to be hoped that the committees outlined in Chapters Seven and Nine, when dealing with environmental matters, will be reinforced by the more sophisticated consultative instruments and procedures prescribed by NAAEC.

A Brief Assessment of NAFTA's Environmental Provisions

Given that trade pacts are designed to facilitate commerce, not environmental progress in the economic area they create, the hyperbolic claim that NAFTA is "the most environmental trade agreement ever signed"[160] nevertheless has some ballast. Indeed, that a trade agreement could go to such lengths to recognize and accommodate envi-

---

160. Supra note 3, Part II.

ronment-related concerns was inconceivable before NAFTA. Today, the scope of challenge-resistant environmental legislation enacted by North American governments at all levels is greater than at any time since the conclusion of old GATT—a fact in no way diminished by criticisms that NAFTA's environmental provisions do not go far enough. Moreover, the effect of many of the environment-related provisions in NAFTA is to foster a legal and political dynamic that may promise ongoing dividends for environmental protection, including, for example, a better consideration of environmental issues at the new World Trade Organization. As Steve Charnovitz rightly observed: "the hyping of the NAFTA's environmental accomplishments transformed the trade and environment debate. For the foreseeable future, all U.S. Trade agreements are going to be evaluated for their greenness."[161] And if NAFTA falls short in remedying the much-feared depressive effect of liberalized trade on environmental regulation, perhaps this deficiency merely reflects the inherent limitations of a trade-enhancing agreement as a vehicle for meaningful advances on this issue. Nevertheless, insofar as a place has been secured for environmental protection in the North American economic constitution that NAFTA forecasts, the agreement contains environmental breakthroughs that can and must be built upon. Another approach, indeed another context, would be needed to take care of unfinished environmental business. Enter the *North American Agreement on Environmental Cooperation*. With the NAAEC (and the Labor side-agreement), NAFTA moves beyond trade and investment to become the NAFTA package, an incomplete yet groundbreaking attempt to integrate the social agenda of trade in and around trade institutions.

---

161. "NAFTA's Social Dimension," supra note 5, Part I at 54. To be fair, however, the 1994 elections for the House of Representatives and the Senate have drastically changed the climate for environmental initiatives in the U.S. Congress. It remains to be seen whether this new context will endure during NAFTA expansion discussions.

Part III

The North American Agreement on Environmental Cooperation

Our discussion in Part III will unfold in the following manner. After a brief history of NAAEC and a description of its relationship with NAFTA, the nascent institution, its ambitious objectives and its broad mandate will be described. With respect to the Commission for Environmental Cooperation's (CEC) mandate, the spotlight will fall on the fact-finding powers and dispute settlement responsibilities conferred under NAAEC. Then, Part III will offer a brief assessment of what has been accomplished by this agreement.

Chapter 5

Why a North American Agreement on Environmental Cooperation?

To be sure, NAFTA is more attentive to environment-related concerns than are most if not all the preceding trade agreements, including the Canada–U.S. FTA, the old GATT, the Uruguay Round package, and the original European trade liberalization texts. Toward the end of the treaty negotiations, however, it was becoming clear that NAFTA's environmental design remained an unfinished structure. A traditional trade agreement remains an awkward instrument to address the emerging social agenda of international economic integration. The extent to which an essentially commercial agreement could provide either for continental substantive environmental norms or for systematic trinational cooperation on the environment is limited. Yet, given the importance of border issues and other environmental concerns that seeped into the NAFTA debate, this is exactly what many in the public and the NGO community in the three countries were demanding. Thus emerged the need for supplemental instruments designed to address the social agenda, including environmental protection, to the satisfaction of vocal interest groups and the citizenry. It was this realization that eventually led to NAAEC. Despite its demonstrable shortcomings, this agreement is still a remarkable development in international environmental law.

The Negotiations

NAFTA's environmental dossier had been opened since the administration of former U.S. President George Bush gave environmental guarantees in May 1991 to obtain fast-track authorization to negotiate a free trade agreement with Mexico. In so doing, he had set out a "parallel track" for environmental issues that did not directly relate to trade in goods. Fifteen months later, little had been achieved on the broader trade and environment agenda.[1] On 16 September 1992, after an agreement in principle between the negotiators (but before the final NAFTA signature ceremony), the environment ministers of Canada and Mexico as well as the head of the American Environmental Protection Agency met in Washington. They agreed to initiate a new negotiation round on environmental issues and announced their goal of creating a trilateral North American environment council. While the parameters of those negotiations remained vague, the ministers were in fact starting the talks on what would become the supplemental environmental agreement. The negotiations finally made headway only in April 1993 when the new administration of President Clinton had begun to take root. Given both NAFTA's timetable for ratification in the three countries and especially the need to present the American Congress with implementing legislation early enough in the Fall of 1993, these second negotiations, as well as a further set on labor standards, were expected to bear fruit within the following months in order for NAFTA to come into force on 1 January 1994. Moreover, NGOs, in particular environmental NGOs, were hot on the trail of the negotiators and never allowed them to negotiate NAAEC with the same relative distance and secrecy that characterized the negotiations of the Canada–United States FTA and NAFTA.

Presidential candidate Bill Clinton had upped the ante when he announced during the campaign that he would back NAFTA only if satisfactory additional agreements on labor and environmental issues were concluded. The attention devoted by American legislators to these issues had already made the negotiation of supplemental accords an important aspect of the Bush Administration's strategy for ratification. Mr. Clinton's electoral victory in November 1992 made critical the

---

1. Magraw, supra note 2, Part I at 17.

completion of a supplemental environmental agreement. Anyone thinking that the combination of bilateral border agreements with Mexico and a more environmentally sensitive NAFTA would be enough to sustain the political drive for ratification, was likely wrong. Without a fairly comprehensive framework for environmental cooperation strengthened with enforcement provisions, many concluded that NAFTA would have no hope for survival in the American ratification process, given the environmental concerns of the legislators, the organized opposition to NAFTA, and the promises made by two Presidents.

For almost a year, negotiations went on, with as many apparent setbacks as encouraging steps forward. The American insistence on enforcement through the use of trade sanctions and the establishment of single-location permanent secretariats to support the labor and environmental parallel agreements undoubtedly met resistance, thus making negotiations difficult.[2] For Canada and Mexico, issues of national sovereignty and political acceptability proved to be particularly delicate.[3] On 13 August 1993, marathon negotiations culminated in an agreement between the three parties. On 13 September 1993, after further refinement by legal experts, the environment ministers of the three countries were able to sign the final legal text of NAAEC in Washington.

NAFTA and the Concept of Side-Agreements

In embarking upon the negotiations leading up to the conclusion of NAAEC, the political leaders of Canada, the United States, and Mexico had agreed on one point: There would be no reopening of the negotiations on the NAFTA text. The intergovernmental environmental side-agreement would have to stand on its own. Beyond this certainty, how-

---

2. Ibid. at 20. "Mexican Environmental Reform," supra note 19, Part I at 95–96; "In fact, Mexican comfort level with NAAEC increased markedly in the early Spring of 1993 when cooperation, rather than enforcement with teeth became the main thrust of NAAEC." John Wirth, personal communication, 29 May 1995.

3. Canadian Prime Minister Kim Campbell apparently played a daring game of brinkmanship that ultimately allowed Canada to be exempted from the trade sanctions procedure of the Agreement. See: "Side-deals and showmanship bring NAFTA closer," *The (Toronto) Globe and Mail* (17 August 1993) A16. See discussion of the negotiations, supra notes 32–52, Part I and accompanying text. For comments on Mexican sensitivity to the issue of national sovereignty, see Aureliano Gonzalez-Baz, "A Mexican Perspective on the North American Free Trade Agreement and the Environment"(1992) 18 Canada–United States Law Journal 235.

ever, the negotiators had no firm idea of the object of their negotiations. After all, NAFTA had created a full-blown legal framework for
trade and investment liberalization. If the trade rules set out in NAFTA
were unchangeable, how could NAAEC, conceived at least initially as
a kind of protocol that would complement the main trade treaty,
achieve the goal of making the trade regime more environmentally
sensitive? Indeed, in the end, it could not directly effect this purpose.
When the parties decided not to reopen NAFTA, they declared that the
trade rules contained therein would have to do. The supplemental
NAAEC would have to "green" NAFTA from the outside, not from the
inside. The debate on how much of what was often considered an
extraneous matter could be incorporated into the North American free
trade context remained difficult.

Several proposals for trinational environmental collaboration had
little or nothing to do with North American trilateral trade and investment. While the environmentalist's goal of making trade disciplines
more environmentally sensitive was at least intelligible to trade negotiators, such goals were often greeted with hostility. The concern over
transboundary pollution as well as the need for continental upward
harmonization in the face of downward competitive pressures went
well beyond the traditional domain of trade law. Looking at NAFTA
itself for guidance provided little help. It is worth recalling that
NAFTA's preamble refers to the promotion of "sustainable development" and that Article 102 speaks of establishing "a framework for further trilateral, regional and multilateral cooperation to expand and
enhance the benefits of this agreement." The text also declares that the
parties will work jointly "to enhance the level of safety and protection
of human, animal and plant life and health, the environment.. . ."[4]
That such provisions may be found in a trade agreement is indeed
unprecedented. They offer, however, a shaky legal and conceptual
foundation for a substantive environmental cooperation agreement.

At the level of principles, there were few anchors. The lack of North
American precedents for such institutional cooperation was most
keenly appreciated. The enforcement of environmental obligations,
the investigatory powers of the new commission, and the channels for
NGO access to this commission were all uncomfortably new issues for
most officials. For example, during the negotiations, the Quebec minister for International Affairs found himself asking how, if, and why citizens could derive from a trade agreement a right to complain about

---

4. NAFTA, supra note 1, Introduction, art. 906.1.

environmental mismanagement in their jurisdiction or that of a trading partner if such practice did not affect trade or traded goods at all? Moreover, many were wondering whether a lower quality of environmental protection practiced by a neighboring party and trading partners was a threat because of the cost competitiveness implications in a liberalized trade regime or because of the inherent costs and danger of environmental degradation in North America? These questions went largely unanswered.

As was mentioned in Part I, transboundary environmental matters were already the subject of a number of arrangements and traditional bilateral treaties.[5] The "parallel track" of the Bush Administration did not distinguish clearly the general environmental portfolio from the U.S.–Mexico transborder pollution issues. In the end, the U.S.–Mexico border area issues were not specifically incorporated into NAAEC.[6] One of the reasons was that the governments of Mexico and the United States had unveiled in February 1992 an *Integrated Environmental Plan for the Mexican–U.S. Border Area*.[7] This agreement, along with the September 1993 *Agreement Between the Government of the United States of America and the Government of the Mexico States Concerning the Establishment of a Border Environmental Commission and a Northern American Development Bank*,[8] is the true heir of the numerous bilateral envi-

---

5. See supra note 5, Part I.

6. Other than a mandate for the CEC to come up with recommendations on transboundary environmental issues within three years of the signing of the NAAEC. See NAAEC, supra note 2, Introduction, art. 10(7).

7. U.S. Environmental Protection Agency, *Integrated Environment Plan for the Mexican–U.S. Border Area: The First Stage* (Washington, D.C.: Environmental Protection Agency, 1992). An initial version, released in August 1991, had met with such criticism that it had to be revised.

8. For a more complete explanation on the nature of these arrangements, to which the government of Canada is not part, see supra note 1, Part I at 22–24. In general the Border Environmental Cooperation Commission (BECC) will coordinate environmental cooperation between local authorities, provide specialized expertise, and certify environmental projects for financing from the North American Development Bank (NAD Bank). By one account, a total of US$ 2 to 3 billions in additional money will be available for the financing of border area environmental infrastructure projects. See Magraw, supra note 2, Part I at 42. See Frederic C. Menz, "The North American Environment: Economic and Public Policy Issues" (March 1994) 4 North American Outlook 3 at 8 [hereinafter "The North American Environment"]; Anne Alonzo and Edward Ranger, "The U.S.–Mexico Border Plan," (May 1992) 2 Business Mexico 35; Jeffrey Schott and Clyde Hufbauer, supra note 23, Part I. See also Runge, supra note 21, Part I at 62–64.

ronmental conventions that preceded NAFTA. The two agreements provide the framework for bilateral U.S.–Mexico cooperation on the environmental future of the border area.[9]

All other outstanding environmental concerns were left to be integrated in the yet to be named environmental side-agreement. This trek through the uncharted territory of trade and the environment proved difficult, and many of the thorny questions raised thus far in this discussion remain unsettled even after the signing of the final text of NAAEC. In general, NAAEC is divided in two. A first set of issues is covered in Parts One through Four, which provide a framework for environmental cooperation that fulfills the environmental pledges of NAFTA, addresses the broad agenda of the environmental community, and literally enumerates the ecological challenges North Americans face today. Part Five, the dispute settlement procedure, concerns itself with a second set of issues related to a peculiar kind of environmental dispute: that which occurs when one party alleges that another is not effectively enforcing its environmental laws.[10]

Nature of NAAEC and Its Relationship with the Main NAFTA Treaty

The centerpiece of NAAEC is the creation of a North American Commission on Environmental Cooperation (CEC). Conferred upon the CEC is a continental environmental cooperation mandate that touches upon the ecological impacts of NAFTA but also extends well beyond the implications of liberalized trade. As well, NAAEC creates a dispute settlement mechanism that seeks to address complaints by one party about the quality of the domestic administration and enforcement of environmental protection schemes of another party. On the other hand, despite the fact that the procedural aspects of the dispute settlement process outlined in NAAEC were shaped largely by that of NAFTA, the relationship between NAAEC and the older NAFTA agreement has been kept to an institutional and legal minimum.

NAAEC is a so-called simple-form treaty that does not require formal instruments of ratification by the national legislatures of Canada, Mex-

---

9. However, the text of these agreements provide the possibility that non-border-area transboundary issues might be addressed as well if they have significant environmental effects.

10. The dispute settlement procedure of NAAEC is analyzed in Part IV, notes 6–30 and accompanying text.

ico, and the United States.[11] In American legal parlance, NAAEC is an executive agreement: It binds the member countries from 1 January 1994 unless they withdraw from NAAEC, and withdrawal from NAAEC does not entail the same level of procedural and legislative formality as withdrawal from NAFTA. A country may withdraw from NAAEC upon six months notice, normally without involving its legislature.[12] Moreover, if one party withdraws in this way, the Agreement would remain in force for the other parties. Furthermore, a party's withdrawal from NAAEC would in no way, *stricto sensu,* affect its membership in NAFTA.[13] The adherence of all NAFTA parties to NAAEC was, however, so important a factor in building support for NAFTA that withdrawal from NAAEC by any party would probably create a serious political crisis, both domestic and international, and put NAFTA itself in jeopardy.[14]

NAAEC remains first and foremost an international legal instrument. Birnie and Boyle remark that among the many roles that international environmental law plays in the field of the environment, two stand out: the constitutional role and the regulatory (or prescriptive) role.[15] Based on this taxonomy, NAAEC is clearly, like many international environmental law instruments, a constitutional document. It provides

---

11. NAAEC is, however, more formal than a simple memorandum of understanding, which could create no binding obligations under international law. H.M. Kindred, et al., *International Law: Chiefly as Interpreted and Applied in Canada,* 4th ed. (Toronto: Emond Montgomery Publications, 1987) at 119–120. "As for NAFTA, although it is commonly referred to as a treaty in the popular press, the NAFTA is not a U.S. treaty. It is an executive agreement entered into under authority from Congress and goes into force only following subsequent legislation. Treaties can be entered into without prior authority from the Congress and go into force only following approval by two-thirds of the Senate and ratification by the President." See "NAFTA's Social Dimension," supra note 5, Part I at 64.

12. NAAEC, supra note 2, Introduction, art. 50. See Appendix III.

13. NAFTA itself has a withdrawal clause that allows a party to leave the agreement after six months notice, under Article 2205. The difference, however, is that all NAFTA parties have adopted long and detailed implementation statutes that would have to be repealed or otherwise modified by their legislature.

14. A domestic political debate on the acceptability of a NAFTA amputated from one or both the side-agreements might become a legal and constitutional confrontation if the argument was put forward that the legislators have accepted the NAFTA proposal of the executive branch only because of such supplemental arrangements. On that basis, the authority of the President or the Canadian Prime Minister to withdraw their country from NAAEC only might be challenged politically and legally.

15. Birnie and Boyle, supra note 128, Part II at 4.

mechanisms for needed environmental cooperation, it creates a dispute settlement procedure, and, most important, it establishes a new institution. It includes no specific protective measures, environmental standards, codes, or substantive rules. Like most international law, NAAEC steers clear of the normative realm and concerns itself with things institutional, primarily because it is the product of an intergovernmental process between entities that each want to set their own standards.

Despite the fact that NAAEC declares that "supporting the environmental goals and objectives of NAFTA" is "an objective of this agreement," the formal links between the NAFTA trade machinery and NAAEC institutions were kept to a minimum.[16] While this probably gave NAAEC's drafters more leeway to venture further outside trade-related aspects, it also meant that some officials were able to keep the new environmental content (which many still associated mostly with protectionism and obstacles to trade) at bay and thus shield the NAFTA Trade Commission from an infusion of environmental thinking.[17]

This inherent separation between the environmental and trade aspects of NAFTA and NAAEC is exemplified through the CEC's mandate to act "as a point of inquiry and receipts for comments from nongovernmental organizations and persons concerning the environmental goals and objectives of the NAFTA."[18] It seems that while the CEC might have limited input into the work of the Free Trade Commission, it will nevertheless have to serve as the official interlocutor of the NGOs seeking to question the environmental record of NAFTA itself. At worst, the CEC could be used by NAFTA institutions and actors as a diversion that enables them to evade difficult environmental questions. Moreover, the CEC is not called upon to enforce or even clarify NAFTA Article 1114's hortatory language against relaxing standards to attract investment. The CEC is simply asked "to provide assistance in consultations under Article 1114 of the NAFTA."[19] This limited role of

---

16. NAAEC, supra note 2, Introduction, art. 1(d).

17. Infra notes 12–29, Part IV and accompanying text on the relationship between NAFTA and NAAEC.

18. NAAEC, supra note 2, Introduction, art. 10(6)(a).

19. NAAEC, ibid. NAAEC 1994-95 Annual Program provides that "[t]he NAAEC will consult with the Free Trade Commission (FTC) to establish a permanent institutional mechanism creating the monetary linkages to assist with consultations regarding trade and environment issues, including, but not limited to, those arising under Article 1114 of the NAFTA." See 1994 Annual Program and Budget for the North American Commission for Environmental Cooperation (NACEC), July 1994, at 3.

the CEC is prefigured by Article 1(e), which includes the avoidance of "trade distortions and new trade barriers" as one of the basic objectives of NAAEC. From the standpoint of the text itself, to the extent that there is a relationship between NAFTA and NAAEC, the latter is almost always subordinate. On the other hand, at the institutional and political level, the ministerial Council could and should act as a counterweight to this imbalance in the NAAEC text.

Such political support for CEC interventions and pronouncements on trade matters will indeed be needed. The CEC has a general mandate to consider, on an ongoing basis, the environmental effects of NAFTA,[20] to assist the Free Trade Commission in environment-related matters,[21] as well as to contribute to "the prevention of environment-related disputes" by making recommendations to the Free Trade Commission.[22] In particular, NAAEC also provides for the CEC's "identifying experts able to provide information or technical advice to NAFTA committees, working groups and other NAFTA bodies."[23] Unfortunately, however, NAFTA does not guarantee that such experts would be consulted. There is no formal provision compelling the Trade Commission, when it convenes a dispute-settlement panel and requires technical support, to request or accept recommendations and expert assistance from the CEC.[24] This is a glaring omission since environmental expertise is plainly necessary to determine whether different standards affecting trade in different and uneven ways are nevertheless legitimate because they do not "result in arbitrary or unjustifiable discrimination" and are "related to" environmental protection. It is to be hoped that the

---

20. Ibid., art. 10(6)(d). The CEC has undertaken, in the Spring of 1995, a long-term evaluation of NAFTA's environmental impact in its annual report to provide new insights on the environment and trade relationship and provide a place of record for the evidence that NAFTA should be made more environmentally sensitive. The CEC has already undertaken a three-year study on NAFTA's environmental impact, Ms. Sarah Richardson, personal communication, 30 May 1995.

21. Ibid., art. 10(6)(e).

22. Ibid., art. 10(6)(c)(ii).

23. Ibid., art. 10(6)(c)(iii). Ideally, the CEC Secretariat and the NAFTA Commission should develop guidelines to identify instances when the environmental advice of the CEC Secretariat will be sought by the trade commission or by a NAFTA panel.

24. However, it should not be taken for granted that the Free Trade Commission and the parties involved in an environment-related commercial dispute will not call on panelists knowledgeable about environmental issues. Under the Canada–U.S. FTA there has generally been a respectable effort to choose panelists who are familiar with the specific commercial subject matter, authoritative in their fields, and well-acquainted with the provinces or states most directly concerned.

optional consultations between the CEC and the NAFTA Dispute Resolution Panel will become established practice.

Mostly detached from the NAFTA system proper, NAAEC will seek to achieve its goals primarily by using two instruments: new institutions to foster trilateral environmental cooperation and new environmental obligations for the signatories.

Chapter 6

Institution Building: Creation of the North American Environmental Commission

Part Three of the NAAEC deals with the creation of the CEC, the environment commission for North America. At the outset it must be repeated that NAAEC is an intergovernmental agreement. The CEC is a ministerial commission just like the Free Trade Commission. While NAAEC creates a central institution in the form of the CEC, this institution will be ultimately controlled by the three governments' representatives, sitting in Council, who will have the final say in all matters. The most important question to ask is whether the CEC is organized and equipped to promote the principles and the objectives presented in the introductory parts of the agreement.[25] More precisely, will it be able to make relevant and effective policy recommendations on the issues the drafters have included in its very broad mandate? It is too

---

25. For some specific proposals on CEC structure and mandate, see Stewart J. Hudson and Rodrigo J. Prudencio, "The North American Commission on Environment and Other Supplemental Environmental Agreements: Part Two of the NAFTA Package," National Wildlife Federation, 4 February 1993; Justin Ward and S. Jacob Scherr, "Environmental Elements of the NAFTA Package: Testimony of the Natural Resources De-

early in the life of NAAEC to know whether the CEC will be properly staffed and funded to do its work.[26] At this stage, the most one can do is to examine closely the three main components of the CEC as set out in the agreement: the Council of Ministers, the permanent Secretariat, and the Joint Public Advisory Committee.[27]

The Structure of the CEC

The Council

The Council comprises "cabinet-level or equivalent representatives of the Parties, or their designees."[28] Unlike the International Joint Commission, the CEC will not have nominally "independent" commissioners but will function as a truly intergovernmental body. Under the terms of the agreement, the environment ministers of Mexico and Canada and the EPA Administrator assembled in Council are "the governing body of the Commission."[29] The Council must oversee the Secretariat and the implementation of the agreement and approve the annual budget as well as the annual program of the CEC.[30] As was mentioned earlier the ministerial quality of the CEC process could be a key component of its eventual credibility and success. The fact that the CEC will be governed by a ministerial Council might help offset the "soft" mandate of the CEC outside dispute settlement, in particular the weak mandate of NAFTA impacts monitoring and mitigation by raising the profile of its activities and recommendations. At the same time, the functioning of the CEC and the administration of the agreement will rest with a Secretariat that will have the key function of pouring both

---

fense Council before the Committee on Environment and Public Works, U.S. Senate," Natural Resources Defense Council, 16 March 1993; J. Michael McClosky and John Audley, " Environmental Concerns Regarding the North American Free Trade Agreement," The Sierra Club, February 1993; "Environmental Provisions" supra note 41, Part II at 10067–73; John Wirth, personal communication, 29 May 1995, supra note 3, Part III.

26. In the Vancouver Declaration of the Council, 28 March 1994, there is a reference to a Secretariat "comprised of approximately 30 professional staff appointed by the Executive Director and drawn from each of the three countries."

27. NAAEC, supra note 2, Introduction, art. 8(2).

28. Ibid., art. 9(1).

29. Ibid., art. 10(1). It must be noted however that nowhere in the NAAEC does it say that the "cabinet-level" representatives must be the minister of the environment, let alone the "EPA administrator" of a party.

30. Ibid., art. 10(1)(e).

substantive clarifications and detailed procedures into the legal container formed by the provisions of the NAAEC.

The Council therefore serves as the political anchor of the CEC, its final authority, and its direct link to the parties. It has to convene at least one public session every year[31] (although it may meet in special session at the request of any party),[32] and it is chaired successively by each party. The decision-making procedure requires unanimity, unless the agreement provides otherwise.[33] The unanimity rule might appear at first an impediment to decisive action. Yet, a membership of 12 has not prevented the European Council of Ministers of the Environment from endorsing the adoption of a variety of Communitywide environmental regulations and directives (though this is, of course, an imperfect analogy).[34] At the same time, the fact that some decisions, by exception to the general rule, require merely a two-thirds majority vote should increase the likelihood of thorough monitoring and more far-reaching Council initiatives.[35] While the CEC and its Council might initially be, in the institutional sense, small players relative to national environmental ministries, it is to be hoped that the rule of consensus will work to increase the importance of Council recommendations and their legitimacy in the eyes of domestic environmental agencies rather than block their adoption.[36] Yet if the recommendations do become

---

31. Ibid., art. 9(3)(a). On 30 June 1994, the governments of the NAAEC parties announced that the first meeting of the CEC Council would take place in Washington, D.C. on 26 July 1994. The ministers have since met again in Mexico in October 1995.

32. Ibid., art. 9(3)(b).

33. Ibid., art. 9(6). There are numerous exceptions to this rule but the unanimity rule is nevertheless an important aspect of the decision-making, particularly with regard to direct enforcement of panel determinations in Canada. See infra notes 140–150 and accompanying text.

34. The analogy is imperfect because the European institutions have more independence and broader powers to regulate at the Union level, particularly with regard to harmonization and direct enforcement of Union environmental standards.

35. Don Munton and John Kirton consider that qualified majority-voting affirms "the single character of the body, and endowing it with genuine supranational characteristics regarding procedures. . .on several important procedural issues." "Bilateral, Trilateral Multilateral" supra note 5, Part I at 75.

36. One successful convention that has many times displayed those characteristics of commitment of political actors and efficacy through compromise is the *International Convention for the Regulation of Whaling*, supra note 106, Part I. In the same fashion as NAAEC, this convention places the responsibility of enforcement squarely upon the state parties and makes them the guarantors of private conduct.

more substantive and consequential, they will also become more delicate to negotiate and craft, which may make them more rare.

Under NAAEC, there are actions that the Council "may" do and
actions that the Council "shall" do. The difference is intentional and
relevant given the broad mandate of the CEC, its inherently limited
resources, and the necessary process of prioritization that has to take
place following the coming into force of NAAEC. Official declarations
of the parties already reflect this difference in the treatment of various
areas of the mandate of the CEC.[37]

The Council may thus explore and make recommendations on a
broad list of topics (to be explored in the next section, on the objectives and the mandate of the CEC). It may also establish standing committees, working groups, or expert groups to help the CEC execute its
mandate.[38] The Council should provide the leadership to push the CEC
forward. It will rely on the Secretariat for logistical and substantive
support as well as orienting these decisions with preliminary analysis
of the issues confronting the CEC.

It is the Executive Director who submits the annual program and
budget of the CEC for approval by the Council.[39] The Council approves
those documents and thus technically controls the undertakings and
activities of the Secretariat and the whole CEC. The Council also has a
role in the initiation of inquiries, and has supervisory prerogatives, as
well as power to prevent, allow, or prompt the release of information.
It approves, in advance, the decision to hold any inquiry into or the
drafting of any report on a matter outside the annual program.[40] It is
the Council's prerogative to prevent the publication of any report submitted to it by the Secretariat.[41] Finally, it is noteworthy that the Coun-

---

37. See Vancouver Declaration, supra note 26, Part III. At the inaugural meeting of
the CEC Council that took place in Vancouver, British Columbia, the priorities chosen
by the Minister of the Environment, the Secretary of SEDESOL, and the EPA administrator were: "conservation and ecosystem protection, NAFTA effects and consultation,
enforcement, pollution prevention, economic instruments, technology cooperation and
transboundary environmental issues." With the exception of economic instruments, all
these elements are found in the Parts of the text where the word "shall" is used.

38. NAAEC, supra note 2, Introduction, art. 9(5)(a).

39. Ibid., art. 11(6).

40. Ibid., art. 13(1); the NAAEC specifically denies the Secretariat the right to venture outside its annual program into issues related to environmental enforcement, it
may only do so in areas related to "the cooperative functions of this agreement."

41. Ibid., art. 13(3); the Council has 60 days to decide against the public release of
a report from its secretariat.

cil issues instructions on the preparation of the annual report, reviews the draft, and approves the final version.[42] It decides whether the submissions and views of NGOs will be included or summarized in the report.[43]

The ministers representing Canada, the United States, and Mexico at the Council could thus retain ultimate control of CEC activities if they so chose. It remains to be seen whether the Council will rely on the letter of the NAAEC to assert its control over the CEC or if it will choose to oversee the activities of a more autonomous Secretariat. There can be no doubt that a more independent Secretariat would increase the flexibility and efficiency of CEC action.

NGOs may present submissions regarding matters that relate to the ineffective enforcement of environmental laws: in this procedure, the Council does not have the power to intervene in the first stage of the process, which involves accepting an appropriate submission and requesting a response from the party involved.[44] It is for the Secretariat to decide on such matters. On the other hand, if the substance of the submission goes past the stage of an unsatisfactory response by a party, the Secretariat must ask the Council for permission to prepare a so-called *factual record* on the matter raised by the submission and provide reasons for going this route.[45] The Council may grant its permission by a two-thirds vote.[46] The Council will then review the draft prepared by the Secretariat and "may by a two-thirds vote, make the final factual record publicly available."[47] The initiative of publication rests with the Council. It is doubtful, however, that the Council would try to block the publication of a factual record once it has allowed its drafting. The political impact would be very negative for the CEC and the NGO community, with whom it must maintain a permanent relationship and which would strongly protest such behavior. In the process of developing a factual record, the Secretariat has to forward any information provided by the JPAC to the Council.[48] But, this obligation is not reciprocal: Instructions from the Council do not have to be

---

42. Ibid., art. 12(1).

43. Ibid., art. 12(2)(d).

44. Ibid., art. 14.

45. Ibid., art. 15(1). For more explanations of the nature of a NAAEC factual record, see infra notes 99–107, Part III with accompanying text.

46. Ibid., art. 15(2).

47. Ibid., art. 15(7).

48. Ibid., art. 15(4).

shared with the JPAC. The factual records are not made available to the JPAC unless the Council decides otherwise by a two-thirds vote. Again, the members of the JPAC, as one of the three pillars on which the CEC rests, would probably not accept to be deprived of such important information. The main instrument of the CEC is information. If technically the Council controls how that information will be gathered, organized, and distributed, the environmental community will be watching closely for lapses in openness and transparency.

In formal dispute settlement under NAAEC, the Council plays an important role. It always has an opportunity to intervene in an effort to bring about a resolution before a request to strike a panel is made. The Council may in this respect call on experts, offer its good offices, and make recommendations. It may even decide, again by two-thirds vote, to communicate such recommendations to the disputing parties.[49] Most important, the Council has the final say on dispute settlement matters: Dispute settlement does not proceed unless the Council agrees by two-thirds vote to convene a panel.[50] The Council also selects the panelists from a roster of those who will eventually sit on a panel.[51] In addition, it approves the Model Rules of Procedure for the panels that are prepared by the secretariat.[52]

The Commission Secretariat

The Commission Secretariat [53] is intended to be a support structure. It is not likely to evolve into a truly separate environment bureaucracy that could, on occasion, square off with the Council or initiate actions and publish recommendations more or less on its own. Rather, the second component of the CEC provides "technical, administrative and operational support to the Council, and other such support as the Council may direct."[54] Realistically however, the Secretariat and its Executive Director will have much leeway in steering the work of the CEC because the Council will not be in a position to micro-manage the various programs it administers. Indeed, the most effective and enduring international environmental agreements have opted for a structure

---

49. Ibid., art. 23(5).

50. Ibid., art. 24(1); see also infra notes 71–86, Part III and accompanying text.

51. Ibid., art. 25(1).

52. Ibid., art. 28(1).

53. Located in Montreal, Canada as per the Vancouver Declaration, supra note 26, Part III.

54. Ibid., art. 11(5).

in which the conference of the parties is supported by a permanent secretariat.[55] The structure adopted by the NAAEC is very similar except that the number of parties is, for the moment, limited to three. Of course, it is a framework that could easily accommodate an increase in the membership.

Acting as the bureaucratic counterpart of the Council, the CEC Secretariat will have a hierarchy of its own. The Secretariat is to be headed by an Executive Director appointed by the Council for three years "and removable solely for cause."[56] The nationality of the Executive Director will rotate among the parties. NAAEC provides that CEC staff is hired "strictly on the basis of efficiency, competence, and integrity"[57] with due regard paid to "the importance of recruiting and equitable proportion of the professional staff from among the nationals of each party."[58] The Council may revoke a Secretariat staff appointment made by the Executive Director by a two-thirds vote.[59] Interestingly, the Director must, in making staff appointments, consider not only lists of candidates supplied by the parties but also suggestions by the Joint Public Advisory Committee (the latter serving to broaden the range of possible candidates outside government circles).[60] These provisions justify high expectations for the quality and independence of the Secretariat personnel.

The Secretariat will produce annual reports for the CEC as well as reports on matters included in its annual program, subject to Council approval. It will also request advice from, and work in collaboration with the third component of the CEC, the Joint Public Advisory Committee.

The fact that there is a centralized, permanent Secretariat to support the work of the CEC is no small victory for those who want environmental issues to be considered consistently and seriously in the NAFTA

---

55. For example, see: The *Convention on the Prevention of Marine Pollution by Dumping of Wastes and Other Matter (The London Dumping Convention)*, 29 December 1972, 26 U.S.T. 2403, T.I.A.S. No. 8165, 1046 U.N.T.S. 120, 11 I.L.M. 1291; the *Convention on International Trade in Endangered Species*, supra note 18, Part I; and the *Montreal Protocol*, supra note 131, Part II.

56. NAAEC, supra note 2, Introduction, art. 11(1). On 30 June 1994, the governments of the NAAEC parties announced that the first Executive Director of the CEC Secretariat will be Mexican economist, and diplomat, Victor Lichtinger.

57. Ibid., art. 11(2)(a).

58. Ibid., art. 11(2)(c).

59. Ibid., art. 11(3).

60. Ibid., art. 11(2)(b).

area. It will establish the CEC's institutional personality in a way that would not have been possible if the Council had been supported only by national sections working in their home countries. While there are many advantages to the creation of a ministerial-level Council, it is fair to say that no international environmental monitoring regime could be successful if its administration remains wholly under the control of member states. Of course, the Secretariat will have to rely heavily on data and information provided by the parties. It is to be hoped, nevertheless, that the appropriate technical counterweight lies in a Secretariat equipped with the resources and the expertise to engage in competent and thorough analyses of the issues it will be asked to study. As Canada and the United States recognized in the *Great Lakes Water Quality Agreement*,[61] there is essential value in independent verification of information supplied by the member states and their national bureaucracies. To adequately accomplish its mandate, the CEC should never be too dependent on the specialists and scientists of the governments of Mexico, the United States, and Canada.

The Joint Public Advisory Committee

NAAEC provides for the creation of a Joint Public Advisory Committee (JPAC) that constitutes an integral part of the CEC. Its main task will be to advise the Council "on any matter within the scope of the agreement . . . and on the implementation and further elaboration of this agreement."[62] This would include the proposed annual program and budget, annual reports, and other Secretariat reports as they are submitted in draft form by the Secretariat to the JPAC.[63] The creation of a nongovernmental advisory committee within the body of the CEC is one of the clearest indications that NAAEC could become much more than an addendum to the NAFTA trade agreement. The JPAC is meant to be a conduit for the input of NGOs and that of the private sector into the undertakings of the CEC. While it remains to be seen how this input will be received by the Council and the Secretariat, the important feature of this arrangement is that the Council and the Secretariat will be unable to ignore the JPAC.

Other features of the JPAC are noteworthy. The parties themselves appoint the members, numbering 15 or more if the parties so decide. Canada, Mexico, and the United States, will each appoint an equal

---

61. Supra note 5, Part I.

62. NAAEC, supra note 2, Introduction, art. 16(4)

63. Ibid., art. 16(6).

number of members.[64] The Council will determine the JPAC's rules of procedure, but the JPAC will select its own chair. The JPAC will meet during the Council's annual session—a fact of no small importance since its credibility may benefit from the political mobilization that surrounds, and the attention that is drawn to a ministerial meeting.[65] It may meet more often if the Council so decides or at the discretion of the JPAC itself. Each party may, at its discretion, create National and Governmental Advisory Committees to advise it on the implementation and further elaboration of the Agreement.[66] No relationship is specified in the Agreement between these national committees and the JPAC.[67] Finally, as noted above, the JPAC will also be able to make suggestions to the Executive Director of the Secretariat on staff appointments.[68]

The existence of the JPAC is truly a mixed blessing for the NGO community. On the one hand, international environmental treaties rarely acknowledge the importance and usefulness of independent advice from outside government circles (even though a recent trend acknowledges the importance of such advice when it relates to scientific findings). NAAEC does so by creating a formal permanent advisory body *inside* the institution, alongside the Secretariat. As explained previously, the JPAC will be allowed to make comments and recommendations on any matter within the scope of NAAEC and will enjoy access to CEC documents in order to undertake its own deliberation.[69] In addition, the visibility afforded by an annual meeting coinciding with the regular Council sessions will give more opportunities for those sitting on the JPAC to make their voices heard. On the other hand, the fact that the JPAC is part of the CEC means that, by definition, the CEC's relationship with the public and NGOs must be broadened

---

64. Ibid., art. 16(1).

65. On 30 June 1994, the governments of the NAAEC parties announced that the first meeting of the JPAC would take place on 25 July 1994, one day before the first meeting of the Council of Ministers.

66. NAAEC, supra note 2, Introduction arts. 17 and 18

67. In both Canada and the United States, there already exist multi-stakeholder national sustainable development advisory bodies attached to the executive branch of government. In Canada there is the National Round Table on the Environment and the Economy, established in 1989 and given legislative support in 1994. In the United States there is the President's Council on Sustainable Development, established by the Clinton administration in 1993.

68. Supra notes 53–61, Part III.

69. Supra notes 62–67, Part III.

beyond the JPAC's activities. The JPAC's 15 members could not possibly be fully representative of the diversity of the NGOs in Canada, Mexico, and the United States. Moreover, JPAC members are appointed by the parties and will likely always include, in addition to environmentalists, representatives from the world of business, academia, aboriginal organizations, labor, and regional or municipal authorities.[70] One, two, or even three representatives to NAAEC from the environmental NGOs of any party will not be sufficient to cover the full spectrum of opinions or to fully represent domestic environmental communities. The conclusion is inescapable: If the CEC is to benefit fully from its efforts to reach the nongovernmental constituency, the JPAC must operate against the backdrop of an open CEC structure, increased transparency, and a variety of proactive instruments that will facilitate NGO participation.

The JPAC could become a critical component of the CEC from the standpoint of public participation in the NAAEC process if certain conditions are met—the quality of the contribution of the individuals appointed, the degree of commitment of the parties to the JPAC, and the relationship that develops, over time, among the CEC, the Secretariat, and the JPAC. There are few precedents in international environmental law for such formalized nongovernmental participation. One particularly open model the JPAC may eventually mimic is the European Environmental Bureau, a forum established in Brussels in which NGO activity is coordinated and which publishes reports and organizes workshops for the purpose of review and criticism of European Union environmental activities.[71]

The CEC is, however, more than the sum of its parts. Though bound by the rules of NAAEC, supported by an independent Secretariat, and advised by a nongovernmental JPAC, the CEC is ultimately governed by the Council of environment ministers. This should ensure the necessary political direction to invigorate and guide the intergovernmental process.

Objectives of NAAEC and Mandate of the CEC

While NAAEC would not exist without NAFTA, the objectives of NAAEC extend well beyond any trade-related matter and embrace tri-

---

70. This is not, of course, a claim that businessmen, native persons, or academics cannot also be "environmentalists." It is simply a comment on the broad diversity of national and sectoral agendas that may legitimately claim representation within the JPAC.

71. Birnie and Boyle, supra note 128, Part II at 77.

lateral cooperation for the improvement of the North American environment. They also venture beyond transboundary pollution issues (the traditional subject matter of international environmental law and previous North American arrangements) to cover domestic governmental activities. These objectives can be found in three different places: the preamble of NAAEC, Part One entitled "Objectives," and the broad and diversified mandate given to the CEC.

Preambles and Objectives

The preamble of the agreement incorporates such principles as "the importance of the conservation, protection and enhancement of the environment," the "essential role of cooperation," and the achievement of "sustainable development for the well-being of present and future generations." Yet, like the Rio Earth Summit's *Declaration on Environment and Development,*[72] (which NAAEC reaffirms) the preamble contains some seemingly conflicting principles that reflect the intrinsic difficulty of integrating environmental concerns into the law of international trade. The parties recognize "the interrelationship of their environments" and emphasize "the importance of public participation." However, they also reaffirm "the sovereign right of states to exploit their own resources pursuant to their own environmental and development policies."[73] They acknowledge the importance of "enhanced levels of protection," but they also note "the existing differences of economic, technological and infrastructural capabilities" among the countries. To be fair, nobody has yet found a way to meaningfully reconcile these different principles in the language in international agreements. It is thus not the letter of the law that will be the ultimate arbiter among these principles but the parties themselves, through the permanent negotiation process NAAEC puts in place.

NAAEC's enumerated objectives, on the other hand, are more straightforward. They include trinational cooperation for environmental conservation and protection, sustainable development, intergener-

---

72. *United Nations Conference on Environment and Development (UNCED),* 3–14 June 1992 (New York: United Nations Department of Public Information, 1993), 14 June 1992, 31 I.L.M. 874 [hereinafter *Rio Declaration*].

73. Both the *Rio Declaration* and the *Stockholm Declaration on the Human Environment,* U.N. Doc. A/CONF. 48/14/Rev.1 (1973), 11 I.L.M. 1416, affirmed state sovereignty over the exploitation of their own resources. It is a fundamental issue for all developing countries and a preoccupation for all states. In the case of the NAAEC preamble, the language would indicate that this sovereignty may only be directly mitigated by the responsibility to prevent damage either "to the environment of other states" or to "areas beyond the limits of national jurisdiction."

ational equity, an emphasis on compliance and enforcement, the avoidance of new trade barriers, the development and enactment of economically efficient measures, and pollution prevention. Moreover, transparency and public participation are presented as keys to accomplishing these goals.

The essential environmental principles are thus all found in these two declaratory sections. Nevertheless, just as NAFTA contains some environmental references that appear to qualify its trade liberalization agenda, Part One of NAAEC features the reverse: References to free trade, economic efficiency, and sovereignty that may be read as restricting the scope of NAAEC's general environmental goals.

Council Recommendations

NAAEC sets forth a detailed program of CEC undertakings.[74] While this list may be too exhaustive to amount to a realistic work plan, it offers a useful guide to the areas where the parties want the CEC to direct its efforts. There are some long-term tasks that the CEC would be unable to sidestep. The Council will prepare a review of the operation and the effectiveness of NAAEC within four years of its entry into force.[75] This means that before 1998, the Council of ministers will report to the parties on the effectiveness of the model of environmental cooperation adopted with the NAFTA/NAAEC package.

The Council must also make recommendations on bilateral transboundary issues "with a view to an agreement between the parties pursuant to this article within three years on obligations."[76] This eventual agreement on transboundary environmental issues would include transboundary impact assessment, notification of affected neighbors, and mitigation. This constitutes a very concrete mandate for the Council to support a new North American agreement on transboundary

---

74. Found under NAAEC, supra note 2, Introduction, art. 10 where "Council Functions" are described.

75. Ibid., art. 10(1)

76. Ibid., art. 10(7). Under its 1994–95 Annual Program, the CEC will initiate a three-phase program of inquiry, reporting any recommendations on transboundary issues. "To avoid duplication, the Commission will develop criteria for determining which activities fall within the scope of the NAAEC Work Program. Discussions will be held with the newly created Border Environment Cooperation Commission, the North American Development Bank, the World Bank, the Inter-American Development Bank, the Canada–U.S. Air Quality Committee and the IJC and other relevant institutions, institutes, agencies, residents and affected parties to solicit their views on relevant transboundary issues." 1994 Annual Program and Budget for the North American Commission for Environmental Cooperation, July 1994, at 4.

environmental issues, especially in light of the provisions for Council recommendations on private rights remedies for transboundary pollution damage[77] and "administrative" legal standing before domestic forums for the governments of aggrieved neighbors.[78] The phraseology used also indicates that the substance of this agreement could be general rules on transboundary environmental pollution to be applied within the NAAEC area, irrespective of the parties involved. It is unclear, however, how this new agreement would relate to the plethora of existing agreements on transboundary pollution between the three NAAEC parties.[79]

Other areas where the Council "shall" make recommendations are likely to form the basis for the Council's work program. The Council shall "strengthen cooperation" on the development of environmental laws and regulation, in particular by "establishing a process for greater compatibility of environmental technical regulations (. . .) in a manner consistent with NAFTA."[80] The Council shall also generally encourage compliance with and enforcement of environmental laws. It must also cooperate with the NAFTA Free Trade Commission to further the environmental goals of NAFTA—to the limited extent described earlier.[81] Further, the Council shall "promote and, as appropriate, develop recommendations" on public access to information on the environment that is held by public authorities,[82] and quite precisely "appropriate limits for specific pollutants, taking into account differences in ecosystems."[83]

---

77. Ibid., art. 10(9); to be granted "(. . .) on a reciprocal basis (. . .) as if the damage was suffered in its territory."

78. Ibid., art. 10(8); "to permit another Party to seek the reduction, elimination or mitigation of transboundary pollution on a reciprocal basis."

79. Article IV of the 1909 *Canada–U.S. Water Boundary Treaty*, supra note 4, Part I already provided that "the waters herein defined as boundary waters and waters flowing across the boundary shall not be polluted on either side to the injury of health or property on the other."

80. NAAEC, supra note 2, Introduction, art. 10(3)(b)

81. Under its 1994–95 Annual Program and Budget, the Secretariat will report on "existing bilateral activities among the Parties concerning enforcement cooperation of the laws and regulations of the Parties." Eventually, an intergovernmental working group will be convened to define guidelines for future work on this subject." 1994 Annual Program and Budget for the North American Commission for Environmental Cooperation, July 1994 at 4.

82. NAAEC, supra note 2, Introduction.

83. Ibid., subparagraph (b). The requirement that the Council make recommendations on "appropriate limits for specific pollutants" is of particular note: pursuant to Article 2(2), a recommendation in this regard is the only kind listed in NAAEC that each

Finally, there is a long list of substantive subject matters on which the Council "may [not shall] consider and develop recommendations."[84] The Council may make recommendations on environmental monitoring and reporting issues such as "data gathering," "common indicators," or "ecologically sensitive national accounts." It may do so on a variety of policy instruments like "economic instruments,"[85] the promotion of "public awareness," "human resources training," methods of "compliance and enforcement," or "eco-labeling." It may, finally, make general recommendations on specific issues like "transboundary pollution," "pollution prevention techniques," "endangered species," "life cycle analysis," or any "other matter it may decide."

One thing is clear: There is hardly an environmental issue that is not included in the mandate of the Council. More specifically, most of the issues included in the CEC work program have only a faint or notional connection with trade, usually through a compliance costs/competitiveness-based argument. Once one goes beyond the arcane legal language of the NAAEC text, however, it becomes apparent that the signatories agreed on certain clear priorities for the Council and the CEC—notably the diligent enforcement of adequate and compatible environmental laws, the management of environmental transboundary issues (with a view to a specific international agreement among the NAFTA/NAAEC parties), and discharge limits for specific pollutants. Not surprisingly, these are on the whole the issues that most preoccupied the U.S. government when it put forth the idea of a separate environmental agreement alongside NAFTA.

The CEC is the first central intergovernmental and political North American institution. If the integration process that spawned the NAFTA/NAAEC package does not falter, this institution will not be the last. Although its beginnings are modest, the future may witness, for example, the CEC taking a more active role in representing the continent, or the region, in international environmental negotiations.

---

party shall specifically "consider implementing in its law." Unfortunately, applying conventional canons of legal interpretation, one would think that all the other recommendations that the CEC or the Council can or shall make to the parties may not be imbued with the same formal character and thus may not merit equal consideration by national governments.

84. Ibid., art. 10(2)

85. Economic instruments are fiscal or other incentives and market instruments— for example green taxes, subsidies withdrawal, and the creation of tradeable pollution permits.

The potential for progress in this area is formidable. If environmental harmonization and coordination efforts proceed swiftly in the NAFTA area, the parties may find it more efficient to speak with a united voice in multilateral forums. Clearly, joint implementation of international environmental agreements would be the natural companion of increased trilateral cooperation. Eventually, when a conference of the parties of the Rio Convention on climate change is convened, the NAFTA/NAAEC parties may want to jointly present the emissions control measures they have chosen as a model. Similarly, with regard to the Biodiversity Convention, eventual NAAEC mechanisms for cooperation on technology transfers and on the funding of conservation efforts may be useful in the articulation of protocols more sensitive to North–South issues. Most major international institutions have some degree of legal personality enabling them to act on the international scene separately from the member states.[86] Maybe one day a different, more powerful CEC will be empowered, like the European Commission, to voice the joint position of NAAEC member states in international environmental negotiations, or, like some UN organizations, to formally enter into treaties and conventions. At the very least, a mandate for environmental cooperation within the territory of the parties will persistently influence the conduct of environmental negotiations and cooperation with nonparties.

Even if drafting recommendations by consensus is likely to be politically difficult and strategically delicate, it is in this section on Council recommendations that NAAEC best presents a shared, wider common interest of the signatories in the conservation of resources, wildlife, and ecosystems by all means available. In Part Two of NAAEC, which outlines the general commitments of the parties, this concern narrows to embrace mainly questions relating to the impact of environmental measures on trade and economic competition and the related question of environmental law enforcement. Such narrowing becomes even more apparent in Part Five, which outlines the dispute settlement mechanism centered around the effectiveness of such enforcement.

---

86. See, for example, the *Vienna Convention on the Law of Treaties between States and International Organizations or between International Organizations,* 20 March 1986, U.N. Doc. A/CONF.129/15 (1986), 25, 25 I.L.M., 543; the case for the international personality of the CEC would be bolstered by references in the text to its role as an autonomous agent. Unfortunately, such references are absent from the text of the NAAEC, either in the list of objectives or in the mandate of the CEC. See also Birnie and Boyle, supra note 128, Part II at 35–36.

General Commitments of the Parties

The parties confer a mandate upon the CEC. They also undertake commitments of their own in Part Two of NAAEC, entitled "Obligations." The nature of these commitments is akin to unilateral declarations of intention since they are not enforceable under the NAAEC, with the notable exception of the commitment to effectively enforce environmental laws, a breach of which may lead to formal dispute settlement. Such commitments can be divided into two distinct sets: a short list of general environmental promises and a more detailed outline of environmental enforcement obligations. Among general commitments, each party promises to adopt policies to promote environmental education, impact assessments,[87] and the use of economic instruments. The parties to the agreement also declare their intention to improve their capabilities in respect of periodic environmental reporting, emergency preparedness, and environmental science and technology. There is, as well, the concrete commitment to implement Council recommendations regarding specific pollutants, described in Chapter 5.[88]

In respect of legal domestic environmental protection matters, the obligations of the parties become more specific. First, NAAEC builds on both NAFTA's recognition of a party's right to choose its own level of domestic environmental protection and on its amorphous principle of upward harmonization. This is accomplished by way of a declaration that "each Party shall ensure that its laws and regulations provide for high levels of environmental protection and shall strive to continue to

---

87. NAAEC, supra note 2, Introduction, Article 2(1)(e) specifies "as appropriate."

88. In one of the few specific substantive commitments in this chapter on general obligations, Article 2(3) provides that each party "shall consider prohibiting the export" to another party of pesticides and toxic substances it has banned or severely restricted. The agreement does not specify that such export prohibitions must be consistent with NAFTA. This prohibition is a recognition that the responsibility of the exporter of dangerous substances is as important as that of the importer, in accordance with Article 21 of the Stockholm Declaration. The "banned or severely restricted" expression is also found in UNEP's nonbinding London Guidelines for the Exchange of Information on Chemicals in International Trade (UNEP GC.15/9/Add.2/Appendix and Supp.3, as amended by UNEP GC.15/30 *Report of the Governing Council on its 15th Session,* GAOR, 44th Sess., UN Doc. A/44/25 (1989) at 156. Importantly, the *London Guidelines,* as well as the *Basel Convention* with relation to hazardous waste, underline the importance of states notifying their trading partners that they have banned substances, and for exporters, of obtaining prior informed consent from the potential importer. Thus, enforcing a commitment to reduce trade in banned or severely restricted hazardous substances such as the one found in the NAAEC really requires the establishment of an elaborate information exchange system.

improve those laws and regulations."[89] Such provisions have been christened "anti-rollback." Second, each party promises to publish and make its laws, regulations, procedures, and administrative rulings pertaining to environmental matters available "in such a manner as to enable interested persons and Parties to become acquainted with them."[90] Third, another general commitment toward cooperation in the legal domain emerges in Article 20, wherein each party undertakes to notify other parties of its environmental initiatives affecting the implementation of NAAEC, to provide information and answer questions with regard to such initiatives, and to follow up on another party's notifications that violations of its environmental law are taking place. The scope of these obligations to allow the other NAAEC parties to become and remain aware of its environmental situation is broad. In many cases, the disclosure of information could be more extensive than what the parties currently share, not only with each other but with their private sector and environmental NGOs.

The other enforcement obligations of the parties in Part Two are related to government enforcement action, private remedies, and procedural guarantees, all for the better enforcement of environmental law. Pivotal Article 5 presents the components of adequate government action for the effective enforcement of environmental laws and regulations. It includes an enumeration of such actions, a description of appropriate remedies and sanctions, and a pledge to make enforcement proceedings available to remedy violations of environmental laws. This obligation to persistently and effectively enforce environmental laws is of paramount importance in NAAEC. It is the only obligation subject to the dispute settlement procedure outlined in Part Five of the agreement, and it is reviewed at length in Part IV of this book.[91]

The parties have also committed themselves to preserve and improve private access to remedies for (1) "interested parties," when they seek to enlist the public authorities of their respective countries to investigate alleged environmental infractions; and for (2) "persons with a legally recognized interest under [the relevant country's] laws," when they seek enforcement of environmental laws and regulations.[92]

---

89. NAAEC, supra note 2, Introduction, art. 3. This type of provision is also known as an "anti-rollback provision." It is a close cousin of NAFTA Article 1114 on pollution havens investments, which is discussed at length in notes 144–146, Part II and accompanying text.

90. Ibid., art. 4

91. See infra notes 66–82, Part IV and accompanying text.

92. NAAEC, supra note 2, Introduction, arts. 6(1) and 6(2).

The difference between interested persons and persons with a "legally recognized interest" is significant. The intention of the drafters appears to be the recognition of a larger constituency of concerned or interested citizens who may petition their government to investigate environmental controversies while restricting the access to formal administrative and judicial enforcement proceedings to persons having domestic legally recognized interest *and* standing. This obligation to improve access to remedies is further refined by a number of specific rights (to be granted "in accordance with the Party's law") to damages, monetary penalties, injunctions, and even to emergency closures.[93]

NAAEC then goes on to enumerate procedural safeguards and due process guarantees that would ensure that the proceedings leading to environmental remedies are "fair, open and equitable." These include procedural transparency and openness to the public, the right to present one's case, the absence of unjustifiable complications or time delays, written and timely decisions, the right to appeal or review, and the right to independent impartial tribunals.[94] Undoubtedly, full compliance with all these standards of judicial and administrative diligence in the administration of justice is a tall order for the governments of all three NAAEC countries. It also raises difficult issues in international law because there are few precedents in respect of internationalized standards for domestic administrative conduct.[95] The development of domestic procedural fairness as an international obligation owed to other states remains in its embryonic stage.

The crucial difference between the obligations of the parties set out in NAAEC, such as the general ones outlined above, and the obligations of the same parties under NAFTA is that most NAAEC obligations are not accompanied by a formal dispute settlement procedure and the possibility of legal sanctions to enforce them. NAAEC's dispute settlement procedure cannot automatically be engaged for *any* dispute "regarding the interpretation or application of this Agreement" as is the case with NAFTA.[96] While the rules of NAAEC are binding on the

---

93. Ibid., art. 6(3).

94. Ibid., arts. 7(1) to (4).

95. These issues are raised again in Part Five of NAAEC on dispute settlement and may become even more difficult to tackle because there could eventually be arbitral panel decisions to be rendered on these yet imprecise standards of adequate governmental conduct in the promotion and enforcement of environmental law. See infra Chapter 9 in Part IV.

96. NAFTA, supra note 1, Introduction, art. 2004.

institutions it creates, such as the Council, the Secretariat, and the JPAC, they are generally not binding on the parties themselves. For example, while consultations may occur, it is *impossible* for a party to request dispute settlement on the grounds that private access to remedies for environmental damage is not available to the citizens of another party. The only exception, which will be discussed in depth in Part IV, is an allegation raised by one party of another's systematic pattern of failure to effectively enforce its existing environmental law (Part Five of the agreement). Other than this specific rule on enforcement, compliance with NAAEC's provisions remains unenforceable. On the other hand, the obligations undertaken under NAAEC constitute an impressive program for cooperation and for effective implementation of the environmental policies to which the parties publicly commit themselves. It will necessarily fall to NGOs and, to a lesser extent, to the Secretariat to monitor the implementation of these obligations and publicize governmental lapses. NAAEC includes some fact-finding and reporting provisions that may facilitate this task.

Fact-Finding and Reporting

In a sense, the CEC and its Secretariat may have no greater power than that of gathering and providing information (perhaps the principal function and primary purpose underlying their establishment). As will be discussed below, NAAEC's dispute settlement provisions are narrow and convoluted, and this will probably restrict their effectiveness. NAAEC is not an environmental treaty like the 1973 MARPOL Convention[97] or the 1972 London Dumping Convention,[98] both of which provide for permanent international supervision of substantive standards of environmental protection. As a multilateral international institution, the CEC's ability to dictate public or private behavior remains minimal. On the other hand, its capacity to publicize environmental mismanagement, broken promises, and government failure to act on behalf of the environment is quite significant. Given the appropriate technical resources and proper access to national sources of information, the CEC could use sound science and objective findings to inform and influence public opinion. Thus, the CEC could prove to be a major contributor to North American environmental efforts. Success

---

97. 2 November 1973, 12 I.L.M. 1319.

98. Supra note 55, Part III and accompanying text.

in this respect would ultimately depend on the extent to which the CEC fulfills its role of supplying political direction and impetus.[99]

The CEC and its Secretariat have three main instruments for communicating recommendations and findings on environmental matters. These are the annual reports, the ordinary or regular Secretariat reports, and the investigation report (which the drafters have designated as a "factual record").

Annual Reports

The Secretariat must submit a draft annual report for review by the Council.[100] Once approved, its final version is to be released publicly. The annual report will cover program activities, budget, and expenses, as well as "the actions taken by each Party in connection with its obligations under this Agreement" (this includes "data on the Party's environmental enforcement activities" and "relevant views and information submitted by nongovernmental organizations and persons . . . and any other matter the Council deems appropriate").[101] As discussed above, the CEC is expressly mandated to monitor the environmental effects of NAFTA.[102] It is to be hoped that such an evaluation becomes a regular and substantial feature of the CEC's annual report.

Again, it is clear that the issue of nonenforcement of environmental laws continues to figure prominently in the system of information management established under NAAEC. NGO submissions may be included in the annual report, particularly if NGOs regularly send relevant submissions on enforcement and other matters to the Secretariat. It is to be hoped that the best NGO contributions will be routinely included or summarized in the annual report, since this is one of the few channels for nongovernmental input into the work of the CEC

---

99. Coordinated systems of fact-finding are more and more frequent in international environmental agreements. See Francesco Franciani, "International Cooperation for the Protection of the Environment: The Procedural Dimension," in W. Lang, H. Newhold, and K. Zemanek, eds., supra note 25, Part I, 203 at 217.

100. NAAEC, supra note 2, Introduction, art. 12(1). According to the 1994–95 Annual Program and Budget, the First Annual Report was expected for 1995: It will be published in February 1996 and will pertain to 1995 activities with some reference to 1994. The first reporting on the state of the environment in the three countries under Article 12(3) is expected to be included in the 1997 Annual Report. 1994 Annual Program and Budget for the North American Commission for Environment and Cooperation, July 1994 at 5, 7.

101. Ibid., art. 12(2).

102. Supra notes 72–85, Part III.

and the documentation it will produce. Furthermore, the annual report could become the most regularly publicized CEC publication, not unlike the annual report of the International Joint Commission on Great Lakes Water Management. It will certainly provide a focal point to evaluate the progress of the new institution and assess the performance of the parties in meeting their obligations. Unfortunately, NAAEC does not provide for regular reporting by the parties on either the fulfillment of their NAAEC obligations—in particular the domestic enforcement obligations—or their efforts at environmental protection. Some international environmental agreements rely on this method of verifying compliance.[103]

Secretariat Reports

The CEC will have the power to publish studies and reports at its discretion. NAAEC provides that the Secretariat may prepare a report for the Council on "any matter within the scope of the annual program."[104] The Secretariat may also report on "other environmental matters related to the cooperative functions of this Agreement" (as long as the matter does not concern issues of nonenforcement of environmental laws and regulations by a party).[105] In respect of subject matter outside the annual program, upon notification by the Secretariat, the Council has 30 days to object by a two-thirds vote. To prepare its reports, the Secretariat may use publicly available information, advice from the JPAC, and information coming from NGOs, governments, hired experts, or conferences, and public consultations. Following submission to the Council, the Secretariat report will be released publicly within 60 days, unless the Council unanimously agrees to prevent such release.[106]

Barring resource constraints, the Secretariat may thus organize meetings of specialists and consultations with outside actors to thoroughly research a specific element of its work program and report its findings to the Council. In that fashion, the CEC could become an appreciably more open institution than traditional multilateral bodies,

---

103. See, for example, Art. 8/9 of the *Protocol Concerning the Control of Emissions of Nitrogen Oxide and their Transboundary Fluxes,* 28 I.L.M. 212; Art. 8, *Montreal Protocol,* supra note 131, Part II.

104. NAAEC, supra note 2, Introduction, art. 13.

105. All issues related to whether a party has failed to enforce its environment laws are considered under the special rules of arts. 14 and 15, ibid.

106. Ibid., arts. 13(2) and 13(3).

bringing into its fold a wide constituency of stakeholders and experts. At the time of writing, the CEC Secretariat was already hosting numerous gatherings of experts on issues such as the environmental impacts of NAFTA and transboundary pollution.

In other respects, it is worth noting that these reports, like the annual reports, can deal extensively with any non-trade-related matter, since the work program of the CEC itself extends well beyond trade and environment issues. In fact, by judiciously applying its reporting powers, the Secretariat can identify significant trends, focus attention on specific environmental priorities, and even (in the words of one author) "create a common factual basis upon which to resolve a dispute."[107]

The CEC and Nongovernmental Organizations

The relationship among the Council, the Secretariat, and the prominent and diverse North American environmental NGO community will be crucial to the credibility and the relevance of the CEC's work. While the relationship with NGOs extends beyond the JPAC and the NGO submissions process, these two elements clearly stand out. The existence of the JPAC has already been explained. As for the NGO submissions procedure, it could very well become the most dynamic and innovative element of the fact-finding and information management mandate of the Secretariat. After examining this procedure, this discussion will spotlight some areas where more could have been accomplished, as well as other opportunities for improved NGO involvement with the CEC.

SUBMISSIONS ON ENFORCEMENT MATTERS AND FACTUAL RECORDS

The Secretariat will consider a submission from NGOs, business enterprises, individuals, any "person" or "organization" "asserting that a Party is failing to effectively enforce its environmental law," thus failing to meet its obligation under NAAEC.[108] Such consideration, how-

---

107. Magraw, supra note 2, Part I at 40.

108. After a rather lengthy tussle over the internal procedures that should be used to process and handle private submissions on enforcement matters the CEC Secretariat produced, in the Spring of 1995, Draft Procedures for submissions on enforcement matters under Articles 14 and 15 of the NAAEC [hereinafter "Draft Procedures"]. The Draft Procedures provide that an acceptable submission is a "documented assertion that a party is failing to effectively enforce its environmental laws" [Article 1.1], made by a party or organization established in the territory of a party [Article 1.2].

ever, is to be done by way of a special procedure distinct from that employed for NGO submissions on other matters.[109] Through this procedure the CEC is empowered, within certain limits, to investigate a party's diligence in enforcing domestic environmental legislation. A special set of rules will apply, different from those used to respond to a public submission not related to enforcement issues. The steeplechase will unfold as follows for complainants: (1) establishing that the submission is of the right kind; (2) persuading the Secretariat to request an explanation from the party; (3) following the explanation, getting the Secretariat to still recommend the establishment of a "factual record"; (4) bringing the Council to approve such recommendation with a two-thirds majority; (5) hoping that the Council will allow the publication of the completed "factual record." As mentioned earlier, it is difficult to imagine that the Council would grant permission to establish a factual record and then prevent its release. In any case, the party complained against would not be able by itself to prevent the publication of a factual record since the authorization procedure simply requires a two-thirds vote.

To accept a submission on enforcement matters, the Secretariat will have to be satisfied that it meets certain criteria. The submission must assert that a party is failing to effectively enforce its environmental laws and must not venture into other areas.[110] A person may allege that park lands are being converted to commercial use without the environmental impact assessment that the law mandates. A claimant may not insist that such conversion be stopped or regulated when domestic laws are silent on the issue. This NAAEC procedure allows the claim that air emissions regulations are not enforced, and not that such regulations are inadequate because they fail to include many pollutants. The Secretariat must also examine whether the submission

---

109. NAAEC, supra note 2, Introduction, art. 14(1). Unlike Part Five dispute settlement provisions, the section on public submissions makes no reference to a "persistent pattern." This points to a different burden of proving the duration or the pervasiveness of the failure to enforce. It may indicate that the evidentiary threshold for an NGO seeking Council action on an enforcement matter is lower than that of a party trying to convince a dispute settlement panel to determine that another is violating the Agreement's enforcement provisions.

110. Under the Draft Procedures, the submitter must identify specific provisions of the applicable environmental law (defined under Article 45(2) [Article 5.1]). The submission must also contain a "succinct account of the facts" and include any documentary evidence in which the submission may be based [Article 5.3].

provides sufficient information and whether it appears "to be aimed at promoting enforcement rather than at harassing industry."[111] The submission must further provide evidence that the matter has been properly brought to the attention of the relevant domestic authorities.[112]

If the Secretariat is satisfied that the submission meets these basic criteria, it may request a response from the party allegedly failing to enforce its environmental law.[113] In deciding whether or not to request a response, the Secretariat will be guided by such principles as the prejudice suffered by the complainant, the advancement of the goals of NAAEC, prior private remedies sought in domestic forums, and, curiously enough, whether "the submission is drawn exclusively from mass media reports."[114] The prejudice to the complainant will be assessed using three criteria: whether the harm is due to the alleged failure to effectively enforce environmental laws, the nature of the harm, and the magnitude of the harm.[115] Following a Secretariat request for a written response to the submission, the party has 30 days to provide an answer.[116] The party implicated may stop the proceed-

---

111. NAAEC, supra note 2, Introduction, art. 14(1)(d). It is to be hoped that this test does not betray a bias that environmental NGOs are in the business of harassing industry more than promoting environmental protection. The Draft Procedures specify that this evaluation will be made in particular through an inquiry into the potential "economic benefits for the submitter," a focus on party actions or omissions "rather than compliance by industry" and the "vexatious or frivolous" character of the submission. See Article 5.4 of the Draft Procedures.

112. Other formal requirements are that the submission be in either English, French, or Spanish and that it does not exceed 15 pages of typed, letter-sized paper, excluding supporting information. See Draft Procedures, Article 3.1 to 3.3.

113. If the submission does not meet the acceptability criteria, the Secretariat under the Draft Procedures will notify the submitter of its reasons and the submitter will have 30 days to resubmit. A second failure to present an acceptable submission will result in the process being terminated without appeal for the submission: see Article 6 of the Draft Procedures.

114. NAAEC, supra note 2, Introduction, art. 14(2). The last criterion may reflect a lack of confidence of the drafters in NGO capacity to present a well-researched brief rather than a stack of newspaper photocopies. On the other hand, the Draft Procedures allow submissions drawn exclusively from mass media reports if no other sources of information are available. See Article 7.4 of the Draft Procedures.

115. See Draft Procedures, Article 7.3. If the Secretariat determines that the submission warrants no response from the party, it will notify the submitter of its reasons. The submitter will have 30 days to supplement the initial submission. If the decision not to request a response from the party does not change following such a supplement of information, the process is terminated. See Draft Procedures, Article 8.

116. The party will have 60 days to respond in "exceptional circumstances."

ings by establishing that the matter is the subject of "pending judicial or administrative proceedings."[117] It may also seek to influence the Secretariat's recommendation to the Council (as to whether or not a factual record should be developed) by submitting previous domestic decisions or describing the private remedies available to the complainant and whether they have been pursued.[118]

Even though a submitter will be given reasons if the party complained against is exempted from giving a response with regards to the submissions, the Secretariat may, nonetheless, recommend to the Council the preparation of a factual record without further consultations with the NGO or person that initially submitted the complaint. The decision to recommend such preparation is not subject to any guidelines in the NAAEC.[119] Following such a recommendation (and if it is granted permission by a two-thirds vote of the Council), the Secretariat will prepare a factual record on the matter raised by the submission.[120] The JPAC may provide the Secretariat relevant information for the purposes of developing such a factual record.[121]

Even if the Secretariat were equipped with adequate research and investigative capabilities, the preparation of a factual report would inevitably require information that only the investigated party could provide. Under NAAEC, the Secretariat first has to consider any infor-

---

117. NAAEC, supra note 2, Introduction, art. 14(3)(a). According to the Draft Procedures, "judicial or administrative proceedings" are defined under NAAEC Article 45(3). This article states: For purposes of Article 14(3), "judicial or administrative proceeding" means:

    (a) a domestic judicial, quasi-judicial or administrative action pursued by the Party in a timely fashion and in accordance with its law. Such actions comprise: mediation; arbitration; the process of issuing a license, permit, or authorization; seeking an assurance of voluntary compliance or a compliance agreement; seeking sanctions or remedies in an administrative or judicial forum; and the process of issuing an administrative order; and

    (b) an international dispute resolution proceeding to which the Party is party.

118. Ibid., subparagraph (b).

119. The Draft Procedures do not provide such guidelines either. They merely allow two or more submissions to be consolidated before the preparation of a factual record is undertaken, if they relate, essentially, to the same facts. See Draft Procedures, Article 10.2. It is noteworthy that the Secretariat will provide reasons to the submitter if the submission process is terminated earlier. However, no reasons are included in the other possible notification to the submitter, which indicates that a factual record will not be constituted. See Draft Procedures, Article 10.3.

120. NAAEC, supra note 2, Introduction, art. 15(1).

121. Ibid., arts. 16(5) and 15(4)(c).

mation submitted by the party complained against before it "may" consider publicly available information, NGO submissions, JPAC submissions, or information "developed by the Secretariat or by independent experts."[122] It appears that the Secretariat will have to rely, at least initially, on the good will of the party complained against and its willingness to allow Secretariat representatives to investigate the complaint. Moreover, in many cases the sole possessor of the information necessary for the preparation of a factual record is the government complained against. While many North American jurisdictions have so-called "sunshine laws," they often remain unwieldy instruments, thus limiting the scope of the information possessed by public authorities that is publicly available. Depending on the circumstances, there might also be a temptation for the party complained against to procrastinate or to be lax in collecting damning evidence. Without a doubt, the reliance on domestic agencies and the need to respect the parties' sovereignty may both pose serious obstacles to the preparation of a complete and reliable factual record. The factual record could include information on the execution by the party complained against of its obligations to swiftly provide the Secretariat with necessary materials.

Indeed, under NAAEC, the party complained against does have an obligation to collaborate with the Secretariat and to diligently provide the information necessary for the preparation of a factual record. The parties must oblige the Secretariat's request for information, "including compliance and enforcement data," subject to some limitations.[123] A party may notify the Council that a request is "excessive or unduly burdensome"—in which case the Council may settle the matter by a two-thirds vote.[124] It is distressing, however, that a party that persistently refuses to provide the requested information would only be required to "promptly advise the Secretariat [and not the Council] of its reasons in writing." This provision could obviously license procrastination and obfuscation. On the other hand, like many other mechanisms prescribed in NAAEC, this obligation of disclosure relies heavily on the smooth operation of the Council and the cooperation of the

---

122. Ibid., art. 15(4).

123. Ibid., art. 21. The phrase "in accordance with its laws" in Article 21(1)(a) probably refers to access to information, protection of privacy, and other sunshine laws. Article 42 also protects matters related to national security, a serious limitation if one considers the well-documented environmental impacts of military establishments and activities, as well as those of the nuclear industry.

124. Ibid., art. 21(2).

ministers who sit at its table. After all, once an NGO submission has triggered the preparation of a factual record, the NGO initiator has no further role in the process other than providing further substantive information that may be used later by the Secretariat.

Once the Secretariat has prepared a draft factual record, it is submitted to the Council and the parties, which have 45 days to make comments.[125] The final version is then presented to the Council. Regrettably, factual records may not be as widely available to the public as will regular Secretariat reports. The latter will automatically be released publicly, unless the Council unanimously decides to veto the release. A factual record, in contrast, will *not* be released publicly unless the Council so decides, by a two-thirds vote.[126] Hopefully, the fact that the Council must act to release the factual record, rather than act to prevent its public distribution, will not give rise to a damaging pattern of secrecy for CEC inquiries in enforcement matters. Similarly, the JPAC will not see the factual record, in draft or final form, even if it contributed information at the drafting stage, unless the Council makes it available to JPAC, again by a two-thirds vote.[127]

With regard to NGO access to procedures for environmental enforcement matters, the outcome of NAAEC negotiations is more encouraging. The drafters could have chosen, in the name of national sovereignty, to confer only upon the nationals of the targeted party the right to make nonenforcement submissions. They could also have restricted the application of this investigative procedure to situations involving only traded goods—thereby formally linking the factual records procedure to the competitiveness aspects of the trade and environment relationship (an avenue chosen in the case of formal dispute settlement). They did neither. Rather, the private submission only has to be filed "by a person or an organization residing or established in the territory of *a* party."[128] Thus, for example, it is possible, for a citizen of Mexico to complain about the inadequate enforcement of environmental standards in Canada, in an industry where the goods produced do not compete with Mexican exports to Canada and never leave Canada to compete in Mexican markets. It is also possible for an NGO based in Vermont to file a submission on forestry management in Washington State. In other words, in the private enforcement submis-

---

125. Ibid., art. 15(4).
126. Ibid., art. 16(7).
127. Ibid., art. 16(7).
128. Ibid., art. 14(1)(f).

sions procedure, the external and internal borders of NAAEC parties are irrelevant. Paradoxically, since, as was shown, the availability of private remedies to the complainant will weigh in the decision of the Secretariat whether or not to develop a factual record following a private complaint, it may actually become easier for a citizen of a foreign party, rather than a citizen of the country complained against, to convince the Secretariat of the need to prepare such a record. The reason is that this person typically will not have legal standing in the jurisdiction where it alleges the violation of NAAEC. A complaint to the CEC may then be the only available recourse.

As for the content of the factual record itself, it will, presumably, be a summary of the nonenforcement allegations and the facts of the matter. According to the Draft Procedures, a factual record will contain: (a) a summary of the submission that initiated the process; (b) a summary of the response, if any, provided by the party concerned; (c) a summary of any other relevant information of a factual nature; and (d) the facts presented by the Secretariat with respect to the matters raised in the submission.

Given its name, it probably cannot include an evaluation or judgment by the Secretariat, despite the numerous NAAEC references to the necessity of effective enforcement of environmental laws.[129] While it is not entirely clear what a factual record would look like, it is expected that a model format will emerge through practice over time. Since it may be publicly released by the Council, the main effect of the factual record may be, on occasion, to alert public opinion and even to prompt another party to initiate procedures for formal dispute settlement. Such a government espousal of the private claim is necessary to proceed from NGO submissions into formal dispute settlement since formal dispute settlement under the NAAEC is the exclusive domain of states.

According to the internal Draft Procedures for Articles in Submissions, the Secretariat will establish a public registry that would allow "any interested nongovernmental organization or person, as well as the JPAC, [to] follow the status of any given submission during the submission process envisaged under Articles 14 and 15 of the Agreement."[130] The Registry will include a list of all submissions and a sum-

---

129. On the other hand, if the production of a factual record eventually leads to formal government dispute settlement, there might be an evidentiary role for the factual record during the proceedings of the panel mandated to determine whether there has been a persistent pattern of failure to enforce the environmental law.

130. Draft Procedures, Article 15.1.

mary of each submission, as well as of the response submitted by the party (if any) and a summary of the various notifications to the submitter. The official documents, whether from the submitter, the party, or the Secretariat, relating to a submission will also be publicly available at CEC headquarters, with appropriate safeguards for confidentiality.[131]

Other Avenues for Access to the CEC

With respect to its recommendations to the parties, the Council is directed to "promote and, as appropriate, develop recommendations regarding public access to" environmental information, including "information on hazardous materials."[132] The parties, however, are under no obligation to implement them. It must be pointed out that this is not a commitment of the parties, only a topic for Council consideration. The inclusion of this reference in the mandate of the Council was mandatory rhetoric.

With regard to the availability of CEC documents, "all decisions and recommendations of the Council shall be made public" unless the Council decides, or NAAEC provides otherwise.[133] In practice, this publication rule can often be set aside, especially with regard to enforcement matters and dispute settlement (as was demonstrated above).[134] The Council could make information on CEC activities difficult to obtain. For example, its recommendations to parties involved in a dispute settlement procedure are not made public unless the Council approves such disclosure by a two-thirds vote.[135] As these recommendations may represent the opinion of the Council as to the fair settlement of a dispute related to environmental enforcement, they would be valuable to the public debate.[136] On the other hand, the creation of a public registry for the documentation surrounding Article 14 submissions is a bold step in the right direction. It is to be hoped that this

---

131. See Draft Procedures, Articles 16 and 17.

132. NAAEC, supra note 2, Introduction, art. 10(5)(a).

133. Ibid., art. 9(7).

134. See supra notes 99–104, Part III and accompanying text.

135. NAAEC, supra note 2, Introduction, art. 23(4).

136. The traditional objection to public disclosure would be that it would make the Council less forthright and candid. It is a legitimate concern. Nevertheless, the final panel report to the disputing parties must be released within five days and, as we will see, it remains one of the few instances where the Council cannot stop the publication of an official CEC document. See ibid., art. 32(3).

openness is indicative of future CEC decisions with regard to the public release of the results of its work.[137]

On the question of the public's involvement in the broader CEC process, NAAEC's performance is also mixed. The CEC Council, the decisional body of the CEC, is obligated only to hold some "public meetings in the course of all regular sessions." Other meetings and special sessions "shall be public where the Council so decides."[138] In general, the Council "may," but does not have to, seek the advice of nongovernmental organizations.[139] Closed meetings are evidently necessary when the Council engages in sensitive discussions (for example, appointments, specific allegations against individuals or corporations, or the fate of a factual record). One can only hope that the practice of regular open meetings of the Council will take root in the CEC.

Scrutiny of the subject matters covered by NAAEC is envisaged as a dynamic and interactive process. However, when the environment-related provisions of NAFTA are at stake, the CEC becomes a one-way street. To be sure, NGOs may ask questions of and provide information to the CEC on the impact of these provisions. In addition, there are no formal mechanisms to ensure that this input will reach the Free Trade Commission or resonate in the NAFTA institutions.

An Assessment of the Commission for Environmental Cooperation

An assessment of the CEC starts from the premise that, dispute settlement being a distinct and fairly self-contained area of NAAEC law, the CEC's formal role therein will be limited (even though it will remain the forum of choice for negotiated settlements). In fulfilling its other

---

137. This is in line with the U.S. priority stated in the environmental executive order that "the United States, as appropriate, shall ensure the transparency and openness of, and opportunities for the public to participate in, activities under the Environmental Cooperation Agreement. (1) In general, pursuant to Articles 15(1) and 15(2), where the Secretariat informs the Council that a factual record is warranted, the United States will support the preparation of such factual record. (2) In general, the United States will support making available to the public all nonconfidential and nonproprietary elements of reports, factual records, decisions, recommendations, and other information gathered or prepared by the Commission. Where requested information is not made publicly available, the United States will endeavor to have the Commission state to the public its reasons for denial of the request in writing." "Draft Executive Order on CEC Secretariat," *Inside NAFTA* (6 April 1994). See Appendix IV.

138. NAAEC, supra note 2, Introduction, art. 9(4).

139. Ibid., art. 9(5)(b).

functions as a multilateral institution, however, the CEC displays, on the one hand, the traditional characteristics of that kind of body (e.g., rules that hand final decision-making power to the official government representatives of the parties) and, on the other hand, characteristics that are prudently innovative (e.g., formal procedures for NGO participation).

Provisions for Effective Council Control

Clearly, the design of the CEC *technically* gives full control of all Commission and Secretariat activities and reporting to the Council of environment ministers. The only documents the release of which cannot be prevented by the Council are the annual reports it has itself approved and the final report of a dispute settlement panel. The Secretariat may make autonomous decisions only in respect of both the implementation of program activities previously approved by the Council and the initial stages of an NGO submission on ineffective environmental enforcement. In practice, however, there is no doubt that the institutional and physical distance between the Council members and the Executive Director, as well as the demands of efficiency and timeliness, will de facto afford a large degree of autonomy to the Secretariat.

Nevertheless, the drafters of the NAAEC have made the decision to make the CEC an intergovernmental body with political representatives at the top of the decision-making ladder. By giving full power to party representatives, however, NAAEC is consistent with a habitual international practice rooted in accepted notions of national sovereignty, of the democratic accountability of the parties' governments, and of the right of the founders and fund providers to control the institution. In this respect, it is not surprising that Canada and the United States have frequently manifested a reluctance to allow the International Joint Commission to perform a truly supervisory role consonant with its more "independent" nature. Close proximity to the political process is not necessarily a weakness in intergovernmental organizations; indeed, by putting NAAEC institutions on a short political leash, the governments of Mexico, Canada, and the United States have also made themselves fully accountable for the successes and the failures of the CEC. If documents are not available without valid reasons, if the Secretariat does not follow up NGO submissions with appropriate requests for responses by governments (and, if need be, investigations), if dispute settlement is derailed when it ought to proceed, if Council decisions shrink beyond recognition of the mandate of the Secretariat, or if recommendations are not forthcoming or relevant, then the Council of ministers and the represented governments will be accountable to a domestic constituency and eventually face blame.

NAAEC is similar to almost all international environmental agreements: Its effectiveness depends largely on autonomous implementation mechanisms. The Secretariat's credibility and NAAEC's relevancy will rest also on sustained cooperation between the parties. The will of the parties to engage in such cooperation ultimately remains driven by domestic political accountability. The provisions for effective Council control prompted criticism from some NGOs which thought that such provisions weakened the CEC. Canada's Pollution Probe and the Sierra Club of Canada commented, two days after the final NAAEC had been unveiled: "the Commission had been strapped into a political straightjacket, limiting its ability to monitor and report on environmental practices and conflicts, and to respond to citizen complaints. Two of three countries must grant permission before the Commission may either investigate a citizen's complaint or release reports to the public."[140]

It is up to the CEC and its Secretariat to demonstrate that such dire predictions were overly pessimistic.

Public Access and NGO Involvement

It has been said, rightly, that the role of individuals, NGOs, and business as formal subjects of law in international environmental law has received too little attention by governments and the negotiators they mandate to draft international agreements.[141] Indeed, underlying public concern for the "greening" of NAFTA is a preoccupation with transparency and public participation.[142] After all, as was shown, it is widely believed in the environmental NGO community that a more open set of institutions would be increasingly sensitive to environmental issues;

---

140. Pollution Probe/Sierra Club of Canada, Joint Press Release, "NAFTA Environment Side Deal: Good Container, Little Content" (14 September 1993).

141. "The Rio Declaration on Environment and Development, adopted in June 1992, established as principle 10 that 'each individual shall have appropriate access to information concerning the environment that is held by public authorities, including information on hazardous materials and activities in their communities, and the opportunity to participate in the decision-making process'." Runge, supra note 21, Part I at 69. See also Günther Handl, "Environmental Security and Global Change: The Challenge to International Law" in Lang, Newhold and Zemanek, eds., supra note 25, Part I, 59 at 72–75. EC, Council Directive 90/313/ECE of 7 June 1990 on Freedom of Access to Information on the Environment, O.J. Legislation (1990) No. L 158/56; OECD, Council, Decision Recommendation of the Council Concerning Provision of Information in Decision-Making Processes Relating to the Prevention of, and Response to, Accidents Involving Hazardous Substances, OECD Doc. C(88)85.

142. For an account of the improvements that took place in the area of public participation in Mexico's environmental institutions in recent years, see: "Mexican Environmental Reform," supra note 19, Part I at 92–94.

that public input would generally translate into more environmentally conscious decision-making.

In time, this assumption could be proven less than true. Lobbies that favor unfettered development can increasingly count on their own network of nonprofit organizations and associations, who are often hostile to environmental initiatives. Some of them are genuine grass roots organizations and some of them are supported by large corporations, but certainly trade institutions will not be able to discriminate against them on that basis. Under Articles 14 and 15 of the NAAEC, private corporations motivated mostly by a desire to prevent foreign competitors from gaining a competitive advantage will be able to trigger CEC activity and inquiries into specific sectors of environmental regulations and enforcement in other member countries. In principle, this is where environmental and commercial objectives will converge. In other areas of CEC activities, development-oriented NGOs and other business associations will be free to participate according to the rules of procedure and may influence the deliberations toward less interventionist stances.[143]

That being said, the NGO preoccupation with accessible trade and environment institutions remains a pressing concern. Thus, GATT is habitually criticized for the secrecy of its dispute settlement procedures, the unavailability of even basic documentation, and the near impossibility of NGOs making their voices heard in the organization.[144] Even government officials have joined in the refrain.[145]

---

143. For an entertaining, if less than accurate account of the state of the pro-development lobby, see C. Deal, *The Greenpeace Guide to Anti-Environmental Organizations* (Berkeley, California: Odonian Press, 1993).

144. To its credit, the GATT Secretariat held its first formal consultation with the nongovernmental community in June 1994. About 300 NGO, government, and GATT representatives met for two days on 10 and 11 June 1994 to discuss transparency and the WTO work program. See Trade and the Environment: News and Views from the General Agreement on Tariffs and Trade, GATT, TE 09 28 July 1994 (94-2051) and TE 010 11 October 1994 (94-1551); see also GATT, Trade, and the Environment, *Report on the GATT Symposium on Trade, Environment and Sustainable Development* (Geneva: GATT, 1994).

145. In February 1994, U.S. Trade Representative Kantor commented on GATT dispute settlement and environmental issues: "it seems to me incredible that in this day in time, that we have what I would call star chamber proceedings that are making the most important decisions that affect the lives of all of our citizens—especially in the environmental area—and there is no accountability whatsoever, because no one knows what those decisions are, what the basis was, who is making the decision, how they're being made, what piece of paper we'll put in front of them." Mickey Kantor, Address (Global Legislators Organization for a Balanced Environment, 28 February 1994)[unpublished].

Despite this background of steady condemnation, the more recently crafted Canada–U.S. FTA proved just as deaf to the calls for more transparency and access. The traditional argument against more access for nongovernment actors is that closed meetings and a degree of secrecy provide the needed elbow room for true intergovernmental negotiation and cooperation; in open institutional architectures, by contrast, diplomats and politicians would be overly cautious. On the need for some degree of privacy, most NGOs will readily agree. Their representatives argue, however, that at some point closed processes cease to facilitate multilateral negotiations and become detrimental to the public good because too many voices go unheard. Simply put, when there is something like a delegation of national sovereignty to the international level, absent direct democratic control, channels must be available for the voice of nongovernmental actors to be heard at that level as well.

In this context, the solutions that were presented in NAFTA, and later in NAAEC, had to meet a very high standard of openness. The NGOs wanted the influence they had in the NAFTA/NAAEC debate, before the conclusion of an agreement, to be matched by unimpeded access to the CEC and its undertakings after the agreement. For its part, NAFTA does not improve the access of NGOs, environmental or otherwise, to its processes and institutions. From the standpoint of access and transparency, it unfortunately replicates previous trade agreements.[146] As for NAAEC, even considering that it *had* to provide for a modicum of transparency and openness, it represents a modest but encouraging improvement over past exclusionary practices. NAAEC's preamble emphasizes "the importance of public participation in conserving, protecting and enhancing the environment."[147] One of the objectives of the agreement is to "promote transparency and public participation in the development of environmental laws, regulations and policies."[148] NAAEC's specific provisions fall somewhat short of realizing these lofty goals.

In particular, NAAEC's drafters have missed some further opportunities to accommodate public input into the work of the CEC. Most important, the implementation of NAFTA Article 1114, the pollution havens investments clause, could have been improved by allowing NGO participation in the relevant consultative role given to the Coun-

---

146. See "Making Trade," supra note 36, Part I at 16.

147. NAAEC, supra note 2, Introduction, Preamble, paragraph 6.

148. Ibid., art. 1(h).

cil. In this regard, there was no reason to restrict the NGO submissions that can lead to the establishment of a factual record outlined earlier to "enforcement" matters. NGOs should have been allowed to present evidence establishing that a NAFTA party is lowering environmental norms in an attempt to attract investments. The possibility of preparing a factual record based on such evidence would have been a useful addition to the NAAEC. If the drafters sought to avoid the difficult questions of party intent raised by the NAFTA provision, they could have allowed the NGO submissions process to include discussions of the anti-rollback provision of NAAEC that seeks to achieve the same objective as NAFTA Article 1114: preventing the competition in trade and investment from putting too much downward pressure on environmental norms.[149]

Moreover, some provisions unduly restrict public access to the submissions procedure. Most ominously, public submissions on enforcement matters have to pass a difficult test of thoroughness and nonharassment (as though a submission would be presumed to be aimed at damaging industry rather than protecting the environment).[150] Furthermore, the Secretariat may refuse to request a response from the party involved, even if the submission is acceptable. On the other hand, the Draft internal Procedure for Handling Article 14 submissions ought to be commended. Due process, administrative fairness and, most of all, the need to enhance the CEC's credibility required that the CEC transcend the minimal requirements of the text and disclose the steps taken in respect of the submissions prepared by NGOs. Implementing the Draft Procedure will largely release the CEC of that burden because these procedures offer much more access and transparency than traditional trade and economic institutions. Indeed, compared to other multilateral organizations outside the UN system (for example, most international development banks, the Asia Pacific Economic Cooperation forum (APEC) and its committees, the OECD, or the NAFTA Free Trade Commission itself), the CEC is likely to have a more sustained and meaningful relationship with NGOs. The public registry of submissions and responses will be a key element of a more open scheme presented by the NAAEC.

That NAAEC provides for public submissions and factual reports is a crucial advance for NGO involvement in the North American environ-

---

149. Ibid., art. 3.
150. Ibid., art. 14(1).

mental dialogue.[151] It has already been noted that one of the CEC's most useful functions will be to cast the spotlight on public authorities that fail to fulfill their obligations—in particular, the obligation to effectively enforce domestic environmental laws. These NAAEC provisions constitute a formal and permanent instrument enabling NGOs to direct the spotlight themselves. It must be noted, however, that the drafters were constrained in their creativity. For example, no private rights of action were created under the NAAEC even if private enforcement of environmental standards is essential to the effectiveness of domestic environmental law.[152] NAAEC-sanctioned NGO activity (and activism) can focus the attention of the Secretariat, the Council, and the parties themselves on the worst areas of environmental neglect. The process of public submission in respect of environmental law enforcement features three notable aspects. First, the initial stage of the process should be, in principle, invulnerable to an attempt by the Council to stop the Secretariat from considering an NGO submission and requesting an explanation from the impugned party. Second, as noted above, NGOs and citizens from any part of North America may make a submission regarding any state or province of their own country or any other party in the NAFTA area. Third, there is neither a trade test nor an expansive "persistent pattern" criterion for public submissions.[153]

The first private submission to the CEC Secretariat occurred on 7 June 1995. A coalition formed of the National Audubon Society, Grupo de los Cien Internacional, and Centro Mexicano de Derencho Ambiental filed a petition asking the CEC to investigate a contamination incident at the Silva Reservoir, in a heavily populated area of Guanajuato

---

151. In the case of Mexico, which arguably still has the government that is least responsive to public calls for environmental action, it has been argued that "[n]ot only does the CEC provide for supranational action against it, an extraordinary and unprecedented concession by itself, it provides an avenue of access to the Mexican policy process that has heretofore been unavailable to Mexican environmental groups, and it has the distinct advantage of linking domestic policy to an external system of accountability." "Mexican Environmental Reform," supra note 19, Part I at 98.

152. See Art. 19.1 of the *Québec Environmental Quality Act* and section 707 of the *Clean Air Act*.

153. NAAEC is thus at the forefront of an evolving international environmental legal order where increasingly, "the body of international practice, as reflected in the abundant manifestation of treaty law, of resolutions of international organizations, of scholarly institutions, and of occasional arbitral decisions, supports the proposition that procedural norms of information, consultation and joint fact-finding and implementation are increasingly accepted as generally applicable rules of international law." Franciani, in W. Lang, H. Newhold, and K. Zemanek, supra note 25, Part I at 219.

state in central Mexico, and the allegedly inadequate response to it by the Mexican government. The petition claimed that the incident had cost the lives of 40,000 migratory and native birds and that residents had drawn reservoir water for domestic use.[154] It is noteworthy that the NGOs chose to submit their brief to the CEC pursuant to Article 13, which deals with general investigations and reports, and not Article 14, as a claim that environmental laws are not enforced. By choosing this path, the NGO coalition avoided a direct confrontation with Mexican authorities. This places the provisions of Articles 14 and 15, which deal with enforcement matters proper, in a new light. It is possible that they may be seen as a last resort to be used when all cooperative approaches have failed. It is also conceivable that Article 13 has been chosen because it involves fewer formal reports to and from the Mexican government. This limits the potential for political polarization and may help the CEC manage its first case in a manner that makes, at once, the NGOs, the Commission, and the Mexican government appear willing to move forward toward a solution. The Commission has agreed to investigate the matter, and there is little doubt that the outcome of the case will constitute a precedent for what the Commission views as the scope of its authority.[155]

At the end of this analysis, three main reasons support cautious optimism: the permanency of the channels for public submissions, the exis-

---

154. "Environmental Coalition Files First Petition with NAFTA Commission to Investigate Massive Bird Kill at Silva Reservoir in Guanajuato, Mexico," Press Release, 7 June 1995 at 1. See also: "Coalicion de égrupos Ambientales Presenta la Primera Denuncia a la Comision de Cooperacion Ambiental Del Tratado de Libre Comercio (TLC), para Investigar la Muerte Masiva de Aves en la Presa de Silva, Guanajuato, Mexico," Press Release, 7 June 1995; Kevin G. Hall "Nafta-Related Watchdog to Study Mexico Bird Kill," Journal of Commerce (19 June 1995) 2A-3A; Howard LaFranchi, "Migratory Birds Die in Droves: Can NAFTA Come to the Rescue?" Christian Science Monitor (18 June 1995)1,9; N. Russer, "NAFTA's Green Arm Swings Into Action," The (Montreal) Gazette (17 June 1995); "Polluted Lake in Mexico Draws Biologists, Officials," The Fort Worth Star-Telegram (17 June 1995); "NAFTA Rules Face Test," The Seattle Post-Intelligencer (14 June 1995); "NAFTA Commission Asked to Check Mexico Bird Kill," Press Release, Reuters Financial Service, 7 June 1995; Anthony DePalma, "Birds' Deaths in Mexico Are a Test for Trade Pact." The New York Times (8 June 1995) A14.

155. See "Nafta-Related Watchdog," ibid. On the other hand, at the time of writing, another coalition of NGOs has submitted a brief to the CEC and this time the allegation of ineffective enforcement is formally made under NAAEC Article 14. [See A Petition Pursuant to Article 14 of the North American Agreement on Environmental Cooperation, Biodiversity Legal Foundation, Consejo Aseor Sierra Madre, Forest Guardians, Greater Gila Biodiversity Project and Southwest Center for Biological Diversity, July 17, 1995.] The NGOs allege that the United States is failing to effectively enforce its Endangered

tence of the JPAC, and the fact that NGOs, particularly the Canadian and American NGOs that played such an important role in the NAFTA/NAAEC debate, are eagerly lining up to exploit NAAEC mechanisms at their disposal. Whether at UNCED in 1992, through the work of mixed organizations like IUCN, or commenting on the works of international financial institutions like the World Bank, the NGO community has long established that it can provide an essential contribution to international environmental debates. The CEC should tap into that potential and refrain from erecting too many walls between itself and the public. True, the existence of the JPAC and the public submissions process should ensure the participation of business actors and environmental groups in monitoring and assessing the implementation of NAAEC.[156] The CEC should, however, institutionalize its relationship with NGOs beyond the JPAC and build on its nascent practice of fostering open forums and gatherings where NGOs can comment on and make recommendations regarding the implementation of NAAEC. The CEC could also adopt a procedure for formal recognition of the advisory or observer status of some NGOs and allow a degree of participation by the recognized NGOs in closed sessions and meetings of committees and groups established by the Council.

One further point deserves mention. It is important to remember that NAAEC is about two distinct types of activity: (1) the discrete procedure for dispute settlement provisions and (2) cooperation, provided for in the rest of the Agreement. Part Five on dispute settlement, both because of its filiation with the trade agreement NAFTA and because of the principle of "green" trade competitiveness it embodies, may be

---

Species Act of 1973 (16 U.S.C. §§1531–1544), since a special budgetary rescission attached to the *Emergency Supplemental Appropriations and Rescissions for the Department of Defense to Preserve and Enhance Military Readiness Act* of 1995 was signed into law on April 10, 1995. This special provision, known as the "Hutchison Rider," effectively prevents the U.S. Fish and Wildlife Service (according to that agency's own interpretation of the Rider) from enforcing, at all, key sections of the Act in 1995 through rescinding a budget item and formal prohibitions. The Rider, however, does not amend the Act. It suspends the application of certain provisions without modifying the underlying statute. The CEC Secretariat thus has to inquire into the nature of this typically American procedure that creates *legislative,* as opposed to administrative, suspension of enforcement through the micromanagement of agency action by lawmakers. At the time of writing, the CEC Secretariat was still wrestling with this difficult issue, which should also be analyzed in the context of NAAEC Article 45(1), which refers to "reasonable discretion" and "bona fide resource allocation."

156. In this sense, the CEC would be closer to the International Labor Organization model than to the GATT/WTO model of international organization.

thought of as new international *economic* law. The rest of NAAEC, centering on the creation of the CEC and party undertakings, is clearly new international *environmental* law. The difference is consequential to this assessment. If one compares NAAEC's public involvement provisions with the opaque and closed system under GATT and the Canada–U.S. FTA, the modest opening of the process to the public through the JPAC as well as through formal submissions on environmental matters is a giant leap forward. When compared, however, with UN institutions dealing with environmental issues, NAAEC fares favorably in most respects. Moreover, compared with current levels of access to domestic environmental administration in Canada and the United States, the access promised under NAAEC still leaves much to be desired. Indeed, environmental cooperation under NAAEC would be well served by a commitment to achieve levels of transparency and participation in the international realm that are at least equal to those that exist in North America's most progressive jurisdictions.

In summary, creating a practice of improved openness and better NGO involvement in CEC procedure is an absolute requirement if the parties hope to demonstrate that regular sessions of the Council outperform dispute settlement as a means of coordinating policy, developing new law, supervising the implementation of national party obligations, putting collective pressure on reluctant players, and resolving disputes. If the CEC excels, dispute settlement will not be the primary method of supervising the performance of NAAEC parties of their new environmental obligations. Given the convoluted, unpredictable, and legalistic nature of NAAEC's dispute settlement procedure, it may be altogether better to rely on it as a measure of very last resort.

Part IV

Dispute Settlement: The Effectiveness of Domestic Environmental Enforcement

The concern of the parties with inadequate enforcement of a country's environmental laws and standards pervades and informs NAAEC. Instead of negotiating substantive environmental standards, NAAEC partners decided to commit themselves to enforcing already existing environmental laws. This procedure seems to be designed to complement NAFTA's pollution havens/investment clause and to address one of the trade community's principal concerns—namely, that spotty enforcement may afford an unfair competitive advantage. The possibility that well-enforced but lax environmental standards gave the same kind of undeserved competitive edge is not addressed by the NAAEC. Clearly there are three assumptions here: (1) Law enforcement is a privileged instrument for implementing environmental protection strategies; (2) Canada, Mexico, and the United States have generally adequate environmental laws; and (3) the benefits of such laws for the environment (and fair trade) could be foregone if their enforcement by public authorities is ineffective. These are controversial assumptions that form the basis of a more in-depth discussion below.

In light of these assumptions, the parties' obligation not to engage in "a persistent pattern of failure to effectively enforce [their] environmental laws and regulations, through appropriate government action" is the centerpiece of NAAEC and the sole subject matter of its formal dispute settlement procedure.[1] This obligation of effective environmental enforcement also raises the most poignant and complicated questions in the implementation process. Most important, while the fear of pollution havens and uneven environmental law enforcement has both environmental and competitiveness underpinnings, the parties have emphasized the competitiveness aspect by restricting dispute settlement to those dispute situations related or somehow linked to trade in goods or services.

One strong tendency in international environmental negotiations, be they bilateral or plurilateral, has been reliance on so-called soft law instruments: declarations, nonbinding principles, guidelines, and other "framework" treaties.[2] The cooperation mandate of the CEC on such subject matters as transboundary pollution and specific contaminants would clearly fall within this category.[3] By contrast, the dispute settlement provisions of NAAEC create, within this intergovernmental framework, "harder," more binding international obligations on the parties. In this way, NAAEC benefited from the flexibility flowing from a small number of actors and a regional scope. The numerous public promises of "binding obligations" and "enforcement with teeth" made by government officials during the negotiations undoubtedly contributed to a relatively strong dispute settlement procedure. It must be remembered, however, that any institutional architecture will have to accommodate the principle of national sovereignty.[4] While NAAEC's enforcement obligations are more formal and binding than their equiv-

---

1. NAAEC, supra note 2, Introduction, arts. 5 and 22.

2. See Hanspeter Newhold, "Commentary" in Lang, Newhold, and Zemanek, eds., supra note 25, Part I at 224.

3. Unless such recommendations are eventually incorporated in formal, binding treaties between the NAAEC parties. See Ralph D'Arge and Allen V. Kneese, "State Liability for Environmental Degradation: An Economic Perspective" (1980) 20 Natural Resources Journal 427.

4. *Trail Smelter Arbitration (Canada v. United States)* (1931–1941) 3 R.I.A.A. 1905 (1941) 33 A.J.I.L. 182; (1941) 35 A.J.I.L. 684. Following the principle set out in Arti-

alent in many other treaties, the legal categories (and the exceptions) used in the Agreement provide some room for accommodating domestic practices. Enforcement through arbitration and dispute settlement is as much a political consensus-building process as it is a quasi-judicial adjudication proceeding.

As well, while international law recognizes, to some degree, the environmental obligations of states toward each other, and while many environmental treaties include dispute settlement provisions, there is a dearth of international arbitral or judicial decisions on environmental issues.[5] Generally, the dispute settlement provisions of environmental treaties are much more rarely used than their counterparts in trade agreements—which can be a sign of either effectiveness or ineffectiveness. Moreover, as discussed in Part II, the more familiar dispute settlement mechanisms found in trade agreements (from which NAAEC's procedure clearly derives), have been denounced (often justifiably) as inherently hostile to environmental concerns.

---

cle IV of the 1909 *Canada–U.S. Water Boundary Treaty,* the Canada–U.S. International Joint Commission (I.J.C.) ruled in favor of American farmers harmed by fumes from the Cominco smelter located on the Canadian side of the border. In awarding damages to the plaintiffs, the I.J.C. asserted that "no state has the right to use or permit the use of its territory in such a manner as to cause damages to another state or to the properties or persons therein." See "Bilateral," supra note 5, Part I at 61.

5. To be fair, outside trade law, there are few judicial or arbitral precedents to draw from in any area of international law. For example, see the *Trail Smelter Arbitration (Canada v. the United States),* ibid.; the *Lake Lanoux Arbitration (France v. Spain),* (1957) 12 R.I.A.A. 281, 24 I.L.R. 101; the *Corfu Channel* case *(United Kingdom v. Albania),* [1949] I.C.J. Rep. 4; Principle 21 of the *Stockholm Declaration on the Human Environment,* UN GA Res. 2996 (XXVII), UN Doc. A/CONF.48/14 (1972), 11 I.L.M. 1416; Principle 19 of the *Rio Declaration,* (UNCED UN DOC. A/Conf.151/5/Rev. 1 (1992); *Canada–United States Air Quality Agreement,* 13 March 1991, 30 I.L.M. 676. Sharon A. Williams, "Public International Law Governing Transboundary Pollution," (1984) International Business Lawyer 43; and Birnie and Boyle supra note 128, Part I at 89 and ff.

Chapter 7

A Strictly Intergovernmental Process

True to NAFTA/NAAEC's intergovernmental spirit, only the governments of the three NAFTA parties can bring about the process of formal dispute settlement in the case of a persistent pattern of failure to effectively enforce domestic environmental law. The only accepted third party interventions are those of another party to the agreement.[6] It must be noted, however, that there are very few examples of international environmental treaties that allow private parties access to the dispute settlement procedure.[7] Consistent with conventional international environmental law, state responsibility is presented in the NAAEC as a state-to-state relation. The environment is not treated as

---

6. A third NAAEC party "that considers it has a substantial interest in the matter" may join the dispute as a full participant under a procedure laid out in supra note 2, Introduction, arts. 22(3), 24(2), and 27(2). Under Article 29 a third party that has not joined the dispute may still attend all hearings, make written or oral submissions to the panel, and receive the disputants' submissions.

7. One possible exception is the important but not yet in force *United Nations Convention on the Law of the Sea* (UNCLOS), 10 December 1982, U.N. Doc. A/CONF. 62/122 (1982), 1295 U.N.T.S. 211; 21 I.L.M. 1261, which would offer some access to dispute settlement for corporations and individuals.

a subject of law granting rights.[8] The initial forum for dispute settlement is the political governmental level that the Council of ministers represents. If the Council's intervention fails, the long and convoluted formal dispute settlement may be initiated.[9] The request for panel convening must be approved by a two-thirds majority of the Council.[10] The dynamics of that Council vote will be important. Should the party complained against agree to have the matter settled by a panel, Council approval would be a formality. If, however, the party complained against opposes the convening of a panel, the third party could be lobbied by both disputing parties in order to secure a two-thirds vote. To be sure, this would involve political bargaining over other issues or a mediation effort by this third party to avoid formal dispute settlement. By contrast, under NAFTA trade dispute settlement rules, once the complaining party has fulfilled all the requirements for a proper request, a panel must automatically be convened, without an approval vote by the Free Trade Commission.[11]

The Trade Connection

To be successful in its demand for formal dispute settlement, the requesting party must meet two criteria. First, it must convince the Council that the alleged persistent pattern of ineffective enforcement: "relates to a situation involving workplace, firms, companies or sectors that produce goods or provide services (a) traded between the territories of the Parties; or (b) that compete, in the territory of the Party complained against, with goods or services produced or provided by

---

8. For a description of conventional international environmental law on the subject of state responsibility, see K. Zemanek, "State Responsibility and Liability" in W. Lang, H. Newhold, and K. Zemanek, eds., supra note 25, Part I at 191–192.

9. The first step in the process of dispute settlement is an allegation by a party that another party has failed to effectively enforce its environmental laws. This is followed by written notification and consultations between the disputing parties for a period of up to 60 days. At this stage, absent a settlement of the dispute, the requesting party may ask for a special session of the CEC Council, which then has 20 days (or more if the Council so decides under Article 23(3)) to intervene and provide its good offices, arrange for expert advice, or make recommendations [Article 24(4)]. If the matter is not resolved within 60 days of the Council's convening a special session, a disputing party may request that the matter be referred to a formal dispute settlement panel. The delay of 60 days can be extended if the parties to the dispute agree [Article 24(1)].

10. NAAEC, supra note 2, Introduction, art. 24(1).

11. NAFTA, supra note 1, Introduction, art. 2008(2).

persons of another Party."[12] At the level of principles, as well as for a developing NAAEC practice, the trade requirement is a pivotal provision.

Environmental Protection as a Competitiveness Issue

The drafters of NAAEC have chosen to restrict the binding application of the environmental enforcement obligations exclusively to trade-related situations—even if that connection may be faint. In the view of the authors, this clearly bespeaks recognition by the parties that the intensity of environmental regulation is a trade and competitiveness issue inasmuch as it affects production/extraction costs, as was explained in Part I. With this provision, the NAAEC parties acknowledge that a country's attractiveness to foreign investors, as well as the relative competitiveness of its exports, varies with the set level of environmental cost internalization across industries. In other words, according to the parties, these two characteristics change with the severity of their environmental regulation and policing of industry. This is within a hair of saying that the environmental cost internalization strategies of trading partners must converge to preserve the competitive playing field. If this were not the case, there would be no need for a trade requirement, and the dispute settlement procedure would have allowed complaints based on other criteria, such as transboundary pollution or the severity of ecological damage.[13] If the underlying purpose of NAAEC's environmental enforcement obligations and dispute settlement procedure is the protection of the natural environment against ecological harm, then the production of traded or competing goods should be irrelevant to a party's call for improvement of its neighbor's environmental enforcement practices. Further evidence of this policy choice is the existence of an alternative within NAAEC: No trade connection is required in the procedure for public submissions to the Secretariat.[14] The production of traded or competing goods was cast aside as a preliminary requirement for private complaints to the

---

12. NAAEC, supra note 2, Introduction, art. 24(1).

13. There are international legal recourses available to Canada, Mexico, and the United States in the case of disputes over transboundary pollution. Conceptually, there was no reason to exclude such disputes in the jurisdiction of NAAEC dispute settlement, unless NAAEC was seen as an instrument designed to complement a trade treaty and address the issue of the impact of environmental protection on trade and competitiveness. See infra notes 110–139, Part IV and accompanying discussion.

14. See supra notes 43 and 44, Part III.

CEC and for the development of factual records. The trade criterion is, however, fully in effect for official government requests for dispute settlement: No trade connection means no panel convening and no formal dispute settlement. Regrettably, the trade test in effect may ultimately limit NAAEC's dispute settlement process exclusively to the role of a safeguard against the problem of ecological dumping.[15]

Moreover, while it is inspired by a preoccupation with the effects of environmental policies on competitiveness and modeled after the NAFTA dispute settlement method, the economic harm approach displayed in the NAAEC dispute settlement procedure is not fully consistent with traditional trade law principles: The allegation would concern environmental dumping but there is no need to show injury. Again, the justification for the emphasis on enforcement seems to be the unfair competitive advantage gained by the exporting country that fails to enforce environmental laws on producers. Some have referred to this practice as ecological dumping since exports end up being sold below their true cost because essential environmental costs are not properly internalized through adequate government enforcement action. While there is no conceptual problem with a dispute settlement procedure based on dumping, environmental, social,[16] or otherwise, the NAAEC procedure does not properly reflect the approach of the GATT *Antidumping Code*[17] or NAFTA's provisions with regard to dumping.[18] Those regimes allow the fair use of domestic trade laws. Under such laws, in order to get reprieve in the form of trade protection, the private party has to show the injury caused by the dumping practices: Loss of sales and loss of market shares amounting to accountable financial losses. The review by an international dispute settlement panel will verify that such an injury indeed was inflicted before allowing the party complained against to maintain duties on imports from the complaining party. If no injury is found, the complaining party is granted the right to retaliate if the offending protection is maintained

---

15. There is one noteworthy difference with NAFTA's dispute settlement procedure (which applies domestic law) in respect of dumping: the requesting party does not have to establish injury to its domestic industry, only the trade connection (NAFTA Chapter Nineteen). For example, see Canada *Special Import Measures Act,* R.S.C. 1985, c.S-15; *U.S. Tariff Act,* 19 U.S.C. § 1337.

16. For example, extremely low wages, slavery-like conditions, and child labor in the production of exported goods as "social dumping."

17. 30 June 1967, 6 I.L.M. 920; 11 April 1979, 18 I.L.M. 621.

18. NAFTA, supra note 1, Introduction, Chapter Nineteen.

by the party complained against. Under NAAEC, even if a trade connection is required, there is no need for the complaining party to show any injury to its producers of goods or services in the sector where lax enforcement of environmental laws by another party is alleged.[19] In other words, there is no need to show economic injury in order to initiate dispute settlement under the NAAEC, only the *potential* for such injury. This means that the trade requirement, while it must be met in order to render receivable complaints of inadequate environmental enforcement, will not be used as it should to demonstrate the commercial injury caused by such ineffective enforcement. Thus emerges the consequence of embodying a *substantive* principle in a *procedural* requirement.

The Case for a Liberal Interpretation

Nevertheless, this procedural quality raises the possibility that the trade test could shrink into a simple formal condition that a party would meet in order to achieve its real goal of forcing another party to change its environmental practices. In that sense, the absence of an obligation to show commercial injury actually broadens the scope of dispute settlement. After all, since the requirement is only to show that the ineffective enforcement "relates to a situation involving" sectors producing competing goods, it might be easy to fulfill it even if the actual trade competition is insignificant. If, for example, Canada really wants to challenge U.S. environmental enforcement practices in the area of aluminum production, or Mexican tolerance for violation of its sulfur dioxide emissions standards, it may only need to show that some of the aluminum or some of the goods produced in Mexican plants that are violating domestic standards end up being bought in Canada or competing at home with Canadian exports. Among three countries that trade so much with one another, as long as the Council adopts a liberal interpretation of the trade test, there will be plenty of opportunity to meet the trade requirement, even if it does not appear that important trade equilibria are affected. It must be remembered, nevertheless, that the trade patterns in the NAFTA area are such that

---

19. This analogy is only valid for the situation described by subparagraph (a) of Article 24: when the party complained against is the exporting country. When the party complained against is the importing country the analogy would not be with dumping rules but with the rule of national treatment, or the rules on subsidies if lax enforcement could be characterized as a disguised subsidy. In that case, according to trade law, a domestic producer is never prohibited from selling below cost on its domestic market.

NAAEC disputes are more likely to be United States–Canada and
United States–Mexico bilateral affairs.

The Danger of a Double Standard

The need for a trade connection may also bring about undesirable
results in the long run. The dispute settlement mechanism will almost
certainly bear some unforeseen consequences once the parties start to
use it or modify their behavior because of its existence. One such
important consequence of resorting to a trade test is the possible creation of two classes of subjects under environmental laws: (1) That
which includes industries or companies producing goods and services
that compete with those of other NAAEC partners, and (2) that which
comprises those industries and companies that do not. When a party
ceases to effectively enforce its environmental laws on the first class of
subjects, the exporters/competitors may be challenged by another
party under NAAEC rules. When it ceases to effectively enforce environmental laws on the second class, no other NAAEC party may initiate formal dispute settlement. A party may thus be inclined to enforce
more effectively environmental laws on the exporters/competitors in
order to avoid dispute settlement.[20] Ultimately, this could mean that
businesses that export to the European Union or to another part of the
world might benefit from higher tolerance from environmental agencies than would those that export to another NAFTA partner. The category of potential benefactors from ineffective enforcement could also
include businesses that sell only domestically and that do not compete
with imports from other NAAEC countries.

Therefore, if a set of industrial water contamination regulations is
unenforced in the St. Lawrence River valley, thus polluting the river,
NAAEC can be invoked to ask Canadian public authorities to more
effectively enforce these regulations since much of what these industries produce (for example, paper products, chemicals, aluminum) is
exported to the United States or competes with U.S. products imported
into Canada. On the other hand, if laws governing waste management
by private contractors in New Jersey or Minnesota are not effectively
enforced, causing widespread pollution, NAAEC may well be of no use

---

20. The argument could also be made that different laws could be administered differently. If NAAEC dispute settlement is regularly used, there could emerge two distinct
classes of environmental laws: (1) those that govern activities related to international
trade and have to be effectively enforced under NAAEC law, and (2) those that govern
activities that do not have such a connection, when public authorities have no new
obligation to make enforcement as effective.

to the other parties for dispute settlement purposes because the trade connection would be difficult to establish.

One of the best examples of the double standard that could evolve is government policing its own activities. Exempt from NAAEC dispute settlement would be the ineffective enforcement of environmental laws on the governments and public agencies of the parties themselves, unless this situation involves such bodies selling or exporting goods or services.[21] If a government disregards its own environmental laws when it builds a bridge or a highway between two cities, NAAEC does not allow dispute settlement to take place. If the same government disregards the same regulations in order to build a dam to produce electricity that is partly exported to another party, or to build a road to open access to a new logging area from which lumber is to be exported, any other party could file a complaint and initiate dispute settlement procedures. This double standard is significant since domestic laws compel governments to conduct environmental impact assessments of public works projects, to improve public lands, to initiate reviews or reauthorization procedures for environmental laws, and to ensure compliance with all environmental norms in public undertakings.[22] The government will not find itself before a dispute settlement panel for an alleged persistent pattern of failure to enforce those important environmental laws that apply to it, unless, in the process, such failure affects the producer of competing goods or services.[23] It is to be hoped that the trade connection will be broadly interpreted to diminish the possibility of such a double standard emerging between environmental laws that affect trade equilibria and those that do not.[24]

---

21. The production of goods is not, however, an insignificant government activity in North America. In Canada for example, governments and their agencies produce and export agricultural goods, electricity, minerals, and steel. In Mexico, publicly owned government agencies are even more involved in the oil and gas sector and other natural resources industries.

22. On the other hand, the language of Article 24 is so broad that a trade connection might be found even if the persistent failure to enforce environmental laws somehow "relates to a situation involving" a sector that produces traded or competing goods. Nevertheless, it is difficult to see how the content of the meaning of the word "relate" could not be linked to an effect on costs and competitiveness.

23. To further illustrate the point, this remains true even if the governmental endeavor has transboundary environmental effects.

24. With regard to the situations where the NAAEC trade connection cannot be established at the international level, NAAEC will still afford the possibility of a CEC investigation and the eventual preparation of a factual record, but only if the domestic recourses have been tried and have failed to provide adequate reprieve.

Panel Convening

Once it is determined that a sufficient connection exists between trading and the alleged ineffective enforcement, the next step is to convene a dispute settlement panel. As was explained, an important two-thirds vote by the Council is required to authorize this. Otherwise, when a panel is convened, the process in NAAEC closely mirrors that of a NAFTA trade dispute settlement.[25] The main difference is the terms of reference of the panel. Unless the parties agree otherwise, the terms of reference of the panel will be: "To examine, in light of the relevant provisions of the Agreement, including those contained in Part Five, whether there has been a persistent pattern of failure by the Party complained against to effectively enforce its environmental law, and to make findings, determinations and recommendations in accordance with Article 31(2)."[26]

The remainder of the procedure mandates the panel to produce first an initial report and then a final report, both of which detail the panel's fact findings, its determination as to the existence of a persistent pattern of ineffective enforcement, and its recommendations for the settlement of the dispute.[27] The final settlement will normally mean that the party complained against shall "adopt and implement an action plan sufficient to remedy the pattern of nonenforcement."[28] The implementation of the final report of the dispute settlement panel

---

25. The parties must agree on a Chair within 15 days and on the panelists within 15 days of the Chairman's selection. A roster of panelists is maintained by the Council (NAAEC Article 27(1)). If there are three parties to a dispute, the rules of Article 27(2) will apply and the delays may be extended. The panel is composed of the Chairman and four more experts from the roster, selected by the parties themselves from among citizens of the other disputing party listed on the roster. Under Article 25, the roster is composed of up to 45 individuals who are nominated for terms of three years and have to demonstrate independence and possess relevant technical, legal, or scientific expertise. Since the disputes will always center on diligence in the application of laws, not the merits of individual environmental controversies, one could assume that qualified experts are likely to be individuals with legal and administrative rather than substantive environmental expertise. On the other hand, scientific expertise will have to intervene in cases where a specific provision or a specific region are concerned to assess the reasonableness of the public authorities' enforcement record in the light of a threat to health or the ecosystems.

26. NAAEC, supra note 2, Introduction, art. 28(3).

27. Ibid., art. 31; within 180 days of the selection of the last panelist.

28. Ibid., art. 31(2). The parties can agree to give the panel more time to produce its initial report. After another 60 day period has elapsed, during which parties can

essentially involves the preparation of a remedial enforcement action plan designed to cure the persistent pattern of failure to effectively enforce environmental laws. If the parties agree on such a plan and the party complained against swiftly carries out its implementation, there would be no need for enforcement measures—the so-called teeth often referred to in the negotiations leading to NAAEC.[29] If, on the contrary, the disputing parties cannot agree on an action plan based on the panel determination, or on whether or not the party complained against is actually honoring the terms of the action plan, sanctions may be put into place under the Agreement.[30] These sanctions and their purposes and possible modalities, which may include fines and trade measures, will be described in Chapter 10.

For now our analysis will focus on the nature of the enforcement obligation. More precisely, we will try to discern what comprises a "persistent pattern of failure to effectively enforce environmental laws." We will look at environmental statutes, regulations, and provisions as contrasted with natural resource management laws and policies. Our inquiry will dwell on the nature of the obligation of due diligence in enforcement undertaken by the parties to NAAEC. In particular the authors will address two issues integrated in the rules of NAAEC: domestic government discretion in the enforcement of environmental laws, and a domestic government's right to allocate scarce resources to different environmental priorities. We will also present some thoughts on useful definitions of a "persistent pattern." Once the matter of the nature of the environmental enforcement obligation is better explained, we will turn to the sanctions put in place to enforce NAAEC obligations.

---

make written comments, the panel presents its final report to the parties, which must in turn transmit it to the Council within 15 days (NAAEC Article 32(2)). The final panel report is then transmitted to the Council along with any written views the parties may want to append. In contrast to the final reports of NAFTA panels, the final report of the panel will be made public, without exception, within five days of its delivery to the Council (NAAEC Article 32(3); *contra* see also NAFTA Annex 1903.2(5) and Article 2017(4)). In contrast also to old GATT rules, the final report does not have to be adopted or approved by the Council to become an official NAAEC legal document.

29. The parties need only to notify the Secretariat and the Council of the agreed solution under NAAEC Article 33.

30. NAAEC, supra note 2, Introduction, art. 34.

Chapter 8

What Is an Environmental Law?

It has been said that the word "environment" is "a term everyone understands but no one is able to define."[31] Yet, defining an "environmental law," for the purposes of describing the NAAEC obligation to enforce such laws, is critical. Lax enforcement of what is in the environmental law basket may entail legal responsibility under NAAEC, whereas the same neglect in respect of a statute lying outside this category has no legal consequences for a member state.[32] Under NAAEC, "environmental laws and regulations" include "any statute or regulation of a Party, or provision thereof, *the primary purpose of which is the protection of the environment,*[33] or the prevention of a danger to human

---

31. Lynton K. Caldwell, *International Environmental Policy and Law,* 1st ed. (New York: Dunham, 1980) at 170.

32. During the negotiations, a "law list" approach, enumerating national legislation covered by NAAEC, was envisaged by some (most notably Canada) and considered by the negotiators, but eventually abandoned because of the sheer complexity and the quantity of legislation involved that would have to be constantly updated.

33. The drafters later added "in the Party's territory," which means that if a Party engaged in extraterritorial enforcement of environmental norms—for example, in the United States through the *Marine Mammal Protection Act,* such enforcement, effective

life or health" (emphasis added).[34] The specific methods of environmental protection listed in NAAEC relate to pollution prevention and control,[35] the control of hazardous and toxic substances,[36] and the conservation of wild flora and fauna and their habitats.[37] To be sure, this definition is uncomfortably broad,[38] and much will be left to legal argument to forge workable parameters.

Environmental Statutes and Regulations

The "primary purpose" approach and the wide diversity of means of environmental protection enumerated in NAAEC's definition of environmental law will render most purportedly environmental statutes in the United States, Canada, and Mexico, both at the federal and the provincial or state level, subject to the enforcement obligation under

---

or ineffective, discriminatory or not, would not fall within the scope of the enforcement obligation found in NAAEC.

34. NAAEC, supra note 2, Introduction, art. 45(2)(a). It is worth noting that the Agreement limits the meaning of "law" to "statutes," "regulations," and "the provisions thereof," thereby seemingly excluding elements such as judicial precedents and interpretations, ministerial directives and guidelines, and various other sources of norms and standards that are an important part of the public authorities' intervention in favor of the environment. Important elements like municipal bylaws may or may not be included in the definition. To diminish their environmental enforcement obligations toward their NAAEC partners, some parties might be tempted to augment the number of rules and norms put in directives and guideline formats. They might then be able to use discretionary power to enforce these nonlegislative instruments without having to concern themselves with the frequency and the intensity of the enforcement.

35. Ibid., art. 45(2)(a)(i).

36. Ibid., arts. 45(2)(a)(i-iii); Article 45(2)(a)(ii) includes "the dissemination of information related thereto," a direct reference to such legislative initiatives as the American *Toxic Release Inventory (TRI) Emergency Planning and Community Right-to-know Act of 1986*, setting up the *Toxic Release Inventory*, and the Canadian *National Pollutant Release Inventory*, instituted under Sect. 16 of the *Canadian Environmental Protection Act*, R.S.C. 1985 (4th Supp.), c.16.

37. NAAEC, supra note 2, Introduction, art. 45(2)(a)(iii).

38. Under Article 45(2) the definition is given "for the purposes of Article 14(1) and Part Five." Article 14(1) is the provision empowering the Secretariat of the Commission to receive a submission from a nongovernmental organization. Part Five is the dispute resolution procedure. The term "environmental law" is also used directly in Articles 5, 6, 10 and, indirectly, in Article 7. It is unclear why the drafters did not choose the formulation "for the purposes of this Agreement." One implication is that the definition of "environmental law" could be even broader, and go beyond the scope of public submission and dispute settlement.

NAAEC. This inclusiveness is reinforced by a general trend toward more comprehensive, umbrella legislation with clearly stated environmental goals and away from statutes addressing specific environmental issues.[39] Moreover, the primary purpose approach does not apply only to whole statutes. Indeed, a regulation or even a single *provision* can fall under NAAEC's definition of environmental law even if either were promulgated under a law whose primary purpose is not the protection of the environment. For instance, a regulation concerning mining waste management but adopted under a statute otherwise aimed at policing general mining activities would qualify as "environmental law" under NAAEC.[40] It is sufficient to establish that the primary purpose of that regulation or provision is the protection of the environment.[41]

In Canada, at the federal level, the best example of consolidated legislation is the *Canadian Environmental Protection Act* (CEPA).[42] Many provinces have now adopted consolidated general environmental "codes." These codes generally include a broad definition of what constitutes the environment and a prohibition on releasing contaminants beyond the levels set by regulations, as well as other environmental

---

39. For example, the purpose of the U.S. *Clean Water Act,* 33 U.S.C. § 1251 is "to restore and maintain the chemical, physical and biological integrity of the Nation's waters."

40. NAAEC, supra note 2, Introduction, art. 45(2)(c).

41. For example, Part XV of the *Canada Shipping Act* R.S.C. 1985, c. S-9, dealing with pollution prevention and control and its oil pollution prevention regulations [SOR/93-3; see A.L. Lucas and R. Cotton, eds., *Canadian Environmental Law,* 2nd ed. (Toronto: Butterworths, 1992) at F.11] would be covered by NAAEC's definition of environmental law while the rest of that legislative scheme is not. Similar articles and regulations exist in American, Mexican, and Canadian laws pertaining to mining, fisheries, energy, oil and gas, and forestry. Article 180(1) on common nuisances and Article 430 on mischief of the *Criminal Code* of Canada R.S.C. 1985, c. C-46, may be more controversial examples of provisions construed as environmental sections of a general statute the primary purpose of which is not environmental. In the United States, good examples of environmental provisions cast in statutes with a nonenvironmental primary purpose would be subsection (a) of the *Port and Tanker Safety Act* 33 U.S.C. § 391, as well as certain sections relating to environmental damage of the *Outer Continental Shelf Lands Act* 43 U.S.C. §§ 1131–1356.

42. Supra note 36, Part IV. Other important federal statutes relating to the environment are: the *Fisheries Act,* R.S.C. 1985, c.F-14; the *Canadian Environmental Assessment Act,* S.C. 1992, c.37; the *National Pollutants Release Inventory Act,* ibid.; the *Pest Control Products Act,* R.S.C. 1985, c.P-9, as amended; and the *Atomic Energy Control Act,* R.S.C. 1985, c.A-12 (A-16).

management provisions.[43] Other provinces may have more scattered environmental protection legislation, although this does not imply that the standards or the enforcement are below the level achieved by the provinces with more general statutes.[44] The issue of competing federal and provincial jurisdictions in the field of environmental protection remains a major feature of Canadian environmental law, which may impact on discussions of Canadian enforcement under NAAEC.[45]

In the United States, the main paradigms of the federal approach to pollution control and environmental protection are found in the *National Environmental Policy Act*.[46] As well, statutes such as the *Clean Air Act*,[47] the *Clean Water Act*,[48] the *Endangered Species Act*,[49] the *Toxic Substances Control Act*,[50] the *Federal Insecticide, Fungicide and Rodenti-*

---

43. For example, Alberta has the *Environment Protection and Enhancement Act,* S.A. 1992 c.E- 13.3; Manitoba has the *Environment Act,* S.M. 1987, c.26; in Manitoba other important environmental statutes include the *Dangerous Goods Handling and Transportation Act,* R.S.M. 1987, c.D-12; the *Rivers and Streams Act,* R.S.M. 1988, c.R-160; and the *Manitoba Hazardous Waste Management Corporation Act,* S.M. 1986-87, c.10; Ontario has its *Environmental Protection Act,* R.S.O. 1990, c.E-19; the *Ontario Water Resources Act,* R.S.O. 1990, c.O-40, is also important; and Quebec has the *Environmental Quality Act,* R.S.Q., 1985, c.Q-2, as amended.

44. In New Brunswick the main environmental statutes are the *Clean Environment Act,* R.S.N.B. 1973, c.C-6, as amended, and the *Clean Water Act,* S.N.B. 1989, c.C-6.1; in Newfoundland the most important law is the *Department of Environment and Lands Act,* R.S.N. 1990, c.D-11; in Nova Scotia the principal environmental laws are the *Environmental Protection Act,* R.S.N.S. 1989, c.150, the *Dangerous Goods and Hazardous Waste Management Act,* R.S.N.S. 1989 c.118, and the *Water Act,* R.S.N.S. 1989, c.500; in Prince Edward Island the main environmental law is the *Environmental Protection Act,* R.S.P.E.I. 1988, c.E-9; in Saskatchewan, the important environmental statutes are the *Environmental Management and Protection Act,* S.S. 1983-84, c.E-10.2, the *Water Corporation Act,* S.S. 1983-84, c.w-4.1, and the *Clean Air Act,* S.S. 1986-7-8, c.12.1; in British Columbia, the most important environmental laws are the *Environment Assessment Act,* S.B.C. 1980-81, c. 41, and the *Waste Management Act* S.B.C. 1982, c. 41.

45. See generally A. St. Pierre, "Impact of Environmental Measures on International Trade," Report 76-91-E (Ottawa: Conference Board of Canada). See also: Michael Jaeger, "Back to the Future: Environmental Federalism in an Era of Sustainable Development" (1993) 3 J. Plan. & Env. L. 1.

46. 42 U.S.C. § 4321; as well see generally Bureau of National Affairs, *U.S. Environmental Laws,* (Washington, D.C.: Bureau of National Affairs, 1988).

47. 42 U.S.C. § 7401.

48. Including the *Water Quality Act* amendments of 1987, 33 U.S.C. § 1251; as well see the *Safe Drinking Water Act,* 42 U.S.C. U.S.C. § 300(f)–300(j-q).

49. 16 U.S.C. § 1531.

50. 15 U.S.C. § 2601.

cide Act,[51] the *Resource Conservation and Recovery Act,*[52] the *Hazardous Materials Transportation Control Act,*[53] and the *Comprehensive Environmental Response, the Compensation and Liability Act* (CERCLA or Superfund)[54] are key federal statutes. Generally, issues of federalism are not as acutely felt in the United States as they are in Canada because, usually, states are given major roles in the implementation and enforcement of national environmental quality standards.[55]

In Mexico, unlike in Canada and the United States, it is the constitution of the country that lays down the main principles of government action. Article 27 of the constitution mandates the federal government to promote resource conservation and ecological equilibrium.[56] Replacing in large part the 1971 *Ley Federal para Prevenir y Controlar la Contaminación* and the 1982 *Ley Federal de Protección al Ambiente*, the 1988 *Ley general del Equilibrio Ecológico y la Protección al Ambiente* addresses all of the important aspects of environmental protection policy and establishes the framework for cooperation between the federal, state, and municipal authorities.[57] Even if all Mexican environmental

---

51. 7 U.S.C. § 136.

52. 42 U.S.C. § 6901.

53. 49 U.S.C. § 1801.

54. 42 U.S.C. § 9601, including the *Superfund Amendments and Reauthorization Act* (SARA) amendments, which itself includes a significant distinct law called the *Emergency Planning and Community Right-to-Know Act* at 42 U.S.C. § 11001.

55. F.R. Anderson, D.R. Mandelker, and A.D. Tarlock, *Environmental Protection: Law and Policy* (Boston: Little, Brown and Co., 1990) at 51–52.

56. Articles 25, 26, and 73 of the Mexican constitution also give public authorities environmental responsibilities.

57. Other important sectoral laws are the *Ley de Aguas Nacionales* on water protection, the *Ley Federal del Mar* on ocean pollution, the *Ley Forestal* on forestry, the *Ley General de Asentamientos Humanos* on health, the *Ley de Pesca* on fisheries, the *Ley de Seguridad Fitopecuaria* on phytosanitary measures, the *Ley Federal sobre Metrología y Normalización* on standardization and the *Ley Minera* on mining. A number of Mexican environmental regulations were promulgated pursuant to the Ecology Law. They are: the Regulation to the Ecology Law for the Prevention and Control of Atmospheric Contamination, effective 26 Nov. 1988; the Regulation to the Ecology Law for Hazardous Wastes, effective 26 Nov. 1989; the Regulation to the Ecology Law for Environmental Impact, effective 8 June 1988; Environmental Technical Standards, promulgated continually; the Decree for the Development and Operation of the In-Bond Export Industry, effective 30 Dec. 1989; the Regulation to the Ecology Law to Promote Mexican Investment and to Regulate Foreign Investment, effective 17 May 1989. See also: Edward M. Ranger, *Environmental Regulation and Enforcement in Mexico,* reprinted from Maquiladora Industry Ann. Rev.; Edward M. Ranger, *A Compliance Checklist,* Bus. Mex., Special Ed. 1993.

statutes pay proper homage to shared jurisdictions, most important decrees, regulations, and directives are prepared by the central government, even if the role of state administrations has steadily become more important. Twenty-seven of the 31 Mexican states have environmental laws of their own.

It must be noted that since domestic environmental laws are sometimes adopted with a view to implementing international environmental agreements, the same failure to effectively enforce such laws would constitute a violation of both NAAEC and this international agreement. In such a case, it is unclear whether the matter should be pursued under the NAAEC Dispute Settlement provisions or under whatever such provisions may be found in the international environmental agreement in question. Absent a future clarification on this issue, NAFTA parties would appear to have the choice.[58]

The Natural Resources Management Exception

It is fair to say that there are very few environmental protection laws, regulations, or provisions that are not included in the NAAEC definition of environmental laws. The same, however, cannot be said for laws and regulations pertaining to natural resource management, unless the concern is a specific regulation or provision addressing directly an environmental or pollution control issue. NAAEC carves out an important exception to the definition of environmental law by excluding from it any statute or regulation, "the primary purpose of which is managing the commercial harvest or exploitation, or subsistence or aboriginal harvesting, of natural resources."[59] A foretaste of this exception can be found in the preamble, wherein the parties *reaffirm* "the sovereign right of States to exploit their own resources pursuant to their own environmental and development policies."[60] This exception in the basic environmental enforcement obligation of the NAAEC parties is thus, from the point of view of the latter, a concrete

---

58. Unless the agreement is one listed under Article 102 of NAFTA and the parties consider that it should have precedence over the NAAEC as well.

59. During the negotiations, Canada considered this exception necessary in light of the constitutionally protected provincial jurisdiction over the management of natural resources.

60. NAAEC preamble, second paragraph. This recognition of national sovereignty over natural resources is rooted in the movement for decolonization of the 1950s and 1960s and has become standard fare in international environmental agreements. See, for example, Principle 2 of the *Rio Declaration,* supra note 72, Part III, Subparagraph 8 of the preamble of the *United Nations Framework Convention on Climate Change,* 9 May

expression of their predating right to manage their own resources. It is also the expression of a belief shared by most states: Few areas are as sovereign as natural resources management and exploitation.

By virtue of this definition, only specifically *environmental* regulations and provisions of natural resource management legislation are considered to be "environmental law" and, thus, covered by the enforcement obligations of NAAEC. For the moment, unsustainable natural resource management caused by governments' failure to effectively enforce their own laws remains beyond the reach of the NAAEC dispute settlement regime.[61] Clearly, the intention is to focus the NAAEC dispute settlement procedure on issues of pollution control rather than conservation and resource and land management. True, the judicial nature of NAAEC's dispute settlement procedure may not readily lend itself to evaluating the relative quality of the "enforcement" of complex resource management policies and schemes. The exclusion from "environmental law" of resource management schemes governing such activities as fishing, mining, and logging might make dispute settlement under NAAEC more manageable and might pay proper homage to national sovereignties. It creates, however, a sense of unfinished business, of incompleteness—especially in light of the references to sustainable development found earlier in NAAEC and in NAFTA itself.[62] Inasmuch as prudent resources management is as fun-

---

1992, UN Doc. A/AC.237/18 Part II Add. 1 and Corr. 1 (1992), 31 I.L.M. 849; Article 193 of UNCLOS, supra note 7, Part IV; UN GA Res. 1803, 17th Sess. (1962); the *Declaration of a New International Economic Order,* UN GA Res. 3201, 29th Sess. (1974); the *Charter of Economic Rights and Duties of States,* UN GA Res. 3281, 29th Sess. (1974). It was referred to in arbitral decisions such as *Texaco Overseas Petroleum Co. and California Asiatic Oil Co. v. Libyan Arab Republic,* 53 I.L.R. 389, 17, I.L.M.1. It is possible that the decolonization origins of this legal principle might, in time, limit its applicability in future environmental disputes. Sustainable development does not imply, in any way, encroachment upon national sovereignty. See statement by UNEP G.C. Doc. UNEP/GC 15/L.37, Annex II (1989).

61. The fact that there is a strong practical argument against including natural resource management in the ambit of NAAEC is one more reason to lament the fact that it includes no substantive environmental provisions, not even general declarations that could be elaborated on at a later stage. A substantive chapter in NAAEC could have included, in addition to limits to specific contaminants and contaminating practices, concrete references to sustainable fish stock management, sustainable forest management, clear-cutting, or improved agricultural practices and so on.

62. There are, however, some precedents for excluding resource policies from the definition of environmental policies. For example, Article 130(r) of the *Single European*

damental to protecting ecosystems and the environment as is preventing pollution, the isolation of resource management schemes leave a gap in the environmental enforcement scheme under NAAEC.

Nevertheless, determining whether the primary purpose of a statute is resource management or environmental protection would, in some cases, be far from straightforward. Consider, for example, that NAAEC's definition of "environmental law" contains references to "the protection of wild flora or fauna, including endangered species, their habitat, and specially protected natural areas."[63] The interplay between such a definition of environmental law and the natural resources exception is far from predictable. For example, the *Canadian Fisheries Act* includes both pollution-prevention provisions and resource protection provisions.[64] While it is clear that the provisions targeting pollution fall under the definition of environmental law set out in the NAAEC, other sections of the Act designed to protect fish stocks might be construed as "primarily aimed at" species conservation or, alternatively, at natural resource management.

The above argues for a narrow interpretation of this exception, which, coupled with a broad understanding of the conservation reference in the definition of environmental law, could likely bring some wilderness and land management laws into the ambit of dispute settlement. At the same time, it is doubtful that a panel would read this exception so narrowly as to rule against the letter of NAAEC and subject entire resource management statutes to the dispute settlement provisions of the agreement. Rather, a panel will likely require a connection between the unenforced provision and the protection of a specific habitat or species (as opposed to resource conservation) before finding that a party is in breach of its obligations under NAAEC.

In theory, therefore, apart from statutes aimed directly at resource management, virtually all environmental statutes and their regulations, as well as the environmental regulations and provisions of other statutes, whether at the federal, state, provincial, or even local level, will fall under NAAEC's definition of environmental law. The defini-

---

Act, 1986 U.K.T.S. 1988 No. 31 establishes the importance of environmental protection and improvement but protects national policy regarding energy resources from interference.

63. NAAEC, supra note 2, Introduction, art. 45(2)(a)(iii).

64. Supra note 42, Part IV; Section 36(3) of the Act prohibits the deposit of "deleterious substances" of any type in water frequented by fish.

tions in the Agreement have paved the way for a comprehensive obligation of the parties to refrain from engaging in a systematic pattern of
failure to effectively enforce their own environmental laws and regulations. The next question raised by NAAEC is what kind of governmental behavior constitutes a breach of that obligation.

Chapter 9

Legal Standard for Enforcement Diligence: What Is Ineffective Environmental Enforcement?

In NAAEC, each party promises to effectively enforce its own environmental laws. The task of the dispute settlement panel is to investigate claims by another party of a failure to do so. The mandate calls for the review of domestic judicial and administrative proceedings (or the absence thereof) with a view to assessing the quality of enforcement in this particular regulatory area.

Environmental enforcement is an enormously complex issue to analyze from a legal, scientific, and economic point of view. While some studies have been conducted on this issue, mostly in the United States, there is a need for more inquiry into the practice of environmental enforcement in all three NAFTA countries.[65] NAAEC seeks to prompt governments into effective environmental enforcement. However, this

---

65. One remarkable such effort is P.B. Downing and K. Hanf, eds., *International Comparison in Implementing Pollution Laws* (Boston: Kluwer-Nijhoff, 1983). A rigorous

begs the question: effective as compared to what? All regulatory agencies have different ways to establish the three main parameters of their action: (1) Defining the standard and what constitutes a violation. (2) How to monitor regulated businesses and detect violations. (3) How to incite the violator to comply with positive incentives like delays, negotiations, and subsidies, or negative incentives like monetary penalties or injunctions. Almost by definition, environmental enforcement is spotty and standards compliance voluntary. An older U.S. study on air pollution concluded that even under ideal circumstances for the enforcing authority, a firm could be in violation 70 percent of the time and never be cited.[66] Most of the evidence in the literature, as well as most of the qualitative inquiries in the nature and practice of environmental enforcement, suggests that "both in the level of control and the date by which the control must be effective are subject to bargaining."[67] Not every environmental degradation is defined as a violation. Not every violation is detected or reported. Few of the documented violations lead to regulatory agency action and follow-up. Numerous such follow-ups never include court action. Court proceedings do not always lead to convictions. The low dollar (or peso) value of the fines imposed on convicted firms will often constitute a poor deterrent for the future. While there are national, regional, and sectoral differences, this is the sobering reality of environmental enforcement everywhere in North America. Indeed, effectiveness in the real world of the administration of pollution control laws is a most relative concept.

There is no obvious place to look in international law either. The appropriate standards to be used in the panels' investigation of the enforcement practices of a party complained against are not hidden in past treaties and arbitrations. The traditional sources of international law are treaties, customary law, and general principles of international law, a well as precedents and legal decisions.[68] International environ-

comparative exercise of the same kind has to be conducted in the three NAFTA countries to illuminate the issue of enforcement that NAAEC has put on center stage.

66. P.B. Downing and W.D. Watson, Jr., "The Economics of Enforcing Air Pollution Controls," (1974) 1 Journal of Environmental Economics and Management 219, cited in ibid. at 249.

67. Ibid., at 252.

68. Some authors add legal doctrine in the form of the "teaching of the most qualified publicists" of international law; see Article 38 of the *Statute of the International Court of Justice*, 26 June 1945, Can. T.S.1945 No. 7, 59 Stat. 1031, 145 U.K.T.S. 805; Birnie and Boyle, supra note 128, Part II at 11; and H.M. Kindred, et al., supra note 11, Part III at 109–110.

mental law relies on the same foundations.[69] One would be hard pressed to find clues in any of these sources as to what the "effective" enforcement of domestic environmental laws might be.[70] Moreover, the dispute settlement procedure, premised on economic harm, focuses on domestic behavior, not ecological damage, so that the principles found in international law precedents concerning transboundary pollution, for instance, would likely be ill-suited.[71] There are, however, such standards of due diligence in the enforcement of laws by public authorities in the administrative law of all three NAAEC parties. While it might be tempting to invoke these standards in presenting before a panel evidence of lax enforcement, a party will likely avoid referring directly to domestic administrative law enforcement standards for fear of creating different enforcement obligations for different NAAEC parties. In the face of this legal void, NAAEC comes to the rescue by elab-

---

69. For example, see A. Kiss, *Droit international de l'environnement*, (Paris: Pédone, 1989) at 49–65.

70. International conventions are replete with expressions such as "best available technology" (*World Charter for Nature*, UNGA Res. No. 37/7 (28 October 1982) at paragraph 11), "best practicable means" (*Paris Convention on the Prevention of Marine Pollutions from Land-Based Sources*, 21 February 1974, 13 I.L.M. 352), or "effective access to remedies" (*Rio Declaration*, supra note 72, Part III, Article 10). Few, however, have been refined and interpreted by judicial or arbitral decisions that would help define a standard of acceptable diligence in the implementation of international environmental agreements. To be sure, good faith attempts and due diligence in the implementation of treaties are considered to be customary international law. [Birnie and Boyle, supra note 128, Part II at 94; see also the 1970 *Declaration on Principles of International Law Concerning Friendly Relations and Co-operation among States in Accordance with the Charter of the United Nations*, UN GA Res. 2625, UN GAOR, 25th Sess., Supp. No. 28, 121, UN Doc. A/8028 (1971).] As well, most authors conclude that in current international environmental law, there is no need to show a guilty mind or a deliberate intent in order to establish that a country is in violation of its treaty obligations. [Ibid., at 142; Ian Brownlie, *State Responsibility* (Oxford: Clarendon Press, 1983) at 38–48; Brian Smith, *State Responsibility and the Marine Environment* (Oxford: Clarendon Press, 1988) at 15–20. Strict liability without the possibility of a defense of due diligence, however, would be imposed only in cases of extreme harm, such as the release of ultrahazardous or radioactive materials; see *Report of the ILC to the UN General Assembly*, 43rd Sess., UN Doc. A/43/10 (1988) at 68.] There is, however, no international legal standard of due diligence (especially not in the application of domestic laws and policies) that is specific enough to help define the enforcement obligations of NAAEC parties.

71. The more direct lineage of the dispute settlement procedure of NAAEC is with trade law, where one generally has to show only a breach of the obligation and some form of economic injury. See A.L. Springer, "Commentary: Due Diligence does not Exist as a Matter of Customary International Law" in Lang, Newhold, and Zemanek, eds., supra note 25, Part I at 199.

orating on what constitutes a breach of that obligation or, more precisely, on what does not constitute such a breach.

Effective Enforcement

To successfully challenge a party's enforcement practices under the Agreement, the complaining party must establish that the party complained against has engaged in a "persistent pattern of failure to effectively enforce its environmental law."[72] The discussion of this concept will be divided into three parts. First, the criteria of effectiveness will be investigated. Then the exceptions to the rule will be explained, as they appear central to the reasoning. Finally, some comments will be made on the notion of the "persistent pattern."

The Vienna Convention on the Law of Treaties suggests three approaches to treaty interpretation: *literal,* involving a preoccupation with the "ordinary meaning of the words"; *effective,* with a view to giving effect to the intentions of the parties; or *teleological,* relying on the aims and objectives of the treaty.[73] None of these approaches appear to the authors to bring improved comprehension to the study of the NAAEC obligation of effective enforcement.[74]

---

72. NAAEC, supra note 2, Introduction, art. 22(1).

73. *Vienna Convention,* supra note 7, Part II, art. 31; see also G.G. Fitzmaurice, "The Law and Procedure of the International Court of Justice: Treaty Interpretation and Certain Other Points" (1951), 28 Br. Y.B. Int'l L., at 1.

74. In this context, the use of the term "effective" seems to open the door to a number of different possibilities. Under a literal approach, effective enforcement could signify either initiating legal proceedings against all known offenders or punishing all offenders. The literal approach suggests that the intention of the drafters might have been to ensure maximum possible compliance with domestic environmental laws. On the other hand, a teleological approach (based on ascertainment of NAAEC's general aim and interpretation of the enforcement obligations in light of this aim) might lead to the conclusion that "effectiveness" entails solving the environmental problem addressed by the particular domestic environmental statute covered (or achieving the stated goal of the statute or the policy underlying it), or preventing the party complained against from acquiring an unfair competitive advantage. The reader will readily see the abortive nature of this interpretative exercise. The "clear" meaning of the text does not shine through the forest of possible interpretations the broadness of the language conjures up. On the other hand, given the intergovernmental and regional nature of NAAEC, we might reasonably expect the panels to rely on a positivist approach in fulfilling their task and not stray far from principles and rules deriving from the will of the three contracting states. Because formal preparatory documents are not available, due to the nature of the NAAEC negotiation process, the evidence of such a collective will lie mostly in the text.

Luckily, certain NAAEC provisions do come to the rescue, even if the range of possible interpretations will remain open until dispute settlement panels have had the chance to assess actual allegations of ineffective environmental enforcement. NAAEC offers guidance in two ways: first, a reference to effective enforcement in the initial sections, and second, a negative definition of effective enforcement through the exceptions to the rule—that is, what such enforcement is not.

Article 5 of the agreement, which was discussed in the chapter devoted to the commitments of the parties (Chapter 6),[75] appears to define effective government enforcement action although it does not specify that this definition is indeed applicable to the dispute settlement provisions of the agreement.[76] Appropriate government enforcement action is illustrated by an enumeration of examples ranging from "appointing and training inspectors" to "providing for search, seizure or detention," through "publicly releasing noncompliance information" and "promoting environmental audits."[77] Virtually all the elements on this list are part of the enforcement arsenal of public authorities in Canada and the United States.[78] Because the relative availability of these instruments is often a function of financial resources, Mexico, like most countries in the hemisphere, does not have at its disposal as complete an array of the listed enforcement measures. Nevertheless, the fact that the drafters chose to target a "failure to effectively enforce" rather than a "failure to enforce," indicates that a violation of NAAEC extends not only to plain nonenforcement but also to inadequate or insufficient enforcement. This choice of words belies a will to link enforcement to a result, and not only to formal procedures.

---

75. Supra notes 87–96, Part III and accompanying text.

76. Because of textual ambiguities, the possibility remains that effective enforcement as a general obligation of the parties and effective enforcement for the purposes of dispute settlement may not be the same thing. Although it might seem incongruous to have two different definitions of effective environmental enforcement—one as a general obligation and one as an obligation subject to dispute settlement—this interpretation could be supported by the wording of Article 45(1), which seems to differentiate between a failure to "effectively enforce its environmental law" and a failure to "comply with article 5(1)."

77. NAAEC, supra note 2, Introduction, art. 5(1).

78. The main instruments used for enforcing environmental statutes in Canada and the United States are fines, imprisonment, injunctions, the recovery of cleanup costs, and the personal liability of administrators and managers, as well as such "softer" mechanisms as monitoring, registration schemes, zoning laws, permits and authorizations, public disclosure, and the like.

In other words, a violation could consist of ineffective administration of environmental laws: fines that are too low, sanctions that are too weak, or prosecutions that consistently allow offenders to escape punishment are not instances of effective enforcement, even if enforcement proceedings take place. An extreme version of this argument would be that effective enforcement is really enforcement that successfully deters and modifies the behavior of environmental offenders.

While NAAEC enumerates specific enforcement *measures*, it makes no reference to enforcement *policies* such as the "polluter pays principle"[79] (despite its long history in international instruments) or the "precautionary principle" (despite numerous recent references).[80] Moreover, the criteria of effectiveness, while implying the achievement of some unnamed objectives, does little to enable the reader to identify which of the enforcement measures are most appropriate under which set of environmental, economic, and legal circumstances.

The only specific definition of a failure to effectively enforce environmental law found in NAAEC is a negative and indirect one; the drafters provided future dispute settlement panelists with two examples of conduct that *does not* constitute such a sanctionable failure: "A Party has not failed to effectively enforce its environmental law or to comply with Article 5(1) in a particular case where the action or inaction in question by agencies or officials of that Party: (a) reflects a rea-

---

79. This omission is particularly glaring since the polluter pays principle is a sound economic policy that tends to have beneficial trade effects by guiding policies toward the goal of true environmental cost internalization, diminishing trade and investment distortions, leading to a better allocation of resources, and helping solve the environmental competitiveness issue underlying the whole dispute settlement procedure of NAAEC. OECD Council, *Recommendation on the Application of the Polluter-Pays Principle to Accidental Pollution*, OECD c(72) 128 (1972); c(74) 223 (1974) and c(89) 88 (1989), 7 July 1989, 28 I.L.M. 1320; OECD, *Economic Instruments for Environmental Protection*, (Paris: OECD, 1989).

80. The precautionary principle refers to the idea of preventing a substance or activity that poses a threat to the environment from affecting the environment "even if there is no conclusive scientific proof linking that particular substance or activity to environmental damage." James Cameron and Juli Abouchar, "The Precautionary Principle: A Fundamental Principle of Law and Policy for the Protection of the Global Environment," (1991) 14 Boston College International and Comparative Law Review 2. *Rio Declaration*, supra note 72, Part III, Principle 15; Report of the Regional Conference at the Ministerial Level on the Follow-up to the Report of the World Commission on Environment and Development in the ECE Region, *Action for A Common Future*, Bergen, Norway, 8–16 May 1990), at 15; *UN Convention on Climate Change*, supra note 60, Part IV; International Law Commission, *Draft Articles on International Liability*, UN Doc. A/CN.4/428 (1990), Article 11; Birnie and Boyle, supra note 128, Part II at 95–98.

sonable exercise of their discretion in respect of investigatory, prose-cutorial, regulatory or compliance matters; or (b) results from *bona fide* decisions to allocate resources to enforcement in respect of other environmental matters determined to have higher priorities."[81] Because this *a contrario* definition is the only one provided by NAAEC, it should play an important role in the process of judging domestic enforcement practices. Thus, it is important to investigate the possible interpretations of expressions like "reasonable discretion" and "*bona fide* decisions."

Reasonable Discretion

The exception in respect of reasonable discretion identifies four types of discretion that might be exercised "reasonably" by a government in making its decisions with regard to enforcement actions: investigation, prosecution, regulation, or compliance. This innovative formulation invites prudence in interpretation when applied to international law.[82] Domestic precedents can provide some guidance about issues of dis-cretion. However, the importance of uniform treatment of all NAAEC parties prevents the reliance on such precedents when preparing a panel determination on the behavior of the party.

In all three NAAEC countries, discretion always remains an impor-tant factor in enforcement and compliance negotiations and proceed-ings because most discovered infractions do not lead to legal action by the regulating agencies and industries. Indeed, the widespread exer-cise of discretion is unavoidable,[83] because of legal requirements such as an exacting burden of proof,[84] as well as the important social, eco-nomic, and political consequences of the enforcement of environmen-

---

81. NAAEC, supra note 2, Introduction, arts. 45(1)(a) and (b).

82. Certainly, in the domestic context of both Canada and the United States, the phrase "reasonable discretion" has received considerable attention in administrative law treatises and judicial decisions. See, for example, Michel Bélanger, *La Responsabil-ité de L'état et de ses sociétés en environnement* (Cowansville, Qué.: Les Éditions Yvon Blais, 1994). See also *Just v. British Columbia,* [1989] 2 S.C.R. 1228; *Kamloops (City of) v. Nielsen,* [1984] 2 S.C.R. 2. It is unclear, however, how much, if any, of that domestic jurisprudence can be carried over into the international regime created by NAAEC. Again, the issue of different standards of review for different NAAEC parties creeps into the debate.

83. Martin H. Scheim and Frédéric Beauvais, "Environmental Law," in Y. Linton, ed. *Doing Business in Canada,*Vol. 3 (New York: Matthew Bender, 1993) at 34–200.

84. Traditionally, this is difficult to establish, particularly in Canadian environmen-tal law where it remains closer to the "beyond reasonable doubt" of criminal law than

tal legislation. Almost without exception, when environmental legislation grants broad discretionary powers to public authorities, it neither imposes clear duties on the minister or agency director nor suggests guidelines for enforcement action. The principal justifications for such vagueness include the protection of economic and political interests and the balancing role of governments. Also supporting the granting of broad discretionary powers are the necessity of adapting new technological and scientific developments and the difficulties in discharging the evidentiary burden a solid legal case normally requires.

In Canada in particular, the question of discretion in environmental enforcement has a familiar ring. As compared to the situation in the United States, litigation and prosecution under environmental statutes in Canada usually give way to so-called negotiated compliance. Even if mandatory rules stipulating coercive sanctions are the hallmarks of most environmental statutes, "strict liability"[85] is rarely fully imposed, and the relevant government will routinely negotiate a schedule of gradual compliance with polluters.[86] If a business generally complies with the terms of such an agreement, there will be no sanctions levied against it.

In some U.S. or Canadian statutes discretion is built-in: It is stated that the minister or the director of the government agency "may" impose sanctions and issue various orders.[87] Where discretion is not explicit, it is necessarily exercised *de facto* because the minister or director can always decide not to investigate a reputed environmental threat or not to take action against an offender. It is possible that this difference between explicit and implicit discretion will matter when a NAAEC panel has to determine whether there has been ineffective environmental enforcement by virtue of an unreasonable exercise of

a civil standard of the balance of probabilities; see *Reference Re S. 94(2) British Columbia Motor Vehicle Act,* [1985] 2 S.C.R. 486. See also: Ibid.

85. In Canadian law a "strict liability" offense means that there is no need for the prosecution to prove any intent *(mens rea)* once the guilty act *(actus reus)* is established beyond a reasonable doubt, leaving only the possibility of a defense of due diligence to the defendant; *R. v. City of Sault Ste-Marie,* [1978] 40 C.C.C. (2nd) 353 (S.C.C.).

86. K. Webb, "La lutte contre la pollution au Canada: La réglementation des années quatre-vingts" (Administrative Law Series, Law Reform Commission of Canada, 1988) 6.

87. As two commentators have remarked, in the case of Canada "most pollution control legislation is comprised of skeleton statutes which confer exceedingly broad discretion on the minister of the environment or on the administrative agency created to administer and enforce the statutes." Supra note 83, Part IV, p. 34-208-9.

discretion. A party complained against will certainly argue that when the government uses built-in statutory discretion to refrain from coercive action, it is, strictly speaking, enforcing (or at least implementing) its legislation and therefore acting in conformity with NAAEC. An interpretation of this sort by a dispute settlement panel would greatly reduce the intensity of the enforcement obligations of the NAAEC parties. In time, it could also influence legislators to recognize discretion more explicitly in environmental protection statutes. On the other hand, NAAEC does not recognize simply any "discretion" but only a "reasonable exercise of discretion" as the valid exception to the effective enforcement obligation. The mere exercise of statutory discretion by public authorities to negotiate compliance (or to do nothing) instead of launching legal proceedings against polluters does not mean that such discretion is *reasonably* exercised. A panel may very well decide, in reviewing the enforcement of such a statute, that explicit statutory discretion extends no special exemption for a government responsible for its enforcement.

Since the early 1970s, both environmentalists and business interests have tried to use the courts either to force environmental agencies to take action against alleged offenders, to prevent them from doing so, or to change regulatory decisions. While most of these cases have to do with a set of specific circumstances rather than patterns of administrative action or inaction, this treatment of discretion in domestic settings may bear some lessons for the NAAEC panels. In true Common Law fashion the Canadian courts, with some notable exceptions,[88] have maintained a tradition of judicial self-restraint in the field of environmental law and have been reluctant to review and quash ministerial decisions.[89] Relying on a classical definition of the separation of pow-

---

88. *Old Man River Society v. Canada (Minister of Transport)*, [1992] 1 S.C.R. 3 [hereinafter *Old Man River*] is the only major decision where the court forced the government to take action to implement environmental legislation (in that case impact assessment legislation was implemented) rather than quash a government action destined to enforce an environmental statute, as in *Re Metal Co. and MacFarlane* (1974), 41 DLR (3d) 161 (Ont. S.C.); and *Stein v. City of Winnipeg* (1975), 41 DLR (3d) 223 (Man. C. A.). It must be noted that the Canadian Constitution does not recognize and protect property rights as does the U.S. Constitution.

89. See *Heineman v. Adventure Charcoal Enterprises Ltd.*, 1 Canadian Environmental Law News, No. 3 at 4 (Ontario High Court 1972); *Nisga's Tribal Council v. British Columbia (Environmental App. Bd.)* (1988), 3 CELR (NS) (BCSC); *Re British Columbia Wildlife Federation and Nu-West Development Corporation* (1977), 72 DLR (3d) 381 (BCSC); *Re Pim and Minister of Environment* (1979), 23 OR (2d) 45 (Ontario Div. Ct.).

ers, they have, for the most part, reviewed the decision-making *process* rather than the *substance* of the decision.

In the United States, requests for judicial review of administrative environmental decision-making, occurring in a somewhat similar legal context, have met with mixed results, but the courts have generally been less deferential to public administrations.[90] According to landmark decisions, agency discretion must never wander into the "arbitrary and capricious," it must involve a "hard look" at the whole set of facts, and it must display a "reasonable choice within a gap left open" by the legislator.[91] Concepts of "substantial evidence," "clear errors of judgment," and the distinction between quasi-judicial agency, "adjudication," and quasi-legislative agency "rule-making" are also important for the American legal standard of judicial review of environmental enforcement decisions. Given the paucity of precedents at the international level, it will be interesting to see if NAAEC dispute settlement panels will pluck some analytical ingredients from this thick legal stew.

The opinion of the authors is that a party complained against must establish that its discretionary decision not to fully or effectively enforce the law is reasonable whether or not an allegedly ineffectively enforced environmental statute, regulation, or provision includes references to discretion. While reasonableness is an elusive legal concept in any context, the positive definition of effective enforcement in Article 5 might help interpret this exception. It provides that "[s]anctions and remedies provided for a violation of a Party's environmental laws and regulations shall, as appropriate, take into consideration the nature and gravity of the violation, any economic benefit derived from the violation by the violator, the economic condition of the violator, and other relevant factors."[92] These provisions clearly suggest that the legitimate exercise of discretion by the parties should be influenced by

---

90. See generally F.R. Anderson, D.A. Mandelker, and A.D. Tarlock, supra note 55, Part IV at 111–144. The possibility for the U.S. Congress to micromanage U.S. environmental agencies' activities and budgets and to directly affect the enforcement of environmental laws and regulations further complicates the interpretation of both the "reasonable discretion" and "bona fide resource allocation" provisions in the U.S. context. See supra note 155, Part III.

91. For example, see *Citizens to Preserve Overton Park v. Volpe,* 401 U.S. 402 (1971), *Block v. Community Nutrition Institute,* 467 U.S. 340 (1984); *Ethyl Corp. v. EPA,* 541 F.2d 1 (D.C. Cir. 1976); *Chevron USA, Inc. v. Natural Resources Defense Council, Inc.* 467 U.S. 837 (1984)

92. NAAEC, supra note 2, Introduction, art. 5(3)(a).

both the severity of the violation and the economic stability of the business enterprise concerned.[93]

Article 5 prescribes a basket of possible environmental enforcement measures including the "seeking of assurances of voluntary compliance and compliance agreements."[94] It further stipulates that government enforcement actions, in addition to the usual array of fines and orders, "include compliance agreements."[95] A stifling interpretation would be to the effect that negotiated compliance *is* effective enforcement. On the other hand, NAAEC's enumeration of a broad panoply of possible enforcement measures does not mean that every one of these policy instruments is a reasonable choice under each and every circumstance. On the contrary, since government enforcement decisions must be made "with the aim of achieving high levels of environmental protection and compliance," each specific context will help the dispute settlement panel determine if the action taken by the party is appropriate and reasonable.[96]

A preliminary analysis of the text of NAAEC suggests, therefore, that the panel will have much leeway in determining what constitutes a "reasonable exercise of discretion." Patterns of prosecutorial and investigatory inaction, as well as patterns of inadequate fines and sanctions, will remain suspect, especially if there is no attempt to come to some agreement on gradual improvement with the violators. Negotiated compliance arrangements that derogate from the strict letter of an environmental statute may indeed be considered to fall within the scope of "reasonable discretion" as set out in the agreement, depending on the attending circumstances. The introduction of a general exception, based on discretionary authority, to the obligation to effectively enforce environmental laws could constitute a significant chal-

---

93. This raises interesting issues with regard to the regulatory context in the country complained against. The stricter the regulations, the more severe the violation and thus the enforcement obligation. On the other hand, the "nature" of the violation may touch on the type and extent of ecological damage inflicted. If the criteria are legal, the regulatory regime is relevant when looking for effective enforcement. If the criteria are ecological, the regulatory regime is not relevant in making such an inquiry. Will a jurisdiction with a comparatively lighter regulatory burden be examined by panelists more severely than another where the amount of regulations to enforce is very large? This touches once more on the tricky notion of an objective standard of review for all three NAAEC countries.

94. NAAEC, supra note 2, Introduction, art. 5(1)(c).

95. Ibid., art. 5(3)(b).

96. Ibid., art. 5(1).

lenge to the idea that NAAEC imposes strict environmental enforcement action on the parties.

Bona Fide Resource Allocation

The second exception to the application of the NAAEC enforcement
provisions is for government inaction based on "*bona fide* decisions to
allocate resources to enforcement in respect of other environmental
matters determined to have higher priorities." This formulation is both
innovative and puzzling. It is unclear whether it means that a country
complained against can justify a poor level of enforcement activity by
explaining either (1) that the overall level of resources it can devote to
environmental protection is limited, (2) that within the environmental
protection envelope there is a set financial amount allocated to
enforcement, or (3) that within the environmental enforcement budget the government chooses other more important priorities than the
subject matter of the complaint. In fact, it would be hard to find a
domain of government action that is more completely protected by the
principle of national sovereignty than the internal budget allocation
process according to national priorities.

On the other hand, in a recent and interesting Canadian case, the
Supreme Court of Canada declared that while the decision to allocate
resources to a governmental department to undertake inspections (in
that case of fraying rock) was political in nature and beyond review,
the implementation of the decision and the reasonableness of the
inspections program was indeed reviewable. The Court considered
that all operational aspects, such as frequency, methods, and equipment had to amount to a reasonable scheme, given the nature and
scope of the risk involved, taking into consideration all surrounding
circumstances, including budgetary constraints.[97] This is precisely the
type of reasoning that a NAAEC panel might have to adopt: exploring
the limits of good faith and diligence of the government of a Party that
has made the decision to regulate the environmental impacts of a particular field of human activity; seeking to assess whether all reasonable
efforts are devoted to the effective enforcement of existing environmental laws.

The expression "determined to have higher priorities" does not seem
precise enough to guide a dispute settlement panel as would an objec-

---

97. *Just,* supra note 82, Part IV. See also, Larry A. Reynolds and David A. Hicks,
"New Directions for the Civil Liability of Public Authorities in Canada," (1992) 71 Canadian Bar Review 1 at 18.

tive standard. Rather, it appears to refer to the government's own determination (i.e., in its exercise of discretion). The inclusion of the qualifier *"bona fide"* is curious because it is to be expected that all decisions of government to allocate resources between priorities are made in good faith, with no desire to intentionally deprive environmental enforcement bodies of the resources they need. On the other hand, this wording could be construed to impose a high threshold of "environmental sincerity" on government action since the good faith requirement gives rise to notions such as true intent and primary motive that underlie government decisions. When a government adopts an environmental law that it knows it does not have the budgetary means to enforce, or when it transfers resources from, for example, effluent pollution control to solid waste regulation enforcement, considerations of good faith may come into play. Considering the fiscal restraint that characterizes the budget processes of all three NAFTA parties, it would be, to say the least, interesting to see how NAAEC panels consider the issue of *bona fide* allocation of resources.

The idea that states may not have all the necessary resources to meet their obligations and that some poorer states are ill-equipped to do so in comparison with wealthier ones has a rich history in international environmental law. Developing countries have often succeeded (and rightly so) in incorporating differential treatment for less-endowed states in environmental conventions;[98] in that sense, while all NAAEC parties have limited resources for environmental enforcement, the resource allocation exception concerns Mexico most directly. Its environmental programs are still severely lacking the financial resources necessary to enforce the new set of environmental laws and, particularly, the hundreds of new regulations and technical standards enacted since 1988.[99] In the NAAEC preamble the parties note "the existence of differences in their respective natural endowments, climatic and geo-

---

98. For example, Article 194 of UNCLOS, supra note 7, Part IV; Principles 6 and 7 of the *Rio Declaration*, Article 23 of the *Stockholm Declaration*, supra note 73, Part III; Article 2 of the *London Dumping Convention*, supra note 55, Part III; Articles 3 and 4 of the *United Nations Framework Convention on Climate Change*, supra note 60, Part IV; Article 16 of the *United Nations Convention on Biological Diversity*, 5 June 1992, Doc. UNEP/Bio. Div/N7- INC.5/4 (1992), 31 I.L.M. 818.

99. As Stephen Mumme convincingly argued: "[i]n 1991, total Mexican spending on environmental protection, including energy conversion programs for industry and vehicular transport, was US$ 1.8 billion, or $21 per capita. The Salinas administration has been effective in generating financing from external and multilateral sources and in focusing expenditures on priority programs like Mexico City's environmental reme-

graphical conditions, and economic, technological and infrastructural capabilities." It is obvious, however, that there were considerable political difficulties in formally branding Mexico a "developing" country and affording it differential treatment in NAAEC, particularly since at the time of the negotiations it was on its way to OECD membership.[100] This would have been a particularly sensitive decision if different treatment translated into lesser obligations for the Mexican government and relaxed enforcement obligations, including the controversial border area.[101] One of the safety valves to accommodate the obvious difference between the parties in enforcement capability could be the possibility of interpreting the provision on resource allocation differently for Mexico than for Canada or the United States. In such a case, for a poorer government this would mean lesser environmental enforcement obligations.[102]

Moreover, in the opinion of the authors, a most intimidating analytical minefield remains in the idea that Mexico, Canada, and the United

---

diation ($4.6 billion through 1995) and border infrastructure ($4.6 million through 1995), but it has fallen considerably short of matching commitments at the level of the industrialized countries. Concealed in the larger figures are very modest allocations to environmental enforcement. SEDUE's, now SEDESOL's, spending on inspection in 1992 was $2.1 million, or $0.24 per capita. Funding of SEDUE field offices along the U.S.–Mexico border scarcely covered salaries, much less operating expenses, for those handling inspections, data analysis, and enforcement. Preliminary indications suggest the situation has not changed substantially under the newly reconfigured administrative system for environmental protection." "Mexican Environmental Reform," supra note 19, Part I at 90–91. See also Tim Golden, "A History of Pollution in Mexico Casts Cloud Over Trade Accord," *The New York Times* (16 August 1993), A1.

100. See Paragraph 7 of the NAAEC preamble. The decision to adopt a uniform approach may, however, complicate the eventual accession to NAFTA and NAAEC of American countries that are even more devoid of environmental enforcement budgets and infrastructure than is Mexico, if the main text of NAAEC is to be kept intact in a future enlargement process.

101. In other environmental conventions and legal instruments, the principle of differentiated obligations for developing countries usually goes hand in hand with the principle of the greater responsibility of the developed countries for the environmental damage that has already occurred. Declaring in NAAEC that the United States and Canada have an overwhelming responsibility for the environmental damage North America has already suffered would also have been very controversial in both these countries.

102. In contrast some observers believe that the level of enforcement in Canada and the United States is a floor that Mexico will be legally bound to attain. See "Greening Free Trade," supra note 19, Part I at 113.

States should be subjected to a uniform standard of review of their enforcement performance. On the one hand, a number of the provisions open the door to an inquiry into the specific economic, institutional, and regulatory circumstances of the party complained against to assess diligence. On the other hand, a "just do your best" standard clashes with both the concept of equal NAAEC obligations for all and the principle of environmentally sound competitiveness underlying the whole dispute settlement procedure.

The distinction between the two above-noted exceptions could become unclear since the issues of reasonable discretion and good faith management of available resources are intimately linked. At worst, a significant easing of the burden placed on public authorities to effectively enforce their environmental laws could result from the limitations placed on NAAEC enforcement obligations on the basis of the exercise of reasonable, prosecutorial, regulatory, or budgetary discretion. At best, such limitations will enable a dispute settlement panel to take into account the practical realities of uneven environmental enforcement and calibrate its determinations and recommendations so as to make them more palatable to the national governments that would ultimately have to implement them.

Against this highly unpredictable background, the party pleading for a restrictive interpretation of the two exceptions to the environmental enforcement obligations will always have the luxury of invoking the customary principle of international law embodied in the maxim *pacta sunt servanda* (the general obligation to observe and respect one's treaties).[103] At the end of the day, the dispute settlement provisions adopted to insure the implementation of the environmental enforcement obligations must be given effect and cannot be disabled on an unsubstantive technical play of legal interpretation.

Persistent Pattern

In addition to dodging the two exceptions outlined above, a complaining party must also prove that there has been a "persistent pattern" of ineffective environmental enforcement. A persistent pattern is defined in the Agreement as a "sustained or recurring course of action or inac-

---

103. Article 26 of the *Vienna Convention on the Law of Treaties,* supra note 7, Part II states that "Every Treaty in force is binding upon the parties to it and must be performed by them in good faith."

tion beginning after the date of entry into force of this Agreement."[104] Lax enforcement practices that existed in Canada, Mexico, or the United States, prior to the coming into force of NAAEC, appear to be "grandfathered" by this wording. A complaining party could not build a case on the basis of a period of ineffective enforcement beginning at any time before 1 January 1994. The fact that enforcement patterns that might have existed up until 1 January 1994 will not be available to assist in a characterization of a "persistent pattern" for the purposes of NAAEC suggests that all three Parties might be held to similar standards starting on that date.[105]

Past enforcement practices, however, may well be available for comparison. Hence, if a panel decides that a "persistent pattern" is akin to a marked divergence from past practice in a given jurisdiction, rather than derived from a more objective international standard, then enforcement practices prior to 1 January 1994 may be offered as evidence in the demonstration of a current, persistent pattern of ineffective enforcement. Paradoxically, under such an interpretation, parties with spotty enforcement records prior to 1994 could end up with a relative advantage under the Agreement because a current pattern of ineffective enforcement would not constitute a decline in enforcement.[106]

Whereas use of the word "persistent" imports an element of duration over time, the meaning of the word "pattern" is less clear. The pattern of ineffective enforcement may be geographic, such as when a particular region is witness to spotty environmental enforcement. It may be legal, if a particular environmental law or regulation is rarely, ineffectively, or never enforced. The pattern may also be related to a distinct industry that is too often excused from its environmental obligations

---

104. NAAEC, supra note 2, Introduction, art. 45 (1). An initial draft of this provision provided that the legal trigger would be a "persistent and unjustifiable pattern of nonenforcement." See "Greening Free Trade," supra note 19, Part I at 110–111. As the author further noted, this implied quasi-perfection on the part of the enforcers.

105. The "persistent pattern" criteria could give rise over time to more objective standards than the two exceptions on discretion and scarce resources precisely because national idiosyncrasies and differences might already be captured by those exceptions.

106. In Canada, for example, some areas of environmental activity are regulated by both levels of government—often with similar standards and measures—which begs the question: What if a law is not enforced by one level of government because the other level of government is effectively enforcing its own statute in that area? Does that restraint constitute a "persistent pattern of failure to enforce an environmental law" under NAAEC?

under various laws. The language of NAAEC provides for all of these possibilities. Once again, dispute settlement panels would have to establish the ground rules as to which systematic pattern of lax enforcement persists long enough to violate NAAEC.

Assessment of the Obligation to Effectively Enforce Environmental Laws

While the implementation of the NAAEC standard is unpredictable because of the two exceptions to the rule and the requirement for a persistent pattern of ineffective enforcement, the emphasis on the international scrutiny of domestic enforcement practices could nevertheless have a double chilling effect on government regulators in the three NAAEC countries. First, the focus on effective enforcement could become a disincentive. Regulators might be wary of adopting new environmental laws and regulations if they are not certain to have the resources necessary or a clear commitment from official decision-makers to adequately enforce the new measures.[107] Second, with respect to existing laws, prosecutors and administrative agencies might hesitate to engage in thorough enforcement if they fear creating a persistent pattern of *effective* enforcement that they might be unable to maintain in the future.[108] As well, an opposite scenario could see a government that favors strong environmental regulatory enforcement deliberately set out to establish a high standard for enforcement, thereby binding succeeding administrations that might not be as committed to enforcing environmental regulations.

In light of the burden of proof on a complaining party, it is possible to get a clearer picture of the effective environmental enforcement obligations of the parties under NAAEC. The broad parameters are set out in Article 5 of the Agreement. The introduction of the reasonable discretion and the *bona fide* resource-allocation exceptions in the legal test for ineffective enforcement is likely to raise the burden of proof of

---

107. Some informal remarks to that effect were made by federal officials at meetings of the Canadian five-year review of the *Canadian Environmental Protection Act* in January 1994.

108. For example, until recent decisions, notably *R. v. Bata Industries Limited et al.* (1992), 7 C.E.L.R. (N.S.) 245 (Ont. Prov. Ct.), the sections of Canadian environmental protection statutes on administrators' and managers' personal liability for environmental damage were largely unused. Now provincial and federal authorities may have to decide whether to put those sanctions back on the shelves or to continue to use them increasingly.

the complaining party. If the exceptions are interpreted very broadly, it can be expected that the federal, state, or provincial governments would be sanctioned by a NAAEC panel only if they engage in conspicuous, protracted, and systematic nonenforcement of an environmental statute (in the absence of a remedial plan or a compliance agreement with the offenders). Even if the exceptions are interpreted narrowly, the task of convincing the dispute settlement panel to issue a determination condemning the enforcement practices of the party complained against might remain difficult. Moreover, the requirement for a persistent pattern will have two effects. First, it could leave only the most protracted and widely spread violations of NAAEC vulnerable to challenges by a complaining party. Second, requests for formal dispute settlement would only slowly percolate up the NAAEC system in the first few years of implementation, while the required systematic patterns emerge or are confirmed.

It can already be expected that NAAEC will be delimiting the margins of tolerable variations between distinct environmental enforcement policies, as much as an instrument for the harmonization of North American environmental practices. Unfortunately there are very few, if any, international legal precedents that shed any light on these matters. For this reason, the first panel awards will be critical in narrowing the broad definitions relating to enforcement and nonenforcement of NAAEC and in establishing general parameters for effective enforcement of environmental laws under NAAEC.[109]

---

109. Despite the relative inclusiveness of the environmental enforcement provisions, and because of the exceptions just surveyed, the obligation for the parties to effectively enforce their own environmental laws may not turn out to be very substantive. It is far less so than the specific obligations one usually finds in the "strong" international environmental treaties like the London Dumping Convention, supra note 55, Part III, or the Montreal Protocol, supra note 131, Part II. We must recall that the expectations of the NGOs that so influenced the environmental debate around NAFTA were very high.

Chapter 10

Sanctions for Noncompliance

Whether in atonement for making it difficult to condemn a party for a persistent pattern of nonenforcement or out of belief that public expectations are more easily met in the realm of sanctions, NAAEC's drafters ensured that the sanctions accompanying the enforcement obligations would be unusually fierce by the normal standards of international environmental agreements. NAAEC's dispute settlement mechanism provides that a party refusing to comply with a panel's final determination can be subjected to two kinds of sanction euphemistically called "monetary enforcement assessments" (or fines) and, as a measure of last resort, "denial of NAFTA benefits" (trade sanctions in the form of tariffs or duties higher than those normally allowed under NAFTA), if the party complained against refuses to pay the fine.[110] Despite Mexico's most emphatic objections, the environmentalist's demands for

---

110. Except when the party complained against is Canada, as explained in Chapter 11 of Part IV. Moreover, there is evidence that the final sanctions provisions of NAAEC are not as sweeping and biting as some U.S. negotiators had envisioned. See Scott Otteman, "Special Report: Near Final NAFTA Greens Text Narrows Scope of Original U.S. Proposal," *Inside U.S. Trade* (20 August 1993) at 1.

trade sanctions as an instrument of enforcement of NAAEC obligations were ultimately accepted, if partially, by the parties.[111]

Following a dispute settlement panel's finding of a party's persistent pattern of failure to effectively enforce its environmental legislation, the disputing parties may agree on "a mutually satisfactory plan, which normally shall conform with the determination and recommendation of the panel."[112] This is a remedial plan designed to cure the country's enforcement failures to the satisfaction of the complaining party and the dispute settlement panel.[113] If the action is mutually agreed upon and implemented to the satisfaction of both parties, the dispute settlement process ends there.

Normally, like most international dispute settlement arrangements, the NAAEC procedure is designed to provide opportunities for the disputing parties to agree on a solution without recourse to sanctions and further panel arbitration. There are, however, two sets of circumstances that may lead to the reconvening of the panel and the further continuation of the dispute settlement process. First, if the disputing parties do not agree on a remedial plan, either may request that the panel be reconvened.[114] Second, if the disputing parties do agree on a remedial plan, but do not agree on whether the party complained against is actually implementing the agreed upon plan, the panel may also be reconvened to assess the situation.[115] Each situation confers new responsibilities on the reconvened panel.

When there is no agreed upon plan, the panel, upon the request of a disputing party, "shall determine whether the action plan proposed

---

111. Mexico's initial negotiating position, like that of Canada's, specified that trade sanctions "were just not on the table." See Gilbert R. Winham, "Enforcement of International Environmental Measures: The North American Agreement on Environmental Cooperation" (Paper presented to the Institute on Global Conflict and Cooperation, UCSD, La Jolla, California, 30 September 1993).

112. NAAEC, supra note 2, Introduction, art. 33.

113. What is a "satisfactory action plan" in the context of NAAEC? It is yet another concept, the shape and content of which remain unclear for the moment. It could be a promise to engage in some of the enforcement activities mentioned in Article 5, or it could be a general promise to spend more on enforcement in the sector concerned. It could also be a very specific commitment by the party complained against to go after some major offenders who have been spared so far. In the worst instance, it could even be a reflection of the "quantitative approach" some favor in trade disputes, outlining quotas for prosecutions, convictions, fines, and other forms of sanctions.

114. NAAEC, supra note 2, Introduction, art. 34(1)(a).

115. Ibid., art. 34(1)(b).

by the party complained against is sufficient to remedy the pattern of nonenforcement,"[116] and will, within 90 days, approve or modify it, as the case may be, in accordance "with the law of the party complained against."[117] Thus, when the reconvened panel undertakes to establish an enforcement action plan, deference to the right of each country to choose and enforce its own laws once again remains paramount. The fact remains that a panel's decision can never in itself modify or preempt national laws in order to improve the effectiveness of its environmental enforcement.

When the parties agree on an enforcement action plan but disagree on whether the party complained against actually complies with it, the reconvened panel *shall* impose a monetary enforcement assessment, if it finds that the party "is not fully implementing the action plan."[118] The use of the word "fully" rather than "effectively" or "appropriately" suggests that the standard for action plan implementation is high and that less than thorough adherence to the terms of the remedial plan will be sanctionable by a dispute settlement panel.[119] The use of the word "shall" forces the dispute settlement panel to impose a monetary enforcement assessment on a party that refuses to implement the binding action plan completely (unless the parties can come to an agreed settlement).

Therefore, if an intractable dispute endures beyond a final panel determination on the matter of effective enforcement of environmental laws, the role of the panel then changes. It becomes the overseer of a process whereby the parties must agree on both a practical solution in the form of an action plan and on the implementation of that action plan. If the party complained against is unable or refuses to reach compromise, the panel first drafts a plan, with which the former must comply, and may accompany this plan with a fine. If the party complained against refuses to implement the plan, the panel *must* impose a fine.

---

116. Ibid., art. 34(4)(a).

117. Ibid., art. 34(4)(a)(ii); in addition, under Article 34(4)(b), the panel *may* impose a monetary enforcement assessment on the party complained against. See supra notes 25–30, Part IV and accompanying text.

118. Ibid., art. 34(5); it is important to note that under Article 34(3) a disputing party has to wait at least 180 days after an action plan has been agreed upon or established before it may request a panel reconvening on the basis of its faulty implementation.

119. The maximum delay for the panel decision is 60 days, or more if the disputing parties so decide.

Hence, under NAAEC dispute settlement, the first sanctions against a country that persists, despite the formal protests of another party, in not enforcing its environmental laws, come in the form of a monetary enforcement assessment. This somewhat new concept in international environmental agreements is premised on the hope that compliance will be enhanced not only by the threat of having to pay a heavy fine but also by the public nature of these sanctions. Such punishment, both costly and highly visible, is clearly a novel technique for international environmental behavior modification.

Fining Misbehaving Governments

The NAAEC has laid out the rules on the nature, the range, and the final destination of the monetary enforcement assessments under Annex 34 of NAAEC. Nevertheless, the dispute settlement panels will have great discretion in fixing the amount of the fine. The monetary enforcement assessments will be paid in national currency, up to a maximum of 20 million dollars (U.S.) for the first year after entry into force. For subsequent years, the fine becomes "0.007 percent of the total trade in goods between the parties."[120] This formula has three main implications. First, the maximum amount of fines will increase as the dollar value of trade between the NAFTA parties increases. This is entirely consistent with the environmental competitiveness rationale for the dispute settlement procedure: More trade means more severe punishment for parties who are improving their competitive position while persistently neglecting environmental protection. Second, the monetary ceiling will also be raised if new countries join the NAFTA trading area and the NAAEC system, unless this provision of NAAEC is amended or newcomers to NAFTA do not sign on to NAAEC. Finally, if dispute settlement ever goes this far, the maximum amount will probably be significant enough to give pause to a country bent on resisting a dispute settlement panel's determination that it is refusing to implement a negotiated or an imposed enforcement action plan.[121]

---

120. NAAEC, supra note 2, Introduction, Annex 34(1). In 1992, this percentage would have amounted to between 21 and 23 million dollars U.S., depending on the estimates. If domestic judicial practices in the environmental field are any indication, a high maximum amount for fines is not a guarantee either of consistent enforcement or of high fines being imposed often. While this would have been the logical choice, there is no evidence that the drafters intended the expression "between the parties" to mean "between the disrupting parties."

121. Another factor that may become important is that the fines are pegged to the U.S. dollar. Devaluation of the Mexican peso or the Canadian dollar against the U.S.

When determining the appropriate amount of a monetary enforcement assessment, the panel is instructed to consider "the duration and pervasiveness" of the failure to enforce, "the level of enforcement that could be expected of a party given its resource constraints," reasons given and efforts made by the party complained against, and "any other relevant factors."[122] The reappearance of good faith and explanations based on resource constraints at this "sentencing" stage of the dispute settlement process means that national characteristics and circumstances will, once again, be considered by the panel and may mitigate the sanctions for persistently ineffective environmental enforcement. There is no mention of the economic harm inflicted on the complaining party by the exports produced in violation of domestic environmental laws, even though, as has been explained, there must be a trade connection in order to engage the dispute settlement procedure in the first place. The competitiveness concern underlying the procedure is not rationally connected to the sanctioning process.

The fine is paid into a fund in the name of the CEC and will be spent, under the supervision of the Council, to improve or enhance either "the environment" or "environmental law enforcement" in the jurisdiction of the party complained against, in a manner "consistent with its law."[123] While funding specific environmental projects is relatively simple to organize, it is questionable whether the allocation of fine money to environmental law enforcement in the territory of the party complained against would be a realistic undertaking at all. No improvement in enforcement patterns in a given country is possible without the full collaboration of public authorities. A country that exhausts a lengthy international dispute settlement process and then pays a fine, would have to be quite intent on maintaining existing enforcement practices. How can one hope that such a resolute government would then agree to collaborate with the CEC, the fine collector, in improving environmental law enforcement within its jurisdiction? It seems more likely that any money collected through the monetary enforcement assessment would be spent on projects of environmental enhancement like cleanup, restoration, water treatment, infrastructure improvement, or reforestation. Even in those instances, the necessary collaboration between the party complained against and fined and the CEC may prove problematic.

---

dollar would result in heavier fines for the governments of those countries, if precedents matter when a panel decides on the amount of the fine.

122. NAAEC, supra note 2, Introduction, Annex 34(2).

123. Ibid., Annex 34(3).

Trade Sanctions: Denial of NAFTA Benefits

There is also the possibility that the monetary enforcement assessment will not be paid by the party complained against, in violation of NAAEC and of the dispute settlement panel's order. In this case two different scenarios are possible. Against Mexico or the United States, the complaining party (or parties) may impose trade sanctions on the other party's exports in the form of a denial of NAFTA benefits.[124] If on the other hand, the party complained against is Canada, there is no possibility of trade sanctions; a special non-trade-related sanctioning process is set up both under NAAEC and Canada's domestic law.[125] The special Canadian procedure is covered at length in the next chapter.

Lawful denial of NAFTA benefits by a disputing party may normally begin six months after the monetary enforcement assessment has been imposed, if no payment is forthcoming. No such delay is required in especially aggravating circumstances where the party failing to pay has already been fined or forced to adopt an enforcement action plan in the same dispute.[126] There is no reference in NAAEC to the legality of these trade measures under NAFTA. Nevertheless, both common sense and the residuary international law rule of the paramountcy of the later treaty mandate that trade sanctions undertaken in conformity with the NAAEC procedure would not be illegal under NAFTA.[127]

The complaining party may not impose trade sanctions in such a manner as to deprive the target party of all NAFTA benefits. Under Annex 36B, the sanctions are limited in two important ways. First, the amount collected must be grossly equivalent to the unpaid monetary enforcement assessment.[128] Thus, the complaining party may impose a

---

124. Ibid., art. 36(1).

125. Under ibid., Annex 36A; see infra notes 140–151, Part IV and accompanying text.

126. Ibid., art. 36(2). The special circumstances are the following: if the monetary enforcement assessment is imposed under Article 34(5)(b) following a determination that the party is not implementing the action plan *and* the panel had previously been forced to impose an action plan or a monetary enforcement assessment, *or* the panel has subsequently determined in further proceedings under Article 35 that the party is still not implementing the action plan. In this instance, there is no 180-day delay before the parties may impose trade sanctions on the party complained against if this party does not pay the fine.

127. For a discussion of the later treaty rule, see I.M. Sinclair, *The Vienna Convention on the Law of Treaties*, 2nd ed. (Manchester: Manchester University Press, 1984) at 93–94.

128. Under Annex 36B(1) the amount of the duty on goods may not exceed the lesser of pre-NAFTA levels or the Most-Favored-Nation rate applicable to those goods.

tariff on a class of goods but this cannot allow it to recuperate an amount of money "manifestly excessive" in comparison with the amount of the fine.[129] Second, under normal circumstances such a tariff cannot be broad-based. The sector it targets must be the sector in which the persistent pattern of lax environmental enforcement has occurred, unless this approach is not "practicable or effective." For example, ineffective enforcement of pollution control legislation may be restricted to a sector like pulp and paper or petrochemicals, in which case the NAFTA benefits would be denied in only those sectors. However, legislation mandating environmental impact assessment may be generally unenforced by the party complained against, in which case, it would be difficult to restrict the denial of benefits to a discrete sector. It appears that the assessment of practicability or effectiveness of trade sanctions is left to the complaining party.[130] The extent to which a complaining party can suspend the benefits it affords another party under NAFTA is measured by reference to the monetary enforcement assessment imposed by the dispute settlement panel. In other words, the scope of the trade sanctions is a function of the amount of the unpaid fine. This would indicate that the deniable benefits referred to are the tariff reductions provided for by NAFTA. This is seemingly corroborated by Annex 36B(1) on trade sanctions, which refers to "increasing the rates of duty on originating goods of the Party complained against."[131]

---

129. NAAEC, supra note 2, Introduction, art. 36(5). If the trade sanctions exceed the level needed to recuperate the amount of the fine, they probably become illegal under NAAEC but also under NAFTA, because the residuary rule of the later treaty would no longer protect the trade measures from NAFTA rules. Interestingly enough, the sanctioned party might be able to use both a NAAEC panel reconvening and a formal complaint under NAFTA to the Free Trade Commission asking for panel review under NAFTA in order to get the exhausted sanctions lifted.

130. Ibid., Annex 36B(2)(b). In principle, any combination of high or low duty rate and long or short period of duty collection might be used by the complaining party to recuperate the fixed amount set by the fine. Unfortunately, NAAEC does not provide for the money collected by the punitive duties undertaken under its rules to be put by the complaining party into the same CEC-controlled fund to which the monetary enforcement assessment will be paid. Since the trade sanctions are in force only long enough to collect the amount of the fine (which they would replace), it would have been a logical choice.

131. On the other hand, paragraph (2) refers to "tariff or other benefits" to be suspended. The implication of this language is that other NAFTA benefits such as the prohibitions on unnecessary import controls or technical barriers to trade could be suspended in case of a violation of the enforcement provisions of NAAEC. It is unclear how such a denial of nontariff benefits, which entails no direct compensatory exchange, would fit into the money-oriented scheme laid out in the other parts of the dispute set-

Once a complaining party has chosen to suspend benefits it affords a second party, the panel can be reconvened to annul such trade sanctions at any time. This would occur if the panel were presented with convincing evidence that the targeted party had paid its fine, or that it was fully implementing the action plan designed to improve its enforcement record.[132]

The Viability and Relevance of Trade Sanctions

As noted in the introduction, the merits and dangers of using trade sanctions to modify another country's environmental behavior are being hotly debated in the international community. In the opinion of the authors, without the benefits and the legitimacy of a multilateral or supranational process, unilateral trade action on behalf of the global commons or the environment of the exporting country, no matter how well-intentioned, is neither easily justifiable nor particularly effective. Many, however, do not share this view and conclude that domestic trade measures remain an important instrument of pressure on states where the environment is not sufficiently protected.[133] In this regard, the NAAEC provisions allowing trade sanctions and the policy choices embodied therein are illuminating in many respects. They may point the way toward the proper use of trade measures as levers to promote more sound environmental practices. NAAEC provisions are noteworthy in at least four respects.

First, there is a bilateral or plurilateral international dispute settlement process that delivers a panel determination, where NAAEC rules, negotiated by all parties, will apply, before any sanctions are allowed and without exception. As well, in contrast to old GATT rules the final report does not have to be adopted or approved by the Council to become an official NAAEC legal document. The trade sanctions may come at the end of the formal dispute settlement process, after consultations, after the possibility of Council recommendations, after the independent international panel's determination, after attempts to

---

tlement section of NAAEC. It would indeed be difficult to measure how long a nontariff benefit has to be suspended before the monetary enforcement assessment can be deemed to have been collected.

132. NAAEC, supra note 2, Introduction, art. 36(4).

133. See, for example, Steve Charnovitz, "Environmental Trade Sanctions," supra note 106, Part I at 805–807. See also the discussion at supra notes 98–116, Part I and accompanying text.

prepare and implement an enforcement action plan, after a disagreement on the plan or its implementation, and after a refusal to pay a monetary fine imposed by a panel. This stands in complete contrast to what is found in habitual national trade legislation, the provisions of the Canada–U.S. FTA, the GATT (old and new), and NAFTA, which normally allow a complaining party to impose countervailing or anti-dumping duties or otherwise deny trade benefits after it has made a *prima facie* case before a *domestic* administrative tribunal that such duties and denials are warranted. Under traditional rules, the trade sanctions are lifted when: (1) the dispute is resolved, or (2) when an international or binational dispute settlement panel determines that the domestic administrative agency or tribunal has erred in applying its own trade remedies and the party imposing sanctions accepts the determination—often months or even years after the initial imposition of a tariff. Because trade sanctions will be less readily available under NAAEC, they are less likely to become instruments of harassment at the beck and call of protection-seeking domestic industries. Moreover, trade sanctions under NAAEC may not have the same damaging impact on the targeted sector as would trade sanctions under NAFTA because the unpaid fine will act as a cap limiting the scope and duration of trade measures. In effect, this multilateral approach is more likely to attain its environmental objectives than is the adoption by national legislation of domestic recourses against "environmental dumping" through "green tariffs" (which have been proposed).[134]

---

134. One could argue that the application of a charge to offset a competitive advantage made possible by lax enforcement could be justified if the advantage were to be characterized as a subsidy. In such an instance, it would be countervailable under national law, based on GATT Article VI, if the "subsidized" imports caused material injury to domestic production in the importing country. Christopher Thomas and Greg A. Tereposky, "The Evolving Relationship Between Trade and Environmental Regulation," (1993) 27 Journal of World Trade 23 at 35. See also: C. Arden-Clarke, "The General Agreement on Tariffs and Trade, Environmental Protection and Sustainable Development," World Wide Fund for Nature, Discussion Paper (June 1991); K.S. Komorosky, "The Failure of Government to Regulate Industry: A Subsidy Under the GATT?" (1988) 10 Houston J. Int'l L. 189; T.K. Plofchan, "Recognizing Countervailing Environmental Subsidies," (1992) 26 Int'l Lawyer 763. See also the Tuna–Dolphin case I, supra note 33, Part I at para. 5.27, 5.32, which rejected this approach. In 1992, the U.S. Congress was presented with: S.984, the proposed *International Pollution Deterrence Act,* which would permit inadequate pollution controls and environmental safeguards (including inadequate enforcement of such controls and safeguards) to be considered as countervailable subsidies; S.1965, the proposed *Global Clean Water Incentives Act,* which would require the Secretary of Commerce to impose fees on imported products subject to or manufactured from processes that do not conform with the *U.S. Clean Water Act* stan-

Second, the intensity of the trade sanction will be limited and the damage suffered by the reluctant party complained against will not be proportional to the size of the market of the complaining party. Normally, wealthier countries with large internal markets, in particular the United States, can make more effective use of trade sanctions (or the threat thereof) to pressure their trading partners. It is axiomatic that under NAFTA, the larger a party's market, the bigger the club it can swing by denying access to that market. In the case of NAAEC, trade sanctions will be limited since the punitive tariff level and its duration are a function of the initial unpaid fine. This means, for instance, that whether the United States faces a denial of NAFTA benefits by Mexico (where, for now, in general, it sells less) or Canada (where, for now, it sells more) American exporters would be punished to the same degree. In Canada, the time required to collect the maximum amount will be shorter because more U.S. exports (in value terms) will be subjected to tariffs. In Mexico, the duration of the sanctions will be longer as fewer American exports will be targeted.

Third, it is important to place this legal experiment with environmentally oriented trade sanctions in the proper context so as to limit the expectations it might create. It provides an opportunity to replace trade sanctions in the broader dispute settlement context. After the preceding survey, it becomes clear that the eventual effectiveness of the NAAEC-sponsored sanctions system against ineffective domestic environmental enforcement practices is mitigated by a series of factors. The term "environmental law" is deemed not to include any system for the management of the harvest or exploitation of natural resources—a severe limitation on the subject matter of dispute settlement.[135] Two big exceptions are also carved out of the definition of ineffective environmental enforcement: the exercise of reasonable discretion or *bona fide* resource allocation decisions are deemed *not* to be instances of lax enforcement. Further, the amount of the fine (which would later determine the breadth of the trade sanctions) must take into account the resource constraints of the party complained against.

---

dards; and with S.59, the proposed General Agreement on Tariffs and Trade for the Environment Act of 1991, which would sanction actions taken under section 301 of the Trade Act of 1974 (19 U.S.C. § 2411) in response to "acts, policies, or practices of foreign countries that would 'diminish the effectiveness' of international agreements on the environment or plant and animal conservation." *Conflicts and Opportunities*, supra note 28, Part I at 92.

135. Supra notes 31–58, Part IV and accompanying text.

Essentially, this means that Mexico would probably be subjected to lower fines than would Canada or the United States. Thus, Mexico, if it refused to pay a monetary enforcement assessment could also face lower tariffs than could the United States, were the dispute settlement process to go this far. Additionally, a crucial point that underlines the intergovernmental nature of the process must be emphasized: The party complained against does not have to conform to the decision of a central body or to North American objective standards enforced by the panels. It need only change its behavior to the satisfaction of the complaining party. One must keep in mind that NAAEC contains provisions for the settlement of disputes between states, not for the supranational enforcement of multilateral standards on states. Even in the face of the most atrocious environmental enforcement record by one NAAEC party, no sanction is imposed unless the other two are willing to seek recourse. Clearly, the potential for behavior-modifying trade measures is therefore limited by the particular characteristics of NAAEC governance and its dispute settlement system.

Finally, the dispute settlement procedure of NAAEC is designed to produce an agreement between disputing parties long before a panel imposes a fine, let alone before trade sanctions are lawfully imposed by a complaining party. It is a convoluted procedure full of delays and meetings that repeatedly encourages the parties to settle before resorting to sanctions. Dan Esty assesses the sanctions procedure of the NAAEC in the following manner: "[w]hether this provision will ever result in penalties being imposed is rather doubtful. Given the layers of conditions and procedural safeguards, the threat of loss of trade benefits seems remote."[136] There are mandatory consultations. The parties will attempt to resolve the dispute at a special session of the Council which, for whatever reason, may even refuse to proceed to formal dispute settlement. Once such a procedure is initiated, the process may stop at any point if there is an agreement by the parties. The least one can say is that clearly the NAAEC rules give a fair chance to the party complained against.

After either a damning initial or final panel report, ample opportunity is given to agree on an enforcement action plan. A panel must then be reconvened to review the implementation of its final report and the action plan. Countries will usually be given six months to pay the monetary enforcement assessment before trade sanctions are allowed, creating yet another settlement opportunity that may, like all

---

136. "Making Trade," supra note 36, Part I at 9.

other such opportunities, involve the bargaining of other ongoing bilateral disputes unrelated to environmental enforcement. On the whole, it may take 18 months, or more, to proceed from the initial request for consultations to a final dispute settlement panel determination. It may take another nine months, or more, for the panel to impose a fine on a party refusing to remedy its enforcement violations, and an additional six months for the imposition of lawful trade sanctions by the complaining party. That is almost three years in total.[137] The only conclusion that can be drawn from this is that the NAAEC procedure is intended to generate settlements and relegates the use of fines and trade sanctions to extreme and perhaps improbably protracted conflicts.[138] Of course, while fears of dilatory tactics may be justified, it must be noted that the best international dispute settlement mechanisms seldom involve sanctions before a satisfactory agreement is reached.

Beyond procedural considerations, the trade sanction provisions of NAAEC betray a confusion of principles that undermines their coherence. On the one hand, a trade connection is required to initiate dispute settlement—implying that at issue are unfair competitive practices akin to dumping at the expense of the environment. The argument neatly follows the NAFTA admonishment against pollution havens. The competitiveness aspect is reaffirmed when the drafters choose to restrict allowable trade sanctions to the sector in which the environmental enforcement has been found to be ineffective. On the other hand, the imposed fines, as has been demonstrated, are not connected to the amount of economic injury caused by ineffective enforcement. What is more, the trade sanctions themselves, restricted as they are to the industry wherein ineffective enforcement is alleged, also are not connected to the injury, because they are proportional to the initial fine. NAAEC sanctions are not tailored toward effecting better environmental cost internalization, even though the motivation appears to be the preservation of a competitive, level playing field, and even if the threat of sanctions might promote a generally higher level of environmental enforcement. Unlike traditional trade law where the aim of

---

137. The 3-year figure is also used by Magraw, see supra note 2, Part I at 41.

138. A less generous interpretation is that trade sanctions are a form of compensation for an overall timid NAAEC: "by relying on such a weak form of international agreement (enforcing one's own law), the administration had to overcompensate by seeking strong remedies to ensure compliance." "NAFTA's Social Dimension," supra note 5, Part I at 60.

trade measures is, in principle, to restore the competitive balance, the NAAEC regime has to rely on an agreement between the parties and the successful implementation of an adequate remedial enforcement action plan because the trade measures it allows are intended to punish, not to correct.

While this formal aspect of dispute settlement is problematic, it may be persuasively argued that the absence of proportionality between the fines/sanctions and the commercial impact of nonenforcement of environmental laws has some merit. Indeed the decision not to mimic traditional anti-dumping remedies may lessen the risk of capture of the dispute settlement process by protectionist interests, seeking to have the highest penalties systematically imposed.

Chapter 11

A Special Regime for Canada

There can be no mistake about it: While all the other provisions of NAAEC bind Canada in the same way as they do the United States or Mexico, dispute settlement involves an altogether different set of rules for Canada.[139] There are two special sections in NAAEC that apply only to Canada. The first is Annex 36A, which exempts Canada from the application of NAAEC provisions on trade sanctions in the case of an unpaid monetary enforcement assessment. The second is Annex 41, which addresses the difficult issue of the implementation of an obligation to effectively enforce environmental laws in a relatively decentralized federation, where the jurisdiction over the environment is shared (and contested) between the federal and provincial governments.[140]

---

139. Presumably, new adherents to the NAAEC (Article 49) would be subjected to the general regime. Nevertheless, they may attempt to obtain the same special exemption from the denial of NAFTA benefits that Canada enjoys.

140. The United States is also a federation, but the parameters of the application of NAAEC to U.S. states were not established in an annex to NAAEC. Rather, they are set out in the Executive Order of the President regarding the CEC Secretariat. "The. . .document outlines procedures by which the executive branch will consult with the U.S. states on issues that arise under NAAEC that affect their interests. It commits the ad-

Canadian Domestic Enforcement and Collection

Scarred by a series of trade disputes with the United States, Canada, throughout the duration of NAAEC negotiations, sought to be exempted from the provisions allowing the application of trade sanctions. Accordingly, under NAAEC rules, there can be no suspension of NAFTA benefits (i.e., no trade sanctions taken against Canada) if it refuses to pay the assessment imposed by the panel.[141] Instead, Annex 36A entitled "Canadian Domestic Enforcement and Collection" constitutes a promise to create a procedure by which the CEC would acquire special standing before the proper Canadian courts to file the panel determination and take proceedings to enforce it "against the person against whom the panel determination is addressed"—that is, either an adhering provincial government or the Government of Canada. For matters involving the Government of Canada, the court of competent jurisdiction is the Federal Court. For the provinces, the courts of competent jurisdiction would be the provincial High Court or the Superior Court, depending on the province.[142]

Until the Summer of 1995, the only jurisdiction that had put forth a law to fulfill that commitment in Canada was the federal government.[143] This bill reflects the commitments undertaken by Canada in paragraph 2 of Annex 36A and the procedures selected therein. The procedure described in Annex 36A is as follows: After 180 days, if Canada fails to pay an assessment, the CEC may, at the request of the complaining party, file the panel determination under its own name before the proper Canadian court. Once filed, the determination becomes an order of the court. The CEC may then take proceedings for

---

ministrator of the Environmental Protection Agency to set up a governmental committee to provide advice on the implementation and further elaboration of the Agreement. A role of the panel will be to inform the states about dispute settlement proceedings or areas of implementation under the side accord which 'directly relate to, or will potentially have a direct impact on the states.'" "Administration to Stress Resolution of PPMs Under NAFTA Side Pact," *Inside NAFTA* (6 April 1994). See Appendix IV.

141. NAAEC, supra note 2, Introduction, Appendix 36A(3).

142. Ibid., Annex 36A(2)(d); in accordance with paragraph 6 of Annex 41, the monetary enforcement assessment is addressed either to "Her Majesty in right of Canada or Her Majesty in right of the province concerned." Provincial accession is governed by Annex 41 of NAAEC. See supra notes 152–177, Part IV and accompanying text.

143. *An Act to Amend the Crown Liability and Proceedings Act,* supra note 2, Introduction. See Appendix V.

the enforcement of that court order. Neither the proceedings nor the order are subject to domestic review or appeal. Any question of fact or of interpretation by the panel will be referred back to the panel, the clarifications and decisions of which will be binding on the court.[144]

Three aspects of this Canadian procedure need to be explained further. First, Annex 36A(1) states that for its purposes a "panel determination" means: "a determination . . . that provides that Canada will pay a monetary enforcement assessment; and a determination by a panel under Article 34(5)(b) that provides that Canada shall fully implement an action plan." This suggests that a panel determination can include *both* a fine and an order for Canada to implement an action plan.[145] This interpretation makes sense; interpreting otherwise the monetary enforcement assessment scheme, particularly in the case of Canada where it is the final sanction, would simply amount to recognizing a system of expensive authorizations for ineffective environmental enforcement. Also, the panel determination which, once filed, would automatically become an order of the Federal Court may be quite detailed. It would involve not only the payment of a fine by the federal government (or any Canadian government complained against) to the CEC but also specific instructions to the government to initiate certain types of remedial action. As noted earlier, there is no definition of "action plan," let alone one that is sufficient to remedy the pattern of nonenforcement in NAAEC. Yet, it would have to include some of the elements listed in Article 5 such as appointing inspectors, carrying out investigations, seeking assurance of voluntary compliance, requiring record keeping and reporting, or even initiating legal proceedings or issuing an administrative order.

Second, no one, including nongovernmental organizations, the complaining country, or the Canadian government itself, may intervene in the proceedings before the Federal Court. The Canadian implementation statute provides that, "no person or body may intervene in any proceedings" of a panel determination filing by the Commission.[146]

---

144. NAAEC, supra note 2, Introduction, art. 1 and Annex 36A(2)(a) to (h).

145. The difficulty here is that Article 34(5)(b) referred to in subparagraph (b) of Annex 36A(1) refers to a determination that Canada is not "fully implementing the action plan, in which case the panel shall impose a monetary enforcement assessment (. . .)." It does not mention a determination that a Party shall fully implement the action plan, as subparagraph (b) indicates. It is only in the following Article 34(6) that the panel is instructed to determine that the party complained against "shall fully implement any action plan."

146. Supra note 2, Introduction, Article 1-20.2(5). See Appendix V.

Only the panel itself may be called upon to explain and interpret its determination. A sweeping privative clause is included that prevents appeals, reviews, and proceedings before any court in the nature of "injunction, *certiorari*, prohibition, *quo warranto*, declaration or otherwise" on any ground, including "excess or loss of jurisdiction" by the panel or by the Federal court. This airtight legal cocoon appears to protect any proceedings related to the filing, determination, or enforcement of the order of the court at any stage. Such a radical shielding of the Canadian enforcement procedure from review by any higher courts may exceed what was required by the language of NAAEC and could be invalid by virtue of standards of Canadian administrative law. This would be the case, particularly if a NAAEC panel were clearly acting outside its terms of reference or if the Federal Court were ruling on matters patently beyond its jurisdiction.

Third, although the direct transformation of a panel determination into a binding court order in Canada does represent, at least conceptually, an encroachment of international law onto Canadian sovereignty, the practical importance of this encroachment could be diminished by the procedure through which panel determinations will be filed and court orders will be enforced. Indeed, it appears that Canada might be able to block the final stages of enforcement of a panel determination before its Federal Court, despite the claim, by some, of European-style direct application of the international panel decision.[147] There are two ways in which Canada might prevent the functioning of the direct sanctioning machinery, both involving governance rules at the Council of ministers, which is the governing body of the CEC.[148] All decisions of the Council are to be taken by consensus, unless otherwise indicated.[149] The Council would ultimately decide on a course of action following a panel determination against Canada and a persistent Canadian refusal to comply. NAAEC provides that "the Commission *may* file . . . a certified copy of a panel determination" in order to transform it into a Federal court order.[150] This decision requires una-

---

147. Saunders, John, "Canada Takes Euro-Style Approach to NAFTA: Analysts" *The (Toronto) Globe and Mail* (18 August 1993) B20.

148. It is also important to remember that in the first instance, under Article 24(1), the request by a complaining party to convene an arbitral panel must be approved by a two-thirds vote of the Council before arbitration may begin. Canada, like any other NAAEC party, can try, if it is the target of such a request, to convince another party to side with it and block the request of the complainant.

149. NAAEC, supra note 2, Introduction, art. 9(6).

150. Ibid., Annex 36(2)(a).

nimity, not a qualified two-thirds majority. Canada could thus veto, at the Council, any decision by the Commission to file the panel determination before the Federal Court. Moreover, even when the panel determination has been incorporated into a court order, further proceedings would be required to enforce it against the Canadian government. According to NAAEC, these proceedings "may" be taken by the Commission, but again the consensus rule would afford Canada the opportunity to block this decision at the Council.[151] Hence, though the legal conduit for the direct application of a panel determination against the Government of Canada now exists in the Canadian judicial system, the NAAEC procedure for using that conduit apparently necessitates Canadian approval. If the Government of Canada felt that a panel determination were unacceptable and wrong, it might be tempted to exercise its veto notwithstanding the inevitable political fallout.

Annex 41 and the Participation of Canadian Provinces in NAAEC

Canada is the object of a special set of rules that recognize the peculiar functioning of its federation. Because the jurisdiction over environmental matters, including enforcement matters, is shared between the provinces and the federal government (and because there are very few political and constitutional opportunities for federal override), NAAEC includes a special clause that grants a virtual veto to the Canadian provinces over the application of formal dispute settlement.[152] Even if the jurisdiction and the power to legislate over environmental matters is divided between the federal government and the provinces,[153] it is simply "Canada" that is bound under NAAEC. Both levels of government must take action to meet the effective enforcement obligations of Canada as a party. Provincial governments must, therefore, be in some way accountable in cases of systematic patterns

---

151. Ibid., Annex 36(2)(d).

152. In May 1993, the Canadian provinces, acting under the aegis of the Canadian Council of ministers of the environment, had put forward Draft Principles for federal–provincial implementation of the NAAEC that were even more restrictive of federal action than the NAAEC. See "Proposed Principles for a Federal–Provincial Agreement Regarding Federal/Provincial Relationships Under NACE," Meeting of the Canadian Council of Ministers of the Environment, 12 May 1993.

153. See S. Richardson and A. Beaulieu, The Implementation of the North American Agreement on Environmental Cooperation, in "NAFTA Law and Policy" (in preparation).

of ineffective environmental enforcement. Otherwise, NAAEC's objective of uniform, diligent enforcement would remain elusive in Canada. The Canadian government cannot, however, bind the provincial governments by signing an international environmental agreement.[154]

Annex 41 of NAAEC, entitled "Extent of Obligations" provides that: "Canada shall set out in a declaration a list of any provinces for which Canada is to be bound in respect of matters within their jurisdiction" (the Declaration).[155] In effect, the solution adopted by the parties to the difficult problem of competing jurisdictions amounts to a formal domestic accession procedure for the Canadian provinces.

The provinces insisted, under this formal agreement, that they control their own environmental fates and play, at the very least, a significant role in the management of the Agreement. Issues to be negotiated included a clear delineation of federal and provincial rights and obligations under the agreement as well as procedures for ongoing management of NAAEC. For instance, Canadian provincial governments wanted clearer guidance on their obligations to provide information, their participation in the dispute settlement procedure, their status and the extent of regional representation on any Canadian delegations, in the CEC Secretariat and on the JPAC of the CEC, as well as the National Advisory Committee (NAC).

The federal and provincial governments negotiated an *Intergovernmental Agreement Regarding the North American Agreement on Environmental Cooperation* in the Spring and Summer of 1994.[156] This Agreement seeks to promote further federal–provincial cooperation, to establish a mechanism for joint NAAEC implementation, and to define the respective roles of the two orders of government in Canada.[157] It binds the provinces to all NAAEC rights and obligations.[158] The Agreement also provides for the creation of a governmental committee to manage Canada's involvement in the NAAEC, including at sessions of

---

154. The federal and provincial governments, in the Agreement regarding provincial participation in the NAAEC (see Appendix VI) have thus agreed, in the Preamble of their agreement, that "nothing in this Agreement affects in any way the respective powers, status or jurisdictional authority of any of the signatories to this Agreement." On the state of the treaty power in Canada, see Hogg, supra note 126, Part II at 281–299; and *A.-G. Can. v. A.-G. Ont. (Labour Conventions Case)* [1937] A.C. 236.

155. NAAEC, supra note 2, Introduction, Annex 41(1).

156. See Appendix VI.

157. See *Canadian Intergovernmental Agreement Regarding the North American Agreement on Environmental Cooperation*, ibid., art. 1.

158. NAAEC, supra note 2, Introduction, art. 2.

the Council.[159] Under the arrangement, a Canadian province that seeks to use NAAEC to challenge the enforcement practices of a NAAEC party will normally be assisted in this matter by the federal government making appropriate representation.[160] In the case of a NAAEC party challenging a province's enforcement practices, it is understood that "the dispute settlement procedures be led and positions established by that province."[161] In general, the economy of the Canadian Intergovernmental Agreement reflects the importance of provincial environmental jurisdiction by acknowledging the provinces as essential partners for NAAEC implementation. The most important aspect of this Agreement however, is the decision of the provincial governments to formally ratify it by amending relevant provincial legislation.

The decision by the provinces to join or not to join will have an important effect on the rights and obligations of all three NAAEC countries with regard to disputes about environmental enforcement.[162] At present, only the Canadian federal government is bound and it can only invoke NAAEC's dispute settlement mechanism in respect of matters that would fall within federal jurisdiction in Canada. Once a sufficient number of provinces have joined the Declaration, both Canada's federal and provincial governments would have expanded, full rights and obligations under the agreement.

Canadian Complaints of a "Persistent Pattern of Failure to Enforce" in the United States or Mexico

In principle, Canada has the right to complain that one of its NAAEC partners is persistently failing to effectively enforce its environmental law.[163] In practice this right is the first one affected by the complete-

---

159. Ibid., art. 3. See also art. 4, which provides that at least one provincial representative will be included in the Canadian delegation to the Council meetings.

160. Ibid., arts. 6(1) and 6(2).

161. Ibid., art. 7.

162. This decision will also affect the capacity of the Commission for Environmental Cooperation to prepare a "factual record" under Article 15 following a submission by a Canadian nongovernmental organization or business enterprise. Paragraph 2 of Annex 41 declares that the Council will "take into account" whether the submission comes from a province that has bound itself to NAAEC. This reduction in the effectiveness of Canadian nongovernmental submissions mirrors that seen in official government action in NAAEC dispute settlement and would be caused by the same factor: lack of provincial support for NAAEC.

163. Under NAAEC, supra note 2, Introduction, art. 24(1) the general test for admissibility of a request for dispute settlement is the existence of an ineffective enforce-

ness or incompleteness of the Declaration. Canada may not request consultations, a Council meeting, or the establishment of a panel "at the instance, or primarily for the benefit, of any government of a province not included in the declaration."[164] This suggests that the Council will not entertain a Canadian request if a province which has not signed on to the Declaration is to be the primary beneficiary of that federal government complaint, whether or not that province has asked the federal government to act on its behalf.[165]

Moreover, even if Canada establishes that its request for the initiation of formal dispute settlement is not primarily for the benefit of a province that does not appear on the Declaration, it must make a further demonstration to access the dispute settlement procedure.[166] Annex 41 requires that the subject matter of the complaint fall in either of two categories: (1) that which falls within federal jurisdiction in Canada; or (2) that which would fall under provincial jurisdiction in Canada as long as provinces representing 55 percent of the Canadian GDP have joined the Declaration, and 55 percent of the industry in question is located in provinces that have joined the Declaration.[167] In other words, a Canadian request for dispute settlement would be followed by the determination as to whether the "matter" at hand would fall either under federal jurisdiction or under provincial jurisdiction "if it were to arise within the territory of Canada." If the matter is deemed to be under federal jurisdiction in Canada, the request is immediately receivable by the Council. If the matter is found, however, to fall within

---

ment situation involving "workplace, firms, companies or sectors that produce goods or provide services: (a) that are traded between the parties; or (b) that compete, in the territory of the Party complained against, with goods or services produced or provided by persons of another Party." See supra notes 12–19, Part IV and accompanying text.

164. Ibid., Annex 41(3).

165. This objective standard could prove an important hurdle if large provinces where Canadian industry and manufacturing is concentrated do not sign the Declaration. Canada has an economy where industry is, in general, concentrated in a few provinces and where specific sectors and resources are often concentrated in small areas. For example, in 1993 three provinces out of ten (British Columbia, Ontario, and Quebec) accounted for 85% of the dollar value of all manufacturing shipments in Canada.

166. A request for consultations under Article 22, however, is not submitted to further review once it is established that it is not made at the instance or for the benefit of a nonmember province.

167. NAAEC, supra note 2, Introduction, Annex 41(4).

provincial jurisdiction, as is likely, such a request is subject to further review before it is acceptable.

CHARACTERIZATION OF THE SUBJECT MATTER

This particular solution and the reasoning it requires (i.e., pretending the matter arose in Canada and then characterizing it as either federal or provincial) is problematic in two respects. First, the "matter" referred to in the NAAEC text is the allegation by Canada that another Party is persistently failing to effectively enforce its environmental laws. Yet, there may be no particular similarity between the relevant environmental management legislation of the three NAAEC parties. Thus, for example, if a party allows mining in a protected area, it may be difficult to properly characterize the issue as relating to conservation, waste and pollution control, or even environmental impact assessment. Second, in light of the porousness of jurisdictional divisions in Canada, even clearly circumscribed matters may not fall under the sole jurisdiction of only one level of government.[168]

It is also worth noting that Canada is responsible for characterizing the dispute and must state, in its written request, whether the subject matter under consideration would fall under federal or provincial legislative authority. This Canadian characterization can subsequently be challenged by the party complained against in order to block the Canadian request for formal dispute settlement. The CEC Council is empowered (by a two-thirds majority) to convene a panel and may entertain arguments about receivability if the right of Canada to request dispute settlement is contested.[169] As well, once Model Rules of Procedure are adopted by the Council,[170] it will be possible for issues such as the characterization of complaints to fall under the jurisdiction of the panel, thus allowing the Party complained against to raise them again as a preliminary objection. A party accused of a persistent failure to enforce might have an interest in establishing that the subject matter of the allegation falls under provincial rather than federal jurisdiction in Canada if, as is the case at present, this would render it beyond the reach of the agreement.

THE 55 PERCENT THRESHOLDS

One will recall that if the matter is characterized as provincial, the Canadian request for dispute settlement will be received by the Coun-

---

168. See generally, *Old Man River,* supra note 88, Part IV.

169. NAAEC, supra note 2, Introduction, art. 24(1).

170. Ibid., art. 28.

cil if "the provinces included in the declaration account for at least 55 percent of Canada's Gross Domestic Product (GDP) for the most recent year in which data are available." Moreover, "where the matter concerns a specific industry or sector, at least 55 percent of total Canadian production in that industry or sector [must be] accounted for by the provinces included in the declaration for the most recent year in which data is available."[171] The first arm of the test prevents Canada from taking a party to dispute settlement over a matter that would be "provincial," unless most of Canada's economy is represented by provinces that have signed the Declaration.[172] The second arm of the test prevents Canada from using the dispute settlement procedure for the benefit of specific industrial sectors located mostly in provinces not appearing on the Declaration. This second arm is likely to be more difficult to handle because industry-specific statistics are less accurate than aggregate provincial shares of GDP and might thus be more open to challenge. As well, the question as to whether the lax enforcement of some environmental laws is peculiar to a "specific industry or sector" as opposed to affecting economic activity or industry and business in general could prove delicate and complex.

U.S. and Mexican Complaints of a "Persistent Pattern of Failure to Enforce" in Canada

The ability of the United States and Mexico to invoke NAAEC's dispute settlement procedure against Canada is also limited by a set of special rules that mirror those limiting Canadian complaints toward the others. In areas of federal jurisdiction, Canada is immediately subject to the provisions of the Agreement.[173] By contrast, neither the United States nor Mexico can initiate enforcement procedures against a province unless that province is listed on the Declaration *and* the 55 percent thresholds of industry and provincial representation are met.[174] There are three main consequences of this provision for Canada's NAAEC partners.

---

171. Ibid., Annex 41(4)(b) and (c).

172. For example, in 1991, the province of Ontario accounted for 40.2% of Canadian GDP (while Quebec represented 23.2% and British Columbia 12.5%) giving it a virtual veto over Canada's right to take another NAAEC Party to arbitration over most environmental issues. Statistics Canada, *Provincial Economic Accounts, Annual Estimates,* 1981–1991 (Ottawa: Queen's Printer, 1993) at 15–23.

173. Other procedural and substantive conditions must also be met; supra notes 15 and 16, Part IV.

174. "No other Party may request a Council meeting under Article 23 or request the establishment of a panel or join a party under Article 24 concerning whether there has

First, no alleged provincial breach of the enforcement obligations can become the responsibility of the federal government if that province is not bound by NAAEC. In effect, it seems that a Canadian province that chooses not to opt into NAAEC may engage in protracted neglect of its environmental enforcement obligations without putting Canada in violation of its NAAEC obligations. In fact, given the language of paragraph 1 of Annex 41, it is doubtful whether the enforcement obligations created by Article 5 exist at all in respect of a provincial government until it accepts to bind itself to the Agreement.[175]

Second, until 55 percent of Canadian GDP is represented on the official Declaration, no dispute settlement can take on the issue of provincial failure to effectively enforce environmental laws, whatever the status of individual provinces targeted by the complaint vis-a-vis the Agreement. This means that if a group of provinces (or a couple of large provinces) refuse to become bound, *all* the Canadian provinces are shielded from the effects of Part Five of the Agreement on dispute settlement. Canada's obligations with regard to provincial behavior will not be enforceable under the NAAEC (even if that province has signed on to the Declaration) until the 55 percent-of-GDP threshold is met. This prompted Canada's Pollution Probe and the Canadian Sierra Club to remark that there is a "[d]e facto exemption of entire Canadian economic sectors (e.g. steel, chemicals, pulp and paper) from penalties for nonenforcement of environmental laws unless provinces representing at least 55 percent of Canada's gross domestic product sign the side deal."[176]

Finally, even if the province has signed on to the Declaration, and even if the 55 percent of GDP threshold is passed, at least 55 percent

---

been a failure to effectively enforce an environmental law of a province unless that province is included in the declaration made under paragraph 1 and the requirements of subparagraph 4(b) and (c) have been met" (NAAEC Annex 41(5)). As in the case of a Canadian complaint in an area that would be under provincial jurisdiction, the possibility is there for another Party to ask for consultations with Canada under Article 22, even if the lack of provincial adherence to the Agreement prevents proceedings from going any further.

175. If this reasoning is correct the provinces themselves are not bound by the obligations on private remedies and procedural guarantees either, until they sign on. The Government of Canada, however, incurs the obligation to meet NAAEC standards on its territory and remains bound in relation to these matters as well as enforcement of provincial decisions.

176. Pollution Probe/Sierra Club of Canada, Joint Press Release (14 September 1993).

of the production capacity of the concerned "sector" or "industry" must be located in the adhering provinces for dispute settlement to be initiated against Canada on grounds of ineffective environmental enforcement in that sector. The questions raised earlier about the particular wording and the methodology that would be used to apply such a test remain unanswered. The lack of adequate definition of the terms "industry" and "sectors" make the functioning of the special regime for Canadian involvement in dispute settlement under NAAEC unpredictable.[177]

Canada and Dispute Settlement Under NAAEC

Therefore the net effect of Annex 41 of NAAEC appears to be granting, until the Declaration is completed and ratified, the provincial level of government in Canada virtual immunity from the environmental enforcement obligations outlined in the Agreement, and, by the same token, to prevent the Government of Canada from resorting to formal dispute settlement in most instances. Provincial willingness to sign on to NAAEC by way of the *Canadian Intergovernmental Agreement* and the Declaration will restore those rights and obligations for the Government of Canada, in a measure proportional to its comprehensiveness. The 55 percent threshold puts pressure on the federal government to complete negotiations with the provinces in a timely fashion in order to give itself the same status as the other NAAEC parties with regard to dispute settlement under the agreement. At the same time, these provisions give the three largest Canadian provinces—Ontario, Quebec, and British Columbia—or a coalition of smaller provinces, a great deal of influence over the reach of the Agreement's environmental enforcement obligations in Canada.

Under NAAEC Canada has promised to "use its best efforts to make this Agreement applicable to as many of its provinces as possible."[178] At the time of writing, only one province, Alberta, had formally ratified

---

177. For example, is the "automobile industry" part of the "manufacturing sector," or is it the other way around? If Canada wants to initiate dispute settlement about enforcement in American paper mills, does it need to have 55 percent of the forest industry in general represented on the declaration of paragraph 1, or simply 55 percent of the pulp and paper sector?

178. NAAEC, supra note 2, Introduction, Annex 41(6). In principle, Canada could try to cast aside the provinces and send a declaration to the other parties saying that it is "bound for matters within their jurisdiction" without the permission of the provincial governments. In practice, it would be extremely perilous, in political and constitutional terms, for the federal government to make such an attempt.

the *Canadian Intergovernmental Agreement*.[179] Other provinces, Quebec and Nova Scotia in particular, have indicated their intention to ratify the *Agreement* and to appear on the Declaration, but it remains clear that implementation of NAAEC dispute settlement in Canada will not be fully underway until most provinces choose to be bound under the *Agreement*.[180]

---

179. At the time of writing, the *International Trade and Investment Agreements Implementation Act* had reached the stage of adoption by the Standing Policy Committee of the Alberta Legislature.

180. It is for this reason that Annex 41 provides that two years after the entry into force of NAAEC, the CEC Council will review "the operation of this annex and in particular, shall consider whether the parties should amend the thresholds established thereunder." See Annex 41(8).

Chapter 12

Assessment of NAAEC Dispute Settlement Procedure

One will inevitably harbor mixed feelings about NAAEC's dispute settlement mechanism. On the one hand, at the formal level the unprecedented has happened: NAAEC is more than a promise, a list of unenforceable obligations, or a new environmental cooperation forum; Canada, Mexico, and the United States have agreed to submit their judicial and quasi-judicial processes for enforcing environmental laws to multilateral, independent, and relatively binding arbitral panel review, thus transcending the well-known general reluctance of states to submit to third party decision-making.[181] NAAEC may not be an override, but it will directly and durably undermine the idea that environmental enforcement is a reserved domestic jurisdiction solely within the exclusive sovereignty of the parties.[182] There are real sanctions for violations in the form of stiff fines and even NAFTA-legal denial of trade benefits, following due process under NAAEC. In addition, NAAEC, as a legal tool for international environmental protec-

---

181. See X. Bilder, "An Overview of International Dispute Settlement" (1986) 1 Emory J. Int'l Disp. Res. 23.

182. This is not very far from saying that environmental *policy* is no longer a strictly sovereign matter within the NAFTA area.

tion, affords real opportunities to refine definitions of state environmental obligations and the notion of environmental protection, as well as to develop innovative rules for sanctions (in particular, trade sanctions) and flexible arrangements for federated states. Anyone who would have predicted such an outcome in 1990, when the NAFTA negotiations started, would have been considered, to say the least, overly optimistic.

On the other hand, the dispute settlement procedure remains lengthy, cumbersome, and full of legal uncertainties. Part Five of NAAEC is laced with constructive ambiguities in relation to definitions, obligations and exceptions, and the most controversial issues are left to dispute settlement panels, the determinations of which are unpredictable. While the difficulty of use might provide an incentive for negotiated settlement, it could also provide shelter for parties that do not live up to their environmental enforcement obligations. It is difficult to determine the extent of the obligations undertaken by Canada, the United States, and Mexico because neither their obligations nor the sanctions are explicitly related to health, property, or the environment. There is a characteristic that NAAEC shares with many earlier environmental treaties, despite its focus on economic impacts rather than ecological consequences: a lack of precise criteria for the determination of the level of risk and degree of potential harm as conditions of interstate cooperation and, eventually, dispute settlement. Rather, the enforcement obligation is only implicitly rooted in a notion of economic harm inflicted through some unfair, environmentally unsound way of obtaining a competitive advantage. Yet, neither the system of fines paid by the governments nor the imposition of duties on the exports of the party complained against seem a particularly appropriate way to allocate the environmental costs of polluting activities. The cost of the fines may well never be passed on to the polluting industries who benefited from lax enforcement. Moreover, even if the money collected through trade sanctions were paid by such industries, it would not go to environmental remediation but into the coffers of the complaining party.[183] The trade measures taken under NAAEC may become effective punishment and may even force the parties complained against to improve their enforcement practices, but such sanctions do not constitute a rational economic solution to unaccounted environmental costs.

---

183. NAAEC, supra note 2, Introduction, Annex 34.

Also, while conventional international environmental law bases compensation on material damage (even if there is a breach or a violation of obligations), the NAAEC dispute settlement regime does not require material damage before sanctions can be imposed. In that sense, this scheme resembles an international quasi-regulation rather than a compensation system like most international environmental legal dispute settlement procedures.[184]

Moreover, the trade connection requirement raises, as we have seen, some very difficult issues of equity and consistency. It is reductive of environmental concerns, it may promote better environmental enforcement in certain areas while not at all in others, and it does not adequately encourage environmental cost internalization. The differences between the provisions on public submissions available to NGOs and Part Five on government dispute settlement mirror the differences in the environmental motivations of both constituencies. NGOs want better protection of the environment for a variety of reasons, many of which have little to do with trade or the competitiveness of exports— such as the inherent aesthetic and spiritual value of nature, the rights of future generations, the protection of human health and welfare, and so on. Accordingly, under NAAEC, when nonenforcement is alleged by *an NGO* or other private party (and thus cannot lead to dispute settlement) there is no need to establish a trade connection. Yet, government officials, especially the trade officials who drafted the NAFTA and, in large part, the NAAEC, are very concerned with the impact of government actions or inactions on the price of traded or competing goods. In fact, they see environmental protection as primarily a trade and competitiveness issue: Environmental laws have to be monitored because (1) their severity may jeopardize hard-to-negotiate market access (thus justifying NAFTA's disciplines), and (2) their permissiveness may afford a country with an unfair competitive advantage acquired at the expense of the environment (thus the inclusion of NAFTA's Article 1114). This is why a trade connection is a *sine qua non* for the initiation of formal dispute settlement, the only procedure in the NAAEC that raises the possibility of sanctions. This difference in the written rules emanates in part from a real gap between the perceptions and motivations of government officials and those of the NGO community.

---

184. "State Responsibility and Liability," in Lang, Newhold, and Zemanek, eds., supra note 25, Part I at 192.

What is more, the decision to concentrate dispute settlement on the quality and the effectiveness of environmental enforcement may detract from the important task of evaluating and upwardly harmonizing the domestic environmental standards themselves. This choice may presage a further judicialization of environmental intervention, at a time when many are questioning this approach and promoting the use of economic instruments and incentives.[185] The American preference for litigation proceedings reflected in Part Five of NAAEC may not be any less commendable than the Canadian taste for protracted compliance negotiations, but it is important that nonlitigious approaches and a range of fiscal and financial incentives remain available to the governments of the NAFTA area.

Clearly, the importance of this precedent for the continent and the hemisphere is not completely diminished by the shortcomings of the text.[186] There should not be too much emphasis on the rule-based nature of NAAEC dispute settlement. Panel determinations, while operative within the environmental regime created by the Agreement, might be found wanting in the broad policy sense. Such determinations should represent encouraging precedents for the environment or the North American polity. Nevertheless, given the expectations it creates, NAAEC's dispute settlement procedure, despite its substantive and procedural weaknesses, will have to perform exceptionally well if it is to become a genuine source of environmental progress.

---

185. Menz, supra note 8, Part III at 10–20. "Instead of relying on regulators to specify appropriate pollution control methods, market-based policies such as effluent charges and emissions trading can achieve the same level of pollution abatement at less cost simply by changing the incentives that individual sources face." Menz, at 12–13.

186. For a more pessimistic account, see "Democratizing International Decision-Making," supra note 14, Part I at 725–726.

Part V

Conclusion

Our survey has shown one thing: The environmental content of NAFTA and the accompanying NAAEC is a complex and difficult issue where many questions remain unresolved. The meshing of trade objectives and environmental concerns in the design of rule-based international regimes is a necessary but nascent undertaking. For the most part, solutions remain best guesses guided as much by instinct and political compromise as by the import of older legal concepts from the environmental and trade domains.

One thing is certain. The environmental effects of trade-related growth, particularly in the border area, have proved a lightning rod for NGO criticism; had it not been for NAFTA it is doubtful that environmental issues would have received the attention they have. Indeed, if NAFTA had been defeated and not ratified, it seems clear that a rare, if not unique opportunity for moving continental environmental cooperation forward would have been lost.

An assessment of what was accomplished depends in part on one's point of departure. First, if one compares the NAAEC, hammered out in 1993, to the NAFTA itself, the former is not as strong a contribution toward environmental protection as is the latter toward trade liberalization. It is less ambitious and less constrictive of government conduct; it does not do for the objectives of sustainable development and environmental protection what NAFTA does for the principle of freer trade. Second, one may compare the whole package with what negotiators concerned with the rational integration of economic and ecological concerns (rather than with liberalizing trade) would have created. In that case, the NAFTA/NAAEC combination probably falls short of protecting and promoting environmental concerns as much as it could have (then again that premise may be flawed since NAFTA is a trade agreement, not an environmental agreement).[1] Third, if one compares the NAFTA/NAAEC package to other trade agreements such as the Canada–U.S. FTA or the Uruguay Round GATT agreements, there is a markedly increased level of environmental sensitivity. In both North American agreements, one finds an unprecedented degree of public commitment to the idea of greening international trade, and of rendering the NAFTA partners accountable for the environmental record of such agreements. Finally, if one wanders outside the realm of trade and compares NAAEC to other international environmental cooperation agreements, one finds that it belongs to the category of very specific and fairly coercive agreements—in no small part because much of its legal and institutional content is borrowed from that of trade agreements, usually more solid and better drafted. Moreover, early indications are that the NAAEC will likely belong to the rare breed of well-funded agreements endowed with efficient follow-up instruments. The draft budget for the last six months of 1994 was set at $2 million. It is expected to climb to $9 million annually.[2] It is plain to see that evaluating the environmental accomplishment of the NAFTA/NAAEC package is largely a measure of perspective and expectations.

---

1. Steve Charnovitz argues that NAAEC, in the end, was a rather weak agreement because "this important issue is being dealt with in the wrong context (NAFTA implementation), in a wrong time frame (quickly), and by the wrong people (USTR as the lead agency)." See "NAFTA's Social Dimension," supra note 5, Part I at 60.

2. 1994 Annual Program and Budget for the North American Commission for Environmental Cooperation, July 1994.

Such a relative assessment is compounded by the fact that both agreements have to be judged on the basis either of elements and principles too recent to have been properly tested, or on the environmental performance of their predecessors (like the Canada–U.S. FTA or the GATT agreements). Nevertheless, there are some lessons that can already be drawn at this early point from the NAFTA/NAAEC experience. We will briefly discuss such lessons in two distinct areas. First, the main arguments raised in the environmental community to challenge trade liberalization will be revisited to see what kind of answers are presented in the NAFTA/NAAEC package. Then, the political and legal consequences of establishing an environmental cooperation framework such as the one outlined in the NAAEC will be explored, both at a general level and in particular as these consequences bear on the ongoing process of hemispheric economic integration.

Chapter 13

NAFTA/NAAEC and the Environmental Agenda of Trade

NAFTA is by far the most important trade agreement planned, discussed, and completed during the 1990s, the high tide of the trade and environment debate (when NGOs and many government officials started considering that environmental implications were a central element of trade negotiations). It is also, as we have seen, a trade agreement that involves partners at very different levels of development. What is more, NAAEC is so far the only such environmental agreement specifically designed to complement a trade treaty—and the CEC it created is, for now, a one-of-a-kind institution. It is thus fair to ask whether the representatives of the three countries have succeeded in properly addressing the issues raised by environmentalists and other experts about the impact of liberalized trade on the environment. Let's recall from Chapter 2 the main environmental arguments against trade liberalization: (1) trade promotes environmentally unsound growth, (2) trade disciplines are a threat to domestic environmental measures, (3) liberalized trade and investment are vehicles for downward harmonization, (4) trade laws are obstacles to the use of domestic trade measures aimed at promoting the protection of the global environment, and (5) the lack of openness and transparency with trade rules and institutions is a critical problem.

Growth and the Importance of Political Leadership

Not surprisingly, the policy choice of NAFTA is unequivocal: economic growth *is* compatible with and probably necessary for improved environmental protection. NAFTA seeks to "increase substantially the investment opportunities in the territories of the Parties"[3] "in a manner consistent with environmental protection and conservation" while promoting "sustainable development."[4] This choice is affirmed in NAAEC as well. Among its objectives, there is an intention to "promote sustainable development based on cooperation and mutually supportive environmental and economic policies."[5]

Both NAFTA and NAAEC embrace growth and explicitly reject the proposition that it takes place only with increased environmental degradation. Yet, some environmental arguments that *support* freer trade are not really emphasized in the text, nor were they featured pre-eminently in the NAFTA debate. This omission is not reassuring because, if the NAFTA package is to be a benchmark for integration of liberalized trade and environmental protection, it should outline some of the principles of integration, rather than simply presenting the reconciliation between both objectives as an arduous and fragile compromise. One of these integrating principles is the positive impact that trade liberalization may have on resource conservation. A declaration in NAFTA and NAAEC that liberalized trade can and does favor more sustainable resource use would have been an indication that the three governments did not treat environmental progress as a "problem," an externality of the trade regime, but rather as a fundamental objective of governance. For example, there is no mention in NAFTA that undistorted markets are consistently the most efficient allocators of scarce resources, and it took the NAAEC text to make reference to economic instruments.

Steady growth may well result in increased financial resources being devoted to environmental protection and sustainable development—particularly in Mexico, where the NAFTA-induced growth could be the fastest and the environmental needs the greatest. There is no recogni-

---

3. NAFTA, supra note 1, Introduction, art. 102(1)(c).

4. Ibid., Preamble.

5. NAAEC, supra note 2, Introduction, art. 1(b).

tion, however, that the positive environmental effects of growth depend on the nature and beneficiaries of that growth. Moreover, at a practical level, an opportunity was probably missed by not providing specifically (and conspicuously) for improved market access for environmentally friendly products and services that provide better instruments for pollution prevention and cleanup.[6] This notion of environment-enhancing trade has been discussed for a number of years; it provides a concrete expression of the positive potential of trade liberalization.[7]

Nevertheless, the five year *history* of NAFTA has changed the face of the debate, probably for good. Most mainstream NGOs have a better sense of the imperative for trade and economic growth. Numerous proponents of free trade accept the fact that the social dimension of trade liberalization must be properly addressed, inside or alongside trade agreements, to produce significant, sustainable economic and social progress. In that respect, we seem to be moving away from the zero-sum game debates of recent years between environmentalists and trade specialists.

The Debate on Trade Disciplines

As was amply shown, international trade disciplines such as the ones found in Chapters Seven and Nine of NAFTA are often denounced by environmentalists as a threat to a sustained high level of environmen-

---

6. In 1992, the environmental market in six Latin American countries (Argentina, Brazil, Chile, Colombia, Mexico, and Venezuela) was estimated at $2.4 billion. See USAID, "Environmental Market Conditions and Business Opportunities in Key Latin American Countries," Business Focus Series (October, 1992).

7. The main difficulty with the idea of bringing down trade barriers in the area of environmental products and services is that the countries that have not yet developed native expertise and capacity in the field could lose the chance to do so. Since the environmental industry is often high-tech and high value added, a country like Mexico might find it unacceptable that the investments it has to make to live up to the environmental obligations of NAFTA and NAAEC would go even more frequently to pay foreign experts, services, and products. According to the OECD, the worldwide environmental market was estimated at a value of $200 billion in 1990 and will grow at a rate of 5.5% to a total of $300 billion by the year 2000. Mexico's market is projected to grow 15% per year during the early part of this decade. See OECD, *The OECD Environment Industry: Situation, Prospects and Government Policies,* OCDE/GD (92)1 (Paris: OECD, 1992). See also U.S. Department of Commerce, International Trade Administration, "Market Research Summary: 1991—The Mexican Market for Pollution Instruments Equipment and Services."

tal protection. The three parties counter that NAFTA trade disciplines can be calibrated to protect environmental laws from unwarranted challenges and foreign harassment (or at least this is what the negotiators have argued). As we have seen, taking into account all relevant aspects, the best available (albeit slim) evidence would suggest that they are right. Most environmental measures simply have no effect on trade or market access. Moreover, the fact that legal recourses are available to attack a neighbor's environmental legislation does not mean such actions will be lightly taken. Trade disciplines are not meant or designed to be applied systematically by a supranational authority.[8] In fact, the political price to be paid by countries bringing forth such challenges has steadily crept up as the debate on NAFTA's environmental impacts has unfolded.[9] As for NAAEC's contribution to the "taming" of trade disciplines, it is marginal, as its advisory mandate in the area of dispute settlement remains thin. Its very existence, however, provides a highly visible forum for discussing the motives and the actions of those invoking trade disciplines to challenge environmental measures. Harmonization committees set up under NAFTA (and possibly by the CEC) will offer states seeking to pressure their partners into loosening their environmental standards the opportunity to do it covertly rather than overtly, thus possibly avoiding public controversy.[10] Harmonization is an important area: Advocating full and vigorous effect to the anti-rollback provisions of NAAEC[11] and opening up the specialized harmonization process to expert NGO representatives could be very productive. Indeed it may be a greater service to the cause of environmental protection than calling for an exemption from NAFTA strictures on technical barriers to trade. While the legal safeguards to protect domestic environmental laws from trade disciplines may not be as comprehensive as needed, both the political context and

---

8. Although at the international level, in the new WTO forum, the ability of states to reject the findings of arbitration panels appears to have been diminished.

9. However, this has not stopped trade challenges to U.S. trade-affecting environmental measures from being brought by the EU. Two U.S. environmental laws were the subject of an EU complaint: the corporate average fuel economy (CAFE) penalties and the gas guzzler tax for automobiles. See "Green Roots, Bad Pruning," supra note 108, Part I at 302. See also: EC, Commission, *Report on U.S. Barriers to Trade and Investment,* (EC, 1993) at 19–20, 51–53.

10. See discussion at notes 143–159, Part II and accompanying text.

11. NAAEC, supra note 2, Introduction, art. 5; see discussion at notes 92–96, Part IV and accompanying text.

regular CEC sessions provide strong incentives against reckless recourses to NAFTA trade disciplines designed to challenge so-called unnecessary trade barriers.

There have been exaggerations about the relative importance of the issue of environmentally insensitive disciplines vis-à-vis other environmental impacts of international trade, such as harmonization mechanisms, institutional cooperation, investment flows, or the relationship with international environmental agreements. A lot of attention in scholarly and popular works has been devoted to allegedly environmentally unsound trade disciplines, in part because of highly publicized cases, in part because they symbolize bureaucratic third-party intrusion in areas heretofore reserved to national sovereignty. Such attention is sometimes but not always warranted. While trade and investment and the international legal framework governing them will have a lasting impact on the human environment and our efforts to protect nature, trade disciplines are not likely to be the dominant operative factor in that relationship. Issues like the impact of environmental policies on the business context, full cost internalization, ecosystem carrying capacity, investment attractiveness, competitiveness, and national priority-setting will probably be more important. The trade and environment debate and its resolution must include careful analysis of trade disciplines. However, it should not be derailed by an esoteric argument weaved around trade disciplines, projected on the international stage by the GATT Tuna–Dolphin affair, but ultimately of relatively little importance outside legal scholarship. After all, even if all environmental laws and regulations were exempted from NAFTA trade disciplines, most of the discussion of the environmental implications of the deal would still be taking place.

Market Pressures: NAAEC's Acknowledgment

The third argument was the claim that the mobility of capital would also put downward pressure on environmental norms because investors would systematically seek to improve their competitiveness by locating in the least regulated areas. This would create an incentive for domestic jurisdictions to establish deregulated or unregulated pollution havens where environmental costs are borne by the community, not the polluter. The intellectual debate on this complex question rages on, as the evidence is slowly collected on the ecological and economic consequences of patterns of trade, investment, and relocations. Nevertheless, the NAFTA/NAAEC package contains, as was demonstrated, an implicit recognition that trade liberalization creates some downward pressures on environmental norms and an admission that some safety mechanisms must be put in place to ward off this phenomenon.

While downward pressures on environmental norms upset both ecological and trade equilibria,[12] the negotiators displayed, throughout the NAFTA and NAAEC negotiations, a bias favoring the preservation or the reestablishment of trade equilibria as the main priority. This bias is rooted in the belief that the impact of environmental policies on North American trade are more worrying than the impact of trade policies on the North American environment. This explains why trade disciplines, while somewhat modified and politically sensitive to use, are still fully enforceable and the pollution havens/investment clause of NAFTA is not. Even more telling, the necessity of showing a trade connection to get a reprieve under NAAEC's dispute settlement procedure suggests that the drafters were mainly concerned not with environmental degradation but with the economic injury inflicted by inadequate domestic environmental practices affecting the price of competing goods (even if the obligation to effectively enforce environmental laws may also have positive ecological effects). This implicit acknowledgment by the NAFTA parties that the thoroughness of environmental protection is a competitiveness issue is very important. In fact, recognizing the environment as a competitiveness issue amounts to recognizing the central importance of adequate and relatively uniform cost internalization in open trade areas.

Overall, the solutions presented by the drafters of the agreements are somewhat half-hearted because not all three scenarios of competitiveness-driven environmental degradation are properly addressed. First, if a party caves in by lowering the environmental norms embodied in its laws (while still enforcing such laws) in an attempt to improve the competitive position of business enterprises already located on its soil, the rules of NAFTA as well as those of NAAEC are silent. There is no way to sanction such behavior, even if it threatens the environment and threatens trade equilibria as they currently exist. Second, if a party tries to attract new investment by lowering environ-

---

12. The notion of trade *equilibrium* is more useful than the notion of trade *fairness* because there is no objective measure of proper environmental cost internalization if all regional variations in economic and ecological circumstances are taken into account. A State that lowers its level of environmental protection changes the equilibrium and violates the principle of upward harmonization. It does not necessarily exceed the carrying capacity of its ecosystems or engage in "unfair" trade practices.

mental standards (again, while still enforcing its laws), NAFTA says it is an undesirable policy that ought not be pursued, yet it provides no enforcement mechanism.[13] Thus, only if a party lowers its level of environmental protection in competing sectors, not by weakening the laws but rather through ineffective enforcement, may another party initiate the protracted and convoluted dispute settlement process under NAAEC. Remedies would come in the form of a change of behavior of the party complained against, or the right to impose fines on that party, or, eventually, the right to impose trade sanctions on the offending goods.

The logic that underpins NAAEC's dispute settlement procedure is not carried to its conclusion. This logic is based on the economic (not the ecological) costs of environmental mismanagement in a liberalized trade area. Indeed, if goods produced in a jurisdiction where environmental laws are not enforced cause economic harm to NAFTA trade partners, so should goods that are produced in jurisdictions where environmental laws are simply inadequate. In both cases inadequate environmental cost internalization upsets trade equilibria. Yet the dispute settlement procedure does not allow challenges against environmental laws that are too permissive, only challenges against ineffective enforcement by a party. Consistency would have demanded that the anti-rollback provision of NAAEC[14] and the pollution havens/investment clause of NAFTA[15] also be enforceable. Such a rule would have helped to prevent trade competition from discouraging attempts at proper environmental cost internalization.

Additionally, NAAEC would not avail a remedy proportional to the injury because the nature of the trade requirement is formal rather than substantive. In other words, such a formal requirement provides no cure for the production cost differential between parties caused by tolerance of noncompliance with environmental laws. A substantive remedy could have been based on the competitive advantage afforded by the violation of the NAAEC enforcement obligation and on the difference between the effective environmental cost internalization realized by the disputing parties' respective environmental enforcement policies.[16] On the other hand, a full-blown sanctioning mechanism that

---

13. NAFTA, supra note 1, Introduction, art. 1114.

14. NAAEC, supra note 2, Introduction art. 3.

15. NAFTA, supra note 1, Introduction art. 1114.

16. This remedy would not, however, address the potentially more important question of the competitive advantage gained through a significant difference between the

seeks to redress instances of environmental dumping would probably be more vulnerable to capture by protectionist interests than would the current dispute settlement procedure, which will rely largely on shame. Nevertheless, devoid of such a legal instrument of economic measurement, NAAEC's dispute settlement procedure, as was demonstrated, would probably culminate either in fines that are not related to the level of injury (and probably not passed on to the exporting firms operating in the territory of the party complained against) or, ultimately, to trade sanctions that are not proportional to the advantage gained at the expense of the environment. Indeed, absent a substantive rule that links the eventual sanctions to the trade impacts of ineffective environmental enforcement, the economic rationality of the trade requirement in NAAEC's dispute settlement procedure remains in question. NAAEC practice may help solve the inconsistencies but since the *ecological* rationale for dispute settlement was not adopted by the drafters of NAAEC, the onus is on them to defend and develop the *economic* concern that is featured in that agreement.

In a more general sense, defining the environmental issues worthy of dispute settlement solely as unfair competitive practices is a reductive approach that relies on one of the seminal ideas of the 1980s: Nations are competing with one another for markets and investments, and international economic law exists simply to police and sustain that competition. While this study is not the proper place to take on this eminently debatable proposition, it must be recognized that this concept of interstate *competition* is at odds with the structure for interstate *cooperation* laid out in the rest of the NAAEC.[17]

Trade Measures and International Law

NAAEC ultimately allows trade sanctions by one of the parties in order to modify another party's environmental behavior; yet the heavy multilateral procedure and the unpredictable legal tests involved make it unlikely that the procedure will be used, thereby sending a mixed message on to the global trading regime. What is particular and unambiguous, however, is a system set out so that the trade sanctions come at the end of the dispute settlement process (not at the beginning). An

---

levels of protection and environmental standards of the disputing parties, not through a difference in enforcement practices.

17. Groupe de Lisbonne, *Limites à la compétitivité* (Montréal: Boréal, 1995); The Lisbon Group, *Limits to Competition* (Cambridge: M.I.T. Press, forthcoming, Fall 1995).

international panel decision comes before any sanctions. Such sanctions become legal only after the consultations, after the Council recommendations, after the independent international panel arbitral determination, after failed attempts to prepare or implement an enforcement action plan, and after the refusal by the party complained against to pay a fine. This process stands in complete contrast to national trade legislation within the framework of the Canada–U.S. FTA, old GATT, and NAFTA procedures, which usually allow countervailing and anti-dumping duties to be imposed by a complaining party at the beginning of a dispute. Under the usual rules, the sanctions would be lifted only months or years after the initial imposition of a tariff or duty. Because of that essential procedural difference, trade sanctions under NAAEC are less likely to be used for harassment. This multilateral approach is more likely to attain its environmental objectives than the national legislations creating a domestic recourse against environmental dumping through "green tariffs" and environmental countervail that some have proposed.[18] There are many reasons for such a state of affairs, but the main one is that, in the multilateral model, the party targeted by a trade measure has participated in the elaboration of both the environmental norm and the trade mechanism designed to enforce it. Given its advantages, it is well worth exploring whether such a multilateral approach could, without undermining current trade regimes, be extended to international environmental norms other than the effective enforcement obligation set under NAAEC.

Openness and Transparency

Finally, the NAFTA package's record is mixed with regard to the necessity of public access to the process and of more transparent proceedings, which are at the core of environmental NGOs' demands for GATT reform and better NAFTA design. This is so despite the fact that NGOs have played a significant and generally constructive role during the NAFTA negotiations, often from within the official teams, working groups, and advisory bodies.[19] On the one hand, NAAEC fails to extend new opportunities for public participation in NAFTA institutions and procedures through *amicus* briefs presented during dispute settlements

---

18. Supra note 134, Part IV.

19. "The NAFTA lesson here is that nongovernmental environmental groups can play an important role in shaping trade agreements without compromising the ability

or otherwise. Moreover, no access to pleadings or other documents filed in NAFTA trade disputes is provided, despite the legitimate demands of NGOs.[20] The only acceptable submissions on NAFTA trade issues proper are the general submissions that can be forwarded to the CEC Secretariat without any specific follow-up process.[21] The type of public submissions that could require a party to respond and lead to some reporting by the CEC (the factual record) have to be directly related to issues of environmental enforcement; other important issues are excluded, such as the environmental impacts of trade and trade rules, and the impact of environmental policies on investment flows and patterns.

On the other hand, as was discussed previously, the CEC structure and its practice could provide windows for increased communication with the outside world and a broader constituency of NGOs. Partly public Council sessions import an element of accountability. The NGO submissions process affords what could become a powerful instrument to prompt slow-moving governments into action. The will and the capacity to fully exploit these opportunities exist in the NGO community.

There are a number of areas where progress can be made without changing the NAFTA/NAAEC package, but simply by supplementing it. One such opportunity is the creation of an official observer status at the CEC, which would fill two important gaps in the institutional architecture. First, granting such status to NGOs that can contribute the most would certainly boost the credibility of the CEC, improve public access and input in the Commission's work, and align it with the most progressive international organizations. There are plenty of precedents for such observer status in intergovernmental bodies and some special arrangement may be tailored specifically for the circumstances of the CEC.[22] Second, another kind of observer status, one for states, might

---

of the parties to negotiate effectively. This experience provides the foundation for in-corporating additional nongovernmental environmental consultation into future trade negotiations." "Reconciling Trade," supra note 41, Part I at 386.

20. "Democratizing International Trade Decision-Making," supra note 14, Part I at 744–745. Robert Housman and Durwood J. Zaelke, "Making Trade and Environmental Policies Mutually Reinforcing: Forging Competitive Sustainability" (1993) 23 Envtl. L. at 545, 570. Daniel C. Esty, "Toward a Greener GATT" Int'l Econ. Insights (March/April 1994) at 17, 20.

21. Under NAAEC, supra note 2, Introduction arts. 10(6), 12(2)(d), and 13(2).

22. See the *Convention on International Trade in Endangered Species of Wild Fauna and Flora,* supra note 18, Part I; the *Basel Convention on the Control of Transboundary*

be very useful in the NAFTA enlargement process. It would allow gradual entry of other American countries into NAAEC and help them measure the nature and the extent of the obligations contained therein.[23] A simple way of bolstering the credibility of the NAAEC dispute settlement panel would be to accept *amicus* briefs from interested NGOs. NAAEC, under the relevant provisions describing what information panels may consider before rendering a determination, is silent on that issue. There is opportunity for proactive behavior on the part of the CEC. There is no decisive reason to exclude quality briefs by NGO intervenors on behalf of the public interest when they may help the panel make its determination (especially if the Secretariat would be at liberty to enact strict guidelines to prevent frivolous, vexatious, or unhelpful interventions).[24] Allowing such interventions has not distorted the domestic legal process in Canada or the United States, and it might provide invaluable added legitimacy to panel findings in the eyes of the North American public. While the current NAAEC rules are constraining, the panels should at least be encouraged to seek information from expert sources when appropriate, and parties should be particularly amenable where such requests for information are directed at NGOs.[25] Moreover, when a factual record in connection with the disputed matter has already been prepared by the Secretariat, it could be given adequate probative value in the proceedings. By so doing, it could provide indirect but tangible access to the dispute settlement process for NGO submissions that have been integrated into such factual records.

Movements of Hazardous Waste and Their Disposal, supra note 97, Part I; and the *Montreal Protocol,* supra note 131, Part II.

23. There should not be the possibility however of states acceding to NAFTA and avoiding their environmental responsibility by getting only observer status at the CEC.

24. Of course, there is also no valid reason to exclude such briefs in the NAFTA dispute settlement process when the dispute has direct environmental implications.

25. NAAEC, supra note 2, Introduction, art. 30; Michael Scott Feeley and Elizabeth Knier, "Environmental Considerations of the Emerging United States–Mexico Free Trade Agreement," (1992) 2 Duke Journal of Comparative and International Law 272.

Chapter 14

Redefining National Sovereignty in the Hemisphere

The historical episode of NAFTA and its side-agreements may profoundly influence future efforts to integrate trade and environmental concerns, as well as the kind of international environmental cooperation that will take place on the continent, in the hemisphere, and beyond. The lessons of the NAFTA debate and its conclusion are likely to endure for two reasons. First, the NAFTA/NAAEC package embodies a number of ideas presented as solutions to our environmental woes and the way that nations should collaborate among themselves to cure them. Many others are bound to adopt these solutions, or at least to attempt to mold some of North America's rules and instruments to their own circumstances. Second, beyond the particular details of the NAFTA/NAAEC package, the process of economic integration in the Americas seems to be firmly under way, with political decision makers sometimes leading the way, sometimes simply adjusting to changing economic realities, but almost always supportive of more integration. While this process remains unpredictable, NAFTA and NAAEC will more than likely be key instruments of its unfolding. Moreover, the NAFTA package remains *the* current experiment in meshing together trade and environment regimes.

Some Implications of the NAFTA/NAAEC Package

Three main ideas stand out in the treatment the NAFTA/NAAEC combination gives to trade and environment issues. The first one is the affirmation that differentiated environmental policies and practices, through their impact on competitiveness, may threaten valuable and important trade, investment, and ecological equilibria. This idea has been discussed at length previously and further elaboration would be superfluous. Nevertheless, such an acknowledgment constitutes one of the strongest conceptual contributions of the North American agreements to the current debate (even if the hard evidence to support either those who deny the linkage or those who see it as fundamental and pervasive has not yet been gathered). A second implication is the focus on the effective enforcement of *domestic* environmental laws as a central goal of *international* environmental cooperation. This concern with enforcement seems to be the main concrete expression of the fear of NAAEC parties that heterogeneous environmental practices within a liberalized trade area will skew the proverbial commercial playing field. The third idea that comes out of the NAFTA/NAAEC combination is expressed in the institutional architecture that was adopted by the negotiators. The creation of a parallel environmental structure comprising a ministerial-level Council, supported by a permanent Secretariat and advised by nongovernmental representatives has some flaws and many strengths.

Focus on Enforcement

The NAAEC displays a constant, unambiguous preoccupation with the obligation for signatory countries to effectively enforce their environmental laws. Of course, there is a direct lineage between the focus on enforcement in the NAAEC and the NAFTA debate that preceded it for three years. Most U.S. environmental organizations saw the 1988–1992 statutory reforms in Mexico as only a necessary foundation for a real quantum leap in enforcement. In that sense, since NAAEC is so much a product of NGO activism, the question was not whether enforcement was going to be a part of the side agreement, but rather how central it was going to be in the text. In fact, it is not without importance that the first provisions of NAAEC pertaining to environmental enforcement are found in Part Three, which is dedicated to institutional cooperation, not in Part Four, which deals with dispute settlement.[26] Since "[t]he whole institutional thrust of the CEC is pred-

---

26. NAAEC, supra note 2, Introduction, arts. 14–15.

icated on the premise that cooperation is the remedy of choice,"[27] the implication is that environmental enforcement, beyond dispute settlement, is a fundamental concern of the parties.

Once the link is established between the competitive position of parties (or firms operating within them) and environmental policy and practice, the equation is forged between effective environmental policy and effective environmental policing. In effect, NAAEC sets up a procedure for the international arbitral review of domestic judicial, quasi-judicial, and administrative enforcement proceedings under environmental legislation. Indeed, NAAEC focuses, first and foremost, on a commitment to protect the *domestic* environment of the parties (through better enforcement of environmental laws). This is very different than most international environmental agreements, which seek to establish "procedures aimed at avoiding or reducing environmental harm to other states or the common environment."[28]

The concern with the quality of environmental enforcement will have some positive impacts as it allows an investigation into the domestic practices of NAAEC parties that formally respects the NAFTA-reaffirmed sovereignty of each party to set the level of environmental protection it desires. NAAEC's dispute settlement procedure gives an international resonance to the public commitment made by a government when it adopts an environmental law; this commitment is no longer undertaken with only nationals watching but also with economic partners as witnesses. While this approach spares substantively inadequate laws, it is more palatable to all NAAEC parties, their politicians, and many important domestic constituencies, as well as to prospective new members of NAFTA and NAAEC. The erosion of national sovereignties will often occur more smoothly by increment than by spectacular leaps forward. Moreover, NAAEC may send a signal to environmental bureaucracies in the Americas that the public promise made by governments when they adopt a new environmental law or regulation should not be trivialized by a failure to implement and enforce such promises and laws. The governments of the NAAEC parties all have to contend with limited or severely limited resources for enforcement. The environmental challenges they face differ, often widely. In that sense, it is somewhat inevitable and probably desirable,

---

27. John Wirth, supra note 2, Part III.

28. "International Cooperation," in Lang, Newhold, and Zemanek, eds., supra note 25, Part I at 203.

that NAAEC recognizes governments' sovereign rights to adopt the environmental legislation of their choice. It may be even better that it contains the instruments to denounce and sanction those governments who would adopt such legislation when they do not have the will to achieve stated goals or the means of effectively enforcing the new laws.

The sharp focus on enforcement rather than the quality of the environmental statutes or the overall level of protection raises some serious problems. Enforcement is expensive and resource-intensive. Furthermore, weak laws or statutes overly tolerant of environmental damage are easier to enforce and may become more attractive, even if the environment would suffer as a result. Notably, there might be a chilling effect on NAAEC parties' environmental regulators unsure of their future capacity to enforce a new statute. There may begin a trend toward purely voluntary standards (unaccompanied by mandatory technical regulations) that governments do not have an obligation to enforce. Such a trend could obviously put into question the undergirding assumption of the NAAEC that most of the parties' environmental laws are generally adequate.

It is at this point that various other instruments, often more political than legal, must be used to prevent the NAAEC from becoming the alibi for a hemispheric environmental regulatory freeze. The process by which NAFTA applicants enter into preliminary discussions with NAFTA parties must involve an assessment of their environmental infrastructures and institutional capabilities. A country that does not have a department or ministry of environment and that is limited to minimal enforcement capabilities should not enter into NAFTA and subject itself to NAAEC, if it is not able to live up to minimal obligations. Moreover, political declarations and domestic policy adjustment that precede signing, ratification, and accession will be very important. In other words, NAFTA parties must seek and obtain clear commitments from eventual partners that they will strengthen their environmental capabilities up to a minimal ability to address their most important and pressing ecological challenges.

Furthermore, as was mentioned earlier, NAAEC also sends a signal about the proper means of implementing environmental policies. One could see a preference for a law-and-order approach managed by prosecutors and tribunals. Such domestic actors are typically more comfortable with all-or-nothing solutions than with the micro- and macro-level balancing of risks and interests involved in environmental policy. For example, the focus on traditional legal enforcement may undermine the use of instruments such as tradeable pollution permits that have begun to take hold in recent years. It is to be hoped that NAAEC's dispute settlement provisions do not have the final effect of narrowing the range of instruments available to the environmentally conscious governments who feel they must be able to "enforce," in a traditional manner, the standards adopted.[29] In fact, NAAEC recognizes the importance of economic instruments in its objectives[30] and in the mandate of the CEC.[31] The practice of NAAEC dispute settlement should reflect such recognition.

The emphasis on legal enforcement may come, as well, at the expense of other emerging or proposed principles of international environmental law such as the precautionary principle, or even of a principle of proportional compensation for economic injury caused by inadequate environmental cost internalization policies.

Even if more effective enforcement of environmental laws generally translates into better protection for the environment, ensuring such protection does not necessarily require tightening enforcement.[32] The drafters of NAAEC selected this particular solution (1) because the environmental laws of Canada, the United States, and Mexico were generally seen as adequate; (2) because enforcement was seen as a particular problem on the U.S.–Mexico border; and (3) because it is easier to reconcile enforcement standards with the principle of national sovereignty. It remains to be seen whether dispute settlement under the NAAEC will implement this approach effectively and

---

29. See "NAFTA's Social Dimension," supra note 5, Part I at 56.

30. NAAEC, supra note 2, Introduction, art. 1(b) and (i).

31. Ibid., art. 10(2)(d).

32. Indeed, as Nicolas Kublicki persuasively argued: "[t]he ultimate goal of the environmental side agreement should be to protect the Mexican environment, not simply to ensure Mexican environmental enforcement. In turn, the priority of Mexican environmental protection must be human health. Millions of Mexicans risk illness and death because they lack clean running water, sewage facilities, emergency planning and knowledge of environmental health risks. Nonetheless, many environmental advocates fail to recognize this primary purpose of the side agreement. They seem to assert that environmental enforcement itself is the goal of the side agreement, evidently assuming that strict enforcement is both the most effective and the most efficient means of environmental protection. While this may be true of developed countries such as the United States or Canada, it is not the case in developing countries such as Mexico. . . .Therefore, concentrated Mexican enforcement can only be justified as a budgetary priority if it constitutes the *most efficient method* of environmental protection—that is, if enforcement yields the greatest amount of environmental protection for human health per each additional peso appropriated for environmental purposes. "Greening Free Trade," supra note 19, Part I at 113–114.

whether it could accommodate a larger number of members from the developing Southern Hemisphere.

The NAFTA/NAAEC Architecture

It is difficult to adequately balance independence and proximity between a CEC governed by environment ministers and the Free Trade Commission headed by the trade ministers. Independence allows the creation of an autonomous voice for the environment, but it may relegate the CEC to the kind of supporting role with which many domestic environmental agencies and departments regularly have to contend. Proximity, on the other hand, makes for more direct channels between the CEC and trade institutions and a better chance to influence decision-making. However, there may be a price in the form of a credibility gap and some difficulty in expressing dissent with the pronouncement of economic actors. Facing this difficulty, the negotiators produced a promising compromise by making the CEC a political ministerial-level body and giving it a separate institutional personality.

More than the NAFTA Trade Commission (which is located in Mexico) the CEC will have the potential to develop scientific positions, devise legal strategies, and eventually generate guidelines and other so-called soft law instruments that can become binding rules related to substantive environmental matters. Despite references to harmonization, NAFTA remains a tool devoted to uprooting obstacles to commerce. The CEC created by the NAAEC, on the contrary, will be able to make positive recommendations, the impact of which will depend on their timeliness, the quality of the scientific expertise behind them, their compatibility with existing practices, and the authoritative quality CEC pronouncements may acquire over time.

True, NAAEC, like NAFTA, is an intergovernmental agreement that sets up a process for the management of obligations that member states undertake toward one another. It contains, however, the seeds of a more fundamental environmental obligation owed by the parties and their citizens to the North American community as a whole.[33] For

33. In fact, some observers of the NAFTA negotiations contend that "[f]or the United States, which has long resisted international organizational constraints on its sovereign prerogatives, and for a U.S.–Canadian relationship that has long avoided formal international organization, these NAFTA institutions represent a significant departure." "Bilateral," supra note 5, Part I at 75. C. Ford Runge is more emphatic: "[t]he CEC reflects incentives to develop transnational institutions, similar to those in the EU, that will be capable of overseeing environmental policies in all three nations. The critical question is whether these institutions will be able to successfully balance independent national policies with the need for oversight and enforcement. The fact that the new

example, the preamble refers to the conviction of the parties that cooperation is essential for the achievement of sustainable development and "the well-being of present and future generations."[34] For environmental groups, the conduit for NGO submissions allows nongovernment actors to monitor the parties' environmental efforts and to publicize the shortcomings. For individual citizens, NAAEC outlines obligations that the member states undertake to guarantee minimum access to environmental information and redress through the judicial system. Despite the fact that all NAAEC provisions are cast in the language of rights and obligations of states vis-à-vis other states, a broader humanistic commitment to the North American environment appears as a watermark through the innovative recognition of the role of NGOs and the environmental rights of individuals.

There are, however, potential weaknesses in the institutional setup created by the NAFTA/NAAEC package. First, the parallel structure centered around the CEC creates a distance. NAFTA, administered by the Free Trade Commission, remains a blunt instrument that can be used against environmental regulations and measures that impinge on the free movement of goods and services. NAAEC, on the other hand, does not grant a corresponding mandate to the CEC to oversee and to formally help to mitigate the potential impacts on the environment of NAFTA parties of measures taken to liberalize trade. In that respect, the CEC gets only an advisory role while being saddled with a mandate to oversee the quality of environmental enforcement in sectors where trade and competition occur (in order to preserve trade equilibria). Second, by avoiding the creation of a more independent CEC not headed by ministers, the parties have disappointed some environmentalists. Elected officials and members of Cabinets,[35] the argument goes, are bound by the pronouncements of their own governments and may be prone to play a more defensive role, trying to steer the CEC away from controversial issues (which are often the most pressing ones) and to slow down the NAAEC's implementation.[36] Third, others have

---

commission is the centerpiece of the environmental side agreement to NAFTA suggests that institutional authority for environmental impacts of trade integration is a real possibility, and that a separate instrument of policy aimed specifically at this target can be created." Runge, supra note 21, Part I at 96–97.

34. NAAEC, supra note 2, Introduction, Preamble, first paragraph; these elements are also present in the objectives of the Agreement in Article 1(a) and (b).

35. Unlike the Canadian and Mexican ministers of the environment, the EPA Administrator is not a member of the Cabinet of the President of the United States.

36. While in theory strong central institutions are good guarantors of the long-term stability and predictability of a rule-based system, we should be careful to differentiate

pointed out the exact opposite problem: Each minister of the environment can decide whether to attend Council meetings or send his or her designated representative. The danger in such a development is obviously that ministers could govern the CEC by proxy, thereby diminishing its visibility, weakening the authority of its pronouncements, and allowing NAAEC to gradually fade in a background of low-level bureaucratic activity.

Ministerial presence is a delicate issue. Most environmentalists want, at once, ministers who are actively involved in the Council, an independent Secretariat, and a CEC sensitive to public pressure. Complete independence from domestic governments is impossible because the CEC is a multilateral intergovernmental political body, not a supranational organization. The governments, through the Council, could effectively control the CEC and its works (no matter who the Council's active members are). The more the Ministers of the Environment are regularly and personally involved in the Council, the more the CEC will lose some autonomy, even if the Council has no inclination for micromanagement. Notwithstanding that risk, continued political interest in the CEC by Canadian, Mexican, and U.S. politicians is probably a condition for its sustained relevance, better funding, and more influence for its recommendations to the Free Trade Commission and the three governments. As two NGO spokespersons commented after the NAAEC was concluded: "[t]he value of the Commission's environmental work, however, is dependent on the political commitment of governments to allow it to act. Other aspects of the agreement, such as the work of the public advisory committee and the effects of citizen complaints, are also dependent on how willing the governments are in practice to candidly address and resolve environmental problems."[37]

The precedent has already been set by two trilateral meetings of the Council: First, an organizing session that took place in March 1994 in

---

between more autonomous central institutions and better area-wide central institutions. The environmental record of the EU is not necessarily better because the environment has ranked high in the European Commission's agenda for intervention. Kirton and Munton paint a vivid portrait of the pessimistic scenario: "It is more likely that any prospective Canadian–Mexican majority would be exercised in the direction of supporting national prerogatives and governmental discretion, given the even greater sensitivity about sovereignty and the less well developed network of ENGOs in the two smaller NAFTA countries. Further, any government that feels consistently outvoted or otherwise discriminated against retains the ability to curtail the operation of ACE by reducing or withholding financial support." See "Bilateral," supra note 5, Part I at 75.

37. Pollution Probe/Sierra Club of Canada, Joint Press Release, "NAFTA Environment Side Deal: Good Container, Little Content" (14 September 1993).

Vancouver; and second, the first official Council session, which occurred in July 1994 in Washington, both attended by Canadian Environment Minister Sheila Copps, EPA Administrator Carol Browner, and Mexican Environment Minister Rojas. After the Oaxaca (Mexico) meeting of October 1995, it is to be hoped that such a practice will endure.

An analysis of the institutional structure and relationship between NAFTA and NAAEC leads to two conclusions. On one hand, by piggybacking on a major trade agreement, NAAEC serves to strike at the core of the global economy–environment relationship. It also enabled the drafters to plug into the rich and solid tradition of international trade law to formalize and strengthen the rules for environmental cooperation and dispute settlement. All the while, the establishment of the CEC headed by a ministerial-level Council enables the environmental agenda to be addressed in its own right by an autonomous yet politically relevant institution. On the other hand, the awkward nature of the link between both agreements, the absence of substantive environmental provisions in NAAEC, and its limited scope indicate that trade agreements may provide poor framework conventions for more specific covenants on environmental and social issues (even if trade treaties negotiations provide the opportunity and incentive to discuss such covenants). In fact, it is NAAEC itself that could, through the continuing work of the CEC, act as an umbrella agreement for future specific protocols on transboundary pollution, minimum levels of specific contaminants, and other environmental issues.

The mandate of the NAAEC is broad in its diversity but it is also modest in view of the traditional list of grievances of the environmental NGOs with regard to international trade. That modesty may be due to a fear by officials that CEC activism might undermine the trade liberalizing agenda of NAFTA. It may also be a recognition of the limits of what a separate agreement could achieve on the trade front. Nevertheless, it is educating to look at what was *not* included in the CEC's mandate.

First, the NAAEC negotiators missed an opportunity to build on some of the environmental provisions of NAFTA (without amending them). The notion of NAAEC or part of NAAEC as a real environmental protocol to NAFTA would have provided an opportunity to clarify some ambiguous NAFTA language that had been criticized by environmentalists. In particular, the extent of the CEC's involvement with the interpretation and implementation of the pollution haven/investment clause of NAFTA Article 1114 is simply to "provide assistance in consultations." It does not specify further the nature of the obligation nor does it supplement it with a more formal dispute resolution process.

Moreover, the CEC can only assist the Free Trade Commission, identify expertise that may be called upon, and make recommendations on the prevention of environment-related trade disputes. As well, no explicit role is given to the CEC with regard to the necessary tasks of extending the lists of international environmental treaties recognized by NAFTA, and of developing criteria for such extension.

Second, beyond its advisory and monitoring role, no real trade functions are given to the CEC. It seems it will not have anything to do with changing or interpreting the legal disciplines on technical barriers and sanitary and phytosanitary measures, nor will it intervene in any dispute raising a challenge to a domestic statute under these provisions. The NAAEC makes no mention of the critical issues of so-called PPMs, with the exception of an obscure reference under Article 10(2)(m) to "the environmental implications of goods throughout their life cycle."[38] There is also no specific mention of environmental subsidies as a trade dispute issue. This is a serious omission, given that NAFTA does not address this matter, while the Uruguay Round negotiators considered it to be important enough to include relevant provisions in the final text. In short, the CEC was given very little responsibility on trade, with the notable exception of administering the convening of arbitral panels that may ultimately allow trade sanctions in the restricted area of nonenforcement of environmental laws.

Third, in the area of dispute settlements, while most bilateral disputes between Canada, the United States, and Mexico are of a transboundary nature, the dispute settlement provisions of the NAAEC do not at all touch the subject. This is a good example of how the NAAEC's implicit preoccupation with the environment, as a competitiveness issue, avails remedies for the *economic* harm, as opposed to *ecological* harm, caused by a party that does not effectively enforce its laws. There is no recourse for a pattern of ineffective enforcement of environmental laws that causes transboundary damage if there is no trade connection. Lax enforcement in one country can cause the pollution of

---

38. On the other hand, "The Environmental Executive Order on CEC Secretariat," puts at the top of the priority list the issue of PPMs. The order states: "[I]t is the national policy of the United States to promote consideration of, with a view toward developing recommendations and reaching agreement on. . .the environmental implications of goods throughout their life cycles, including the environmental effects of processes and production methods and the internalization of environmental costs associated with products from raw material to disposal." See *Inside NAFTA* (6 April 1994) at 12–13. See Appendix IV.

shared rivers or the atmosphere over its neighbor's territory. If the industry that pollutes does not export or compete with imports, there is no redress through formal dispute settlement under the NAAEC. If NAAEC were to have properly addressed transboundary issues, then it would have been fully in line with the intergovernmental nature of the document and its dispute settlement process. There was an opportunity to codify and build on a body of international law and North American precedents that dealt, albeit incompletely, with the issue of transboundary pollution. After all, the standard in transboundary pollution matters is also one of due diligence.[39] These international law recourses are still available but there seems to have been a conscious decision not to venture into that area during the NAAEC negotiations.

The difficult issue raised by these omissions is one that the environmental movement and the global trading regime have to face as well: Are environmental concerns better promoted by the creation of a separate environmental committee or institution or does such a separation undermine the agenda for making trade rules more environmentally friendly?

Economic Integration in the Americas

Trade liberalization and economic integration are, in the mid-1990s, the order of the day in the Americas.[40] While former U.S. President George Bush's 1990 description of NAFTA as the first step toward free trade "from Alaska to Tierra Del Fuego" may yet take a few detours and some time to materialize, there is a strong pattern of bringing down barriers to trade and investment in Latin America and the Caribbean countries. Outside NAFTA, there are four important and relatively successful trade initiatives involving the nations of the Americas: Mercosur,[41] the Andean Group,[42] the Central American Common

---

39. OECD, *Legal Aspects of Transfrontier Pollution*, (Paris: OECD, 1977) at p. 385 and ff.

40. There is little doubt that failure to ratify NAFTA, however, would have slowed down considerably the momentum of trade integration in the region. See "Greening Free Trade," supra note 19, Part I at 109–110.

41. Mercosur comprises Argentina, Brazil, Uruguay, and Paraguay, and is to become a customs union following an agreement signed in August 1994.

42. The Andean Group, which includes Bolivia, Peru, Ecuador, Colombia, and Venezuela, dates back to 1969 and was "relaunched" in 1988 with much success since.

Market,[43] and the Group of Three (or G-3).[44] There are also a large number of bilateral trade and economic cooperation agreements in the region. As well, the new Association of Caribbean States has indicated that it will seek to contribute to regional trade liberalization efforts. Bolivia is looking for association with Mercosur. Chile, long relying on a network of bilateral agreements, has manifested a similar interest in Mercosur in case its knocking at NAFTA's door remains unanswered. Other NAFTA hopefuls include, among others, Venezuela, Honduras, Argentina, and Trinidad and Tobago. The vision expressed in June 1994 by Colombian President Cesar Gaviria of "the Americas integrated from North to South" seems to be within the reach of committed governments.[45]

There are, to be sure, some significant roadblocks to American economic integration. Protectionist constituencies in all the countries of the region remain forces to be reckoned with. Many "special cases" involving currency and price controls (as in Venezuela), inflationary outbursts (as in Brazil), agricultural goods and export subsidies (as in every other trade area in the world) have recently caused tensions. Indeed, political leaders often find themselves besieged as the pain of adjustment often comes before the more diffuse benefits of increased trade. As well, the energies devoted to building regional and subregional trade alliances cannot always be harnessed for the benefit of larger arrangements. Moreover, the complex and sensitive nature of the political and cultural issues related to the social agenda of trade slow down progress and take aback many a trade negotiator. For example, a U.S. offer of something called "NAFTA parity" to Caribbean and Central American countries received a cool reception in July 1994.[46] As for Brazil, it has become a genuine "trading giant torn between its by now traditional trade diversification strategy and its newfound interest in the United States market which takes more and more of its high value added manufactures. [I]t may come to accept the environmental obligation of NAFTA as the price for moving closer to North America

---

43. The Central American Common Market has five members (Guatemala, El Salvador, Nicaragua, Honduras, and Costa Rica) and was also formally relaunched in October 1993.

44. The so-called Group of Three (or G-3), the most recent such initiative, is a partnership between Mexico, Venezuela, and Colombia that was sealed in May 1994.

45. "NAFTA Is not Alone," *The Economist*, (18 June 1994) 47, at 48.

46. "After NAFTA, AFTA?," *The Economist*, (13–19 August 1994) 13–14.

and expunging, thus, its terrible image as the burner of forests. Brazil has in the past been quick to condemn 'conditionality'."[47]

Nevertheless, as one commentator aptly put it, "the growing economic and social interaction in North America, although far from the daily headlines, is one of the most significant developments of our time."[48] The objective of making trade treaties and environmental protection policies more mutually compatible (for the benefit of both) must be pursued with renewed efforts in the face of this oncoming wave of change. This is where the existence and future development of the NAAEC, alongside NAFTA, become vitally important.

The momentum is obvious as witnessed by the flurry of activity surrounding the preparations for the mid-December 1994 Miami Pan-American Summit when President Clinton hosted the 34 heads of state and government from all Latin and South American as well as Caribbean countries.[49] The agenda of the Miami Summit was broadly divided into three parts: (1) Governance, including democratic development; (2) economic integration, including trade, investment, and possibly a general discussion of NAFTA accession; and (3) sustainable development, which comprises both *natural* environment issues and *human* environment issues. Early on, there was some discussion of a preparatory meeting of environment ministers in October to canvass the environmental agenda for the Summit.[50] No such meeting took place. Indeed, whether in the general context of sustainable economic development or in discussing the modalities of future trade initiatives like NAFTA expansion, environmental issues were expected to figure preeminently at the Miami Summit.[51]

In the end, environmental protection and the social agenda of trade did not receive much attention at the Summit. Again, it seems that U.S.

---

47. John Wirth, supra note 2, Part III.

48. Jeffrey E. Garten, "The Changing Face of North America in the Global Economy" (Address before the Americas Society and the Council of the Americas, 17 May 1994)[unpublished].

49. Only Cuba has not been asked to send representatives.

50. Ambassador C. Gillespie, "An American Perspective on the Summit of the Americas" (Address to the National Round Table on the Environment and the Economy Workshop on Advancing Sustainable Development at the Summit of the Americas, 11 July 1994) [unpublished].

51. As one White House official has said, "the environment will be a critical component of a broader sustainable development agenda for the Summit." M. Rentschler, "Memo to U.S. Non-Governmental Organizations" (Washington, D.C., 14 March 1994) [unpublished].

politics played an important role in influencing the treatment of environmental issues at the Summit, much like they did in NAFTA. The November 1994 congressional election weakened severely the Democratic party, which had championed the social agenda of trade. Elected were Republicans, who, even if in favor of trade liberalization, tended to prefer trade and environment "de-linked," NAFTA without NAAEC or the labor agreement.[52] What is more, the NGOs that had enjoyed so much political clout during the NAFTA talks were lacking both strong congressional allies and the mobilizing issue of the *maquiladoras*. In addition, most South and Latin American countries were much more interested in freer trade than environmental cooperation and did not want environmental references included in the final communiqué.[53] The final result was equivocal. The key decision was a commitment to creating a "Free Trade for the Americas Area" by the year 2005. The countries agreed to "strive to make our trade liberalization and environmental policies mutually supportive." The precise mechanisms leading to such an objective however were not concretely delineated. The other important announcement that surrounded the Miami Summit was the intention of Canada, Mexico, and the United States to enter into formal talks with Chile on NAFTA accession.[54]

After the Miami Summit, two great uncertainties persist with regard to the future of trade liberalization in the region: (1) Will NAFTA be the main instrument? Will the United States enter into a series of bilateral treaties with those countries that are now seeking access to its markets, or, alternatively, seek to enlarge NAFTA to include more Southern American nations? And (2) will the NAAEC be the key instrument for greening trade in the Americas? What are the proper means

---

52. It is also noteworthy that the U.S. *North American Free Trade Agreement Implementation Act* does not include, in its list of objectives for future NAFTA accessions, the goal of concomitant NAAEC accession for new NAFTA partners. See *NAFTA Implementation Act*, supra note 1, Introduction, at §108 (a)(5).

53. D.E. Sanger, "U.S. Envisions an Expansion of Free Trade in Hemisphere," *The New York Times* (8 December 1994) A7.

54. D. Fagan, "Chile to begin NAFTA Talks," *The (Toronto) Globe and Mail* (7 December 1994) B4. NAFTA accession is governed by Article 2204, which reads: "1. Any country or group of countries may accede to this Agreement subject to such terms and conditions as may be agreed between such country or countries and the Commission and following approval in accordance with the applicable legal procedures of each country. 2. This Agreement shall not apply as between any Party and any acceding country or group of countries if, at the time of accession, either does not consent to such application."

for addressing the social agenda of trade liberalization (in particular environmental concerns) as integration proceeds?

Multilateralism and Bilateralism

The United States, by any measure, towers as the hub of the economic and geopolitical system of the Americas. The United States is the biggest trading partner of most countries in the area. The actions and pronouncements of the U.S. government will be decisive in the next phase of economic integration—just as they were during the previous phase, the one that delivered the Canada–U.S. FTA, NAFTA, and NAAEC. Moreover, despite changing political times, the United States still is, much more than any other major actor in the region, the champion of the social agenda of trade, particularly its environmental component. The moods and idiosyncrasies of both houses of the Congress and the Executive branch remain, therefore, at the epicenter of the process of regional economic integration.

The United States has sent conflicting signals on the issue of NAFTA enlargement. The U.S. government is publicly committed to more trade agreements in the region (with Chile heading the list). Even if both NAFTA and NAAEC provide for the accession of new partners, many in the United States seem to favor bilateral agreements, especially those politicians who are skeptical of the NAAEC. Overall the approach is cautious and for good reason: The passage of NAFTA cost the Clinton administration dearly in political capital, the ratification of the new GATT and the WTO has proved tricky, and even those pushing for more free trade agreements admit it may take a while for U.S. industry, labor, and environmental NGOs to digest NAFTA, let alone take another mouthful.[55]

There are indications that the United States will, in the end, choose the multilateral route of enlarging the membership of NAFTA. The U.S. administration is clearly on record as supporting the establishment of a Pan-American trading area. Officials have been formally mandated to advise the President on the optimal approach to move beyond NAFTA and into discussions of a regional multilateral trade area.[56] Representatives of the U.S. governments have suggested a "building block" or

---

55. On the other hand, Chile has an economy 100 times smaller than that of the United States, and most of its exports to the United States are already duty-free.

56. In December 1993, the U.S. Trade Representative was mandated to report on the best strategy and pace to follow. U.S. NAFTA implementing legislation called for a 1 May 1994 deadline for USTR to report to the President and Congress on post-NAFTA

"step-by-step" approach for the numerous countries where the economy is not sufficiently developed and the labor and environmental reform efforts have not progressed sufficiently to allow them to live up to NAFTA package obligations.[57] Such suggestions lead to the concept of "associate" or "candidate" membership on a ladder that eventually may end with full NAFTA status. These expositions by high officials clearly indicate the interest of the U.S. government in building on existing agreements through NAFTA expansion. In addition, with every newcomer the NAFTA package would crystallize a little more and be presented "as is" to applicants, thus simplifying the accession process.

It is easy to see, however, why the so-called "hub-and-spoke" approach, a series of bilateral agreements with either individual Latin American countries or subregional trade groups like Mercosur or the G-3, can be attractive for U.S. policy-makers. In such circumstances, the negotiating power of the United States is undiluted. It can freely choose among the applicants, and could decide what kind of agreements and compromises it wants on trade, investment, and the social agenda issues (with the possibility of varying from the parameters of NAFTA and NAAEC). Moreover, Mexico and Canada would not be present to run interference or complicate the discussions with their own agenda. Many think it also would consecrate and reinforce the American position as the economic center of the hemisphere, making it the obligatory gateway for trade and investment. This view has been expressed by many important U.S. policy-makers. Clearly, the bilateral route would put a cloud of uncertainty over the NAAEC, as well as over any effort to integrate environmental concerns with trade negotiations. In 1992 some NGO representatives could claim that a new agreement with Chile would allow for strengthened environmental provisions. In 1995, however, the desire of House Minority Leader Rep. Richard A. Gephart that NAFTA be the "floor for any future negotiations" linking trade and environment seems largely unattainable without going the NAFTA route.[58]

---

scenarios, and a 1 July 1994 deadline for the President to recommend to the Congress a "list" of countries with which discussion should begin.

57. M. Kantor, Address (Georgetown University Law Center, 21 January 1994) [unpublished]; J.E. Garten, Address (*Consejo Profesional de Ciebdas Economicas,* 25 March 1994) [unpublished].

58. J.M. Goshko and P. Bher, "34 Hemispheric Leaders to Seek Free Trade Pact," *Washington Post* (8 December 1994) A31 at A42

Other governments have also been somewhat at odds over the nature and scope of future trade agreements in the hemisphere. Mexico, it has been suggested, could benefit from a slowdown of the NAFTA enlargement process by acting as an economic nexus between North America and Latin America through its membership in NAFTA, the G-3, and its bilateral agreements (as with Chile and Costa Rica). Mexico may thus be reluctant to share its NAFTA status so soon. High-level trade officials have indicated, however, that Mexico is amenable to an extension of NAFTA in the Americas.[59] Canada, which was caught a little off guard by Mexico's NAFTA bid in 1991, has strongly voiced its opposition to a proliferation of bilateral and subregional trade agreements and has expressed, on several occasions, explicit support for NAFTA expansion, despite meager support in Canada for the agreement.[60] Most Latin American countries seem more concerned with the goal of improving access to the U.S. market than with the means of achieving such access, whether it be NAFTA membership or some other form of trade treaty. In that sense, arrangements such as the NAAEC are perceived by many Latin and South American countries as conditionality, a concept defined by developing countries as abusive duress and by industrialized countries as a necessity to guarantee progress, including in the environmental field.

The main stumbling block for NAFTA accession remains the requirement for unanimous consent among the three existing parties, since this procedure grants Canada, Mexico, and the United States virtual veto power over the enlargement of membership to new countries. Although objections from Canada and Mexico seem unlikely at this point, such objections to the accession of Latin American or Caribbean countries would probably push the United States toward the "multibilateral" solution of the hub-and-spoke approach.

While multilateralism is no doubt messier and more cumbersome than is bilateralism, a comprehensive approach to economic integration that takes into account trade, investment, environmental aspects, and the rest of the social agenda will best emerge out of the enlargement of NAFTA, not bilateral agreements. Notably with regard to environmental issues, a series of tailor-made side-agreements would rapidly prove unmanageable, undermine the importance and signifi-

---

59. H. Blanco, Address (Institute of the Americas, 4 March 1994) [unpublished].

60. Most explicitly in a 14 January 1994 speech by Canada's Minister for International Trade, reported in *Inside U.S. Trade* (26 January 1994) at 11. See also "Open Trade Door, MacLaren Warns," *Financial Post*, 24 September 1994, at 1.

cance of such agreements, and defeat the purpose of preserving trade equilibria through the convergence of environmental policies and practices. The hub-and-spoke approach where the United States would be multiplying bilateral trade agreements is much less likely to lead to the kind of predictable, principled, rule-based system that commands the respect of both environmentalists and industrialists. The environmental agenda (as well as other reasons) requires that the process of economic integration abbreviate NAFTA into AFTA, the *American Free Trade Agreement,* not generate a carnival of acronyms standing for as many bilateral agreements.

Building on the NAAEC

If the assumption that economic integration in the Americas will take place one way or another is correct, then, setting aside for trade activists the matter of the choice between multilateralism or bilateralism, a question must be answered: How can such integration be shaped so as to take full account of environmental concerns? Generally, the legal and institutional innovations of the NAFTA/NAAEC package, if they are adequately funded and swiftly implemented, will constitute a very significant precedent with respect to the level of international environmental cooperation that ought to accompany economic integration. Such a precedent could buttress a pattern of intergovernmental activity on behalf of the environment, and raise expectations about what is achievable and desirable. The main pitfall lies in the issue of effective enforcement. The main opportunity lies in building up the strength and capacity of the CEC. The inescapable conclusion is thus that all new NAFTA members should enter the NAAEC as well and become partners in the CEC.

Because of the focus on environmental issues and the inflation of expectations, Chile and other NAFTA hopefuls like Honduras and Argentina are adopting new far-reaching environmental legislation, creating or designing new environmental agencies, and evaluating their environmental infrastructure.[61] In principle, this new appreciation of environmental issues, even if it is not entirely disinterested, ought to be welcomed. There is, however, a danger that such would-

---

61. On the other hand, it is readily evident that Argentina lacks sufficient budgetary resources to be able to make environmental protection a priority. "Greening Free Trade," supra note 19, Part I at 109 n.235. See also Don Podesta, "The Environment Running Second: Argentina Skips Protections In Rush to Improve Economy," *Washington Post* (4 February 1993) at A14.

be NAFTA members may be overly ambitious: They are adopting laws for which they may not have the resources to effectively implement. NAAEC, on the other hand, is geared toward maximizing environmental enforcement. Indeed, in the words of one official, few countries in Latin America and the Caribbean "are at this time likely to be far enough in their reform efforts, or in their labor and environmental policies to meet the NAFTA standard."[62] It must be remembered that the Mexican environmental laws and practices that were so scrutinized during the NAFTA debate are within or above the Latin and South American average.

In the case of Chile, where the economy largely relies on the exploitation of natural resources and where environmental legislation is thus most important, there have already been visits by U.S. EPA officials to assess Chilean environmental laws and regulations. Obviously, one central issue, besides the soundness of the norms and the aptness of the regulations, is the capacity of Chilean public authorities to effectively enforce such standards and regulations, at least at a level comparable to that practiced in Canada and the United States. All the comments made above about the difficulties in applying the standard of effective enforcement to NAAEC partners, particularly Mexico, are magnified in the case of most southern NAFTA hopefuls. Unless at the time of accession a candidate country has the resources to engage in minimal enforcement of its environmental laws, one of three unwanted developments would occur: (1) Those laws will have to be modified (which means loosened); (2) the government will have to be disciplined by other parties into devoting more resources to environmental enforcement; or (3) the NAAEC effective enforcement standard will have to become overly elastic, probably by relying on the two exceptions based on discretion and resource allocation.[63] The first possibility would be an entirely undesirable and perverse effect of the dispute settlement procedure and it would contradict both the letter and the spirit of the NAAEC. The second possibility is unappetizing because it may involve dealing with the enforcement issue in the charged atmosphere and fixed parameters of formal dispute settlement, which is less conducive to optimal solutions. The last possibility would empty NAAEC's Part Five of its content, making it a dead letter and hindering the pursuit of environmental objectives. Clearly, a thorough negotia-

---

62. Garten, supra note 48, Part V.

63. See discussion of NAAEC Article 45(a) and (b) at supra notes 81–103, Part IV and accompanying text.

tion of environmental enforcement issues and a series of commitments and adjustments on the part of NAFTA applicants could help prevent those three unappealing scenarios. In particular, political declarations and special environmental cooperation agreements over and above the NAAEC may help to insure that the implementation of the NAFTA does not have perverse effects on environmental protection and conservation efforts. As well, the foreseeable difficulties indicate that swiftness may be the enemy of solidity and efficiency. An incremental approach to NAAEC membership (which could be synchronized with the pace of the NAFTA membership ladder evoked earlier) might be a preferred avenue.

The greatest environmental opportunity springing from the process of economic integration in the Americas now lies in the chance to build up the CEC. At the global and regional level, there is a most regrettable dearth of strong, credible, and authoritative international environmental institutions. The Inter-American Development Bank and the Organization of American States, despite their renewed interest in environmental issues, have neither the expertise nor the mandate to manage the kind of environmental regime that NAFTA expansion requires. The NAFTA process just spawned the CEC, a new entity that has the potential to become such a strong, effective institution for the Americas. Enlarging the membership of NAAEC would make it increasingly relevant and important as the main international environmental cooperation in the hemisphere. As well, it would likely expand the pool of human and financial resources available to the CEC, increasing its capacity to intervene and advise, as well as providing it with promising economies of scale. Failure to make adherence to NAAEC mandatory for all new NAFTA countries would carry an exceedingly high opportunity cost and jeopardize all the efforts that governments and NGOs have dedicated to reconciling trade and environmental agendas in the region. A proliferation of bilateral environmental agreements between the United States and its trading partners would dilute the potential of the CEC, maybe even marginalize it before it has the opportunity to take flight. Compounding these difficulties is the unpredictable legal *Capernaum* that would be left after such a proliferation of similar but different environmental protocols. In other words, bilateralism would likely weaken the CEC, threaten the achievement of its crucial mandate for environmental cooperation, and undermine attempts at deepening the environmental regime any further.

Thus, three elements stand out in this cursory cost/benefit analysis of the impacts of economic integration in the Americas on the environmental regime that emerges through NAAEC. First, trade agreements that do not seriously take into account environmental concerns, at least as much as does NAFTA, are simply no longer acceptable from an environmental point of view. Second, coherence and consistency, the need for a rule-based predictable commercial context, and the imperative of environmental progress all demand that the scope of the environmental regime match as closely as possible the scope of the trade agreement. Third, a multilateral approach makes more environmental and economic sense than does a multiplication of bilateral deals. Therefore, ideally, the chosen route for economic integration would entail the gradual enlargement of NAFTA, along with obligatory membership in NAAEC for countries that accede to NAFTA. Since from an applicant's point of view NAFTA is more of a prize and NAAEC more of a burden, allowing NAFTA accession without a commitment to NAAEC would seem quite imprudent.

Nevertheless, economic integration in the Americas cannot be a process turned inward. All American countries are part of a much larger club now called the World Trade Organization (a club which also has decided to take on the issue of trade and the environment). Their partners in Asia, Europe, and Africa will follow closely the unfolding events and noisily voice their concerns if measures taken to address environmental concerns in the Americas affect their trade and investment interests. Most important, many of the region's countries, including the United States, Canada, and Mexico, produce similar goods and thus *need* to trade with partners outside the Americas. Mercosur countries already trade more with Western Europe than with the three NAFTA parties, including the United States. The lasting prosperity of the constituents of a future AFTA thus requires not only greater access to the giant markets of the United States but also to the ones of Western Europe and Asia. The free flow of trade and investment in such a broader (indeed global) area will also demand complementary environmental regimes on the same scale. This is why even the possible enlargement of the membership of the NAFTA/NAAEC combination is only the first step (albeit an important one) toward a true reconciling of environmental imperatives with an integrating global economy. The next round of discussions at the WTO level will thus be even more complex and difficult than were the negotiations leading to the NAAEC. However, just like the NAAEC, this round could also be a critical moment on the way to trade-supported and more environmentally sustainable economic development.

Appendix I

Appendix I(a)

PRIVATE SUBMISSIONS ON ENFORCEMENT MATTERS AND FACTUAL RECORDS

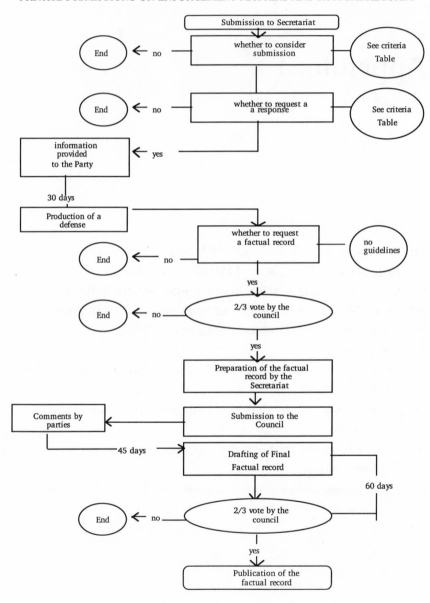

Appendix I(b)

Table 1. Requirements for Private Submissions

Requirements as to form

1. RESIDENCE (14:1(f))
Submitter must be a person or an organization residing or established in the territory[1] of any Party.

2. LANGUAGES (14:1(a))
Submitter must have notified the Secretariat of the language to be used in the submission.

3. IDENTIFICATION (14:1(b))
The submission must "clearly identify" the person or organization making the submission.

Requirements as to content

4. COMMUNICATION TO PARTY (14:1(e))
The submission must contain proof that the matter has been communicated to the relevant authorities of the Party complained against and indicate its response if any.

5. INFORMATION (14:1(c))
The submission must provide sufficient information including documentary evidence to "allow the Secretariat to review the submission."

6. INDUSTRIAL HARASSMENT (14:1(d))
The submission must appear to be aimed to promote enforcement rather than at harassment of industry.

7. HARM (14:2(a))
The Secretariat will consider whether the submitter alleges harm to itself.

8. PURSUING PRIVATE REMEDIES (14:2(c))
The Secretariat will consider whether the submitter pursued private remedies available in the Party's domestic forum.

9. MASS MEDIA REPORT (14:2(d))
Another factor considered is whether the submission is "drawn exclusively from mass media reports."

Objectives

10. ADVANCING THE GOALS OF THE AGREEMENT (14:2(b))
The Secretariat will consider whether the submission alone or combined with other submissions "raises matters whose further study in this process would advance the goals of the Agreement." N.B. The objectives pursued by the Agreement are set out in Article 1(a-j).

---

[1]For a definition of territory see Annex 45 of the Agreement regarding country-specific definitions.

Appendix I(c)

CONSULTATION AND RESOLUTION OF DISPUTES
Consultations

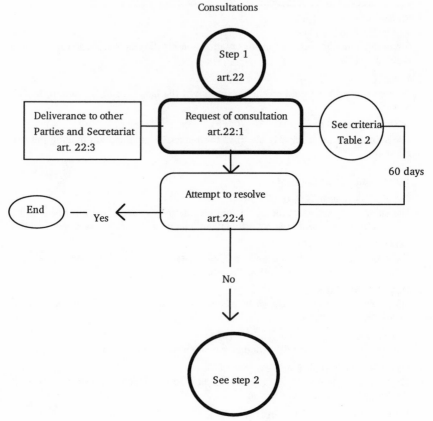

Appendix I(d)

Table 2. Criteria for Request of Consultation and Resolution of
Disputes

Burden of proof	Means
Persistent pattern of failure	The complaining Party must establish that the ineffective enforcement began after January 1st, 1994, and that it formed a consistent pattern over a certain period of time.
by other Party	
to effectively enforce	The complaining Party must demonstrate, if the legislation in question allows for discretion as to compliance matters, that such discretion was exercised unreasonably by the public authorities of the Party complained against.
	If the defense is to the effect that non-enforcement is due to allocation of resources, then the complaining Party must prove that such allocation does not follow from a bona fide decision by the public authorities of the Party complained against.
its environmental laws	The complaining Party must establish that the primary purpose of the law, regulation, or provision is the protection of the environment.

Appendix I(e)

CONSULTATION AND RESOLUTION OF DISPUTES
Initiation of Procedures

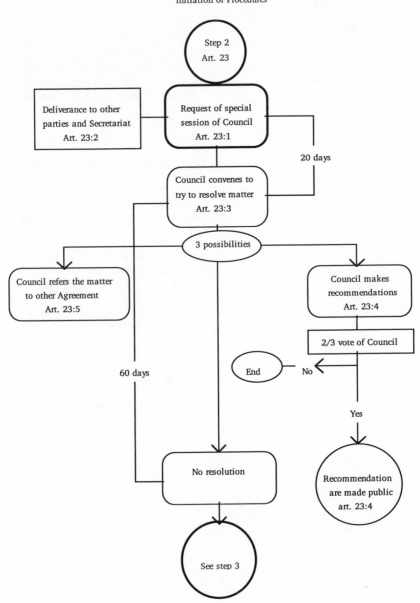

Appendix I(f)

CONSULTATION AND RESOLUTION OF DISPUTES
Request for an Arbitral Panel

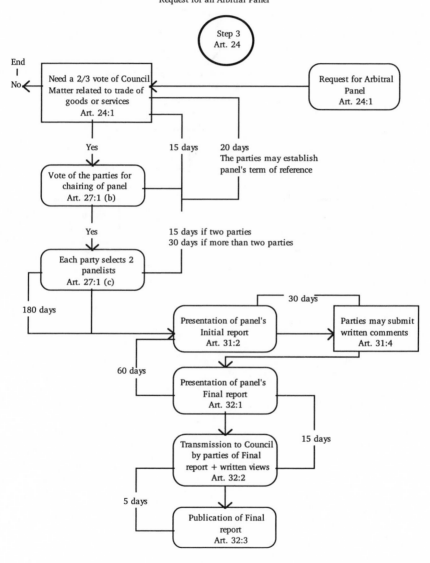

Appendix I(g)

CONSULTATION AND RESOLUTION OF DISPUTES
Implementation of Final Report

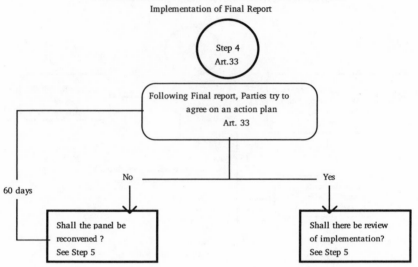

Appendix I(h)

CONSULTATION AND RESOLUTION OF DISPUTES
Review of Implementation

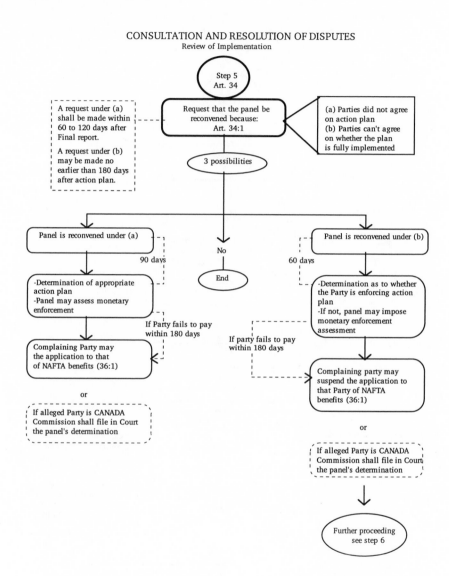

Step 5
Art. 34

A request under (a)
shall be made within
60 to 120 days after
Final report.

A request under (b)
may be made no
earlier than 180 days
after action plan.

Request that the panel be
reconvened because:
Art. 34:1

(a) Parties did not agree
on action plan
(b) Parties can't agree
on whether the plan
is fully implemented

3 possibilities

No

End

Panel is reconvened under (a)

90 days

-Determination of appropriate
action plan
-Panel may assess monetary
enforcement

If Party fails to pay
within 180 days

Complaining Party may
the application to that
of NAFTA benefits (36:1)

or

If alleged Party is CANADA
Commission shall file in Court
the panel's determination

Panel is reconvened under (b)

60 days

-Determination as to whether
the Party is enforcing action
plan
-If not, panel may impose
monetary enforcement
assessment

If party fails to pay
within 180 days

Complaining party may
suspend the application to
that Party of NAFTA
benefits (36:1)

or

If alleged Party is CANADA
Commission shall file in Court
the panel's determination

Further proceeding
see step 6

Appendix I(i)

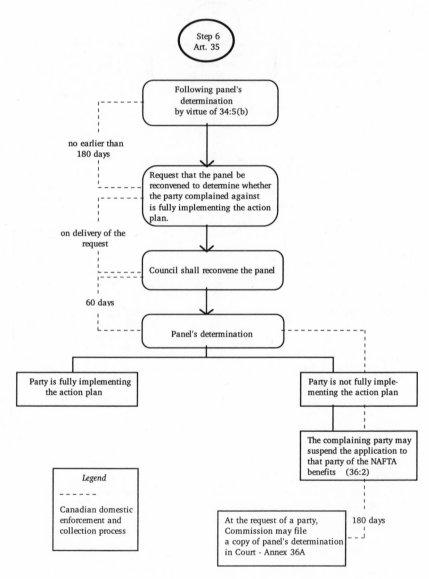

CONSULTATION AND RESOLUTION OF DISPUTES

Further Proceeding

Step 6
Art. 35

Following panel's
determination
by virtue of 34:5(b)

no earlier than
180 days

Request that the panel be
reconvened to determine whether
the party complained against
is fully implementing the action
plan.

on delivery of the
request

Council shall reconvene the panel

60 days

Panel's determination

Party is fully implementing
the action plan

Party is not fully imple-
menting the action plan

The complaining party may
suspend the application to
that party of the NAFTA
benefits   (36:2)

Legend

- - - - - -

Canadian domestic
enforcement and
collection process

At the request of a party,   180 days
Commission may file
a copy of panel's determination
in Court - Annex 36A

Appendix II
Selected Provisions of NAFTA Related to the Environment

Preamble

The Government of Canada, the Government of the United Mexican States, and the Government of the United States of America, resolved to:

STRENGTHEN the special bonds of friendship and cooperation among their nations;

CONTRIBUTE to the harmonious development and expansion of world trade and provide a catalyst to broader international cooperation;

CREATE an expanded and secure market for the goods and services produced in their territories;

REDUCE distortions to trade;

ESTABLISH clear and mutually advantageous rules governing their trade;

ENSURE a predictable commercial framework for business planning and investment;

BUILD on their respective rights and obligations under the *General Agreement on Tariffs and Trade* and other multilateral and bilateral instruments of cooperation;

ENHANCE the competitiveness of their firms in global markets;

FOSTER creativity and innovation, and promote trade in goods and services that are the subject of intellectual property rights;

CREATE new employment opportunities and improve working conditions and living standards in their respective territories;

UNDERTAKE each of the preceding in a manner consistent with environmental protection and conservation;

PRESERVE their flexibility to safeguard the public welfare;

PROMOTE sustainable development;

STRENGTHEN the development and enforcement of environmental laws and regulations; and

PROTECT, enhance, and enforce basic workers' rights;

HAVE AGREED as follows:

PART ONE
GENERAL PART

Chapter One

Objectives

Article 101: Establishment of the Free Trade Area

The Parties to this Agreement, consistent with Article XXIV of the *General Agreement on Tariffs and Trade,* hereby establish a free trade area.

Article 102: Objectives

1. The objectives of this Agreement, as elaborated more specifically through its principles and rules, including national treatment, most-favored-nation treatment, and transparency, are to:

   (a) eliminate barriers to trade in, and facilitate the cross-border movement of, goods and services between the territories of the Parties;

   (b) promote conditions of fair competition in the free trade area;

   (c) increase substantially investment opportunities in the territories of the Parties;

   (d) provide adequate and effective protection and enforcement of intellectual property rights in each Party's territory;

   (e) create effective procedures for the implementation and application of this Agreement, for its joint administration, and for the resolution of disputes; and

   (f) establish a framework for further trilateral, regional, and multilateral cooperation to expand and enhance the benefits of this Agreement.

2. The Parties shall interpret and apply the provisions of this Agreement in the light of its objectives set out in paragraph 1 and in accordance with applicable rules of international law.

Article 103: Relation to Other Agreements

1. The Parties affirm their existing rights and obligations with respect to each

other under the *General Agreement on Tariffs and Trade* and other agreements to which such Parties are party.

2. In the event of any inconsistency between this Agreement and such other agreements, this Agreement shall prevail to the extent of the inconsistency, except as otherwise provided in this Agreement.

Article 104: Relation to Environmental and Conservation Agreements

1. In the event of any inconsistency between this Agreement and the specific trade obligations set out in:

(a) the *Convention on International Trade in Endangered Species of Wild Fauna and Flora,* done at Washington, 3 March 1973, as amended 22 June 1979;

(b) the *Montreal Protocol on Substances that Deplete the Ozone Layer,* done at Montreal, 16 September 1987, as amended 29 June 1990;

(c) the *Basel Convention on the Control of Transboundary Movements of Hazardous Wastes and Their Disposal,* done at Basel, 22 March 1989, on its entry into force for Canada, Mexico, and the United States; or

(d) the agreements set out in Annex 104.1;

such obligations shall prevail to the extent of the inconsistency, provided that where a Party has a choice among equally effective and reasonably available means of complying with such obligations, the Party chooses the alternative that is the least inconsistent with the other provisions of this Agreement.

2. The Parties may agree in writing to modify Annex 104.1 to include any amendment to an agreement referred to in paragraph 1 and any other environmental or conservation agreement.

Article 105: Extent of Obligations

The Parties shall ensure that all necessary measures are taken in order to give effect to the provisions of this Agreement, including their observance, except as otherwise provided in this Agreement, by state and provincial governments.

Annex 104.1
Bilateral and Other Environmental and Conservation Agreements

1. The *Agreement Between the Government of Canada and the Government of the United States of America Concerning the Transboundary Movement of Hazardous Waste,* signed at Ottawa, 28 October 1986.

2. The *Agreement Between the United States of America and the United Mexican States on Cooperation for the Protection and Improvement of the Environment in the Border Area,* signed at La Paz, Baja California Sur, 14 August 1983.

Chapter Two

General Definitions

Article 201: Definitions of General Application

1. For purposes of this Agreement, unless otherwise specified:

Commission means the Free Trade Commission established under Article 2001(1) (The Free Trade Commission);

Customs Valuation Code means the Agreement on Implementation of Article VII of the *General Agreement on Tariffs and Trade,* including its interpretative notes;

days means calendar days, including weekends and holidays;

enterprise means any entity constituted or organized under applicable law, whether or not for profit, and whether privately owned or governmentally owned, including any corporation, trust, partnership, sole proprietorship, joint venture, or other association;

enterprise of a Party means an enterprise constituted or organized under the law of a Party;

existing means in effect on the date of entry into force of this Agreement;

Generally Accepted Accounting Principles means the recognized consensus or substantial authoritative support in the territory of a Party with respect to the recording of revenues, expenses, costs, assets and liabilities, disclosure of information, and preparation of financial statements. These standards may be broad guidelines of general application as well as detailed standards, practices, and procedures;

goods of a Party means domestic products as these are understood in the *General Agreement on Tariffs and Trade* or such goods as the Parties may agree, and includes originating goods of that Party;

Harmonized System (HS) means the *Harmonized Commodity Description and Coding System,* and its legal notes and rules, as adopted and implemented by the Parties in their respective tariff laws;

measure includes any law, regulation, procedure, requirement, or practice;

national means a natural person who is a citizen or permanent resident of a Party and any other natural person referred to in Annex 201.1;

originating means qualifying under the rules of origin set out in Chapter Four (Rules of Origin);

person means a natural person or an enterprise;

person of a Party means a national, or an enterprise of a Party;

Secretariat means the Secretariat established under Article 2002(1) (The Secretariat);

state enterprise means an enterprise that is owned, or controlled through ownership interests, by a Party; and

territory means for a Party the territory of that Party as set out in Annex 201.1.

2. For purposes of this Agreement, unless otherwise specified, a reference to a state or province includes local governments of that state or province.

Annex 201.1
Country-Specific Definitions

For purposes of this Agreement, unless otherwise specified:

national also includes:

(a) with respect to Mexico, a national or a citizen according to Articles 30 and 34, respectively, of the Mexican Constitution; and

(b) with respect to the United States, "national of the United States" as defined in the existing provisions of the *Immigration and Nationality Act;*

territory means:

(a) with respect to Canada, the territory to which its customs laws apply, including any areas beyond the territorial seas of Canada within which, in accordance with international law and its domestic law, Canada may exercise rights with respect to the seabed and subsoil and their natural resources;

(b) with respect to Mexico,

    (i) the states of the Federation and the Federal District;

    (ii) the islands, including the reefs and keys, in adjacent seas;

    (iii) the islands of Guadalupe and Revillagigedo situated in the Pacific Ocean;

    (iv) the continental shelf and the submarine shelf of such islands, keys, and reefs;

    (v) the waters of the territorial seas, in accordance with international law, and its interior maritime waters;

    (vi) the space located above the national territory, in accordance with international law; and

    (vii) any areas beyond the territorial seas of Mexico within which, in accordance with international law, including the *United Nations Convention on the Law of the Sea,* and its domestic law, Mexico may exercise rights with respect to the seabed and subsoil and their natural resources; and

(c) with respect to the United States,

    (i) the customs territory of the United States, which includes the 50 states, the District of Columbia and Puerto Rico;

    (ii) the foreign trade zones located in the United States and Puerto Rico; and

(iii) any areas beyond the territorial seas of the United States within which, in accordance with international law and its domestic law, the United States may exercise rights with respect to the seabed and subsoil and their natural resources.

Chapter Seven

Agriculture and Sanitary and Phytosanitary Measures

Section A: Agriculture

Article 701: Scope and Coverage

1. This Section applies to measures adopted or maintained by a Party relating to agricultural trade.

2. In the event of any inconsistency between this Section and another provision of this Agreement, this Section shall prevail to the extent of the inconsistency.

Article 702: International Obligations

1. Annex 702.1 applies to the Parties specified in that Annex with respect to agricultural trade under certain agreements between them.

2. Prior to adopting pursuant to an intergovernmental commodity agreement, a measure that may affect trade in an agricultural good between the Parties, the Party proposing to adopt the measure shall consult with the other Parties with a view to avoiding nullification or impairment of a concession granted by that Party in its Schedule to Annex 302.2.

3. Annex 702.3 applies to the Parties specified in that Annex with respect to measures adopted or maintained pursuant to an intergovernmental coffee agreement.

Article 703: Market Access

1. The Parties shall work together to improve access to their respective markets through the reduction or elimination of import barriers to trade between them in agricultural goods.

Customs Duties, Quantitative Restrictions, and Agricultural Grading and Marketing Standards

2. Annex 703.2 applies to the Parties specified in that Annex with respect to customs duties and quantitative restrictions, trade in sugar and syrup goods, and agricultural grading and marketing standards.

Special Safeguard Provisions

3. Each Party may, in accordance with its Schedule to Annex 302.2, adopt or

maintain a special safeguard in the form of a tariff rate quota on an agricultural good listed in its Section of Annex 703.3. Notwithstanding Article 302(2), a Party may not apply an over-quota tariff rate under a special safeguard that exceeds the lesser of:

(a) the most-favored-nation (MFN) rate as of 1 July 1 1991; and

(b) the prevailing MFN rate.

4. No Party may, with respect to the same good and the same country, at the same time:

(a) apply an over-quota tariff rate under paragraph 3 and

(b) take an emergency action covered by Chapter Eight (Emergency Action).

Article 708: Definitions

For purposes of this Section:

agricultural good means a good provided for in any of the following:

Note: For purposes of reference only, descriptions are provided next to the corresponding tariff provision.

(a) Harmonized System (HS) Chapters 1 through 24 (other than a fish or fish product); or

(b) HS subheading   2905.43   manitol
    HS subheading   2905.44   sorbitol
    HS heading   33.01   essential oils
    HS headings   35.01 to 35.05   albuminoidal substances,
                                                modified starches, glues
    HS subheading   3809.10   finishing agents
    HS subheading   3823.60   sorbitol n.e.p.
    HS headings   41.01 to 41.03   hides and skins
    HS heading   43.01   raw furskins
    HS headings   50.01 to 50.03   raw silk and silk waste
    HS headings   51.01 to 51.03   wool and animal hair
    HS headings   52.01 to 52.03   raw cotton, cotton waste,
                                                and cotton carded or
                                                combed
    HS heading   53.01   raw flax
    HS heading   53.02   raw hemp

customs duty means "customs duty" as defined in Article 318 (National Treatment and Market Access for Goods-Definitions);

duty-free means "duty-free" as defined in Article 318;

fish or fish product means a fish or crustacean, mollusk or other aquatic invertebrate, marine mammal, or a product thereof provided for in any of the following:

Note: For purposes of reference only, descriptions are provided next to the corresponding tariff provision.

HS Chapter	03	fish and crustaceans, mollusks and other aquatic invertebrates
HS heading	05.07	tortoise-shell, whalebone and whalebone hair, and those fish or crustaceans, mollusks or other aquatic invertebrates, marine mammals, and their products within this heading
HS heading	05.08	coral and similar materials
HS heading	05.09	natural sponges of animal origin
HS heading	05.11	products of fish or crustaceans, mollusks or other aquatic invertebrates; dead animals of Chapter 3
HS heading	15.04	fats and oils and their fractions, of fish or marine mammals
HS heading	16.03	"non-meat" extracts and juices
HS heading	16.04	prepared or preserved fish
HS heading	16.05	prepared preserved crustaceans, mollusks and other aquatic invertebrates;
HS subheading	2301.20	flours, meals, pellets of fish

material means "material" as defined in Article 415 (Rules of Origin-Definitions);

over-quota tariff rate means the rate of customs duty to be applied to quantities in excess of the quantity specified under a tariff rate quota;

sugar or syrup good means "sugar or syrup good" as defined in Annex 703.2;

tariff item means a "tariff item" as defined in Annex 401; and

tariff rate quota means a mechanism that provides for the application of a customs duty at a certain rate to imports of a particular good up to a specified quantity (in-quota quantity), and at a different rate to imports of that good that exceed that quantity.

Annex 702.1

Incorporation of Trade Provisions

1. Articles 701, 702, 704, 705, 706, 707, 710, and 711 of the *Canada-United States Free Trade Agreement,* which Articles are hereby incorporated into and made a part of this Agreement, apply as between Canada and the United States.

2. The definitions of the terms specified in Article 711 of the *Canada-United States Free Trade Agreement* shall apply to the Articles incorporated by paragraph 1.

3. For purposes of this incorporation, any reference to Chapter Eighteen of the *Canada-United States Free Trade Agreement* shall be deemed to be a reference

to Chapter Twenty (Institutional Arrangements and Dispute Settlement Procedures) of this Agreement.

4. The Parties understand that Article 710 of the *Canada-United States Free Trade Agreement* incorporates the GATT rights and obligations of Canada and the United States with respect to agricultural, food, beverage, and certain related goods, including exemptions by virtue of paragraph (1)(b) of the Protocol of Provisional Application of the GATT and waivers granted under Article XXV of the GATT.

Annex 702.3
Intergovernmental Coffee Agreement

Notwithstanding Article 2101 (General Exceptions), neither Canada nor Mexico may adopt or maintain a measure, pursuant to an intergovernmental coffee agreement, that restricts trade in coffee between them.

Section B: Sanitary and Phytosanitary Measures
Article 709: Scope and Coverage

In order to establish a framework of rules and disciplines to guide the development, adoption, and enforcement of sanitary and phytosanitary measures, this Section applies to any such measure of a Party that may, directly or indirectly, affect trade between the Parties.

Article 710: Relation to Other Chapters

Articles 301 (National Treatment) and 309 (Import and Export Restrictions), and the provisions of Article XX(b) of the GATT as incorporated into Article 2101(1) (General Exceptions), do not apply to any sanitary or phytosanitary measure.

Article 711: Reliance on Nongovernmental Entities

Each Party shall ensure that any nongovernmental entity on which it relies in applying a sanitary or phytosanitary measure acts in a manner consistent with this Section.

Article 712: Basic Rights and Obligations

Right to Take Sanitary and Phytosanitary Measures

1. Each Party may, in accordance with this Section, adopt, maintain, or apply any sanitary or phytosanitary measure necessary for the protection of human, animal, or plant life or health in its territory, including a measure more stringent than an international standard, guideline, or recommendation.

Right to Establish Level of Protection

2. Notwithstanding any other provision of this Section, each Party may, in protecting human, animal, or plant life or health, establish its appropriate levels of protection in accordance with Article 715.

Scientific Principles

3. Each Party shall ensure that any sanitary or phytosanitary measure that it adopts, maintains, or applies is:

(a) based on scientific principles, taking into account relevant factors including, where appropriate, different geographic conditions;

(b) not maintained where there is no longer a scientific basis for it; and

(c) based on a risk assessment, as appropriate to the circumstances.

Non-Discriminatory Treatment

4. Each Party shall ensure that a sanitary or phytosanitary measure that it adopts, maintains, or applies does not arbitrarily or unjustifiably discriminate between its goods and like goods of another Party, or between goods of another Party and like goods of any other country, where identical or similar conditions prevail.

Unnecessary Obstacles

5. Each Party shall ensure that any sanitary or phytosanitary measure that it adopts, maintains, or applies is applied only to the extent necessary to achieve its appropriate level of protection, taking into account technical and economic feasibility.

Disguised Restrictions

6. No Party may adopt, maintain, or apply any sanitary or phytosanitary measure with a view to, or with the effect of, creating a disguised restriction on trade between the Parties.

Article 713:　　International Standards and Standardizing Organizations

1. Without reducing the level of protection of human, animal, or plant life or health, each Party shall use, as a basis for its sanitary and phytosanitary measures, relevant international standards, guidelines, or recommendations with the objective, among others, of making its sanitary and phytosanitary measures equivalent or, where appropriate, identical to those of the other Parties.

2. A Party's sanitary or phytosanitary measure that conforms to a relevant international standard, guideline, or recommendation shall be presumed to be consistent with Article 712. A measure that results in a level of sanitary or phytosanitary protection different from that which would be achieved by a measure based on a relevant international standard, guideline, or recommendation shall not for that reason alone be presumed to be inconsistent with this Section.

3. Nothing in Paragraph 1 shall be construed to prevent a Party from adopting, maintaining, or applying, in accordance with the other provisions of this Section, a sanitary or phytosanitary measure that is more stringent than the relevant international standard, guideline, or recommendation.

4. Where a Party has reason to believe that a sanitary or phytosanitary measure of another Party is adversely affecting or may adversely affect its exports and the measure is not based on a relevant international standard, guideline, or recommendation, it may request, and the other Party shall provide in writing, the reasons for the measure.

5. Each Party shall, to the greatest extent practicable, participate in relevant international and North American standardizing organizations, including the *Codex Alimentarius Commission,* the *International Office of Epizootics,* the *International Plant Protection Convention,* and the *North American Plant Protection Organization,* with a view to promoting the development and periodic review of international standards, guidelines, and recommendations.

Article 714: Equivalence

1. Without reducing the level of protection of human, animal, or plant life or health, the Parties shall, to the greatest extent practicable and in accordance with this Section, pursue equivalence of their respective sanitary and phytosanitary measures.

2. Each importing Party:

(a) shall treat a sanitary or phytosanitary measure adopted or maintained by an exporting Party as equivalent to its own where the exporting Party, in cooperation with the importing Party, provides to the importing Party scientific evidence or other information, in accordance with risk assessment methodologies agreed on by those Parties, to demonstrate objectively, subject to subparagraph (b), that the exporting Party's measure achieves the importing Party's appropriate level of protection;

(b) may, where it has a scientific basis, determine that the exporting Party's measure does not achieve the importing Party's appropriate level of protection; and

(c) shall provide to the exporting Party, on request, its reasons in writing for a determination under subparagraph (b).

3. For purposes of establishing equivalence, each exporting Party shall, on the request of an importing Party, take such reasonable measures as may be available to it to facilitate access in its territory for inspection, testing, and other relevant procedures.

4. Each Party should, in the development of a sanitary or phytosanitary measure, consider relevant actual or proposed sanitary or phytosanitary measures of the other Parties.

Article 715: Risk Assessment and Appropriate Level of Protection

1. In conducting a risk assessment, each Party shall take into account:

   (a) relevant risk assessment techniques and methodologies developed by international or North American standardizing organizations;

   (b) relevant scientific evidence;

   (c) relevant processes and production methods;

   (d) relevant inspection, sampling, and testing methods;

   (e) the prevalence of relevant diseases or pests, including the existence of pest-free or disease-free areas or areas of low pest or disease prevalence;

   (f) relevant ecological and other environmental conditions; and

   (g) relevant treatments, such as quarantines.

2. Further to paragraph 1, each Party shall, in establishing its appropriate level of protection regarding the risk associated with the introduction, establishment, or spread of an animal or plant pest or disease, and in assessing the risk, also take into account the following economic factors, where relevant:

   (a) loss of production or sales that may result from the pest or disease;

   (b) costs of control or eradication of the pest or disease in its territory; and

   (c) the relative cost-effectiveness of alternative approaches to limiting risks.

3. Each Party, in establishing its appropriate level of protection:

   (a) should take into account the objective of minimizing negative trade effects; and

   (b) shall, with the objective of achieving consistency in such levels, avoid arbitrary or unjustifiable distinctions in such levels in different circumstances, where such distinctions result in arbitrary or unjustifiable discrimination against a good of another Party or constitute a disguised restriction on trade between the Parties.

4. Notwithstanding paragraphs (1) through (3) and Article 712(3)(c), where a Party conducting a risk assessment determines that available relevant scientific evidence or other information is insufficient to complete the assessment, it may adopt a provisional sanitary or phytosanitary measure on the basis of available relevant information, including from international or North American standardizing organizations and from sanitary or phytosanitary measures of other Parties. The Party shall, within a reasonable period after information sufficient to complete the assessment is presented to it, complete its assessment, review and, where appropriate, revise the provisional measure in the light of the assessment.

5. Where a Party is able to achieve its appropriate level of protection through the phased application of a sanitary or phytosanitary measure, it may, on the request of another Party and in accordance with this Section, allow for such a

phased application, or grant specified exceptions for limited periods from the measure, taking into account the requesting Party's export interests.

Article 716: Adaptation to Regional Conditions

1. Each Party shall adapt any of its sanitary or phytosanitary measures relating to the introduction, establishment, or spread of an animal or plant pest or disease, to the sanitary or phytosanitary characteristics of the area where a good subject to such a measure is produced and the area in its territory to which the good is destined, taking into account any relevant conditions, including those relating to transportation and handling, between those areas. In assessing such characteristics of an area, including whether an area is, and is likely to remain, a pest-free or disease-free area or an area of low pest or disease prevalence, each Party shall take into account, among other factors:

(a) the prevalence of relevant pests or diseases in that area;

(b) the existence of eradication or control programs in that area; and

(c) any relevant international standard, guideline, or recommendation.

2. Further to paragraph 1, each Party shall, in determining whether an area is a pest-free or disease-free area or an area of low pest or disease prevalence, base its determination on factors such as geography, ecosystems, epidemiological surveillance and the effectiveness of sanitary or phytosanitary controls in that area.

3. Each importing Party shall recognize that an area in the territory of the exporting Party is, and is likely to remain, a pest-free or disease-free area or an area of low pest or disease prevalence, where the exporting Party provides to the importing Party scientific evidence or other information sufficient to so demonstrate to the satisfaction of the importing Party. For this purpose, each exporting Party shall provide reasonable access in its territory to the importing Party for inspection, testing, and other relevant procedures.

4. Each Party may, in accordance with this Section:

(a) adopt, maintain, or apply a different risk assessment procedure for a pest-free or disease-free area than for an area of low pest or disease prevalence, or

(b) make a different final determination for the disposition of a good produced in a pest-free or disease-free area than for a good produced in an area of low pest or disease prevalence,

taking into account any relevant conditions, including those relating to transportation and handling.

5. Each Party shall, in adopting, maintaining, or applying a sanitary or phytosanitary measure relating to the introduction, establishment, or spread of an animal or plant pest or disease, accord a good produced in a pest-free or disease-free area in the territory of another Party no less favorable treatment than it accords a good produced in a pest-free or disease-free area, in another country, that poses the same level of risk. The Party shall use equivalent risk

assessment techniques to evaluate relevant conditions and controls in the pest-free or disease-free area and in the area surrounding that area and take into account any relevant conditions, including those relating to transportation and handling.

6. Each importing Party shall pursue an agreement with an exporting Party, on request, on specific requirements the fulfillment of which allows a good produced in an area of low pest or disease prevalence in the territory of an exporting Party to be imported into the territory of the importing Party and achieves the importing Party's appropriate level of protection.

Article 717: Control, Inspection, and Approval Procedures

1. Each Party, with respect to any control or inspection procedure that it conducts:

 (a) shall initiate and complete the procedure as expeditiously as possible and in no less favorable manner for a good of another Party than for a like good of the Party or of any other country;

 (b) shall publish the normal processing period for the procedure or communicate the anticipated processing period to the applicant on request;

 (c) shall ensure that the competent body

   (i) on receipt of an application, promptly examines the completeness of the documentation and informs the applicant in a precise and complete manner of any deficiency;

   (ii) transmits to the applicant as soon as possible the results of the procedure in a form that is precise and complete so that the applicant may take any necessary corrective action;

   (iii) where the application is deficient, proceeds as far as practicable with the procedure if the applicant so requests; and

   (iv) informs the applicant, on request, of the status of the application and the reasons for any delay;

 (d) shall limit the information the applicant is required to supply to that necessary for conducting the procedure;

 (e) shall accord confidential or proprietary information arising from, or supplied in connection with, the procedure conducted for a good of another Party

   (i) treatment no less favorable than for a good of the Party; and

   (ii) in any event, treatment that protects the applicant's legitimate commercial interests, to the extent provided under the Party's law;

 (f) shall limit any requirement regarding individual specimens or samples of a good to that which is reasonable and necessary;

 (g) should not impose a fee for conducting the procedure that is higher for a good of another Party than is equitable in relation to any such fee it imposes for its like goods or for like goods of any other country, taking into account communication, transportation, and other related costs;

(h) should use criteria for selecting the location of facilities at which the procedure is conducted that do not cause unnecessary inconvenience to an applicant or its agent;

(i) shall provide a mechanism to review complaints concerning the operation of the procedure and to take corrective action when a complaint is justified;

(j) should use criteria for selecting samples of goods that do not cause unnecessary inconvenience to an applicant or its agent; and

(k) shall limit the procedure, for a good modified subsequent to a determination that the good fulfills the requirements of the applicable sanitary or phytosanitary measure, to that necessary to determine that the good continues to fulfill the requirements of that measure.

2. Each Party shall apply, with such modifications as may be necessary, paragraphs 1(a) through (i) to its approval procedures.

3. Where an importing Party's sanitary or phytosanitary measure requires the conduct of a control or inspection procedure at the level of production, an exporting Party shall, on the request of the importing Party, take such reasonable measures as may be available to it to facilitate access in its territory and to provide assistance necessary to facilitate the conduct of the importing Party's control or inspection procedure.

4. A Party maintaining an approval procedure may require its approval for the use of an additive, or its establishment of a tolerance for a contaminant, in a food, beverage, or feedstuff, under that procedure prior to granting access to its domestic market for a food, beverage, or feedstuff containing that additive or contaminant. Where such Party so requires, it shall consider using a relevant international standard, guideline, or recommendation as the basis for granting access until it completes the procedure.

Article 718: Notification, Publication, and Provision of Information

1. Further to Articles 1802 (Publication) and 1803 (Notification and Provision of Information), each Party proposing to adopt or modify a sanitary or phytosanitary measure of general application at the federal level shall:

(a) at least 60 days prior to the adoption or modification of the measure, other than a law, publish a notice and notify in writing the other Parties of the proposed measure and provide to the other Parties and publish the full text of the proposed measure, in such a manner as to enable interested persons to become acquainted with the proposed measure;

(b) identify in the notice and notification the good to which the measure would apply, and provide a brief description of the objective and reasons for the measure;

(c) provide a copy of the proposed measure to any Party or interested person that so requests and, wherever possible, identify any provision that deviates in substance from relevant international standards, guidelines, or recommendations; and

(d) without discrimination, allow other Parties and interested persons to make comments in writing and shall, on request, discuss the comments and take the comments and the results of the discussions into account.

2. Each Party shall seek, through appropriate measures, to ensure, with respect to a sanitary or phytosanitary measure of a state or provincial government:

(a) that, at an early appropriate stage, a notice and notification of the type referred to in paragraph 1(a) and (b) are made prior to their adoption; and

(b) observance of paragraph 1(c) and (d).

3. Where a Party considers it necessary to address an urgent problem relating to sanitary or phytosanitary protection, it may omit any step set out in paragraph 1 or 2, provided that, on adoption of a sanitary or phytosanitary measure, it shall:

(a) immediately provide to the other Parties a notification of the type referred to in paragraph 1(b), including a brief description of the urgent problem;

(b) provide a copy of the measure to any Party or interested person that so requests; and

(c) without discrimination, allow other Parties and interested persons to make comments in writing and shall, on request, discuss the comments and take the comments and the results of the discussions into account.

4. Each Party shall, except where necessary to address an urgent problem referred to in paragraph 3, allow a reasonable period between the publication of a sanitary or phytosanitary measure of general application and the date that it becomes effective to allow time for interested persons to adapt to the measure.

5. Each Party shall designate a government authority responsible for the implementation at the federal level of the notification provisions of this Article, and shall notify the other Parties thereof. Where a Party designates two or more government authorities for this purpose, it shall provide to the other Parties complete and unambiguous information on the scope of responsibility of each such authority.

6. Where an importing Party denies entry into its territory of a good of another Party because it does not comply with a sanitary or phytosanitary measure, the importing Party shall provide a written explanation to the

exporting Party, on request, that identifies the applicable measure and the reasons that the good is not in compliance.

Article 719: Inquiry Points

1. Each Party shall ensure that there is one inquiry point that is able to answer all reasonable inquiries from other Parties and interested persons, and to provide relevant documents, regarding:

(a) any sanitary or phytosanitary measure of general application, including any control or inspection procedure or approval procedure, proposed, adopted, or maintained in its territory at the federal, state, or provincial government level;

(b) the Party's risk assessment procedures and factors it considers in conducting the assessment and in establishing its appropriate levels of protection;

(c) the membership and participation of the Party, or its relevant federal, state, or provincial government authorities in international and regional sanitary and phytosanitary organizations and systems, and in bilateral and multilateral arrangements within the scope of this Section, and the provisions of those systems and arrangements; and

(d) the location of notices published pursuant to this Section or where such information can be obtained.

2. Each Party shall ensure that where copies of documents are requested by another Party or by interested persons in accordance with this Section, they are supplied at the same price, apart from the actual cost of delivery, as the price for domestic purchase.

Article 720: Technical Cooperation

1. Each Party shall, on the request of another Party, facilitate the provision of technical advice, information, and assistance, on mutually agreed terms and conditions, to enhance that Party's sanitary and phytosanitary measures and related activities, including research, processing technologies, infrastructure, and the establishment of national regulatory bodies. Such assistance may include credits, donations, and grants for the acquisition of technical expertise, training, and equipment that will facilitate the Party's adjustment to and compliance with a Party's sanitary or phytosanitary measure.

2. Each Party shall, on the request of another Party:

(a) provide to that Party information on its technical cooperation programs regarding sanitary or phytosanitary measures relating to specific areas of interest; and

(b) consult with the other Party during the development of, or prior to the adoption or change in the application of, any sanitary or phytosanitary measure.

Article 721: Limitations on the Provision of Information

Nothing in this Section shall be construed to require a Party to:

(a) communicate, publish texts, or provide particulars or copies of documents other than in an official language of the Party; or

(b) furnish any information the disclosure of which would impede law enforcement or otherwise be contrary to the public interest or would prejudice the legitimate commercial interests of particular enterprises.

Article 722: Committee on Sanitary and Phytosanitary Measures

1. The Parties hereby establish a Committee on Sanitary and Phytosanitary Measures, comprising representatives of each Party who have responsibility for sanitary and phytosanitary matters.

2. The Committee should facilitate:

(a) the enhancement of food safety and improvement of sanitary and phytosanitary conditions in the territories of the Parties;

(b) activities of the Parties pursuant to Articles 713 and 714;

(c) technical cooperation between the Parties, including cooperation in the development, application, and enforcement of sanitary or phytosanitary measures; and

(d) consultations on specific matters relating to sanitary or phytosanitary measures.

3. The Committee:

(a) shall, to the extent possible, in carrying out its functions, seek the assistance of relevant international and North American standardizing organizations to obtain available scientific and technical advice and minimize duplication of effort;

(b) may draw on such experts and expert bodies as it considers appropriate;

(c) shall report annually to the Commission on the implementation of this Section;

(d) shall meet on the request of any Party and, unless the Parties otherwise agree, at least once each year; and

(e) may, as it considers appropriate, establish and determine the scope and mandate of working groups.

Article 723: Technical Consultations

1. A Party may request consultations with another Party on any matter covered by this Section.

2. Each Party should use the good offices of relevant international and North

American standardizing organizations, including those referred to in Article 713(5), for advice and assistance on sanitary and phytosanitary matters within their respective mandates.

3. Where a Party requests consultations regarding the application of this Section to a Party's sanitary or phytosanitary measure, and so notifies the Committee, the Committee may facilitate the consultations, if it does not consider the matter itself, by referring the matter for nonbinding technical advice or recommendations to a working group, including an ad hoc working group, or to another forum.

4. The Committee should consider any matter referred to it under paragraph 3 as expeditiously as possible, particularly regarding perishable goods, and promptly forward to the Parties any technical advice or recommendations that it develops or receives concerning the matter. Each Party involved shall provide a written response to the Committee concerning the technical advice or recommendations within such time as the Committee may request.

5. Where the involved Parties have had recourse to consultations facilitated by the Committee under paragraph 3, the consultations shall, on the agreement of the Parties involved, constitute consultations under Article 2006 (Consultations).

6. The Parties confirm that a Party asserting that a sanitary or phytosanitary measure of another Party is inconsistent with this Section shall have the burden of establishing the inconsistency.

Article 724: Definitions

For purposes of this Section:

animal includes fish and wild fauna;

appropriate level of protection means the level of protection of human, animal, or plant life or health in the territory of a Party that the Party considers appropriate;

approval procedure means any registration, notification, or other mandatory administrative procedure for:

(a) approving the use of an additive for a stated purpose or under stated conditions, or

(b) establishing a tolerance for a stated purpose or under stated conditions for a contaminant,

in a food, beverage or feedstuff prior to permitting the use of the additive or the marketing of a food, beverage or feedstuff containing the additive or contaminant;

area means a country, part of a country, or all or parts of several countries;

area of low pest or disease prevalence means an area in which a specific pest or disease occurs at low levels;

contaminant includes pesticide and veterinary drug residues and extraneous matter;

control or inspection procedure means any procedure used, directly or indirectly, to determine that a sanitary or phytosanitary measure is fulfilled, including sampling, testing, inspection, evaluation, verification, monitoring, auditing, assurance of conformity, accreditation, registration, certification, or other procedure involving the physical examination of a good, of the packaging of a good, or of the equipment or facilities directly related to production, marketing, or use of a good, but does not mean an approval procedure;

international standard, guideline, or recommendation means a standard, guideline, or recommendation:

(a) regarding food safety, adopted by the *Codex Alimentarius Commission,* including one regarding decomposition elaborated by the *Codex Committee on Fish and Fishery Products,* food additives, contaminants, hygienic practice, and methods of analysis and sampling;

(b) regarding animal health and zoonoses, developed under the auspices of the *International Office of Epizootics;*

(c) regarding plant health, developed under the auspices of the *Secretariat of the International Plant Protection Convention* in cooperation with the *North American Plant Protection Organization;* or

(d) established by or developed under any other international organization agreed on by the Parties;

pest includes a weed;

pest-free or disease-free area means an area in which a specific pest or disease does not occur;

plant includes wild flora;

risk assessment means an evaluation of:

(a) the potential for the introduction, establishment, or spread of a pest or disease and associated biological and economic consequences; or

(b) the potential for adverse effects on human or animal life or health arising from the presence of an additive, contaminant, toxin, or disease-causing organism in a food, beverage, or feedstuff;

sanitary or phytosanitary measure means a measure that a Party adopts, maintains, or applies to:

(a) protect animal or plant life or health in its territory from risks arising from the introduction, establishment, or spread of a pest or disease;

(b) protect human or animal life or health in its territory from risks arising from the presence of an additive, contaminant, toxin, or disease-causing organism in a food, beverage, or feedstuff;

(c) protect human life or health in its territory from risks arising from a disease-causing organism or pest carried by an animal or plant, or a product thereof; or

(d) prevent or limit other damage in its territory arising from the introduction, establishment, or spread of a pest;

including end product criteria; a product-related processing or production method; a testing, inspection, certification, or approval procedure; a relevant statistical method; a sampling procedure; a method of risk assessment; a packaging and labeling requirement directly related to food safety; and a quarantine treatment, such as a relevant requirement associated with the transportation of animals or plants or with material necessary for their survival during transportation; and

scientific basis means a reason based on data or information derived using scientific methods.

PART THREE
TECHNICAL BARRIERS TO TRADE

Chapter Nine

Standards-Related Measures

Article 901: Scope and Coverage

1. This Chapter applies to standards-related measures of a Party, other than those covered by Section B of Chapter Seven (Sanitary and Phytosanitary Measures), that may, directly or indirectly, affect trade in goods or services between the Parties, and to measures of the Parties relating to such measures.

2. Technical specifications prepared by governmental bodies for production or consumption requirements of such bodies shall be governed exclusively by Chapter Ten (Government Procurement).

Article 902: Extent of Obligations

1. Article 105 (Extent of Obligations) does not apply to this Chapter.

2. Each Party shall seek, through appropriate measures, to ensure observance of Articles 904 through 908 by state or provincial governments and by non-governmental standardizing bodies in its territory.

Article 903: Affirmation of Agreement on Technical Barriers to Trade and Other Agreements

Further to Article 103 (Relation to Other Agreements), the Parties affirm with respect to each other their existing rights and obligations relating to standards-related measures under the *GATT Agreement on Technical Barriers to Trade* and all other international agreements, including environmental and conservation agreements, to which those Parties are party.

Article 904: Basic Rights and Obligations

Right to Take Standards-Related Measures

1. Each Party may, in accordance with this Agreement, adopt, maintain, or apply any standards-related measure, including any such measure relating to safety, the protection of human, animal, or plant life or health, the environment or consumers, and any measure to ensure its enforcement or implementation. Such measures include those to prohibit the importation of a good of another Party or the provision of a service by a service provider of another Party that fails to comply with the applicable requirements of those measures or to complete the Party's approval procedures.

Right to Establish Level of Protection

2. Notwithstanding any other provision of this Chapter, each Party may, in pursuing its legitimate objectives of safety or the protection of human, animal, or plant life or health, the environment or consumers, establish the levels of protection that it considers appropriate in accordance with Article 907(2).

Non-Discriminatory Treatment

3. Each Party shall, in respect of its standards-related measures, accord to goods and service providers of another Party:

    (a) national treatment in accordance with Article 301 (Market Access) or Article 1202 (Cross-Border Trade in Services); and

    (b) treatment no less favorable than that it accords to like goods, or in like circumstances to service providers, of any other country.

Unnecessary Obstacles

4. No Party may prepare, adopt, maintain, or apply any standards-related measure with a view to or with the effect of creating an unnecessary obstacle to trade between the Parties. An unnecessary obstacle to trade shall not be deemed to be created where:

    (a) the demonstrable purpose of the measure is to achieve a legitimate objective, and

    (b) the measure does not operate to exclude goods of another Party that meet that legitimate objective.

Article 905: Use of International Standards

1. Each Party shall use, as a basis for its standards-related measures, relevant international standards or international standards whose completion is imminent, except where such standards would be an ineffective or inappropriate means to fulfill its legitimate objectives—for example because of fundamental climatic, geographical, technological, or infrastructural factors, scientific justification, or the level of protection that the Party considers appropriate.

2. A Party's standards-related measure that conforms to an international standard shall be presumed to be consistent with Article 904(3) and (4).

3. Nothing in paragraph 1 shall be construed to prevent a Party, in pursuing its legitimate objectives, from adopting, maintaining, or applying any standards-related measure that results in a higher level of protection than would be achieved if the measure were based on the relevant international standard.

Article 906: Compatibility and Equivalence

1. Recognizing the crucial role of standards-related measures in achieving legitimate objectives, the Parties shall, in accordance with this Chapter, work jointly to enhance the level of safety and of protection of human, animal, and plant life and health, the environment, and consumers.

2. Without reducing the level of safety or of protection of human, animal, or plant life or health, the environment or consumers, without prejudice to the rights of any Party under this Chapter, and taking into account international standardization activities, the Parties shall, to the greatest extent practicable, make compatible their respective standards-related measures, so as to facilitate trade in a good or service between the Parties.

3. Further to Articles 902 and 905, a Party shall, on request of another Party, seek, through appropriate measures, to promote the compatibility of a specific standard or conformity assessment procedure that is maintained in its territory with the standards or conformity assessment procedures maintained in the territory of the other Party.

4. Each importing Party shall treat a technical regulation adopted or maintained by an exporting Party as equivalent to its own where the exporting Party, in cooperation with the importing Party, demonstrates to the satisfaction of the importing Party that its technical regulation adequately fulfills the importing Party's legitimate objectives.

5. The importing Party shall provide to the exporting Party, on request, its reasons in writing for not treating a technical regulation as equivalent under paragraph 4.

6. Each Party shall, wherever possible, accept the results of a conformity assessment procedure conducted in the territory of another Party, provided that it is satisfied that the procedure offers an assurance, equivalent to that provided by a procedure it conducts or a procedure conducted in its territory the results of which it accepts, that the relevant good or service complies with the applicable technical regulation or standard adopted or maintained in the Party's territory.

7. Prior to accepting the results of a conformity assessment procedure pursuant to paragraph 6, and to enhance confidence in the continued reliability of each other's conformity assessment results, the Parties may consult on such matters as the technical competence of the conformity assessment bodies involved, including verified compliance with relevant international standards through such means as accreditation.

Article 907: Assessment of Risk

1. A Party may, in pursuing its legitimate objectives, conduct an assessment of risk. In conducting an assessment, a Party may take into account, among other factors relating to a good or service:

(a) available scientific evidence or technical information;

(b) intended end uses;

(c) processes or production, operating, inspection, sampling, or testing methods; or

(d) environmental conditions.

2. Where pursuant to Article 904(2) a Party establishes a level of protection that it considers appropriate and conducts an assessment of risk, it should avoid arbitrary or unjustifiable distinctions between similar goods or services in the level of protection it considers appropriate, where the distinctions:

(a) result in arbitrary or unjustifiable discrimination against goods or service providers of another Party;

(b) constitute a disguised restriction on trade between the Parties; or

(c) discriminate between similar goods or services for the same use under the same conditions that pose the same level of risk and provide similar benefits.

3. Where a Party conducting an assessment of risk determines that available scientific evidence or other information is insufficient to complete the assessment, it may adopt a provisional technical regulation on the basis of available relevant information. The Party shall, within a reasonable period after information sufficient to complete the assessment of risk is presented to it, complete its assessment, review and, where appropriate, revise the provisional technical regulation in the light of that assessment.

Article 908: Conformity Assessment

1. The Parties shall, further to Article 906 and recognizing the existence of substantial differences in the structure, organization, and operation of conformity assessment procedures in their respective territories, make compatible those procedures to the greatest extent practicable.

2. Recognizing that it should be to the mutual advantage of the Parties concerned and except as set out in Annex 908.2, each Party shall accredit, approve, license, or otherwise recognize conformity assessment bodies in the territory of another Party on terms no less favorable than those accorded to conformity assessment bodies in its territory.

3. Each Party shall, with respect to its conformity assessment procedures:

(a) not adopt or maintain any such procedure that is stricter, nor apply the procedure more strictly, than necessary to give it confidence that a good or a service conforms with an applicable technical regulation or standard, taking into account the risks that nonconformity would create;

(b) initiate and complete the procedure as expeditiously as possible;

(c) in accordance with Article 904(3), undertake processing of applications in nondiscriminatory order;

(d) publish the normal processing period for each such procedure or communicate the anticipated processing period to an applicant on request;

(e) ensure that the competent body

  (i)   on receipt of an application, promptly examines the completeness of the documentation and informs the applicant in a precise and complete manner of any deficiency;

  (ii) transmits to the applicant as soon as possible the results of the conformity assessment procedure in a form that is precise and complete so that the applicant may take any necessary corrective action;

  (iii) where the application is deficient, proceeds as far as practicable with the procedure where the applicant so requests; and

  (iv) informs the applicant, on request, of the status of the application and the reasons for any delay;

(f) limit the information the applicant is required to supply to that necessary to conduct the procedure and to determine appropriate fees;

(g) accord confidential or proprietary information arising from, or supplied in connection with, the conduct of the procedure for a good of another Party or for a service provided by a person of another Party

  (i)   the same treatment as that for a good of the Party or a service provided by a person of the Party, and

  (ii) in any event, treatment that protects an applicant's legitimate commercial interests to the extent provided under the Party's law;

(h) ensure that any fee it imposes for conducting the procedure is no higher for a good of another Party or a service provider of another Party than is equitable in relation to any such fee imposed for its like goods or service providers or for like goods or service providers of any other country, taking into account communication, transportation, and other related costs;

(i) ensure that the location of facilities at which a conformity assessment procedure is conducted does not cause unnecessary inconvenience to an applicant or its agent;

(j) limit the procedure, for a good or service modified subsequent to a determination that the good or service conforms to the applicable technical regulation or standard, to that necessary to determine that the good or service continues to conform to the technical regulation or standard; and

(k) limit any requirement regarding samples of a good to that which is reasonable, and ensures that the selection of samples does not cause unnecessary inconvenience to an applicant or its agent.

4. Each Party shall apply, with such modifications as may be necessary, the relevant provisions of paragraph 3 to its approval procedures.

5. Each Party shall, on request of another Party, take such reasonable measures as may be available to it to facilitate access in its territory for conformity assessment activities.

6. Each Party shall give sympathetic consideration to a request by another Party to negotiate agreements for the mutual recognition of the results of that other Party's conformity assessment procedures.

Article 909: Notification, Publication, and Provision of Information

1. Further to Articles 1802 (Publication) and 1803 (Notification and Provision of Information), each Party proposing to adopt or modify a technical regulation shall:
   (a) at least 60 days prior to the adoption or modification of the measure, other than a law, publish a notice and notify in writing the other Parties of the proposed measure in such a manner as to enable interested persons to become acquainted with the proposed measure, except that in the case of any such measure relating to perishable goods, each Party shall, to the greatest extent practicable, publish the notice and provide the notification at least 30 days prior to the adoption or modification of the measure, but no later than when notification is provided to domestic producers;
   (b) identify in the notice and notification the good or service to which the measure would apply, and shall provide a brief description of the objective of, and reasons for the measure;
   (c) provide a copy of the proposed measure to any Party or interested person that so requests, and shall, wherever possible, identify any provision that deviates in substance from relevant international standards; and
   (d) without discrimination, allow other Parties and interested persons to make comments in writing and shall, on request, discuss the comments and take the comments and the results of the discussions into account.

2. Each Party proposing to adopt or modify a standard or any conformity assessment procedure not otherwise considered to be a technical regulation shall, where an international standard relevant to the proposed measure does not exist or such measure is not substantially the same as an international standard, and where the measure may have a significant effect on the trade of the other Parties:

(a) at an early appropriate stage, publish a notice and provide a notification of the type required in paragraph 1(a) and (b); and

(b) observe paragraph 1(c) and (d).

3. Each Party shall seek, through appropriate measures, to ensure, with respect to a technical regulation of a state or provincial government other than a local government:

(a) that, at an early appropriate stage, a notice and notification of the type required under paragraph 1(a) and (b) are made prior to their adoption; and

(b) observance of paragraph 1(c) and (d).

4. Where a Party considers it necessary to address an urgent problem relating to safety or to protection of human, animal, or plant life or health, the environment or consumers, it may omit any step set out in paragraph 1 or 3, provided that on adoption of a standards-related measure it shall:

(a) immediately provide to the other Parties a notification of the type required under paragraph 1(b), including a brief description of the urgent problem;

(b) provide a copy of the measure to any Party or interested person that so requests; and

(c) without discrimination, allow other Parties and interested persons to make comments in writing, and shall, on request, discuss the comments and take the comments and the results of the discussions into account.

5. Each Party shall, except where necessary to address an urgent problem referred to in paragraph 4, allow a reasonable period between the publication of a standards-related measure and the date that it becomes effective to allow time for interested persons to adapt to the measure.

6. Where a Party allows nongovernmental persons in its territory to be present during the process of development of standards-related measures, it shall also allow nongovernmental persons from the territories of the other Parties to be present.

7. Each Party shall notify the other Parties of the development of, amendment to, or change in the application of its standards-related measures no later than the time at which it notifies nongovernmental persons in general or the relevant sector in its territory.

8. Each Party shall seek, through appropriate measures, to ensure the observance of paragraphs 6 and 7 by a state or provincial government, and by nongovernmental standardizing bodies in its territory.

9. Each Party shall designate by 1 January 1994 a government authority responsible for the implementation at the federal level of the notification provisions of this Article, and shall notify the other Parties thereof. Where a Party

designates two or more government authorities for that purpose, it shall provide to the other Parties complete and unambiguous information on the scope of responsibility of each such authority.

Article 910: Inquiry Points

1. Each Party shall ensure that there is an inquiry point that is able to answer all reasonable inquiries from other Parties and interested persons, and to provide relevant documents regarding:

(a) any standards-related measure proposed, adopted, or maintained in its territory at the federal, state, or provincial government level;

(b) the membership and participation of the Party, or its relevant federal, state, or provincial government authorities, in international and regional standardizing bodies and conformity assessment systems, and in bilateral and multilateral arrangements regarding standards-related measures, and the provisions of those systems and arrangements;

(c) the location of notices published pursuant to Article 909, or where the information can be obtained;

(d) the location of the inquiry points referred to in paragraph 3; and

(e) the Party's procedures for assessment of risk, and factors it considers in conducting the assessment and in establishing, pursuant to Article 904(2), the levels of protection that it considers appropriate.

2. Where a Party designates more than one inquiry point, it shall:

(a) provide to the other Parties complete and unambiguous information on the scope of responsibility of each inquiry point; and

(b) ensure that any inquiry addressed to an incorrect inquiry point is promptly conveyed to the correct inquiry point.

3. Each Party shall take such reasonable measures as may be available to it to ensure that there is at least one inquiry point that is able to answer all reasonable inquiries from other Parties and interested persons and to provide relevant documents or information as to where they can be obtained regarding:

(a) any standard or conformity assessment procedure proposed, adopted, or maintained by nongovernmental standardizing bodies in its territory; and

(b) the membership and participation of relevant nongovernmental bodies in its territory in international and regional standardizing bodies and conformity assessment systems.

4. Each Party shall ensure that where copies of documents are requested by another Party or by interested persons in accordance with this Chapter, they are supplied at the same price, apart from the actual cost of delivery, as the price for domestic purchase.

Article 911: Technical Cooperation

1. Each Party shall, on request of another Party:

   (a) provide to that Party technical advice, information, and assistance on mutually agreed terms and conditions to enhance that Party's standards-related measures and related activities, processes, and systems;

   (b) provide to that Party information on its technical cooperation programs regarding standards-related measures relating to specific areas of interest; and

   (c) consult with that Party during the development of, or prior to the adoption or change in the application of, any standards-related measure.

2. Each Party shall encourage standardizing bodies in its territory to cooperate with the standardizing bodies in the territories of the other Parties in their participation, as appropriate, in standardizing activities, such as through membership in international standardizing bodies.

Article 912: Limitations on the Provision of Information

Nothing in this Chapter shall be construed to require a Party to:

   (a) communicate, publish texts, or provide particulars or copies of documents other than in an official language of the Party; or

   (b) furnish any information the disclosure of which would impede law enforcement or otherwise be contrary to the public interest, or would prejudice the legitimate commercial interests of particular enterprises.

Article 913: Committee on Standards-Related Measures

1. The Parties hereby establish a Committee on Standards-Related Measures, comprising representatives of each Party.

2. The Committee's functions shall include:

   (a) monitoring the implementation and administration of this Chapter, including the progress of the subcommittees and working groups established under paragraph 4, and the operation of the inquiry points established under Article 910;

   (b) facilitating the process by which the Parties make compatible their standards-related measures;

   (c) providing a forum for the Parties to consult on issues relating to standards-related measures, including the provision of technical advice and recommendations under Article 914;

   (d) enhancing cooperation on the development, application, and enforcement of standards-related measures; and

(e) considering non-governmental, regional and multilateral developments regarding standards-related measures, including under the
GATT.

3. The Committee shall:

(a) meet on request of any Party and, unless the Parties otherwise agree,
at least once each year; and

(b) report annually to the Commission on the implementation of this
Chapter.

4. The Committee may, as it considers appropriate, establish and determine
the scope and mandate of subcommittees or working groups, comprising representatives of each Party. Each subcommittee or working group may:

(a) as it considers necessary or desirable, include or consult with

(i) representatives of nongovernmental bodies, including standardizing bodies,

(ii) scientists, and

(iii) technical experts; and

(b) determine its work program, taking into account relevant international
activities.

5. Further to paragraph 4, the Committee shall establish

(a) the following subcommittees:

(i) Land Transportation Standards Subcommittee, in accordance
with Annex 913.5.a-1;

(ii) Telecommunications Standards Subcommittee, in accordance
with Annex 913.5.a-2;

(iii) Automotive Standards Council, in accordance with Annex
913.5.a-3;

(iv) Subcommittee on Labeling of Textile and Apparel Goods, in accordance with Annex 913.5.a-4; and

(b) such other subcommittees or working groups as it considers appropriate to address any topic, including

(i) identification and nomenclature for goods subject to standards-
related measures;

(ii) quality and identity standards and technical regulations;

(iii) packaging, labeling, and presentation of consumer information,
including languages, measurement systems, ingredients, sizes,
terminology, symbols, and related matters;

(iv) product approval and post-market surveillance programs;

(v) principles for the accreditation and recognition of conformity
assessment bodies, procedures and systems;

(vi)   development and implementation of a uniform chemical hazard classification and communication system;

(vii) enforcement programs, including training and inspections by regulatory, analytical, and enforcement personnel;

(viii) promotion and implementation of good laboratory practices;

(ix)   promotion and implementation of good manufacturing practices;

(x)   criteria for assessment of potential environmental hazards of goods;

(xi)   methodologies for assessment of risk;

(xii) guidelines for testing of chemicals, including industrial and agricultural chemicals, pharmaceuticals, and biologicals;

(xiii) methods by which consumer protection, including matters relating to consumer redress, can be facilitated; and

(xiv) extension of the application of this Chapter to other services.

6. Each Party shall, on request of another Party, take such reasonable measures as may be available to it to provide for the participation in the activities of the Committee, where and as appropriate, of representatives of state or provincial governments.

7. A Party requesting technical advice, information, or assistance pursuant to Article 911 shall notify the Committee, which shall facilitate any such request.

Article 914: Technical Consultations

1. Where a Party requests consultations regarding the application of this Chapter to a standards-related measure, and so notifies the Committee, the Committee may facilitate the consultations, if it does not consider the matter itself, by referring the matter for nonbinding technical advice or recommendations to a subcommittee or working group, including an ad hoc subcommittee or working group, or to another forum.

2. The Committee should consider any matter referred to it under paragraph 1 as expeditiously as possible and promptly forward to the Parties any technical advice or recommendations that it develops or receives concerning the matter. The Parties involved shall provide a written response to the Committee concerning the technical advice or recommendations within such time as the Committee may request.

3. Where the involved Parties have had recourse to consultations facilitated by the Committee under paragraph 1, the consultations shall, on the agreement of the Parties involved, constitute consultations under Article 2006 (Consultations).

4. The Parties confirm that a Party asserting that a standards-related measure of another Party is inconsistent with this Chapter shall have the burden of establishing the inconsistency.

Article 915: Definitions

1. For purposes of this Chapter:

approval procedure means any registration, notification, or other mandatory administrative procedure for granting permission for a good or service to be produced, marketed, or used for a stated purpose or under stated conditions;

assessment of risk means evaluation of the potential for adverse effects;

conformity assessment procedure means any procedure used, directly or indirectly, to determine that a technical regulation or standard is fulfilled, including sampling, testing, inspection, evaluation, verification, monitoring, auditing, assurance of conformity, accreditation, registration, or approval used for such a purpose, but does not mean an approval procedure;

international standard means a standards-related measure, or other guide or recommendation, adopted by an international standardizing body and made available to the public;

international standardizing body means a standardizing body whose membership is open to the relevant bodies of at least all the parties to the *GATT Agreement on Technical Barriers to Trade,* including the *International Organization for Standardization* (ISO), the *International Electrotechnical Commission* (IEC), *Codex Alimentarius Commission,* the *World Health Organization* (WHO), the *Food and Agriculture Organization* (FAO), the *International Telecommunication Union* (ITU); or any other body that the Parties designate;

land transportation service means a transportation service provided by means of motor carrier or rail;

legitimate objective includes an objective such as:

    (a) safety;

    (b) protection of human, animal, or plant life or health, the environment or consumers, including matters relating to quality and identifiability of goods or services; and

    (c) sustainable development,

considering, among other things, where appropriate, fundamental climatic or other geographical factors, technological or infrastructural factors, or scientific justification but does not include the protection of domestic production;

make compatible means bring different standards-related measures of the same scope approved by different standardizing bodies to a level such that they are either identical, equivalent, or have the effect of permitting goods or services to be used in place of one another or fulfill the same purpose;

services means land transportation services and telecommunications services;

standard means a document, approved by a recognized body, that provides, for common and repeated use, rules, guidelines or characteristics for goods or related processes and production methods, or for services or related operating methods, with which compliance is not mandatory. It may also include or deal exclusively with terminology, symbols, packaging, marking, or labeling requirements as they apply to a good, process, or production or operating method;

standardizing body means a body having recognized activities in standardization;

standards-related measure means a standard, technical regulation, or conformity assessment procedure;

technical regulation means a document that lays down goods' characteristics or their related processes and production methods, or services' characteristics or their related operating methods, including the applicable administrative provisions, with which compliance is mandatory. It may also include or deal exclusively with terminology, symbols, packaging, marking, or labeling requirements as they apply to a good, process, or production or operating method; and

telecommunications service means a service provided by means of the transmission and reception of signals by any electromagnetic means, but does not mean the cable, broadcast, or other electromagnetic distribution of radio or television programming to the public generally.

2. Except as they are otherwise defined in this Agreement, other terms in this Chapter shall be interpreted in accordance with their ordinary meaning in context and in the light of the objectives of this Agreement, and where appropriate by reference to the terms presented in the sixth edition of the ISO/IEC Guide 2: 1991, General Terms and Their Definitions Concerning Standardization and Related Activities.

Chapter Twenty

Institutional Arrangements and Dispute Settlement Procedures

Section B: Dispute Settlement

Article 2003: Cooperation

The Parties shall at all times endeavor to agree on the interpretation and application of this Agreement, and shall make every attempt through cooperation and consultations to arrive at a mutually satisfactory resolution of any matter that might affect its operation.

Article 2004: Recourse to Dispute Settlement Procedures

Except for the matters covered in Chapter Nineteen (Review and Dispute Settlement in Antidumping and Countervailing Duty Matters) and as otherwise provided in this Agreement, the dispute settlement provisions of this Chapter shall apply with respect to the avoidance or settlement of all disputes between the Parties regarding the interpretation or application of this Agreement or wherever a Party considers that an actual or proposed measure of another Party is or would be inconsistent with the obligations of this Agreement or cause nullification or impairment in the sense of Annex 2004.

Article 2005: GATT Dispute Settlement

1. Subject to paragraphs 2, 3, and 4, disputes regarding any matter arising under both this Agreement and the *General Agreement on Tariffs and Trade*, any agreement negotiated thereunder, or any successor agreement (GATT), may be settled in either forum at the discretion of the complaining Party.

2. Before a Party initiates a dispute settlement proceeding in the GATT against another Party on grounds that are substantially equivalent to those available to that Party under this Agreement, that Party shall notify any third Party of its intention. If a third Party wishes to have recourse to dispute settlement procedures under this Agreement regarding the matter, it shall inform promptly the notifying Party and those Parties shall consult with a view to agreement on a single forum. If those Parties cannot agree, the dispute normally shall be settled under this Agreement.

3. In any dispute referred to in paragraph 1 where the responding Party claims that its action is subject to Article 104 (Relation to Environmental and Conservation Agreements) and requests in writing that the matter be considered under this Agreement, the complaining Party may, in respect of that matter, thereafter have recourse to dispute settlement procedures solely under this Agreement.

4. In any dispute referred to in paragraph 1 that arises under Section B of Chapter Seven (Sanitary and Phytosanitary Measures) or Chapter Nine (Standards-Related Measures):

(a) concerning a measure adopted or maintained by a Party to protect its human, animal, or plant life or health, or to protect its environment, and

(b) that raises factual issues concerning the environment, health, safety, or conservation, including directly related scientific matters,

where the responding Party requests in writing that the matter be considered under this Agreement, the complaining Party may, in respect of that matter, thereafter have recourse to dispute settlement procedures solely under this Agreement.

5. The responding Party shall deliver a copy of a request made pursuant to paragraph 3 or 4 to the other Parties and to its Section of the Secretariat. Where the complaining Party has initiated dispute settlement proceedings regarding any matter subject to paragraph 3 or 4, the responding Party shall deliver its request no later than 15 days thereafter. On receipt of such request, the complaining Party shall promptly withdraw from participation in those proceedings and may initiate dispute settlement procedures under Article 2007.

6. Once dispute settlement procedures have been initiated under Article 2007 or dispute settlement proceedings have been initiated under the GATT, the forum selected shall be used to the exclusion of the other, unless a Party makes a request pursuant to paragraph 3 or 4.

7. For purposes of this Article, dispute settlement proceedings under the GATT are deemed to be initiated by a Party's request for a panel, such as under Article XXIII:2 of the *General Agreement on Tariffs and Trade* 1947, or for a committee investigation, such as under Article 20.1 of the Customs Valuation Code.

Article 2006: Consultations

1. Any Party may request in writing consultations with any other Party regarding any actual or proposed measure or any other matter that it considers might affect the operation of this Agreement.

2. The requesting Party shall deliver the request to the other Parties and to its Section of the Secretariat.

3. Unless the Commission otherwise provides in its rules and procedures established under Article 2001(4), a third Party that considers it has a substantial interest in the matter shall be entitled to participate in the consultations on delivery of written notice to the other Parties and to its Section of the Secretariat.

4. Consultations on matters regarding perishable agricultural goods shall commence within 15 days of the date of delivery of the request.

5. The consulting Parties shall make every attempt to arrive at a mutually satisfactory resolution of any matter through consultations under this Article or other consultative provisions of this Agreement. To this end, the consulting Parties shall:

(a) provide sufficient information to enable a full examination of how the actual or proposed measure or other matter might affect the operation of this Agreement;

(b) treat any confidential or proprietary information exchanged in the course of consultations on the same basis as the Party providing the information; and

(c) seek to avoid any resolution that adversely affects the interests under this Agreement of any other Party.

Article 2007: Commission—Good Offices, Conciliation, and Mediation

1. If the consulting Parties fail to resolve a matter pursuant to Article 2006 within:

(a) 30 days of delivery of a request for consultations,

(b) 45 days of delivery of such request if any other Party has subsequently requested or has participated in consultations regarding the same matter,

(c) 15 days of delivery of a request for consultations in matters regarding perishable agricultural goods, or

(d) such other period as they may agree,

any such Party may request in writing a meeting of the Commission.

2. A Party may also request in writing a meeting of the Commission where:

(a) it has initiated dispute settlement proceedings under the GATT regarding any matter subject to Article 2005(3) or (4), and has received a request pursuant to Article 2005(5) for recourse to dispute settlement procedures under this Chapter; or

(b) consultations have been held pursuant to Article 513 (Working Group on Rules of Origin), Article 723 (Sanitary and Phytosanitary Measures-Technical Consultations) and Article 914 (Standards-Related Measures-Technical Consultations).

3. The requesting Party shall state in the request the measure or other matter complained of and indicate the provisions of this Agreement that it considers relevant, and shall deliver the request to the other Parties and to its Section of the Secretariat.

4. Unless it decides otherwise, the Commission shall convene within 10 days of delivery of the request and shall endeavor to resolve the dispute promptly.

5. The Commission may:

(a) call on such technical advisers or create such working groups or expert groups as it deems necessary;

(b) have recourse to good offices, conciliation, mediation, or such other dispute resolution procedures; or

(c) make recommendations,

as may assist the consulting Parties to reach a mutually satisfactory resolution of the dispute.

6. Unless it decides otherwise, the Commission shall consolidate two or more proceedings before it pursuant to this Article regarding the same measure. The Commission may consolidate two or more proceedings regarding other matters before it pursuant to this Article that it determines are appropriate to be considered jointly.

Article 2008: Request for an Arbitral Panel

1. If the Commission has convened pursuant to Article 2007(4), and the matter has not been resolved within:

(a) 30 days thereafter,

(b) 30 days after the Commission has convened in respect of the matter most recently referred to it, where proceedings have been consolidated pursuant to Article 2007(6), or

(c) such other period as the consulting Parties may agree,

any consulting Party may request in writing the establishment of an arbitral panel. The requesting Party shall deliver the request to the other Parties and to its Section of the Secretariat.

2. On delivery of the request, the Commission shall establish an arbitral panel.

3. A third Party that considers it has a substantial interest in the matter shall be entitled to join as a complaining Party on delivery of written notice of its intention to participate to the disputing Parties and its Section of the Secretariat. The notice shall be delivered at the earliest possible time, and in any event no later than seven days after the date of delivery of a request by a Party for the establishment of a panel.

4. If a third Party does not join as a complaining Party in accordance with paragraph 3, it normally shall refrain thereafter from initiating or continuing:

(a) a dispute settlement procedure under this Agreement, or

(b) a dispute settlement proceeding in the GATT on grounds that are substantially equivalent to those available to that Party under this Agreement,

regarding the same matter in the absence of a significant change in economic or commercial circumstances.

5. Unless otherwise agreed by the disputing Parties, the panel shall be established and perform its functions in a manner consistent with the provisions of this Chapter.

Article 2009: Roster

1. The Parties shall establish by 1 January 1994 and maintain a roster of up to 30 individuals who are willing and able to serve as panelists. The roster members shall be appointed by consensus for terms of three years, and may be reappointed.

2. Roster members shall:

(a) have expertise or experience in law, international trade, other matters covered by this Agreement or the resolution of disputes arising under international trade agreements, and shall be chosen strictly on the basis of objectivity, reliability, and sound judgment;

(b) be independent of, and not be affiliated with or take instructions from, any Party; and

(c) comply with a code of conduct to be established by the Commission.

Article 2010: Qualifications of Panelists

1. All panelists shall meet the qualifications set out in Article 2009(2).

2. Individuals may not serve as panelists for a dispute in which they have participated pursuant to Article 2007(5).

Article 2011: Panel Selection

1. Where there are two disputing Parties, the following procedures shall apply:

(a) The panel shall comprise five members.

(b) The disputing Parties shall endeavor to agree on the chair of the panel within 15 days of the delivery of the request for the establishment of the panel. If the disputing Parties are unable to agree on the chair within this period, the disputing Party chosen by lot shall select within five days as chair an individual who is not a citizen of that Party.

(c) Within 15 days of selection of the chair, each disputing Party shall select two panelists who are citizens of the other disputing Party.

(d) If a disputing Party fails to select its panelists within such period, such panelists shall be selected by lot from among the roster members who are citizens of the other disputing Party.

2. Where there are more than two disputing Parties, the following procedures shall apply:

(a) The panel shall comprise five members.

(b) The disputing Parties shall endeavor to agree on the chair of the panel within 15 days of the delivery of the request for the establishment of the panel. If the disputing Parties are unable to agree on the chair within this period, the Party or Parties on the side of the dispute chosen by lot shall select within 10 days a chair who is not a citizen of such Party or Parties.

(c) Within 15 days of selection of the chair, the Party complained against shall select two panelists, one of whom is a citizen of a complaining Party, and the other of whom is a citizen of another complaining Party. The complaining Parties shall select two panelists who are citizens of the Party complained against.

(d) If any disputing Party fails to select a panelist within such period, such panelist shall be selected by lot in accordance with the citizenship criteria of subparagraph (c).

3. Panelists shall normally be selected from the roster. Any disputing Party may exercise a peremptory challenge against any individual not on the roster who is proposed as a panelist by a disputing Party within 15 days after the individual has been proposed.

4. If a disputing Party believes that a panelist is in violation of the code of conduct, the disputing Parties shall consult and if they agree, the panelist shall be removed and a new panelist shall be selected in accordance with this Article.

Article 2012: Rules of Procedure

1. The Commission shall establish by 1 January 1994 Model Rules of Procedure, in accordance with the following principles:

(a) the procedures shall assure a right to at least one hearing before the panel as well as the opportunity to provide initial and rebuttal written submissions; and

(b) the panel's hearings, deliberations, and initial report, and all written submissions to and communications with the panel shall be confidential.

2. Unless the disputing Parties otherwise agree, the panel shall conduct its proceedings in accordance with the Model Rules of Procedure.

3. Unless the disputing Parties otherwise agree within 20 days from the date of the delivery of the request for the establishment of the panel, the terms of reference shall be:

"To examine, in the light of the relevant provisions of the Agreement, the matter referred to the Commission (as set out in the request for a Commission meeting) and to make findings, determinations and recommendations as provided in Article 2016(2)."

4. If a complaining Party wishes to argue that a matter has nullified or impaired benefits, the terms of reference shall so indicate.

5. If a disputing Party wishes the panel to make findings as to the degree of adverse trade effects on any Party of any measure found not to conform with the obligations of the Agreement or to have caused nullification or impairment in the sense of Annex 2004, the terms of reference shall so indicate.

Article 2013: Third Party Participation

A Party that is not a disputing Party, on delivery of a written notice to the disputing Parties and to its Section of the Secretariat, shall be entitled to attend all hearings, to make written and oral submissions to the panel, and to receive written submissions of the disputing Parties.

Article 2014: Role of Experts

On request of a disputing Party, or on its own initiative, the panel may seek information and technical advice from any person or body that it deems appropriate, provided that the disputing Parties so agree and subject to such terms and conditions as such Parties may agree.

Article 2015: Scientific Review Boards

1. On request of a disputing Party or, unless the disputing Parties disapprove, on its own initiative, the panel may request a written report of a scientific

review board on any factual issue concerning environmental, health, safety, or other scientific matters raised by a disputing Party in a proceeding, subject to such terms and conditions as such Parties may agree.

2. The board shall be selected by the panel from among highly qualified, independent experts in the scientific matters, after consultations with the disputing Parties and the scientific bodies set out in the Model Rules of Procedure established pursuant to Article 2012(1).

3. The participating Parties shall be provided:

(a) advance notice of, and an opportunity to provide comments to the panel on, the proposed factual issues to be referred to the board; and

(b) a copy of the board's report and an opportunity to provide comments on the report to the panel.

4. The panel shall take the board's report and any comments by the Parties on the report into account in the preparation of its report.

Article 2016: Initial Report

1. Unless the disputing Parties otherwise agree, the panel shall base its report on the submissions and arguments of the Parties and on any information before it pursuant to Article 2014 or 2015.

2. Unless the disputing Parties otherwise agree, the panel shall, within 90 days after the last panelist is selected or such other period as the Model Rules of Procedure established pursuant to Article 2012(1) may provide, present to the disputing Parties an initial report containing:

(a) findings of fact, including any findings pursuant to a request under Article 2012(5);

(b) its determination as to whether the measure at issue is or would be inconsistent with the obligations of this Agreement or cause nullification or impairment in the sense of Annex 2004, or any other determination requested in the terms of reference; and

(c) its recommendations, if any, for resolution of the dispute.

3. Panelists may furnish separate opinions on matters not unanimously agreed.

4. A disputing Party may submit written comments to the panel on its initial report within 14 days of presentation of the report.

5. In such an event, and after considering such written comments, the panel, on its own initiative or on the request of any disputing Party, may:

(a) request the views of any participating Party;

(b) reconsider its report; and

(c) make any further examination that it considers appropriate.

Article 2017: Final Report

1. The panel shall present to the disputing Parties a final report, including any separate opinions on matters not unanimously agreed, within 30 days of presentation of the initial report, unless the disputing Parties otherwise agree.

2. No panel may, either in its initial report or its final report, disclose which panelists are associated with majority or minority opinions.

3. The disputing Parties shall transmit to the Commission the final report of the panel, including any report of a scientific review board established under Article 2015, as well as any written views that a disputing Party desires to be appended, on a confidential basis within a reasonable period of time after it is presented to them.

4. Unless the Commission decides otherwise, the final report of the panel shall be published 15 days after it is transmitted to the Commission.

Article 2018: Implementation of Final Report

1. On receipt of the final report of a panel, the disputing Parties shall agree on the resolution of the dispute, which normally shall conform with the determinations and recommendations of the panel, and shall notify their Sections of the Secretariat of any agreed resolution of any dispute.

2. Wherever possible, the resolution shall be non-implementation or removal of a measure not conforming with this Agreement or causing nullification or impairment in the sense of Annex 2004 or, failing such a resolution, compensation.

Article 2019: Non-Implementation—Suspension of Benefits

1. If in its final report a panel has determined that a measure is inconsistent with the obligations of this Agreement or causes nullification or impairment in the sense of Annex 2004 and the Party complained against has not reached agreement with any complaining Party on a mutually satisfactory resolution pursuant to Article 2018(1) within 30 days of receiving the final report, such complaining Party may suspend the application to the Party complained against of benefits of equivalent effect until such time as they have reached agreement on a resolution of the dispute.

2. In considering what benefits to suspend pursuant to paragraph 1:

    (a) a complaining Party should first seek to suspend benefits in the same sector or sectors as that affected by the measure or other matter that the panel has found to be inconsistent with the obligations of this Agreement or to have caused nullification or impairment in the sense of Annex 2004; and

    (b) a complaining Party that considers it is not practicable or effective to suspend benefits in the same sector or sectors may suspend benefits in other sectors.

3. On the written request of any disputing Party delivered to the other Parties and its Section of the Secretariat, the Commission shall establish a panel to determine whether the level of benefits suspended by a Party pursuant to paragraph 1 is manifestly excessive.

4. The panel proceedings shall be conducted in accordance with the Model Rules of Procedure. The panel shall present its determination within 60 days after the last panelist is selected or such other period as the disputing Parties may agree.

Section C: Domestic Proceedings and Private Commercial Dispute Settlement

Article 2020: Referrals of Matters from Judicial or Administrative Proceedings

1. If an issue of interpretation or application of this Agreement arises in any domestic judicial or administrative proceeding of a Party that any Party considers would merit its intervention, or if a court or administrative body solicits the views of a Party, that Party shall notify the other Parties and its Section of the Secretariat. The Commission shall endeavor to agree on an appropriate response as expeditiously as possible.

2. The Party in whose territory the court or administrative body is located shall submit any agreed interpretation of the Commission to the court or administrative body in accordance with the rules of that forum.

3. If the Commission is unable to agree, any Party may submit its own views to the court or administrative body in accordance with the rules of that forum.

Article 2021: Private Rights

No Party may provide for a right of action under its domestic law against any other Party on the ground that a measure of another Party is inconsistent with this Agreement.

Article 2022: Alternative Dispute Resolution

1. Each Party shall, to the maximum extent possible, encourage and facilitate the use of arbitration and other means of alternative dispute resolution for the settlement of international commercial disputes between private parties in the free trade area.

2. To this end, each Party shall provide appropriate procedures to ensure observance of agreements to arbitrate and for the recognition and enforcement of arbitral awards in such disputes.

3. A Party shall be deemed to be in compliance with paragraph 2 if it is a party to and is in compliance with the 1958 *United Nations Convention on the Recognition and Enforcement of Foreign Arbitral Awards* or the 1975 *Inter-American Convention on International Commercial Arbitration*.

4. The Commission shall establish an Advisory Committee on Private Commercial Disputes comprising persons with expertise or experience in the resolution of private international commercial disputes. The Committee shall report and provide recommendations to the Commission on general issues referred to it by the Commission respecting the availability, use, and effectiveness of arbitration and other procedures for the resolution of such disputes in the free trade area.

Appendix III

North American Agreement on Environmental Cooperation (Final Draft)

Between the Government of Canada, the Government of the United Mexican States, and the Government of the United States of America, 13 September 1993

Preamble

The Government of Canada, the Government of the United Mexican States, and the Government of the United States of America:

CONVINCED of the importance of the conservation, protection, and enhancement of the environment in their territories and the essential role of cooperation in these areas in achieving sustainable development for the well-being of present and future generations;

REAFFIRMING the sovereign right of States to exploit their own resources pursuant to their own environmental and development policies and their responsibility to ensure that activities within their jurisdiction or control do not cause damage to the environment of other States or of areas beyond the limits of national jurisdiction;

RECOGNIZING the interrelationship of their environments;

ACKNOWLEDGING the growing economic and social links between them, including the North American Free Trade Agreement (NAFTA);

RECONFIRMING the importance of the environmental goals and objectives of the NAFTA, including enhanced levels of environmental protection;

EMPHASIZING the importance of public participation in conserving, protecting, and enhancing the environment;

NOTING the existence of differences in their respective natural endowments, climactic and geographical conditions, and economic, technological, and infrastructural capabilities;

REAFFIRMING the *Stockholm Declaration on the Human Environment* of 1972 and the *Rio Declaration on Environment and Development* of 1992;

RECALLING their tradition of environmental cooperation and expressing their desire to support and build on international environmental agreements and existing policies and laws, in order to promote cooperation between them; and

CONVINCED of the benefits to be derived from a framework, including a Commission, to facilitate effective cooperation on the conservation, protection and enhancement of the environment in their territories;

Have Agreed as Follows:

PART ONE
OBJECTIVES

Article 1: Objectives

The objectives of this Agreement are to:

(a) foster the protection and improvement of the environment in the territories of the Parties for the well-being of present and future generations;

(b) promote sustainable development based on cooperation and mutually supportive environmental and economic policies;

(c) increase cooperation between the Parties to better conserve, protect, and enhance the environment, including wild flora and fauna;

(d) support the environmental goals and objectives of the NAFTA;

(e) avoid creating trade distortions or new trade barriers;

(f) strengthen cooperation on the development and improvement of environmental laws, regulations, procedures, policies, and practices;

(g) enhance compliance with, and enforcement of, environmental laws and regulations;

(h) promote transparency and public participation in the development of environmental laws, regulations, and policies;

(i) promote economically efficient and effective environmental measures; and

(j) promote pollution prevention policies and practices.

PART TWO
OBLIGATIONS

Article 2: General Commitments

1. Each Party shall, with respect to its territory:

(a) periodically prepare and make publicly available reports on the state of the environment;

(b) develop and review environmental emergency preparedness measures;

(c) promote education in environmental matters, including environmental law;

(d) further scientific research and technology development in respect of environmental matters;

(e) assess, as appropriate, environmental impacts; and

(f) promote the use of economic instruments for the efficient achievement of environmental goals.

2. Each Party shall consider implementing in its law any recommendation developed by the Council under Article 10(5)(b).

3. Each Party shall consider prohibiting the export to the territories of the other Parties of a pesticide or toxic substance whose use is prohibited within the Party's territory. When a Party adopts a measure prohibiting or severely restricting the use of a pesticide or toxic substance in its territory, it shall notify the other Parties of the measure, either directly or through an appropriate international organization.

Article 3: Levels of Protection

Recognizing the right of each Party to establish its own levels of domestic environmental protection and environmental development policies and priorities, and to adopt or modify accordingly its environmental laws and regulations, each Party shall ensure that its laws and regulations provide for high levels of environmental protection and shall strive to continue to improve those laws and regulations.

Article 4: Publication

1. Each Party shall ensure that its laws, regulations, procedures, and administrative rulings of general application respecting any matter covered by this Agreement are promptly published or otherwise made available in such a manner as to enable interested persons and Parties to become acquainted with them.

2. To the extent possible, each Party shall:

(a) publish in advance any such measure that it proposes to adopt; and

(b) provide interested persons and Parties a reasonable opportunity to comment on such proposed measures.

Article 5: Government Enforcement Action

1. With the aim of achieving high levels of environmental protection and compliance with its environmental laws and regulations, each Party shall effec-

tively enforce its environmental laws and regulations through appropriate governmental action, subject to Article 37, such as:

(a) appointing and training inspectors;

(b) monitoring compliance and investigating suspected violations, including through on-site inspections;

(c) seeking assurances of voluntary compliance and compliance agreements;

(d) publicly releasing noncompliance information;

(e) issuing bulletins or other periodic statements on enforcement procedures;

(f) promoting environmental audits;

(g) requiring record keeping and reporting;

(h) providing or encouraging mediation and arbitration services;

(i) using licenses, permits, or authorizations;

(j) initiating, in a timely manner, judicial, quasi-judicial, or administrative proceedings to seek appropriate sanctions or remedies for violations of its environmental laws and regulations;

(k) providing for search, seizure, or detention; or

(l) issuing administrative orders, including orders of a preventative, curative, or emergency nature.

2. Each Party shall ensure that judicial, quasi-judicial, or administrative enforcement proceedings are available under its law to sanction or remedy violations of its environmental laws and regulations.

3. Sanctions and remedies provided for a violation of a Party's environmental laws and regulations shall, as appropriate:

(a) take into consideration the nature and gravity of the violation, any economic benefit derived from the violation by the violator, the economic condition of the violator, and other relevant factors; and

(b) include compliance agreements, fines, imprisonment, injunctions, the closure of facilities, and the cost of containing or cleaning up pollution.

Article 6: Private Access to Remedies

1. Each Party shall ensure that interested persons may request the Party's competent authorities to investigate alleged violations of its environmental laws and regulations and shall give such requests due consideration in accordance with law.

2. Each Party shall ensure that persons with a legally recognized interest under its law in a particular matter have appropriate access to administrative, quasi-judicial, or judicial proceedings for the enforcement of the Party's environmental laws and regulations.

3. Private access to remedies shall include rights, in accordance with the Party's law, such as:

(a) to sue another person under that Party's jurisdiction for damages;

(b) to seek sanctions or remedies such as monetary penalties, emergency closures, or orders to mitigate the consequences of violations of its environmental laws and regulations;

(c) to request the competent authorities to take appropriate action to enforce that Party's environmental laws and regulations in order to protect the environment or to avoid environmental harm; or

(d) to seek injunctions where a person suffers, or may suffer, loss, damage, or injury as a result of conduct by another person under that Party's jurisdiction contrary to that Party's environmental laws and regulations or from tortious conduct.

Article 7: Procedural Guarantees

1. Each Party shall ensure that its administrative, quasi-judicial, and judicial proceedings referred to in Articles 5(2) and 6(2) are fair, open, and equitable, and to this end shall provide that such proceedings:

(a) comply with due process of law;

(b) are open to the public, except where the administration of justice otherwise requires;

(c) entitle the parties to the proceedings to support or defend their respective positions and to present information or evidence; and

(d) are not unnecessarily complicated and do not entail unreasonable charges or time limits or unwarranted delays.

2. Each Party shall provide that final decisions on the merits of the case in such proceedings are:

(a) in writing and preferably state the reasons on which the decisions are based;

(b) made available without undue delay to the parties to the proceedings and, consistent with its law, to the public; and

(c) based on information or evidence in respect of which the parties were offered the opportunity to be heard.

3. Each Party shall provide, as appropriate, that parties to such proceedings have the right, in accordance with its law, to seek review and, where warranted, correction of final decisions issued in such proceedings.

4. Each Party shall ensure that tribunals that conduct or review such proceedings are impartial and independent and do not have any substantial interest in the outcome of the matter.

PART THREE
COMMISSION FOR ENVIRONMENTAL
COOPERATION

Article 8: The Commission

1. The Parties hereby establish the Commission for Environmental Cooperation.

2. The Commission shall comprise a Council, a Secretariat, and a Joint Public Advisory Committee.

Section A: The Council

Article 9: Council Structure and Procedures

1. The Council shall comprise cabinet-level or equivalent representatives of the Parties, or their designees.

2. The Council shall establish its rules and procedures.

The Council shall convene:

    (a) at least once a year in regular session; and

    (b) in special session at the request of any Party.

Regular sessions shall be chaired successively by each Party.

4. The Council shall hold public meetings in the course of all regular sessions. Other meetings held in the course of regular or special sessions shall be public where the Council so decides.

5. The Council may:

    (a) establish, and assign responsibilities to, ad hoc or standing committees, working groups or expert groups;

    (b) seek the advice of nongovernmental organizations or persons, including independent experts; and

    (c) take such other action in the exercise of its functions as the Parties may agree.

6. All decisions and recommendations of the Council shall be taken by consensus, except as the Council may otherwise decide or as otherwise provided in this Agreement.

7. All decisions and recommendations of the Council shall be made public, except as the Council may otherwise decide or as otherwise provided in this Agreement.

Article 10: Council Functions

1. The Council shall be the governing body of the Commission and shall:

(a) serve as a forum for the discussion of environmental matters within the scope of this Agreement;

(b) oversee the implementation and develop recommendations on the further elaboration of this Agreement and, to this end, the Council shall, within four years after the date of entry into force of this Agreement, review its operation and effectiveness in the light of experience;

(c) oversee the Secretariat;

(d) address questions and differences that may arise between the Parties regarding the interpretation or application of this Agreement;

(e) approve the annual program and budget of the Commission; and

(f) promote and facilitate cooperation between the Parties with respect to environmental matters.

2. The Council may consider, and develop recommendations regarding:

(a) comparability of techniques and methodologies for data gathering and analysis, data management, and electronic data communications on matters covered by this Agreement;

(b) pollution prevention techniques and strategies;

(c) approaches and common indicators for reporting on the state of the environment;

(d) the use of economic instruments for the pursuit of domestic and internationally agreed environmental objectives;

(e) scientific research and technology development in respect of environmental matters;

(f) promotion of public awareness regarding the environment;

(g) transboundary and border environmental issues, such as the long-range transport of air and marine pollutants;

(h) exotic species that may be harmful;

(i) the conservation and protection of wild flora and fauna and their habitat, and specially protected natural areas;

(j) the protection of endangered and threatened species;

(k) environmental emergency preparedness and response activities;

(l) environmental matters as they relate to economic development;

(m) the environmental implications of goods throughout their life cycles;

(n) human resource training and development in the environmental field;

(o) the exchange of environmental scientists and officials;

(p) approaches to environmental compliance and enforcement;

(q) ecologically sensitive national accounts;

(r) eco-labeling; and

(s) other matters as it may decide.

3. The Council shall strengthen cooperation on the development and continuing improvement of environmental laws and regulations, including by:

(a) promoting the exchange of information on criteria and methodologies used in establishing domestic environmental standards; and

(b) without reducing levels of environmental protection, establishing a process for developing recommendations on greater compatibility of environmental technical regulations, standards, and conformity assessment procedures in a manner consistent with the NAFTA.

4. The Council shall encourage:

(a) effective enforcement by each Party of its environmental laws and regulations;

(b) compliance with those laws and regulations; and

(c) technical cooperation between the Parties.

5. The Council shall promote and, as appropriate, develop recommendations regarding:

(a) public access to information concerning the environment that is held by public authorities of each Party, including information on hazardous materials and activities in its communities, and opportunity to participate in decision-making processes related to such public access; and

(b) appropriate limits for specific pollutants, taking into account differences in ecosystems.

6. The Council shall cooperate with the NAFTA Free Trade Commission to achieve the environmental goals and objectives of the NAFTA by:

(a) acting as a point of inquiry and receipt for comments from nongovernmental organizations and persons concerning those goals and objectives;

(b) providing assistance in consultations under Article 1114 of the NAFTA where a Party considers that another Party is waiving or derogating from, or offering to waive or otherwise derogate from, an environmental measure as an encouragement to establish, acquire, expand, or retain an investment of an investor, with a view to avoiding any such encouragement;

(c) contributing to the prevention or resolution of environment-related trade disputes by:

(i) seeking to avoid disputes between the Parties,

(ii) making recommendations to the Free Trade Commission with respect to the avoidance of such disputes, and

(iii) identifying experts able to provide information or technical advice to NAFTA committees, working groups and other NAFTA bodies;

(d) considering on an ongoing basis the environmental effects of the NAFTA; and

(e) otherwise assisting the Free Trade Commission in environment-related matters.

7. Recognizing the significant bilateral nature of many transboundary environmental issues, the Council shall, with a view to agreement between the Parties pursuant to this Article within three years on obligations, consider and develop recommendations with respect to:

(a) assessing the environmental impact of proposed projects subject to decisions by a competent government authority and likely to cause significant adverse transboundary effects, including a full evaluation of comments provided by other Parties and persons of other Parties;

(b) notification, provision of relevant information, and consultation between Parties with respect to such projects; and

(c) mitigation of the potential adverse effects of such projects.

8. The Council shall encourage the establishment by each Party of appropriate administrative procedures pursuant to its environmental laws to permit another Party to seek the reduction, elimination, or mitigation of transboundary pollution on a reciprocal basis.

9. The Council shall consider and, as appropriate, develop recommendations on the provision by a Party, on a reciprocal basis, of access to and rights and remedies before its courts and administrative agencies for persons in another Party's territory who have suffered or are likely to suffer damage or injury caused by pollution originating in its territory as if the damage or injury were suffered in its territory.

Section B: The Secretariat

Article 11: Secretariat Structure and Procedures

1. The Secretariat shall be headed by an Executive Director, who shall be chosen by the Council for a three-year term, which may be renewed by the Council for one additional three-year term. The position of Executive Director shall rotate consecutively between nationals of each Party. The Council may remove the Executive Director solely for cause.

2. The Executive Director shall appoint and supervise the staff of the Secretariat, regulate their powers and duties, and fix their remuneration in accordance with general standards to be established by the Council. The general standards shall provide that:

(a) staff shall be appointed and retained, and their conditions of employment shall be determined, strictly on the basis of efficiency, competence, and integrity;

(b) in appointing staff, the Executive Director shall take into account lists of candidates prepared by the Parties and by the Joint Public Advisory Committee;

(c) due regard shall be paid to the importance of recruiting an equitable proportion of the professional staff from among the nationals of each Party; and

(d) the Executive Director shall inform the Council of all appointments.

3. The Council may decide, by a two-thirds vote, to reject any appointment that does not meet the general standards. Any such decision shall be made and held in confidence.

4. In the performance of their duties, the Executive Director and the staff shall not seek or receive instructions from any government or any other authority external to the Council. Each Party shall respect the international character of the responsibilities of the Executive Director and the staff and shall not seek to influence them in the discharge of their responsibilities.

5. The Secretariat shall provide technical, administrative, and operational support to the Council and to committees and groups established by the Council, and such other support as the Council may direct.

6. The Executive Director shall submit for the approval of the Council the annual program and budget of the Commission, including provision for proposed cooperative activities and for the Secretariat to respond to contingencies.

7. The Secretariat shall, as appropriate, provide the Parties and the public information on where they may receive technical advice and expertise with respect to environmental matters.

8. The Secretariat shall safeguard:

(a) from disclosure information it receives that could identify a nongovernmental organization or person making a submission if the person or organization so requests or the Secretariat otherwise considers it appropriate; and

(b) from public disclosure any information it receives from any nongovernmental organization or person where the information is designated by that nongovernmental organization or person as confidential or proprietary.

Article 12: Annual Report of the Commission

1. The Secretariat shall prepare an annual report of the Commission in accordance with instructions from the Council. The Secretariat shall submit a draft of the report for review by the Council. The final report shall be released publicly.

2. The report shall cover:

(a) activities and expenses of the Commission during the previous year;

(b) the approved program and budget of the Commission for the subsequent year;

(c) the actions taken by each Party in connection with its obligations under this Agreement, including data on the Party's environmental enforcement activities;

(d) relevant views and information submitted by nongovernmental organizations and persons, including summary data regarding submissions, and any other relevant information the Council deems appropriate;

(e) recommendations made on any matter within the scope of this Agreement; and

(f) any other matter that the Council instructs the Secretariat to include.

3. The report shall periodically address the state of the environment in the territories of the Parties.

Article 13: Secretariat Reports

1. The Secretariat may prepare a report for the Council on any matter within the scope of the annual program. Should the Secretariat wish to prepare a report on any other environmental matter related to the cooperative functions of this Agreement, it shall notify the Council and may proceed unless, within 30 days of such notification, the Council objects by a two-thirds vote to the preparation of the report. Such other environmental matters shall not include issues related to whether a Party has failed to enforce its environmental laws and regulations. Where the Secretariat does not have specific expertise in the matter under review, it shall obtain the assistance of one or more independent experts of recognized experience in the matter to assist in the preparation of the report.

2. In preparing such a report, the Secretariat may draw upon any relevant technical, scientific, or other information, including information:

(a) that is publicly available;

(b) submitted by interested nongovernmental organizations and persons;

(c) submitted by the Joint Public Advisory Committee;

(d) furnished by a Party;

(e) gathered through public consultations, such as conferences, seminars, and symposia; or

(f) developed by the Secretariat, or by independent experts engaged pursuant to paragraph 1.

3. The Secretariat shall submit its report to the Council, which shall make it publicly available, normally within 60 days following its submission, unless the Council otherwise decides.

Article 14: Submissions on Enforcement Matters

1. The Secretariat may consider a submission from any nongovernmental organization or person asserting that a Party is failing to effectively enforce its environmental law, if the Secretariat finds that the submission:

(a) is in writing in a language designated by that Party in a notification to the Secretariat;

(b) clearly identifies the person or organization making the submission;

(c) provides sufficient information to allow the Secretariat to review the submission, including any documentary evidence on which the submission may be based;

(d) appears to be aimed at promoting enforcement rather than at harassing industry;

(e) indicates that the matter has been communicated in writing to the relevant authorities of the Party and indicates the Party's response, if any; and

(f) is filed by a person or organization residing or established in the territory of a Party.

2. Where the Secretariat determines that a submission meets the criteria set out in paragraph 1, the Secretariat shall determine whether the submission merits requesting a response from the Party. In deciding whether to request a response, the Secretariat shall be guided by whether:

(a) the submission alleges harm to the person or organization making the submission;

(b) the submission, alone or in combination with other submissions, raises matters whose further study in this process would advance the goals of this Agreement;

(c) private remedies available under the Party's law have been pursued; and

(d) the submission is drawn exclusively from mass media reports.

Where the Secretariat makes such a request, it shall forward to the Party a copy of the submission and any supporting information provided with the submission.

3. The Party shall advise the Secretariat within 30 days or, in exceptional circumstances and on notification to the Secretariat, within 60 days of delivery of the request:

(a) whether the matter is the subject of a pending judicial or administrative proceeding, in which case the Secretariat shall proceed no further; and

(b) of any other information that the Party wishes to submit, such as

(i) whether the matter was previously the subject of a judicial or administrative proceeding, and

(ii) whether private remedies in connection with the matter are available to the person or organization making the submission and whether they have been pursued.

Article 15: Factual Record

1. If the Secretariat considers that the submission, in the light of any response provided by the Party, warrants developing a factual record, the Secretariat shall so inform the Council and provide its reasons.

2. The Secretariat shall prepare a factual record if the Council, by a two-thirds vote, instructs it to do so.

3. The preparation of a factual record by the Secretariat pursuant to this Article shall be without prejudice to any further steps that may be taken with respect to any submission.

4. In preparing a factual record, the Secretariat shall consider any information furnished by a Party and may consider any relevant technical, scientific, or other information:

(a) that is publicly available;

(b) submitted by interested nongovernmental organizations or persons;

(c) submitted by the Joint Public Advisory Committee; or

(d) developed by the Secretariat or by independent experts.

5. The Secretariat shall submit a draft factual record to the Council. Any Party may provide comments on the accuracy of the draft within 45 days thereafter.

6. The Secretariat shall incorporate, as appropriate, any such comments in the final factual record and submit it to the Council.

7. The Council may, by a two-thirds vote, make the final factual record publicly available, normally within 60 days following its submission.

Section C: Advisory Committees

Article 16: Joint Public Advisory Committee

1. The Joint Public Advisory Committee shall comprise 15 members, unless the Council otherwise decides. Each Party or, if the Party so decides, its National Advisory Committee convened under Article 17, shall appoint an equal number of members.

2. The Council shall establish the rules of procedure for the Joint Public Advisory Committee, which shall choose its own chair.

3. The Joint Public Advisory Committee shall convene at least once a year at the time of the regular session of the Council and at such other times as the Council, or the Committee's chair with the consent of a majority of its members, may decide.

4. The Joint Public Advisory Committee may provide advice to the Council on any matter within the scope of this Agreement, including on any documents provided to it under paragraph 6, and on the implementation and further

elaboration of this Agreement, and may perform such other functions as the Council may direct.

5. The Joint Public Advisory Committee may provide relevant technical, scientific, or other information to the Secretariat, including for purposes of developing a factual record under Article 15. The Secretariat shall forward to the Council copies of any such information.

6. The Secretariat shall provide to the Joint Public Advisory Committee at the time they are submitted to the Council copies of the proposed annual program and budget of the Commission, the draft annual report, and any report the Secretariat prepares pursuant to Article 13.

7. The Council may, by a two-thirds vote, make a factual record available to the Joint Public Advisory Committee.

Article 17: National Advisory Committees

Each Party may convene a national advisory committee, comprising members of its public, including representatives of nongovernmental organizations and persons, to advise it on the implementation and further elaboration of this Agreement.

Article 18: Governmental Committees

Each Party may convene a governmental committee, which may comprise or include representatives of federal and state or provincial governments, to advise it on the implementation and further elaboration of this Agreement.

Section D: Official Languages

Article 19: Official Languages

The official languages of the Commission shall be English, French, and Spanish. All annual reports under Article 12, reports submitted to the Council under Article 13, factual records submitted to the Council under Article 15(6) and panel reports under Part Five shall be available in each official language at the time they are made public. The Council shall establish rules and procedures regarding interpretation and translation.

PART FOUR
COOPERATION AND PROVISION
OF INFORMATION

Article 20: Cooperation

1. The Parties shall at all times endeavor to agree on the interpretation and application of this Agreement, and shall make every attempt through coop-

eration and consultations to resolve any matter that might affect its operation.

2. To the maximum extent possible, each Party shall notify any other Party with an interest in the matter of any proposed or actual environmental measure that the Party considers might materially affect the operation of this Agreement or otherwise substantially affect that other Party's interests under this Agreement.

3. On request of any other Party, a Party shall promptly provide information and respond to questions pertaining to any such actual or proposed environmental measure, whether or not that other Party has been previously notified of that measure.

4. Any Party may notify any other Party of, and provide to that Party, any credible information regarding possible violations of its environmental law, specific and sufficient to allow the other Party to inquire into the matter. The notified Party shall take appropriate steps in accordance with its law to so inquire and to respond to the other Party.

Article 21: Provision of Information

1. On request of the Council or the Secretariat, each Party shall, in accordance with its law, provide such information as the Council or the Secretariat may require, including:

   (a) promptly making available any information in its possession required for the preparation of a report or factual record, including compliance and enforcement data; and

   (b) taking all reasonable steps to make available any other such information requested.

2. If a Party considers that a request for information from the Secretariat is excessive or otherwise unduly burdensome, it may so notify the Council. The Secretariat shall revise the scope of its request to comply with any limitations established by the Council by a two-thirds vote.

3. If a Party does not make available information requested by the Secretariat, as may be limited pursuant to paragraph 2, it shall promptly advise the Secretariat of its reasons in writing.

PART FIVE
CONSULTATION AND RESOLUTION OF DISPUTES

Article 22: Consultations

1. Any Party may request in writing consultations with any other Party regarding whether there has been a persistent pattern of failure by that other Party to effectively enforce its environmental law.

2. The requesting Party shall deliver the request to the other Parties and to the Secretariat.

3. Unless the Council otherwise provides in its rules and procedures established under Article 9(2), a third Party that considers it has a substantial interest in the matter shall be entitled to participate in the consultations on delivery of written notice to the other Parties and to the Secretariat.

4. The consulting Parties shall make every attempt to arrive at a mutually satisfactory resolution of the matter through consultations under this Article.

Article 23: Initiation of Procedures

1. If the consulting Parties fail to resolve the matter pursuant to Article 22 within 60 days of delivery of a request for consultations, or such other period as the consulting Parties may agree, any such Party may request in writing a special session of the Council.

2. The requesting Party shall state in the request the matter complained of and shall deliver the request to the other Parties and to the Secretariat.

3. Unless it decides otherwise, the Council shall convene within 20 days of delivery of the request and shall endeavor to resolve the dispute promptly.

4. The Council may:

   (a) call on such technical advisers or create such working groups or expert groups as it deems necessary;

   (b) have recourse to good offices, conciliation, mediation, or such other dispute resolution procedures; or

   (c) make recommendations

as may assist the consulting Parties to reach a mutually satisfactory resolution of the dispute. Any such recommendations shall be made public if the Council, by a two-thirds vote, so decides.

5. Where the Council decides that a matter is more properly covered by another agreement or arrangement to which the consulting Parties are party, it shall refer the matter to those Parties for appropriate action in accordance with such other agreement or arrangement.

Article 24: Request for an Arbitral Panel

1. If the matter has not been resolved within 60 days after the Council has convened pursuant to Article 23, the Council shall, on the written request of any consulting Party and by a two-thirds vote, convene an arbitral panel to consider the matter where the alleged persistent pattern of failure by the Party complained against to effectively enforce its environmental law relates to a situation involving workplaces, firms, companies, or sectors that produce goods or provide services:

   (a) traded between the territories of the Parties; or

(b) that compete, in the territory of the Party complained against, with goods or services produced or provided by persons of another Party.

2. A third Party that considers it has a substantial interest in the matter shall be entitled to join as a complaining Party on delivery of written notice of its intention to participate to the disputing Parties and the Secretariat. The notice shall be delivered at the earliest possible time, and in any event no later than seven days after the date of the vote of the Council to convene a panel.

3. Unless otherwise agreed by the disputing Parties, the panel shall be established and perform its functions in a manner consistent with the provisions of this Part.

Article 25: Roster

1. The Council shall establish and maintain a roster of up to 45 individuals who are willing and able to serve as panelists. The roster members shall be appointed by consensus for terms of three years, and may be reappointed.

2. Roster members shall:

(a) have expertise or experience in environmental law or its enforcement, or in the resolution of disputes arising under international agreements, or other relevant scientific, technical, or professional expertise or experience;

(b) be chosen strictly on the basis of objectivity, reliability, and sound judgment;

(c) be independent of, and not be affiliated with or take instructions from, any Party, the Secretariat, or the Joint Public Advisory Committee; and

(d) comply with a code of conduct to be established by the Council.

Article 26: Qualifications of Panelists

1. All panelists shall meet the qualifications set out in Article 25(2).

2. Individuals may not serve as panelists for a dispute in which:

(a) they have participated pursuant to Article 23(4); or

(b) they have, or a person or organization with which they are affiliated has, an interest, as set out in the code of conduct established under Article 25(2)(d).

Article 27: Panel Selection

1. Where there are two disputing Parties, the following procedures shall apply:

(a) The panel shall comprise five members.

(b) The disputing Parties shall endeavor to agree on the chair of the panel within 15 days after the Council votes to convene the panel. If the disputing Parties are unable to agree on the chair within this period, the disputing Party chosen by lot shall select within five days a chair who is not a citizen of that Party.

(c) Within 15 days of selection of the chair, each disputing Party shall select two panelists who are citizens of the other disputing Party.

(d) If a disputing Party fails to select its panelists within such period, such panelists shall be selected by lot from among the roster members who are citizens of the other disputing Party.

2. Where there are more than two disputing Parties, the following procedures shall apply:

(a) The panel shall comprise five members.

(b) The disputing Parties shall endeavor to agree on the chair of the panel within 15 days after the Council votes to convene the panel. If the disputing Parties are unable to agree on the chair within this period, the Party or Parties on the side of the dispute chosen by lot shall select within 10 days a chair who is not a citizen of such Party or Parties.

(c) Within 30 days of selection of the chair, the Party complained against shall select two panelists, one of whom is a citizen of a complaining Party, and the other of whom is a citizen of another complaining Party. The complaining Parties shall select two panelists who are citizens of the Party complained against.

(d) If any disputing Party fails to select a panelist within such period, such panelist shall be selected by lot in accordance with the citizenship criteria of subparagraph (c).

3. Panelists shall normally be selected from the roster. Any disputing Party may exercise a peremptory challenge against any individual not on the roster who is proposed as a panelist by a disputing Party within 30 days after the individual has been proposed.

4. If a disputing Party believes that a panelist is in violation of the code of conduct, the disputing Parties shall consult and, if they agree, the panelist shall be removed and a new panelist shall be selected in accordance with this Article.

Article 28: Rules of Procedure

1. The Council shall establish Model Rules of Procedure. The procedures shall provide:

(a) a right to at least one hearing before the panel;

(b) the opportunity to make initial and rebuttal written submissions; and

(c) that no panel may disclose which panelists are associated with majority or minority opinions.

2. Unless the disputing Parties otherwise agree, panels convened under this Part shall be established and conduct their proceedings in accordance with the Model Rules of Procedure.

3. Unless the disputing Parties otherwise agree within 20 days after the Council votes to convene the panel, the terms of reference shall be:

> "To examine, in light of the relevant provisions of the Agreement, including those contained in Part Five, whether there has been a persistent pattern of failure by the Party complained against to effectively enforce its environmental law, and to make findings, determinations and recommendations in accordance with Article 31(2)."

Article 29: Third Party Participation

A Party that is not a disputing Party, on delivery of a written notice to the disputing Parties and to the Secretariat, shall be entitled to attend all hearings, to make written and oral submissions to the panel, and to receive written submissions of the disputing Parties.

Article 30: Role of Experts

On request of a disputing Party, or on its own initiative, the panel may seek information and technical advice from any person or body that it deems appropriate, provided that the disputing Parties so agree and subject to such terms and conditions as such Parties may agree.

Article 31: Initial Report

1. Unless the disputing Parties otherwise agree, the panel shall base its report on the submissions and arguments of the Parties and on any information before it pursuant to Article 30.

2. Unless the disputing Parties otherwise agree, the panel shall, within 180 days after the last panelist is selected, present to the disputing Parties an initial report containing:

(a) findings of fact;

(b) its determination as to whether there has been a persistent pattern of failure by the Party complained against to effectively enforce its environmental law, or any other determination requested in the terms of reference; and

(c) in the event the panel makes an affirmative determination under subparagraph (b), its recommendations, if any, for the resolution of the dispute, which normally shall be that the Party complained against adopt and implement an action plan sufficient to remedy the pattern of nonenforcement.

3. Panelists may furnish separate opinions on matters not unanimously agreed.

4. A disputing Party may submit written comments to the panel on its initial report within 30 days of presentation of the report.

5. In such an event, and after considering such written comments, the panel, on its own initiative or on the request of any disputing Party, may:

(a) request the views of any participating Party;

(b) reconsider its report; and

(c) make any further examination that it considers appropriate.

Article 32: Final Report

1. The panel shall present to the disputing Parties a final report, including any separate opinions on matters not unanimously agreed, within 60 days of presentation of the initial report, unless the disputing Parties otherwise agree.

2. The disputing Parties shall transmit to the Council the final report of the panel, as well as any written views that a disputing Party desires to be appended, on a confidential basis within 15 days after it is presented to them.

3. The final report of the panel shall be published five days after it is transmitted to the Council.

Article 33: Implementation of Final Report

If, in its final report, a panel determines that there has been a persistent pattern of failure by the Party complained against to effectively enforce its environmental law, the disputing Parties may agree on a mutually satisfactory action plan, which normally shall conform with the determinations and recommendations of the panel. The disputing Parties shall promptly notify the Secretariat and the Council of any agreed resolution of the dispute.

Article 34: Review of Implementation

1. If, in its final report, a panel determines that there has been a persistent pattern of failure by the Party complained against to effectively enforce its environmental law, and:

(a) the disputing Parties have not agreed on an action plan under Article 33 within 60 days of the date of the final report, or

(b) the disputing Parties cannot agree on whether the Party complained against is fully implementing

   (i) an action plan agreed under Article 33,

   (ii) an action plan deemed to have been established by a panel under paragraph 2, or

(iii) an action plan approved or established by a panel under paragraph 4,

any disputing Party may request that the panel be reconvened. The requesting Party shall deliver the request in writing to the other Parties and to the Secretariat. The Council shall reconvene the panel on delivery of the request to the Secretariat.

2. No Party may make a request under paragraph 1(a) earlier than 60 days, or later than 120 days, after the date of the final report. If the disputing Parties have not agreed to an action plan and if no request was made under paragraph 1(a), the last action plan, if any, submitted by the Party complained against to the complaining Party or Parties within 60 days of the date of the final report, or such other period as the disputing Parties may agree, shall be deemed to have been established by the panel 120 days after the date of the final report.

3. A request under paragraph 1(b) may be made no earlier than 180 days after an action plan has been:

(a) agreed under Article 33;

(b) deemed to have been established by a panel under paragraph 2; or

(c) approved or established by a panel under paragraph 4;

and only during the term of any such action plan.

4. Where a panel has been reconvened under paragraph 1(a), it:

(a) shall determine whether any action plan proposed by the Party complained against is sufficient to remedy the pattern of nonenforcement and

(i)   if so, shall approve the plan, or

(ii) if not, shall establish such a plan consistent with the law of the Party complained against, and

(b) may, where warranted, impose a monetary enforcement assessment in accordance with Annex 34,

within 90 days after the panel has been reconvened or such other period as the disputing Parties may agree.

5. Where a panel has been reconvened under paragraph 1(b), it shall determine either that:

(a) the Party complained against is fully implementing the action plan, in which case the panel may not impose a monetary enforcement assessment; or

(b) the Party complained against is not fully implementing the action plan, in which case the panel shall impose a monetary enforcement assessment in accordance with Annex 34,

within 60 days after it has been reconvened or such other period as the disputing Parties may agree.

6. A panel reconvened under this Article shall provide that the Party complained against shall fully implement any action plan referred to in paragraph 4(a)(ii) or 5(b), and pay any monetary enforcement assessment imposed under paragraph 4(b) or 5(b), and any such provision shall be final.

Article 35: Further Proceeding

A complaining Party may, at any time beginning 180 days after a panel determination under Article 34(5)(b), request in writing that a panel be reconvened to determine whether the Party complained against is fully implementing the action plan. On delivery of the request to the other Parties and the Secretariat, the Council shall reconvene the panel. The panel shall make the determination within 60 days after it has been reconvened or such other period as the disputing Parties may agree.

Article 36: Suspension of Benefits

1. Subject to Annex 36A, where a Party fails to pay a monetary enforcement assessment within 180 days after it is imposed by a panel:

 (a) under Article 34(4)(b), or

 (b) under Article 34(5)(b), except where benefits may be suspended under paragraph 2(a),

any complaining Party or Parties may suspend, in accordance with Annex 36B, the application to the Party complained against of NAFTA benefits in an amount no greater than that sufficient to collect the monetary enforcement assessment.

2. Subject to Annex 36A, where a panel has made a determination under Article 34(5)(b) and the panel:

 (a) has previously imposed a monetary enforcement assessment under Article 34(4)(b) or established an action plan under Article 34(4)(a)(ii); or

 (b) has subsequently determined under Article 35 that a Party is not fully implementing an action plan;

the complaining Party or Parties may, in accordance with Annex 36B, suspend annually the application to the Party complained against of NAFTA benefits in an amount no greater than the monetary enforcement assessment imposed by the panel under Article 34(5)(b).

3. Where more than one complaining Party suspends benefits under paragraph 1 or 2, the combined suspension shall be no greater than the amount of the monetary enforcement assessment.

4. Where a Party has suspended benefits under paragraph 1 or 2, the Council shall, on the delivery of a written request by the Party complained against to the other Parties and the Secretariat, reconvene the panel to determine whether the monetary enforcement assessment has been paid or collected, or

whether the Party complained against is fully implementing the action plan, as the case may be. The panel shall submit its report within 45 days after it has been reconvened. If the panel determines that the assessment has been paid or collected, or that the Party complained against is fully implementing the action plan, the suspension of benefits under paragraph 1 or 2, as the case may be, shall be terminated.

5. On the written request of the Party complained against, delivered to the other Parties and the Secretariat, the Council shall reconvene the panel to determine whether the suspension of benefits by the complaining Party or Parties pursuant to paragraph 1 or 2 is manifestly excessive. Within 45 days of the request, the panel shall present a report to the disputing Parties containing its determination.

PART SIX
GENERAL PROVISIONS

Article 37: Enforcement Principle

Nothing in this Agreement shall be construed to empower a Party's authorities to undertake environmental law enforcement activities in the territory of another Party.

Article 38: Private Rights

No Party may provide for a right of action under its law against any other Party on the ground that another Party has acted in a manner inconsistent with this Agreement.

Article 39: Protection of Information

1. Nothing in this Agreement shall be construed to require a Party to make available or allow access to information:

(a) the disclosure of which would impede its environmental law enforcement; or

(b) that is protected from disclosure by its law governing business or proprietary information, personal privacy, or the confidentiality of governmental decision making.

2. If a Party provides confidential or proprietary information to another Party, the Council, the Secretariat, or the Joint Public Advisory Committee, the recipient shall treat the information on the same basis as the Party providing the information.

3. Confidential or proprietary information provided by a Party to a panel under this Agreement shall be treated in accordance with the rules of procedure established under Article 28.

Article 40: Relation to Other Environmental Agreements

Nothing in this Agreement shall be construed to affect the existing rights and obligations of the Parties under other international environmental agreements, including conservation agreements, to which such Parties are party.

Article 41: Extent of Obligations

Annex 41 applies to the Parties specified in that Annex.

Article 42: National Security

Nothing in this Agreement shall be construed:

   (a) to require any Party to make available or provide access to information the disclosure of which it determines to be contrary to its essential security interests; or

   (b) to prevent any Party from taking any actions that it considers necessary for the protection of its essential security interests relating to

      (i) arms, ammunition, and implements of war, or

      (ii) the implementation of national policies or international agreements respecting the nonproliferation of nuclear weapons or other nuclear explosive devices.

Article 43: Funding of the Commission

Each Party shall contribute an equal share of the annual budget of the Commission, subject to the availability of appropriated funds in accordance with the Party's legal procedures. No Party shall be obligated to pay more than any other Party in respect of an annual budget.

Article 44: Privileges and Immunities

The Executive Director and staff of the Secretariat shall enjoy in the territory of each Party such privileges and immunities as are necessary for the exercise of their functions.

Article 45: Definitions

1. For purposes of this Agreement:

A Party has not failed to "effectively enforce its environmental law" or to comply with Article 5(1) in a particular case where the action or inaction in question by agencies or officials of that Party:

   (a) reflects a reasonable exercise of their discretion in respect of investigatory, prosecutorial, regulatory, or compliance matters; or

(b) results from *bona fide* decisions to allocate resources to enforcement in respect of other environmental matters determined to have higher priorities;

nongovernmental organization means any scientific, professional, business, nonprofit, or public interest organization or association which is neither affiliated with, nor under the direction of, a government;

persistent pattern means a sustained or recurring course of action or inaction beginning after the date of entry into force of this Agreement;

province means a province of Canada, and includes the Yukon Territory and the Northwest Territories and their successors; and

territory means for a Party the territory of that Party as set out in Annex 45.

2. For purposes of Article 14(1) and Part Five:

(a) **environmental law** means any statute or regulation of a Party, or provision thereof, the primary purpose of which is the protection of the environment, or the prevention of a danger to human life or health, through

    (i)   the prevention, abatement, or control of the release, discharge, or emission of pollutants or environmental contaminants;

    (ii) the control of environmentally hazardous or toxic chemicals, substances, materials, and wastes, and the dissemination of information related thereto; or

    (iii) the protection of wild flora or fauna, including endangered species, their habitat, and specially protected natural areas

in the Party's territory, but does not include any statute or regulation, or provision thereof, directly related to worker safety or health.

(b) For greater certainty, the term **environmental law** does not include any statute or regulation, or provision thereof, the primary purpose of which is managing the commercial harvest or exploitation, or subsistence or aboriginal harvesting, of natural resources.

(c) The primary purpose of a particular statutory or regulatory provision for purposes of subparagraphs (a) and (b) shall be determined by reference to its primary purpose, rather than to the primary purpose of the statute or regulation of which it is part.

3. For purposes of Article 14(3), **judicial or administrative proceeding** means:

(a) a domestic judicial, quasi-judicial, or administrative action pursued by the Party in a timely fashion and in accordance with its law. Such actions comprise: mediation; arbitration; the process of issuing a license, permit, or authorization; seeking an assurance of voluntary compliance or a compliance agreement; seeking sanctions or remedies in an administrative or judicial forum; and the process of issuing an administrative order; and

(b) an international dispute resolution proceeding to which the Party is party.

PART SEVEN
FINAL PROVISIONS

Article 46: Annexes

The Annexes to this Agreement constitute an integral part of the Agreement.

Article 47: Entry into Force

This Agreement shall enter into force on 1 January 1994, immediately after entry into force of the NAFTA, on an exchange of written notifications certifying the completion of necessary legal procedures.

Article 48: Amendments

1. The Parties may agree on any modification of or addition to this Agreement.

2. When so agreed, and approved in accordance with the applicable legal procedures of each Party, a modification or addition shall constitute an integral part of this Agreement.

Article 49: Accession

Any country or group of countries may accede to this Agreement subject to such terms and conditions as may be agreed between such country or countries and the Council and following approval in accordance with the applicable legal procedures of each country.

Article 50: Withdrawal

A Party may withdraw from this Agreement six months after it provides written notice of withdrawal to the other Parties. If a Party withdraws, the Agreement shall remain in force for the remaining Parties.

Article 51: Authentic Texts

The English, French, and Spanish texts of this Agreement are equally authentic.

IN WITNESS WHEREOF, the undersigned, being duly authorized by the respective Governments, have signed this Agreement.

Appendix III   357

Annex 34
Monetary Enforcement Assessments

1. For the first year after the date of entry into force of this Agreement, any monetary enforcement assessment shall be no greater than 20 million dollars (U.S.) or its equivalent in the currency of the Party complained against. Thereafter, any monetary enforcement assessment shall be no greater than 0.007 percent of total trade in goods between the Parties during the most recent year for which data are available.

2. In determining the amount of the assessment, the panel shall take into account:

   (a) the pervasiveness and duration of the Party's persistent pattern of failure to effectively enforce its environmental law;

   (b) the level of enforcement that could reasonably be expected of a Party given its resource constraints;

   (c) the reasons, if any, provided by the Party for not fully implementing an action plan;

   (d) efforts made by the Party to begin remedying the pattern of nonenforcement after the final report of the panel; and

   (e) any other relevant factors.

3. All monetary enforcement assessments shall be paid in the currency of the Party complained against into a fund established in the name of the Commission by the Council and shall be expended at the direction of the Council to improve or enhance the environment or environmental law enforcement in the Party complained against, consistent with its law.

Annex 36A
Canadian Domestic Enforcement and Collection

1. For the purposes of this Annex, panel determination means:

   (a) a determination by a panel under Article 34(4)(b) or 5(b) that provides that Canada shall pay a monetary enforcement assessment; and

   (b) a determination by a panel under Article 34(5)(b) that provides that Canada shall fully implement an action plan where the panel:

   (i) has previously established an action plan under Article 34(4)(a)(ii) or imposed a monetary enforcement assessment under Article 34(4)(b); or

   (ii) has subsequently determined under Article 35 that Canada is not fully implementing an action plan.

2. Canada shall adopt and maintain procedures that provide that:

   (a) subject to subparagraph (b), the Commission, at the request of a complaining Party, may in its own name file in a court of competent jurisdiction a certified copy of a panel determination;

(b) the Commission may file in court a panel determination that is a panel determination described in paragraph 1(a) only if Canada has failed to comply with the determination within 180 days of when the determination was made;

(c) when filed, the panel determination, for purposes of enforcement, shall become an order of the court;

(d) the Commission may take proceedings for enforcement of a panel determination that is made an order of the court, in that court, against the person against whom the panel determination is addressed in accordance with paragraph 6 of Annex 41;

(e) proceedings to enforce a panel determination that has been made an order of the court shall be conducted by way of summary proceedings;

(f) in proceedings to enforce a panel determination that is a panel determination described in paragraph 1(b) and that has been made an order of the court, the court shall promptly refer any question of fact or any question of interpretation of the panel determination to the panel that made the panel determination, and the decision of the panel shall be binding on the court;

(g) a panel determination that has been made an order of the court shall not be subject to domestic review or appeal; and

(h) an order made by the court in proceedings to enforce a panel determination that has been made an order of the court shall not be subject to review or appeal.

3. Where Canada is the Party complained against, the procedures adopted and maintained by Canada under this Annex shall apply and the procedures set out in Article 36 shall not apply.

4. Any change by Canada to the procedures adopted and maintained by Canada under this Annex that have the effect of undermining the provisions of this Annex shall be considered a breach of this Agreement.

Annex 36B

Suspension of Benefits

1. Where a complaining Party suspends NAFTA tariff benefits in accordance with this Agreement, the Party may increase the rates of duty on originating goods of the Party complained against to levels not to exceed the lesser of:

(a) the rate that was applicable to those goods immediately prior to the date of entry into force of the NAFTA, and

(b) the Most-Favored-Nation rate applicable to those goods on the date the Party suspends such benefits,

and such increase may be applied only for such time as is necessary to collect, through such increase, the monetary enforcement assessment.

2. In considering what tariff or other benefits to suspend pursuant to Article 36(1) or (2):

(a) a complaining Party shall first seek to suspend benefits in the same sector or sectors as that in respect of which there has been a persistent pattern of failure by the Party complained against to effectively enforce its environmental law; and

(b) a complaining Party that considers it is not practicable or effective to suspend benefits in the same sector or sectors may suspend benefits in other sectors.

Annex 41
Extent of Obligations

1. On the date of signature of this Agreement, or of the exchange of written notifications under Article 47, Canada shall set out in a declaration a list of any provinces for which Canada is to be bound in respect of matters within their jurisdiction. The declaration shall be effective on delivery to the other Parties, and shall carry no implication as to the internal distribution of powers within Canada. Canada shall notify the other Parties six months in advance of any modification to its declaration.

2. When considering whether to instruct the Secretariat to prepare a factual record pursuant to Article 15, the Council shall take into account whether the submission was made by a nongovernmental organization or enterprise incorporated or otherwise organized under the laws of a province included in the declaration made under paragraph 1.

3. Canada may not request consultations under Article 22 or a Council meeting under Article 23 or request the establishment of a panel or join as a complaining Party under Article 24 against another Party at the instance, or primarily for the benefit, of any government of a province not included in the declaration made under paragraph 1.

4. Canada may not request a Council meeting under Article 23, or request the establishment of a panel or join as a complaining Party under Article 24 concerning whether there has been a persistent pattern of failure by another Party to effectively enforce its environmental law, unless Canada states in writing that the matter would be under federal jurisdiction if it were to arise within the territory of Canada, or:

(a) Canada states in writing that the matter would be under provincial jurisdiction if it were to arise within the territory of Canada; and

(b) the provinces included in the declaration account for at least 55 percent of Canada's Gross Domestic Product (GDP) for the most recent year in which data are available; and

(c) where the matter concerns a specific industry or sector, at least 55 percent of total Canadian production in that industry or sector is accounted for by the provinces included in the declaration for the most recent year in which data are available.

5. No other Party may request a Council meeting under Article 23 or request the establishment of a panel or join as a complaining Party under Article 24

concerning whether there has been a persistent failure to effectively enforce an environmental law of a province unless that province is included in the declaration made under paragraph 1 and the requirements of subparagraphs 4(b) and (c) have been met.

6. Canada shall, no later than the date on which an arbitral panel is convened pursuant to Article 24 respecting a matter within the scope of paragraph 5 of this Annex, notify in writing the complaining Parties and the Secretariat of whether any monetary enforcement assessment or action plan imposed by a panel under Article 34(4) or 34(5) against Canada shall be addressed to Her Majesty in right of Canada or Her Majesty in right of the province concerned.

7. Canada shall use its best efforts to make this Agreement applicable to as many of its provinces as possible.

8. Two years after the date of entry into force of this Agreement, the Council shall review the operation of this Annex and, in particular, shall consider whether the Parties should amend the thresholds established in paragraph 4.

Annex 45
Country-Specific Definitions

For purposes of this Agreement:

territory means:

(a) with respect to Canada, the territory to which its customs laws apply, including any areas beyond the territorial seas of Canada within which, in accordance with international law and its domestic law, Canada may exercise rights with respect to the seabed and subsoil and their natural resources;

(b) with respect to Mexico,

    (i)   the states of the Federation and the Federal District;

    (ii) the islands, including the reefs and keys, in adjacent seas;

    (iii) the islands of Guadalupe and Revillagigedo situated in the Pacific Ocean;

    (iv) the continental shelf and the submarine shelf of such islands, keys, and reefs;

    (v) the waters of the territorial seas, in accordance with international law, and its interior maritime waters;

    (vi) the space located above the national territory, in accordance with international law; and

    (vii) any areas beyond the territorial seas of Mexico within which, in accordance with international law, including the *United Nations Convention on the Law of the Sea,* and its domestic law, Mexico may exercise rights with respect to the seabed and subsoil and their natural resources; and

(c) with respect to the United States,

(i)   the customs territory of the United States, which includes the 50 states, the District of Columbia, and Puerto Rico;

(ii) the foreign trade zones located in the United States and Puerto Rico; and

(iii) any areas beyond the territorial seas of the United States within which, in accordance with international law and its domestic law, the United States may exercise rights with respect to the seabed and subsoil and their natural resources.

Appendix IV

Executive Order 12915 of 13 May 1994

Federal Implementation of the North American Agreement on Environmental Cooperation

59 F.R. 25775

By the authority vested in me as President by the Constitution, and the laws of the United States of America, including the North American Free Trade Agreement Implementation Act, Public Law 103-182; 107 Stat. 2057 ("NAFTA Implementation Act"), and section 301 of title 3, United States Code, it is hereby ordered as follows:

Section 1. Policy. (a) The North American Agreement on Environmental Cooperation ("Environmental Cooperation Agreement") shall be implemented consistent with United States policy for the protection of human, animal or plant life or health, and the environment. The Environmental Cooperation Agreement shall also be implemented to advance sustainable development, pollution prevention, environmental justice, ecosystem protection, and biodiversity preservation and in a manner that promotes transparency and public participation in accordance with the North American Free Trade Agreement ("NAFTA") and the Environmental Cooperation Agreement.

(b) Effective implementation of the Environmental Cooperation Agreement is essential to the realization of the environmental objectives of NAFTA and the NAFTA Implementation Act and promotes cooperation on trade and environmental issues between the United States, Canada, and Mexico.

Section 2. Implementation of the Environmental Cooperation Agreement.

(a) Policy Priorities. In accordance with Article 10(2) of the Environmental Cooperation Agreement, it is the policy of the United States to promote consideration of, with a view toward developing recommendations and reaching agreement on, the following priorities within the Council of the Commission for Environmental Cooperation ("Council"):

(1) pursuant to Article 10(2)(m), the environmental impact of goods throughout their life cycles, including the environmental effects of processes and production methods and the internalization of environmental costs associated with products from raw material to disposal;

(2) pursuant to Articles 10(2)(b), (g), (i), (j), and (k), pollution prevention techniques and strategies, transboundary and border environmental issues, the conservation and protection of wild flora and fauna (including endangered species), their habitats and specially protected natural areas, and environmental emergency preparedness and response activities:

(3) pursuant to Articles 10(3) and 10(4), implementation of Environmental Cooperation Agreement provisions and the exchange of information among the United States, Canada, and Mexico concerning the development, continuing improvement, and effective enforcement of, and compliance with, environmental laws, policies, incentives, regulations, and other applicable standards;

(4) pursuant to Article 10(5)(a), public access to environmental information held by public authorities of each party to the Environmental Cooperation Agreement, including information on hazardous materials and activities in its communities and the opportunity to participate in decision-making processes related to such public access;

(5) pursuant to Article 10(2)(1), environmental matters as they relate to sustainable development; and

(6) other priorities as appropriate or necessary.

(b) *United States Representation on Council.* The Administrator of the Environmental Protection Agency ("EPA") shall be the representative of the United States on the Council. The policies and positions of the United States in the Council shall be coordinated through applicable interagency procedures.

(c) *Environmental Effects of NAFTA.* Pursuant to Article 10(6)(d) of the Environmental Cooperation Agreement, the Administrator of the EPA shall work actively within the Council to consider on an ongoing basis the environmental effects of the NAFTA and review progress toward the objectives of the Environmental Cooperation Agreement.

(d) *Transparency and Public Participation.* The United States, as appropriate, shall endeavor to ensure the transparency and openness of, and opportunities for the public to participate in, activities under the Environmental Cooperation Agreement.

(1) To the greatest extent practicable, pursuant to Articles 15(1) and 15(2), where the Secretariat of the Commission for Environmental Cooperation ("Secretariat") informs the Council that a factual record is warranted, the United States shall support the preparation of such factual record.

(2) To the greatest extent practicable, the United States shall support public disclosure of all nonconfidential and nonproprietary elements of reports, factual records, decisions, recommendations, and other information gathered or prepared by the Commission for Environmental Cooperation ("Commission"). Where requested information is not made available, the United States shall endeavor to have the Commission state in writing to the public its reasons for denial of the request.

(3) The United States shall provide public notice of the opportunity to apply for inclusion on a roster of qualified individuals available to serve on arbitral panels under the Environmental Cooperation Agreement.

(4) The United States shall seek to ensure that the Model Rules of Procedure for dispute settlement established pursuant to Articles 28(1) and 28(2) of the Environmental Cooperation Agreement provide for the preparation of public versions of written submissions and arbitral reports not otherwise made publicly available, and for public access to arbitral hearings.

(5) Consistent with the Environmental Cooperation Agreement, the EPA Administrator shall develop procedures to inform the public of arbitral proceedings and Commission activities under the Environmental Cooperation Agreement, and to provide appropriate mechanisms for receiving public comment with respect to such arbitral proceedings and Commission activities involving the United States.

(6) As a disputing party, the United States shall seek to ensure, pursuant to Article 30 of the Environmental Cooperation Agreement, that the arbitral panels consult with the appropriate experts for information and technical advice.

(e) *Consultation with States* (1) Pursuant to Article 18 of the Environmental Cooperation Agreement, the EPA Administrator shall establish a governmental committee to furnish advice regarding implementation and further elaboration of the Agreement. Through this committee, or through other means as appropriate, the EPA Administrator and other relevant Federal agencies shall:

(A) inform the States on a continuing basis of matters under the Environmental Cooperation Agreement that directly relate to, or will potentially have a direct impact on, the States, including: (i) dispute settlement proceedings and other matters involving enforcement by the States of environmental laws; and (ii) implementation of the Environmental Cooperation Agreement, including Council committee, and working group activities, in any area in which the States exercise concurrent or exclusive legislative, regulatory, or enforcement authority;

(B) provide the States with an opportunity to submit information and advice with respect to matters identified in Section 2 (e)(1)(A) of this order; and

(C) involve the States to the greatest extent practicable at each stage of the development of United States positions regarding matters identified in Section 2(e)(1)(A) of this order that will be addressed by the Council, committees, subcommittees, or working groups established under the Environmental Cooperation Agreement, or through dispute settlement processes prescribed under the Environmental Cooperation Agreement (including involvement through the inclusion of appropriate representatives of the States).

(2) When formulating positions regarding matters identified in Section 2(e)(1)(A) of this order, the United States shall take into account the information and advice received from States.

(3) The United States, where appropriate, shall include representatives of interested States as Members of the United States delegations to the Council and other Commission bodies, including arbitral panels.

Section 3. National Advisory Committee. The EPA Administrator shall utilize a National Advisory Committee as provided under Article 17 of the Environmental Cooperation Agreement.

Section 4. United States Contributions to the Commission for Environmental Cooperation. In accordance with section 532(a)(2) of the NAFTA Implementation Act, the EPA is designated as the agency authorized to make the contributions of the United States from funds available for such contributions to the annual budget of the Commission for Environmental Cooperation.

Section 5. Judicial Review. This order is intended only to improve the internal management of the executive branch and is not intended to, and does not, create any right to administrative or judicial review, or any other right or benefit or trust responsibility, substantive or procedural, enforceable by a party against the United States, its agencies or instrumentalities, its officers or employees, or any other person.

THE WHITE HOUSE
13 May 1994.

Appendix V

An Act to Amend the Crown Liability and Proceedings Act

Summary

The North American Agreement on Environmental Cooperation and the North American Agreement on Labor Cooperation each establish a mechanism for the resolution of disputes between Parties to the Agreement with respect to whether there has been a persistent pattern of failure by a Party to effectively enforce its environmental law or to effectively enforce its occupational safety and health child labor or minimum wage technical labor standards.

Each Agreement provides for the establishment of panels to make findings of fact and determinations with respect to the matter in dispute. A panel may, in its determination, require a Party to adopt an action plan and, in certain cases, to pay a monetary enforcement assessment.

This enactment amends the *Crown Liability and Proceedings Act* so as to permit domestic enforcement by the Federal Court of Canada of any panel determination that is addressed to the Crown in right of Canada.

The major elements of the enactment are as follows:

1. The enactment sets out a procedure by which a panel determination may be filed in the Federal Court. On filing, the panel determination would become an order of the Federal Court.

2. A panel determination that is made an order of the Federal Court would be enforceable in the same manner as any other order of that Court, subject to certain limitations.

3. There would be no right of appeal against a panel determination or an order or decision made by the Court in any enforcement proceedings. The enactment also contains a privative clause to exclude domestic judicial review

of panel proceedings, panel determinations, enforcement proceedings taken in Federal Court, and orders and decisions made by the Federal Court in any enforcement proceedings.

An Act to Amend the Crown Liability and Proceedings Act

[Assented to 12 May 1994]

Her Majesty, by and with the advice and consent of the Senate and House of Commons of Canada, enacts as follows:

1. The *Crown Liability and Proceedings Act* is amended by adding the following after Section 20:

Environmental and Labor Cooperation Agreements

20.1 In this section and Sections 20.2 to 20.4,

"appropriate Commission" means

(a) in respect of a panel determination as defined in Annex 36A of the Environmental Cooperation Agreement, the Commission for Environmental Cooperation established under Article 8 of that Agreement; and

(b) in respect of a panel determination as defined in Annex 41A of the Labor Cooperation Agreement, the Commission for Labor Cooperation established under Article 8 of that Agreement;

"Environmental Cooperation Agreement" means the North American Agreement on Environmental Cooperation entered into by the Government of Canada, the Government of the United Mexican States, and the Government of the United States of America and signed on 14 September 1993, as amended from time to time in accordance with Article 48 of that Agreement;

"Labor Cooperation Agreement" means the North American Agreement on Labor Cooperation entered into by the Government of Canada, the Government of the United Mexican States, and the Government of the United States of America and signed on 14 September 1993, as amended from time to time in accordance with Article 52 of that Agreement;

"panel" means an arbitral panel convened under Article 24 of the Environmental Cooperation Agreement or Article 29 of the Labor Cooperation Agreement;

"Panel determination" means a panel determination as defined in Annex 36A of the Environmental Cooperation Agreement or Annex 41A of the Labor Cooperation Agreement.

20.2 (1) A panel determination that is addressed to the Crown may, for the purpose of its enforcement only, be made an order of the Federal Court.

(2) To make a panel determination an order of the Federal Court, the appropriate Commission shall file a certified copy of the determination in the

Registry of that Court and, on filing, the determination becomes an order of that Court.

20.3 (1) Subject to subsections (2) to (5), a panel determination that is made an order of the Federal Court is enforceable in the same manner as any other order of that Court.

(2) Proceedings for enforcement of a panel determination that is made an order of the Federal Court may be taken against the Crown only in that Court and only by the appropriate Commission.

(3) Any proceedings referred to in subsection (2) shall be heard and determined in a summary way.

(4) If any question of fact or interpretation of a panel determination arises in any proceedings referred to in subsection (2), the Federal Court shall refer the question to the panel that made the determination, and the decision of the panel on the question is binding on that Court.

(5) No person or body may intervene in any proceedings referred to in subsection (2).

20.4 (1) Panel determinations, including panel determinations that are made orders of the Federal Court, and orders and decisions made by the Federal Court in any proceedings referred to in subsection 20.3(2) are final and binding and are not subject to appeal to any court.

(2) Subject to Section 20.3, no panel determination, including a panel determination that is made an order of the Federal Court, no determination or proceedings of a panel made or carried on or purporting to be made or carried on under the Environmental Cooperation Agreement or the Labor Cooperation Agreement, no order or decision made by the Federal Court in any proceedings referred to in subsection 20.3(2), and no proceedings of that Court made or carried on or purporting to be made or carried on under that subsection shall be

(a) questioned, reviewed, set aside, removed, prohibited, or restrained; or

(b) made the subject of any proceedings in, or any process or order of, any court, whether by way of or in nature of injunction, certiorari, prohibition, quo warrantor declaration or otherwise,

on any ground, including the ground that the determination, proceedings, order, or decision is beyond the jurisdiction of the panel or the Federal Court, as the case may be, or that, in the course of any proceedings, the panel or the Federal Court for any reason exceeded or lost its jurisdiction.

Coming Into Force

2. This Act shall come into force on a day to be fixed by order of the Governor in Council.

Loi Modifiant la Loi sur la responsabilité civile de l'État et le contentieux administratif

Sommaire

L'Accord nord-américain de coopération dans le domaine de l'environnement et l'Accord nord-américain de coopération dans le domaine du travail prévoient l'instauration d'un mode de règlement des différends entre les parties au cas où l'une d'elles aurait omis de façon systématique d'assurer l'application efficace de sa législation de l'environnement ou l'application efficace de ses normes techniques du travail concernant la santé et la securité au travail, le travail des enfants ou le salaire minimum.

À cet égard, chacun des accords prévoit l'institution de groupes spéciaux chargés de faire les constatations de fait et de rendre des décisions quant aux questions qui font l'objet des différends. Ces décisions peuvent imposer l'adoption d'un plan d'action ou le versement d'une compensation monétaire pour non-application.

Le texte, par la modification de la *Loi sur la responsabilité civile de l'État et le contentieux administratif,* permet à la Cour fédérale de donner force exécutoire aux décisions des groupes spéciaux rendues contre l'État canadien.

Points saillants du texte:

1. Est établie une procédure par laquelle la décision d'un groupe spécial peut être considérée comme une ordonnance de la Cour fédérale.

2. Les modalités s'exécution de l'ordonnance sont, sauf exceptions prévues, semblables à celles des autres ordonnances de la Cour fédérale.

3. Les décisions d'un groupe spécial et les ordonnances et décisions de la Cour fédérale sur les procédures d'exécution ne sont pas susceptibles d'appel et l'action des groupes spéciaux et celle de la Cour fédérale sont exclues du pouvoir de révision judiciaire.

Loi Modifiant la Loi sur la responsabilité civile de l'État et le contentieux administratif

[Donnés le 12 mai 1994]

Sa Majesté, sur l'avis et avec le consentement du Sénat et de la Chambre des communes du Canada, édicte:

1. La Loi sur la responsabilité civile de l'État et le contentieux administratif est modifiée par adjonction, après l'article 20, de ce qui suit:

Accords sur l'environnement et le travail

20.1 Les définitions qui suivent s'appliquent au présent article et aux articles 20.2 à 20.4.

« Accord sur l'environnement » L'Accord nord-américain de coopération dans le domaine de l'environnement conclu entre le gouvernement du Canada, le gouvernement des États-Unis d'Amérique et le gouvernement des États-Unis du Mexique et signé le 14 septembre 1993, dans la version incorporant les modifications éventuellement apporteés aux termes de son article 48.

« Accord sur le travail » L'Accord nord-américain de coopération dans le domaine du travail conclu entre le gouvernement du Canada, le gouvernement des Etats-Unis d'Amérique et le gouvernement des États-Unis du Mexique et signé le 14 septembre 1993, dans la version incorporant les modifications éventuellement apportées aux termes de son article 52.

« commission compétente » La Commission de coopération environnementale constitueé aux termes de l'article 8 de l'Accord sur l'environnement ou la Commission de coopération dans le domaine du travail constituée aux termes de l'article 8 de l'Accord sur le travail, selon qu'il s'agit d'une décision d'un groupe spécial visée à l'annexe 36A de l'Accord sur l'environnement ou de la décision d'un groupe spécial visée à l'annexe 41A de l'Accord sur le travail.

« décision d'un groupe spécial » Décision d'un groupe spécial visée, selon le cas, à l'annexe 36A de l'Accord sur l'environnement ou à l'annexe 41A de l'Accord sur le travail.

« groupe spécial » Groupe spécial arbitral réuni aux termes, selon le cas, de l'article 24 de l'Accord sur l'environnement ou de l'article 29 de l'Accord sur le travail.

20.2 (1) La décision d'un groupe spécial qui vise l'État peut, uniquement en vue de son exécution, être assimilée à une ordonnance de la Cour fédérale.

(2) L'assimilation se fait par dépôt au greffe de la Cour fédérale, par la commission compétente, d'une copie certifiée conforme de la décision. Elle s'effectue au moment du dépôt.

20.3 (1) La décision d'un groupe spécial assimilée à une ordonnance de la Cour fédérale est sous réserve des paragraphes (2) à (5), exécutable comme les autres ordonnances de ce tribunal.

(2) Les procédures relatives à l'exécution de la décision d'un groupe spécial assimilée à une ordonnance de la Cour fédérale peuvent être engagées contre l'État mais seulement devant ce tribunal et seulement par la commission compétente.

(3) La Cour fédérale statue sur les procédures d'exécution visées au paragraphe (2) selon une procédure sommaire.

(4) La Cour fédérale défère au groupe spécial qui a rendu la décision toute question de fait ou d'interprétation qui se soulève au cours des procédures d'exécution. La décision du groupe spécial sur la question lie le tribunal.

(5) Aucune intervention n'est permise dans les procédures prévues au paragraphe (2).

20.4 (1) Les décisions d'un groupe spécial, y compris celles qui sont assimilées à une ordonnance de la Cour fédérale, et les ordonnances ou décisions de la Cour fédérale rendues au cours des procédures prévues au paragraphe 20.3(2) sont obligatoires et définitives et ne sont pas susceptibles d'appel.

(2) Sous réserve de l'article 20.3, l'action-décision, y compris celle qui a été assimilée à une ordonnance de la Cour fédérale, ou procédure-du groupe spécial, dans la mesure où elle s'exerce ou est censée s'exercer dans le cadre de l'Accord sur l'environnement ou de l'Accord sur le travail, et l'action-décision, ordonnance ou procédure-de la Cour fédérale, dans la mesure où elle s'exerce ou est censée s'exercer dans le cadre du paragraphe 20.3(2), ne peuvent, pour quelque motif que ce soit, y compris l'excès de pouvoir ou l'incompétence à une étape quelconque de la procédure:

(a) être contestées, révisées, annulées, empêchées ou limitées;

(b) faire l'objet d'un recours judiciaire, notamment par voie d'injonction, de certiorari, de prohibition, de quo warranto ou de jugement déclaratoire.

Entrée en Vigueur

2. La présente loi entre en vigueur à la date fixée par décret du gouverneur en conseil.

Appendix VI
Canadian Intergovernmental Agreements

Canadian Intergovernmental Agreement Regarding the North American Agreement on Environmental Cooperation

Preamble

GIVEN that Canada has entered into the North American Free Trade Agreement (NAFTA) and the North American Agreement on Environmental Cooperation (NAAEC) with the United Mexican States and the United States of America;

RECOGNIZING that partnership and cooperation between the federal, provincial, and territorial governments are essential in order to achieve the goals of the NAAEC and the environmental goals of the NAFTA;

REAFFIRMING the importance of interjurisdictional cooperation as set out in the "Statement of Interjurisdictional Cooperation on Environmental Matters" adopted by the Canadian Council of Ministers of the Environment (CCME) on 20 March 1990 in Vancouver;

AFFIRMING that cooperation for the conservation, protection, and enhancement of the environment is an essential element for achieving sustainable development;

RECOGNIZING the important roles and respective responsibilities of the federal, provincial, and territorial governments in the area of the environment; and

CONFIRMING that nothing in this Agreement affects in any way the respective powers, status or jurisdictional authority of any of the signatories to this Agreement;

The undersigned governments have agreed as follows:

[Note: In this Agreement, when the context requires, words in the singular include the plural.]

Objectives

Article 1

The objectives of this Agreement are to:

(a) continue to ensure cooperation with regard to environmental matters and to better conserve, protect, and enhance the environment through the effective and efficient implementation of the NAAEC;

(b) establish a mechanism that will provide for the full participation of the provincial and territorial governments with the federal government in the implementation, management, and further elaboration of the NAAEC in accordance with the terms of this Agreement; and

(c) define roles in the implementation, management, and further elaboration of the NAAEC.

Rights and Obligations of the NAAEC

Article 2

The signatory governments to this Agreement shall enjoy the rights of the NAAEC and shall be bound by its obligations in accordance with their respective jurisdictions.

Governmental Committee

Article 3

1. A Governmental Committee is hereby created to develop and manage Canada's involvement in the NAAEC including, without limiting the foregoing, the establishment of Canada's positions and approaches as well as the preparation for, participation at, and follow-up to meetings of the Council of the Commission for Environmental Cooperation (Council).

2. The Governmental Committee will be composed of the ministers responsible for the environment, or their designees, from each signatory government. It will be co-chaired by the federal minister and a minister from one of the other signatory governments, the latter chosen for a one-year term and in a manner to be determined by the Governmental Committee. The Governmental Committee will meet at the ministerial level at least once a year and as necessary.

3. The Governmental Committee will be supported by a Committee of Senior Officials composed of representatives from each signatory government. It will be co-chaired and operate on the same basis as the Governmental Committee.

4. Both Committees will function on the basis of consensus, unless otherwise specified in this Agreement.

5. Both Committees will cooperate with the appropriate intergovernmental

committees on international trade when addressing trade-related matters under the NAAEC or the NAFTA.

6. Representatives of governments that have not signed this Agreement may participate in the meetings of both Committees. They will have the opportunity to comment and will normally be invited to participate in cooperative activities of the NAAEC and, as appropriate, in other activities under this Agreement. They shall not be included in the determination of consensus under paragraph 4 above.

7. The Committees will perform their functions in a cost-effective manner. To this end, existing intergovernmental mechanisms such as the CCME may be invited to provide support as appropriate.

8. Secretariat services for and as assigned by the Governmental Committee will be provided by the federal government. Other signatory governments may second officials for this purpose.

9. The Governmental Committee will adopt its own rules of procedure.

Representation on the Commission for Environmental Cooperation

Article 4

The federal Minister of the Environment will represent Canada on the Council. Canadian delegations to Council meetings will be determined by the Governmental Committee and will normally include a representative of at least one other signatory government. Participation in the Council working groups and other bodies of the Commission for Environmental Cooperation will be established by the Governmental Committee.

Provision of Information

Article 5

1. The Governmental Committee will provide a forum for the ongoing mutual exchange of information between and among the federal government and the provincial and territorial governments regarding issues related to the NAAEC.

2. As a general rule, all documents relating to the operation of this Agreement and to Canadian activities under the NAAEC will be provided promptly to all governments. All governments will be advised promptly of all other NAAEC documents and will be provided with the documents upon request.

3. With respect to matters arising under Articles 14 and 20 of the NAAEC, the Canadian Representative will immediately convey to provincial and territorial governments any submission or question that relates to an enforcement practice in Canada. The government concerned will prepare an appropriate response, consulting with other interested governments.

4. Where information is requested from the Canadian Representative under Article 21 of the NAAEC, the signatory governments shall ensure that all the rights and obligations of Articles 21 (Provision of Information) and 39 (Protection of Information) of the NAAEC are respected. Pursuant to Article 21 of the NAAEC, the Canadian Representative will only convey to the Council or Secretariat of the Commission for Environmental Cooperation information on or regarding a province or territory after the provincial or territorial government concerned has been afforded a reasonable opportunity to provide written advice to the federal government regarding the information that may be conveyed and the information that must be withheld in accordance with the NAAEC and domestic law.

Cooperation, Consultation, and Resolution of Disputes

Article 6

1. Notwithstanding the general rule of consensus, if a signatory to this Agreement brings to the attention of the Governmental Committee practices on the part of another Party to the NAAEC that may be inconsistent with that Party's obligations, the Canadian Representative, after an opportunity for discussion and comment in the Governmental Committee, will as a general rule pursue the matter in accordance with the terms of the NAAEC.

2. If, exceptionally, the Canadian Representative should wish to delay or not to pursue a matter, the Canadian Representative will cooperate with the government that raised the matter, with a view to developing an agreed course of action.

Article 7

1. When the Canadian Representative is notified of a request for consultations under Article 22 of the NAAEC, the Canadian Representative shall immediately notify the signatory government concerned. The signatory government shall report to the Governmental Committee on the circumstances and there shall be an opportunity for the Committee to discuss and comment. Where the request involves a provincial or territorial enforcement practice, the consultations under the NAAEC shall involve, and include representation from, both the federal government and the other signatory government concerned.

2. When a special session of the Council is requested under Article 23 of the NAAEC, the Canadian delegation to the Council will include representation from the provincial or territorial government whose enforcement practice is the subject of the dispute.

3. Notwithstanding the general rule of consensus, in the event that a signatory government is the subject of a request for an arbitral panel under Article 24 of the NAAEC, the dispute settlement procedures will be led and positions established by the government or governments whose enforcement practice is the subject of the dispute.

4. Where a provincial or territorial government enforcement practice is the subject of an arbitral panel, the federal government shall participate in all proceedings. Where a federal enforcement practice is the subject of an arbitral panel, any province or territory may provide appropriate advice or assistance.

5. A provincial or a territorial government may invite the federal government to co-manage an arbitral panel procedure where the provincial or territorial enforcement practice is the subject of the dispute.

6. The Governmental Committee will be kept informed and have an opportunity to comment on arbitral panels in progress.

Article 8

Each signatory to this Agreement shall take all necessary measures within its jurisdiction to implement any action plan or ensure payment of any monetary enforcement assessment, with respect to the nonenforcement of its environmental law, imposed by an arbitral panel pursuant to the NAAEC.

Article 9

1. Any implementation of an action plan or payment of a monetary enforcement assessment shall be the responsibility of the government whose environmental law is the subject of the complaint under the NAAEC.

2. The Canadian Representative will consult with the government whose enforcement practice is the subject of a dispute prior to making a written declaration pursuant to paragraph 6 of Annex 41 of the NAAEC.

3. Further to paragraph 3 of Annex 34 of the NAAEC, the Canadian Representative will seek to ensure that any monetary enforcement assessment expended in Canada will be expended in the jurisdiction whose enforcement practice was the subject of the complaint.

National Advisory Committee

Article 10

The Governmental Committee will establish and appoint members to a National Advisory Committee to advise it on the implementation and further elaboration of the NAAEC. The National Advisory Committee may provide advice on its own initiative or at the request of the Governmental Committee.

Funding

Article 11

Each government shall bear the cost of its own participation in the ongoing implementation of this Agreement, including costs related to its participation in delegations, committees, or working groups established under the NAAEC.

Amendments

Article 12

Any modification of or addition to this Agreement shall be by agreement of the signatory governments.

Entry Into Force

Article 13

1. This Agreement shall enter into force upon the signature of the federal government and a minimum of one provincial government. The federal government will notify the other Parties accordingly under Annex 41 of the NAAEC.

2. A provincial or territorial government may sign this Agreement at any time and the federal government will amend the declaration under Annex 41 of the NAAEC accordingly.

Withdrawal

Article 14

A government may withdraw from this Agreement six months after it provides written notice of its intent to withdraw to the other signatory governments and the federal government will amend the declaration under Annex 41 of the NAAEC accordingly. If a government, other than the federal government, withdraws, the Agreement remains in force for the remaining governments.

Authentic Texts

Article 15

The English and French texts of this Agreement are equally authentic.

Bibliography and Further Reference Sources

Books

Anderson, F.R., D.R. Mandelker, and A.D. Tarlock. 1990. *Environmental Protection: Law and Policy*. Boston: Little, Brown and Co.

Anderson, K., and R. Blackburst, eds. 1992. *The Greening of World Trade Issues*. London: Harvester Wheatsheaf.

Baumol, W.J., and W.E. Oates. 1988. *The Theory of Environmental Policy*, 3d ed. Cambridge: Cambridge University Press.

Bélanger, Michel. 1994. *La responsabilité de l'état et de ses sociétés en environnement*. Cowansville, Qué.: Les Éditions Yvon Blais Inc.

Bernstam, M.S. 1991. *The Wealth of Nations and Environment*. London: Institute of Economic Affairs.

Bhagwati, J.N. 1991. *The World Trading System at Risk*. New York and London: Harvester Wheatsheaf.

Birnie, Patricia W., and Alan Boyle. 1992. *International Law and the Environment*, 2d ed. Oxford: Clarendon Press.

Boardman, Robert. 1981. *International Organization and the Conservation of Nature*. Bloomington: Indiana University Press.

Bovard, J. 1991. *The Fair Trade Fraud*. New York: St. Martin's Press.

Brownlie, Ian. 1983. *State Responsibility*. Oxford: Clarendon Press.

Burrows, F. 1987. *Free Movement in European Community Law*. Oxford: Clarendon Press.

Caldwell, Lynton K. 1980. *International Environmental Policy and Law*, 1st ed. New York: Dunham.

Cooper, R.N. 1989. *Can Nations Agree? Issues in International Economic Cooperation*. Washington, D.C.: The Brookings Institute.

Daly, Herman E., and John B. Cobb Jr. 1989. *For the Common Good: Redirecting the Economy Toward Continuity, the Environment, and a Sustainable Future*. Boston: Beacon Press.

Deal, C. 1993 *The Greenpeace Guide to Anti-Environmental Organizations*. Berkeley, California: Odonian Press.

Deardoff, A.V., and R.M. Stern, eds. 1991. *Analytical and Negotiating Issues in the Global Trading System*. Ann Arbor: University of Michigan Press.

Downing, P.B., and K. Hanf, eds. 1983. *International Comparison in Implementing Pollution Laws*. Boston: Kluwer-Nijhoff.

Dwivedi, O.P., ed. 1980. *Resources and the Environment: Policy Perspectives for Canada*. Toronto: McClelland and Stewart.

Grinspun, Ricardo, and Maxwell A. Cameron, eds. 1993. *The Political Economy of North American Free Trade*. Ottawa: Canadian Centre for Policy Alternatives; Montreal: McGill-Queen's University Press.

Groupe de Lisbonne. 1995. *Limites à la compétitivité*. Montreal: Boréal.

Hillman, A.L. 1989. *The Political Economy of Protection*. London and New York: Harwood.

Hogg, Peter W. 1992. *Constitutional Law of Canada*, 3d ed. Toronto: Carswell.

Housman, Robert F. 1992. *The Interaction of International Trade and Environmental Agreements*. Washington, D.C.: Center for International Environmental Law.

Hudec, Robert E. 1990. *The GATT Legal System and World Trade Diplomacy*, 2d ed. Salem: Butterworths.

Jackson, John. 1989. *The World Trading System: Law and Policy of International Economic Relations*. Cambridge: MIT Press.

Jacobson, H., and W. Gimmerman, eds. *New Approaches to International Conflict*. Ann Arbor: University of Michigan Press, forthcoming.

Johnson, Stanley, and Guy Corcelle. 1989. *The Environmental Policy of the European Communities*, International Environmental Law and Policy Series. London: Graham and Trotman.

Keyes, Cameron. 1991. *The European Community and Environmental Policy: An Introduction for Americans*. Baltimore: World Wildlife Fund Publications.

Kindred, H.M., et al. 1987. *International Law: Chiefly as Interpreted and Applied in Canada*, 4th ed. Toronto: Emond Montgomery Publications.

Kiss, A. 1989. *Droit International de l'énvironnement*. Paris: Pédone.

Lang, W., H. Newhold, and K. Zemanek, eds. 1990. *Environmental Protection and International Law*. London: Graham and Trotman.

Leonard, H. *Are Environmental Regulations Driving U.S. Industry Overseas?* Washington, D.C.: The Conservation Foundation.

Linton, Yvan, ed. 1993. *Doing Business in Canada*, Vol. 3. New York: Matthew Bender.

Lisbon Group. *The Limits to Competition.* Cambridge: MIT Press, forthcoming.

Lucas, A.L., and R. Cotton, eds. 1992. *Canadian Environmental Law*, 2d ed. Toronto: Butterworths.

MacDonald, Doug. 1991. *The Politics of Pollution.* Toronto: McClelland and Stewart.

Manning, William R. 1916. *Early Diplomatic Relations Between the United States and Mexico.* Baltimore: Johns Hopkins University Press.

Matthews, J.T. 1991. *Preserving the Global Environment.* New York and London: W.W. Norton.

Paquin, Marc. 1992. *Le droit de l'environnement et les administrateurs d'enterprises.* Cowansville, Qué.: Les Éditions Yvon Blais Inc.

Pearce, D., ed. 1991. *Blueprint 2: Greening the World Economy.* London: Earthscan Publications.

Pescatore, Pierre, et al. 1991. *Handbook of GATT Dispute Settlement.* Ardsley-on-Hudson, New York: Transnational Juris Publications.

Porter, M. 1990. *The Competitive Advantage of Nations.* London: MacMillan.

Prudencio, Rodrigo J., and Stewart J. Hudson. 1994. *The Road to Marrakech: An Interim Report on Environmental Reform of the GATT and International Trade System.* Washington, D.C.: National Wildlife Federation.

Repetto, Robert. 1993. *Trade and Environmental Policies: Achieving Complementarities and Avoiding Conflict.* Washington, D.C.: World Resources Institute.

Ricardo, David. 1965. *The Principles of Political Economy and Taxation.* London: Dent; New York: Dutton.

Richardson, Sarah, ed. 1993. *Shaping Consensus: The North American Commission on the Environment and NAFTA.* Ottawa: National Round Table on the Environment and the Economy.

Rubin, Seymour J., and Thomas R. Graham, eds. 1982. *Environment and Trade: The Relation of International Trade and Environmental Policy.* Totowa, New Jersey: Allan Held, Osmun.

Runge, C. Ford, François Ortalo-Magne, and Philip Van de Kamp. 1994. *Freer Trade, Protected Environment: Balancing Trade Liberalization and Environmental Interests.* New York: Council on Foreign Relations.

Schott, Jeffrey J., and Gary Clyde Hufbauer. 1993. *NAFTA: An Assessment.* Washington, D.C.: Institute for International Economics.

Sinclair, I.M. 1984. *The Vienna Convention on the Law of Treaties*, 2d ed. Manchester: Manchester University Press.

Smith, Brian D. 1988. *State Responsibility and the Marine Environment.* Oxford: Clarendon Press.

Swenarchuk, Michelle. 1993. "The Environmental Implications of NAFTA: A Legal Analysis." In Canadian Environmental Law Association, ed.: *The Environmental Implications of Trade Agreements.* Toronto: Queen's Printer.

Tinbergen, Jan. 1950. *On the Theory of Economic Policy.* Amsterdam: Elsevier, North Holland.

Tucker, W. 1982. *Progress and Privilege: America in the Age of Environmentalism.* Garden City, New Jersey: Anchor Press/Doubleday.

Wiktor, Christian L., ed. 1976. *Unperfected Treaties of the United States of America.* Dobbs Ferry: Oceana.

Yandle, B. 1989. *The Political Limits of Environmental Regulation.* New York: Quorum Books.

Zaelke, Durwood, et al., eds. 1993. *Trade and the Environment: Law, Economics, and Policy.* Washington, D.C.: Island Press.

Articles

"Administration to Stress Resolution of PPMs Under NAFTA Side Pact." *Inside NAFTA* (6 April 1994).

"After NAFTA, AFTA?" *The Economist* (13–19 August 1994), 13.

Alonzo, Anne, and Edward M. Ranger. "The U.S.–Mexico Border Plan." (May 1992) 2 *Business Mexico* 35.

Anderson, Belina. "Unilateral Trade Measures and Environmental Protection Policy." (1993) 66 *Temple Law Review* 751.

Audley, J.J., and E.M. Uslaner. "NAFTA. the Environment and American Domestic Politics." (1994) 4 *North American Outlook* 23.

Bailey, James E. "Free Trade and the Environment—Can NAFTA Reconcile the Irreconcilable?" (1993) *Westlaw* 6.

Bergsman, Michael. "EPA to Change Clean Air Rule to Ward Off Threatened GATT Challenge." *Inside U.S. Trade* (25 March 1994).

Beyers, Carol J. "The U.S./Mexico Tuna Embargo Dispute: A Case Study of the GATT and Environmental Progress." (1992) 16 *Maryland Journal of International Law and Trade* 229.

Bhagwati, Jagdish. "The Case for Free Trade." (November 1993) 269 *Scientific American* 42.

Bialos, Jeffrey, and Deborah Siegel. "Dispute Resolution Under NAFTA: The Newer and Improved Model." (1993) 27 *International Lawyer* 603.

Bilder, X. "An Overview of International Dispute Settlement." (1986) 1 *Emory Journal of International Dispute Resolution* 23.

Bradsher, Keith. "Impasse Ends on Sanctions for American Trade Pact." *International Herald Tribune* (14–15 August 1993) 1.

———. "U.S. Appeals Trade-Accord Requirement." *The New York Times* (25 August 1993) C1.

Brooke, James. "America—Environmental Dictator?" *The New York Times* (3 May 1992).

Buckley, Ralf. "International Trade, Investment and Environmental Regulation—An Environmental Management Perspective." (1993) 27 *Journal of World Trade* 101.

Cameron, James, and Juli Abouchar. "The Precautionary Principle: A Fundamental Principle of Law and Policy for the Protection of the Global Environment." (1991) 14 *Boston College International and Comparative Law Review* 2.

"Candidates' Trade Policy Statements Show There May Be Substance After All." (1988) 59 *Metals Week* 3.

Casteñeda, Jorge G. "Can NAFTA Change Mexico?" *Foreign Affairs* (September-October 1993) 66.

Charnovitz, Steve. "Exploring the Environmental Exceptions in GATT Article XX." (1991) 25 *Journal of World Trade* 37.

———. "GATT and the Environment: Examining the Issues." (1992) 4 *International Environmental Affairs* 203.

———. "NAFTA: An Analysis of Its Environmental Provisions." (1993) 23 *Environmental Law Reporter* 10067.

———. "The Environment vs Trade Rules: Defogging the Debate." (1993) 23 *Environmental Law* 475.

———. "Dolphins and Tuna: An Analysis of the Second GATT Panel Report." (1994) 24 *Environmental Law Reporter* 10567.

———. "Encouraging Environmental Cooperation Through the Pelly Amendment." (1994) *J. Env. & Dev.* 3.

———. "Environmental Trade Sanctions and the GATT: An Analysis of the Pelly Amendment on Foreign Environmental Practices." (1994) 9 *The American University Journal of International Law* 751.

———. "NAFTA's Social Dimension: Lessons from the Past and Framework for the Future." (1994) 8 *The International Trade Journal* 39.

———. "Green Roots, Bad Pruning: GATT Rules and Their Application to Environmental Trade Measures." (1994) 7 *Tulane Environmental Law Journal* 299.

Clinton, Bill. "Expanding Trade and Creating American Jobs." (1993) 23 *Environmental Law* 683.

Cooper, Kenneth J. "To Compel or Encourage: Seeking Compliance with International Trade Agreements at the State Level." (1993) 2 *Minnesota Journal of Global Trade* 143.

Daly, Herman E. "The Perils of Free Trade." (November 1993) 269 *Scientific American* 50.

D'Arge, Ralph C., and Allen V. Kneese. "State Liability for Environmental Degradation: An Economic Perspective." (1980) 20 *Natural Resources Journal* 427.

DePalma, Anthony. "Birds' Deaths in Mexico Are a Test for Trade Pact." *The New York Times* (8 June 1995) A14.

Downing, P.B., and W.D. Watson Jr. "The Economics of Enforcing Air Pollution Controls." (1974) 1 *Journal of Environmental Economics and Management* 219.

Dunham, Will. "Wildlife Group Backs Free Trade." *Houston Chronicle* (17 September 1992) 2.

Dunoff, Jeffrey L. "Reconciling International Trade with Preservation of the Global Commons: Can We Prosper and Protect?" (1992) 49 *Washington and Lee Law Review* 1407.

Eckes, Alfred. "U.S.–Mexican Trade, 1880s Style." *Journal of Commerce* (10 September 1992).

"Effects of National Environmental Regulation on International Trade and Investment." (1991) 10 *UCLA Pacific Basin Law Journal* 212.

Emerson, Peter M. "NAFTA Passage Can Protect the Environment." *Austin American Statesman* (8 January 1993).

"Environment and Development: The Founex Report." (1972) 586 *International Conciliation* 28.

"The Environment and Free Trade: Meeting Halfway at the Mexican Border." (1991) 10 *UCLA Pacific Basin Law Journal* 193.

"Environmentalists' Assessment of NAFTA Green Language." *Inside U.S. Trade* (17 July 1992).

Esty, Daniel C. "Toward a Greener GATT." (March/April 1994) *Int'l Econ. Insights*.

———. "Making Trade and Environmental Policies Work Together: Lessons from NAFTA." *Aussenwirtschaft*, 19 Jahrgang (1994), Heft I.

Fagan, D. "Chile to begin NAAFTA Talks." *The Globe and Mail* (7 December 1994) B4.

Feeley, Michael Scott, and Elizabeth Knier. "Environmental Considerations of the Emerging United States–Mexico Free Trade Agreement." (1992) 2 *Duke Journal of Comparative and International Law* 259.

Finger, J.M., and T. Murray. "Policing Unfair Imports: The United States Example." (1990) 24 *Journal of World Trade* 39.

Fitzmaurice, G.G. "The Law and Procedure of the International Court of Justice: Treaty Interpretation and Certain Other Points." (1951) 28 *British Yearbook of International Law* 1.

Friedman, Thomas L. "U.S. Puts Sanctions on Taiwan." *The New York Times* (11 April 1995) B1.

"GATT Argues Over Response to Earth Summit on Trade and Environment." *Inside U.S. Trade* (30 October 1992).

"GATT—Will Liberalized Trade Aid Global Environmental Protection?" (1992) 21 *Denver Journal of International Law and Policy* 55.

"GATT TBT Agreement Reveals Failure of U.S. to Secure Changes." *Inside U.S. Trade* (24 December 1993).

"GATT Trade and Environment Subcommittee Sets Workplan for Fall." *Inside U.S. Trade* (15 July 1994).

Golden, Tim. "A History of Pollution in Mexico Casts Cloud Over Trade Accord." *The New York Times* (16 August 1993) A1.

Gonzalez-Baz, Aureliano. "A Mexican Perspective on the North American Free Trade Agreement and the Environment." (1992) 18 *Canada–United States Law Journal* 235.

Goshko, J.M., and P. Bher. "34 Hemispheric Leaders to Seek Free Trade Pact." *Washington Post* (8 December 1994) A31.

Gramm, Phil., Sen. "Leaving Mexico at the Altar." *Washington Post* (1 June 1993) A17.

Gregory, Michael. "Environment, Sustainable Development, Public Participation and the NAFTA: A Retrospective." (1992) 7 *Journal of Environmental Law and Litigation* 99.

Hahn, R.W., and K.R. Richards. "The Internationalization of Environmental Regulation." (1989) 30 *Harvard International Law Journal* 421.

Haigh, Nigel, and Konrad von Moltke. "The European Community: An Environmental Force." (July/August 1990) 16 *EPA Journal*.

Hair, Jay D. "Turning a Perceived Threat Into a Positive Step." *International Wildlife* (March-April 1993).

Hall, Kevin. "NAFTA-Related Watchdog to Study Mexico Bird Kill." *Journal of Commerce* (19 June 1995) 2A.

Hammonds, Holly. "A U.S. Perspective on the EC Hormones Directive." (1990) 11 *Michigan Journal of International Law* 840.

Heckart, Robert L., and Tira Harpaz. "Critics Ask if NAFTA Is Green Enough." (1992) 15 *The National Law Journal* 17.

Hills, Carla. "America's Free Trade 'Firsts'." *Journal of Commerce* (14 August 1992) 8A.

Hofgard, Kurt C. "Is This Land Really Our Land? Impacts of Free Trade Agreements on U.S. Environmental Protection." (1993) 23 *Environmental Law* 635.

Holmer, Alan F., and Judith H. Bello. "Trade and the Environment: A Snapshot from Tuna/Dolphins to the NAFTA and Beyond." (1993) 27 *International Lawyer* 169.

Horlick, Gary, and F. Amanda DeBusk. "Dispute Resolution under NAFTA: Building on the U.S.–Canada FTA, GATT and ICSID." (1993) 10 *Journal of International Arbitration* 51.

Housman, Robert F. "A Kantian Approach to Trade and the Environment." (1992) 49 *Washington and Lee Law Review* 1373.

———. "The North American Free Trade Agreement's Lesson for Reconciling Trade and the Environment." (1994) 30 *Stanford Journal of International Law* 379.

———. "Democratizing International Trade Decision-Making." (1994) 27 *Cornell International Law Journal* 699.

Housman, Robert F., and Paul Orbuch. "Integrating Labor and Environmental Concerns into the North American Free Trade Agreement: A Look Back and a Look Ahead." (1993) 8 *American University Journal of International Law and Policy* 719.

Housman, Robert F., and Durwood Zaelke. "The Collision of the Environment and Trade: The GATT Tuna–Dolphin Decision." (1992) 22 *Environmental Law Reporter* 10268.

———. "Trade, Environment and Sustainable Development: A Primer." (1992) 15 *Hastings International & Comparative Law Review* 535.

———. "Making Trade and Environmental Policies Mutually Reinforcing: Forging Competitive Sustainability." (1993) 23 *Environmental Law* 545.

Hudec, Robert E. "Retaliation Against 'Unreasonable' Foreign Trade Practices: The New Section 301." (1975) 59 *Minnesota Law Review* 461.

Husser, Nancy. "NAFTA's Green Arm Swings into Action." *The (Montreal) Gazette* (17 June 1995).

Hustiis, Brenda S. "The Environmental Implications of the North American Free Trade Agreement." (1993) 28 *Texas International Law Journal* 589.

Ikegawa, Jima. "NAFTA: How Will It Affect U.S. Environmental Regulations?" (1993) 6 *The Transnational Lawyer* 225.

"International Trade and the Environment: Implications of GATT for Future Environmental Protection Efforts." (1992) 3 *Colorado Journal of International Environmental Law and Policy* 655.

Jackson, John. "World Trade Rules and Environmental Policies: Congruence or Conflict?" (1992) 49 *Washington and Lee Law Review* 1227.

Jaeger, Michael. "Back to the Future: Environmental Federalism in an Era of Sustainable Development." (1993) 3 *Journal of Environmental Law and Practice* 3.

Johnson, Pierre Marc, and André Beaulieu. "NAFTA's Green Opportunities." (1994) 5 *Journal of Environmental Law and Practice* 5.

Kass, Stephen L., and Michael B. Gerrard. "The North American Commission on the Environment." (1993) 209 *New York Law Journal* 3.

Komorosky, K.S. "The Failure of Government to Regulate Industry: A Subsidy under GATT?" (1988) 10 *Houston Journal of International Law* 189.

Krutilla, Kerry. "Environmental Regulation in an Open Economy." (1991) 20 *Journal of Environmental Economics and Management* 127.

Kublicki, Nicolas. "The Greening of Free Trade: NAFTA, Mexican Environmental Law, and Debt Exchanges for Mexican Environmental Infrastructure Development." (1994) 19 *Columbia Journal of Environmental Law* 59.

LaFranchi, Howard. "Migratory Birds Die in Droves: Can NAFTA Come to the Rescue?" *Christian Science Monitor* (18 January 1995) 1.

Lallas, Peter L. "NAFTA and Evolving Approaches to Identify and Address 'Indirect' Environmental Impacts of International Trade." (1993) 5 *Geo. Int'l Envt'l L. Rev.* 519.

"Let them eat pollution." *The Economist* (8 February 1992) 66.

Lowry, Andrew. "North American Free Trade and the Environment." *Business America* (19 October 1992) 22.

Maggs, John. "G.M. to Treat Sewage at 35 Mexican Factories." *Austin American Statesman* (15 May 1991).

Magraw, D. "NAFTA's Repercussions: Is Green Trade Possible?" (1994) 35 *Environment* 14.

Maloney, M.T., and R.E. McCormick. "A Positive Theory of Environmental Quality Regulation." (1982) 25 *Journal of Law and Economics* 99.

McDorman, Ted L. "The 1991 U.S.–Mexico GATT Panel Report on Tuna and Dolphin." (1992) 17 *North Carolina Journal of International Law and Commercial Regulation* 461.

McKeith, Malissa H. "The Environment and Free Trade: Meeting Halfway at the Mexican Border." (1991) 10 *Pacific Basin Law Journal* 183.

Meng, Werner P. "The Hormone Conflict Between the EEC and the United States Within the Context of GATT." (1990) 11 *Michigan Journal of International Law* 818.

Menz, Frederic C. "The North American Environment: Economic and Public Policy Issues." (March 1994) 4 *North American Outlook* 3.

Mumme, Stephen P. "Clearing the Air: Environmental Reform in Mexico." (1991) 16 *Environment* 7.

——. "State and Local Influence in Transboundary Environmental Policy-Making Along the U.S.–Mexico Border: The Case of Air Quality Management." 2 *Journal of Borderlands Studies* 1.

——."Mexican Environmental Reform and NAFTA." (March 1994) 4 *North American Outlook* 87.

Munton, Don, and John Kirton. "North American Environmental Cooperation:

Bilateral, Trilateral, Multilateral." (March 1994) 4 *North American Outlook* 59.

"NAFTA is not Alone." *The Economist* (18 June 1994) 47.

"NAFTA Rules Face Test." *Seattle Post-Intelligencer* (14 June 1995).

"National Wildlife Federation Endorses Green Provisions in Trade Pact with Mexico." *International Wildlife* (Jan.-Feb. 1993).

"Open Trade Door, MacLaren Warns." *Financial Post* (24 September 1994) 1.

Otteman, Scott. "Special Report: Near Final NAFTA Greens Text Narrows Scope of Original U.S. Proposal." *Inside U.S. Trade* (20 August 1993).

Pasurka, Carl. "Environmental Control Costs and U.S. Effective Rates of Protection." (1985) 13 *Public Finance Quarterly* 161.

Petersmann, E-U. "Trade Policy, Environmental Policy and GATT: Why Trade Rules and Environmental Rules Should Be Mutually Consistent." (1991) 46 *Aussenwirtschaft* 197.

Plofchan, T.K. "Recognizing Countervailing Environmental Subsidies." (1992) 26 *International Lawyer* 763.

Podesta, Don. "The Environment Running Second: Argentina Skips Protections in Rush to Improve Economy." *Washington Post* (4 February 1993) A14.

"Polluted Lake in Mexico Draws Biologists, Officials." *Fort Worth Star-Telegram* (17 June 1995).

Poges, Amelia. "Harmonization in the EU." (1993) Geneva: Office of Legal Affairs, GATT Secretariat.

Ranger, Edward M. "Environmental Regulation and Enforcement in Mexico." (1991) *Maquiladora Industry Annual Review.*

———. "Mexican Environmental Regulations." (1992) *Business Mexico: Special Edition.*

———. "A Compliance Checklist." (1993) *Business Mexico: Special Edition.*

Raul, Alan Charles, and Paul E. Hagen. "The Convergence of Trade and Environmental Law." (1993) 8 *Natural Resources and Environment* 3.

Reilly, William K. "Pollution Won't Be a Byproduct." *L.A. Times* (August 1992) M5.

Reynolds, Larry A., and David A. Hicks. "New Directions for the Civil Liability of Public Authorities in Canada." (1992) 71 *Revue du Barreau canadien* 1.

Richardson Sarah, and André Beaulieu. "The Implementation of the North American Agreement on Environmental Cooperation." In *NAFTA Law and Policy* (forthcoming).

Riding, Alan. "Gore Insists Environment Is a Trade Issue." *The New York Times* (15 April 1994).

Ross, David J. "Making GATT Dolphin Safe: Trade and the Environment." (1992) 2 *Duke Journal of Comparative International Law* 345.

Runge, C. Ford. "Trade Protectionism and Environmental Regulations: The New Nontariff Barriers." (1990) 11 *Northwestern Journal of International Law and Business* 47.

Sanchez, Roberto. "Health and Environmental Risks of the Maquiladora in Mexicali." (1990) 30 *Natural Resources Journal* 163.

Sanger, D.E. "U.S. Envisions an Expansion of Free Trade in Hemisphere." *The New York Times* (8 December 1994) A7.

Saunders, John. "Canada Takes Euro-Style Approach to NAFTA: Analysts." *The (Toronto) Globe and Mail* (18 August 1993) B20.

Schwenker, Carl F. "Protecting the Environment and U.S. Competitiveness in the Era of Free Trade: A Proposal." (1993) 71 *Texas Law Review* 1355.

"Side-deals and showmanship bring NAFTA closer." *The (Toronto) Globe and Mail* (17 August 1993) A16.

Skilton, Thomas E. "GATT and the Environment in Conflict: The Tuna–Dolphin Dispute and the Quest for an International Conservation Strategy." (1993) 26 *Cornell International Law Journal* 455.

Szekely, Alberto. "Emerging Boundary Environmental Challenges and Institutional Issues: Mexico and the United States." (1993) 33 *Natural Resources Journal* 33.

Terrell, Gaynell. "Tragic Puzzle Grips Families on the Border: Plant Pollution May Cause Brain Not to Develop." *Houston Post* (17 May 1991) A1.

Thomas, Christopher. "The Future: The Impact of Environmental Regulations on Trade." (1992) 18 *Canada–United States Law Journal* 383.

Thomas, Christopher, and Greg A. Tereposky. "The Evolving Relationship Between Trade and Environmental Regulation." (1993) 27 *Journal of World Trade* 23.

Tobey, James. "The Effects of Domestic Environmental Policies on Patterns of World Trade: An Empirical Test." (1990) 43 *Kiklos* 193.

"Trade and Environment: Draft Decision by TNC." *Inside U.S. Trade—Special Report* (14 December 1993).

"The U.S.–EC Hormone Beef Controversy and the Standards Code: Implications for the Application of Health Regulations to Agricultural Trade." (1989) 14 *North Carolina Journal of International Law* 135.

"The Use of Trade Provisions in International Environmental Agreements and Their Compatibility with the GATT." (1991) 2 *Yearbook of International Environmental Law* 3.

"The Vital Treaty That Must Not Die: Dealing with Legitimate Criticism of NAFTA." *L.A. Times* (25 March 1993) B6.

"Un nouveau spectre hante le tiers-monde: l'éco-colonialisme'." *Courier International* (11 March 1993) 8.

"USTR Draft Reveals Intention to Implement GATT Dispute Panels." *Inside U.S. Trade* (4 March 1994).

Voigt, David. "The Maquiladora Problem in the Age of NAFTA: Where Will We Find Solutions?" (1993) 2 *Minnesota Journal of Global Trade* 329.

Ward, J., and G.T. Prickett. "Prospects for a Green Trade Agreement." (1992) 33 *Environment* 3.

Williams, Sharon A. "Public International Law Governing Transboundary Pollution." (1984) *International Business Lawyer* 243.

Zagaris, Bruce. "The Transformation of Environmental Enforcement Cooperation Between Mexico and the United States in the Wake of NAFTA." (1992) 18 *North Carolina Journal of International Law and Commercial Regulation* 59.

Zarcostas, John. "GATT Snubs U.S. Request to Open Tuna–Dolphin Debate to Public." *Journal of Commerce* (21 July 1994) 6A.

Canadian Statutes and Regulations

An Act to Amend the Crown Liability and Proceedings Act, S.C. 1994, c.11.

Atomic Energy Control Act, R.S.C. 1985, c.A-16.

Canada Shipping Act, R.S.C. 1985, c.S-9.

Canadian Environmental Assessment Act, S.C. 1992, c.37.

Canadian Environmental Protection Act, R.S.C. 1985 (4th Supp.), c.16.

Clean Air Act, S.S. 1986-7-8-, c.12.1

Clean Environment Act, R.S.N.B. 1973, c.C-6.

Clean Water Act, S.N.B. 1989, c.C-61.

Dangerous Goods and Hazardous Waste Management Act, R.S.N.S. 1989, c.118.

Dangerous Goods Handling and Transportation Act, R.S.M. 1987, c.D-12.

Department of Environment and Lands Act, R.S.N. 1990, c.D-11.

Environment Act, S.M. 1987, c.26.

Environment Assessment Act, S.B.C. 1980-81, c.41.

Environmental Management and Protection Act, S.S. 1983-84, c.E-10.2.

Environmental Protection Act, R.S.N.S. 1989, c.150.

Environmental Protection Act, R.S.O. 1990 c.E-19.

Environmental Protection Act, R.S.P.E.I. 1988, c.E-9.

Environmental Protection and Enhancement Act, S.A. 1992, c.E-13.3.

Environmental Quality Act, R.S.Q. 1985, c.Q-2.

Fisheries Act, R.S.C. 1985, c.F-14.

Manitoba Hazardous Waste Management Corporation Act, S.M. 1986-87. c.10.

North American Free Trade Agreement Implementation Act, S.C. 1993, c.44.

Ontario Water Resources Act, R.S.O. 1990, c.O-40.

Pest Control Products Act, R.S.C. 1985, c.P-9.

Rivers and Streams Act, R.S.M. 1988, c.R-160.

Special Import Measures Act, R.S.C. 1985, c.S-15.

Waste Management Act, S.B.C. 1982, c.41.

Water Act, R.S.N.S. 1989, c.500.

Water Corporation Act, S.S. 1983-84, c.W-4.1.

U.S. Statutes and Regulations

Clean Air Act, 42 U.S.C. § 7401.

Clean Water Act, U.S.C. 1251(a)(1982).

Comprehensive Environmental Response, the Compensation and Liability Act, 42 U.S.C. § 9601.

Elephant Conservation Act, 16 U.S.C. § 420.

Emergency Planning and Community Right-to-Know Act, 42 U.S.C. § 11001.

Endangered Species Act, 16 U.S.C. § 1531.

Federal Implementation of the North American Agreement on Environmental Cooperation, Executive Order 12915 U.S.C.C.A.N. (108 Stat.) B42.

Federal Insecticide, Fungicide, and Rodenticide Act, 7 U.S.C. § 136.

Fishermen's Protective Act, 22 U.S.C. 1978.

Fishery Conservation and Management Act, 16 U.S.C. 1821(e)(2).

Hazardous Materials Transportation Control Act, 49 U.S.C. § 1801.

Marine Mammal Protection Act, 22 U.S.C. § 1978 and 16 U.S.C. § 1821.

National Environmental Policy Act, 42 U.S.C. § 4321.

North American Free Trade Agreement Implementation Act, Pub. L. No. 103-182, 107 Stat. 2057.

Omnibus Trade and Competitiveness Act, 19 U.S.C. §§ 2902-2903.

Outer Continental Shelf Lands Act, U.S.C §§ 1131-1356.

Port and Tanker Safety Act, 33 U.S.C. § 391.

Regulation of Fuels and Fuel Additives; Standards for Reformulated and Conventional Gasoline, 57 Fed. Reg. 13,416 (1992).

Resource Conservation and Recovery Act, 42 U.S.C. § 6901.

Safe Drinking Water Act, 42 U.S.C. § 300(f)-300(j-q).

Tariff Act, 19 U.S.C. § 1337.

Toxic Substances Control Act, 15 U.S.C. § 2601.

Trade Act, 19 U.S.C. §§ 2101, 2111-2112, 2191.

Mexican Statutes and Regulations

Decree for the Development and Operation of the In-Bond Export Industry, effective 30 December 1989.

Ley General Del Equilibrio Ecologico Y La Proteccion Al Ambiente, D.O. 28 January 1988, 4 Inter-American Legal Materials (ABA) 664.

Regulation to the Ecology Law for the Prevention and Control of Atmospheric Contamination, effective 26 November 1988.

Regulation to the Ecology Law for Hazardous Wastes, effective 26 November 1988.

Regulation to the Ecology Law for Environmental Impact, effective 8 June 1988.

Regulation to the Ecology Law to Promote Mexican Investment and to Regulate Foreign Investment, effective 17 May 1989.

International Agreements and Treaties

Adjustment and Amendments to the Montreal Protocol on Substances that Deplete the Ozone Layer, 29 June 1990, 30 I.L.M. 537.

Agreement Between the Government of Canada and the Government of the United States of America Concerning the Transboundary Movement of Hazardous Waste, 28 October 1986, Can. T.S. 1986 No. 39, T.I.A.S. No. 11099.

Agreement Establishing the World Trade Organization, 15 December 1993, GATT Doc. MTN/FA II, art. V.2.

Agreement on the Application of Sanitary and Phytosanitary Measures, 15 December 1993, GATT Doc. MTN/FA II, art. V.2.

Basel Convention on the Control of Transboundary Movements of Hazardous Wastes and Their Disposal, 22 March 1989, Doc. UNEP/WG. 190/4 (1989), Can. T.S. 1992 No. 19, 28 I.L.M. 649.

Canada–United States Agreement on Great Lakes Water Quality. 15 April 1972, CAN. T.S. 1972 No. 12, 23 U.S.T. 301, 837 U.N.T.S. 213, T.I.A.S. No. 7312, 11 I.L.M. 694.

Canada–United States Air Quality Agreement, 13 March 1991, 30 I.L.M. 676.

Canada–United States Free Trade Agreement, 22 December 1987, Can. T.S. 1989 No. 3, 27 I.L.M. 281.

Convention on International Trade in Endangered Species of Wild Fauna and Flora, 3 March 1973, 27 U.S.T. 1087. T.I.A.S. No. 8349, 993 U.N.T.S. 243.

Convention on Nature Protection and Wild Life Preservation in the Western Hemisphere, 12 October 1940, 565 Stat. 1354, 1368.

Convention on the Prevention of Marine Pollution by Dumping of Wastes and Other Matter (The London Dumping Convention), 29 December 1972, 26 U.S.T. 2403, T.I.A.S. No. 8165, 1046 U.N.T.S. 120, 11 I.L.M. 1291.

Declaration on Principles of International Law Concerning Friendly Relations and Cooperation among States in Accordance with the Charter of the United Nations, UN GA Res. 2625, UN GAOR, 25th Sess., Supp. No. 28, 121, UN Doc. a/8028 (1971).

Final Act Embodying the Results of the Uruguay Round of Multilateral Trade Negotiations, GATT Secretariat Document MTN/FA (signed at Marrakech in April 1994).

General Agreement on Tariffs and Trade (GATT), 30 October 1947, Can. T.S. 1947 No. 27, 61 Stat. All, 55 U.N.T.S. 187, T.I.A.S. No. 1700.

Great Lakes Water Quality Agreement, 22 November 1978, United States–Canada, Can. T.S. 1978 No. 20, 30 U.S.T.1384, T.I.A.S. No. 9257.

International Convention for the Prevention of Pollution from Ships (MARPOL), 2 November 1973, 12 I.L.M. 1319.

International Convention for the Regulation of Whaling, 2 December 1946, 1 U.S.T. 506, 161 U.N.T.S. 72.

Mexico–United States Agreement Concerning the Establishment of a Border Environmental Commission and a Northern American Development Bank, 16 November 1993, 32 I.L.M. 1545.

Mexico–United States Agreement on Cooperation for the Protection and the Improvement of the Environment of the Metropolitan Area of Mexico City, 3 October 1989, 29 I.L.M. 25.

Mexico–United States Agreement to Cooperate in the Solution of Environmental Problems in the Border Area, 14 August 1983, 22 I.L.M. 1025.

Montreal Protocol on Substances That Deplete the Ozone Layer, 16 September 1987, 26 I.L.M. 1541.

North American Agreement on Environmental Cooperation, 8 September 1993, Canada–Mexico–United States, 32 I.L.M. 1480.

North American Free Trade Agreement, 8 December 1992, Canada–Mexico–United States, 32 I.L.M. 289.

North American Plant Protection Agreement, 28 October 1976, Canada–Mexico–United States, 28 U.S.T. 6223, T.I.A.S. No. 8680.

Paris Convention on the Prevention of Marine Pollutions from Land-Based Sources, 21 February 1974, 13 I.L.M. 352.

Protocol Concerning the Control of Emissions of Nitrogen Oxide and Their Transboundary Fluxes, 31 October 1988, 28 I.L.M. 212.

Treaty Relating to Boundary Waters and Questions Arising Along the Boundary Between the U.S. and Canada, 11 January 1909, United States–United Kingdom, 36 Stat. 2448, U.S.T.548.

United Nations Convention on Biological Diversity, 5 June 1992, Doc. UNEP/Bio. Div/N7-INC.5/4 (1992), 31 I.L.M. 818.

United Nations Convention on the Law of the Sea (UNCLOS), 10 December 1982, UN Doc. A/CONF. 62/122 (1982), 1295 U.N.T.S. 211, 21 I.L.M. 1261.

United Nations Framework Convention on Climate Change, 9 May 1992, UN Doc. A/AC.237/18 Part II Add. I and Corr. I (1992), 31 I.L.M. 849.

United States–Costa Rica Convention for the Establishment of an Inter-American Tropical Tuna Commission, 31 May 1949, 1 U.S.T. 230, T.I.A.S. No. 2044.

United States–Israel Free Trade Agreement, 22 April 1985, 24 I.L.M. 653.

United States–Mexico Convention Touching the Boundary Line Between the Two Countries Where It Follows the Bed of the Rio Grande and the Rio Colorado, 12 November 1884, Stat. 1011, 9 Bevans 865, T.S. 226.

Vienna Convention on the Law of Treaties, 23 May 1969, UN Doc. A/CONF. 39/27 (1969), 8 I.L.M. 679.

Vienna Convention on the Law of Treaties Between States and International Organizations or Between International Organizations, 20 March 1986, UN Doc. A/CONF. 129/15 (1986), 25 I.L.M. 543.

Government Documents

Description of the Proposed North American Free Trade Agreement, prepared by the governments of Canada, the United Mexican States, and the United States of America, 12 August 1992.

Canada

Canadian Intergovernmental Agreement Regarding the North American Agreement on Environmental Cooperation (see Appendix VI).

Department of Foreign Affairs and International Trade, *Stacking the Deck: Compliance and Dispute Settlement in International Environmental Agreements,* (Policy Staff Paper No. 93/15) by K.H. Christie (Ottawa: Queen's Printer, December 1993).

Government of Canada. *North American Free Trade Agreement: Canadian Environmental Review* (Queen's Printer: Ottawa, October 1992).

United States

Environmental Implications of the Uruguay Round of GATT: Hearing Before the Subcommittee on Economic Policy, Trade and the Environment, of the House Committee on Foreign Affairs, 103d Cong., 2d Sess. (1994).

House Congressional Resolution 246, Congressional Record, 6 August 1992 at 117699.

Impacts of Trade Agreements on U.S. Environmental Protection and Natural Resource Conservation Efforts. Hearing before the Subcommittee on Environment and Natural Resources of the House Committee on Merchant Marine Fisheries, 103d Cong., 1st Sess., 23-24 (1993).

Report of Environmental Issues, in addendum to the *Message from the President of the United States Transmitting North American Free Trade Agreement Supplemental Agreements,* 103d Cong., 1st Sess., 4 November 1993, H. Doc. 103-160.

Trade and Environment: Hearing Before the Subcommittee on Foreign Commerce and Tourism of the Senate Committee on Commerce, Science and Transportation, 103d Cong., 2d Sess. (1994).

U.S. Congress, General Accounting Office. *International Environment: International Agreements Are Not Well Monitored.* GA/RCED-92-43 (Gaithersburg, MD: U.S. General Accounting Office, 1992).

————. *U.S.–Mexico Trade: Assessment of Mexico's Environmental Controls for New Companies,* GAO/GGD-92-113 (Washington, D.C.: U.S. Government Printing Office, 1992).

————. *U.S.–Mexico Trade: Some U.S. Wood Furniture Firms Relocated from Los Angeles Area to Mexico,* GAO/NSAID-91-191 (Gaithersburg, MD: U.S. General Accounting Office, 1991).

U.S. Congress, Office of Technology Assessment. *Development Assistance, Export Promotion and Environmental Technology—Background Paper,* OTA-BP-ITE-107 (Washington, D.C.: U.S. Government Printing Office, 1993).

————. *Trade and the Environment: Conflicts and Opportunities,* OTA-BP-ITE-94 (Washington, D.C.: U.S. Government Printing Office, 1992).

U.S. Department of Commerce, International Trade Administration. "Market Research Summary: 1991-The Mexican Market for Pollution Instruments Equipment and Services."

U.S. Government. The White House. *May 1 Action Plan in Response to Concerns Raised by Congress Regarding a North American Free Trade Agreement,* 1 May 1991.

U.S. House of Representatives. Committee on Ways and Means. *Exchange of Letters on Issues Concerning the Negotiation of a North American Free Trade Agreement,* WMCP 102-10, 1 May 1991.

International Documents and Decisions

Australian Subsidy on Ammonium Sulphate, (Chile v. Australia) (1950), GATT Doc. CP.4/39, 2 B.I.S.D. (1952) 188.

Canada—Measures Affecting Exports of Unprocessed Herring and Salmon (United States v. Canada) (1988), GATT Doc. L/6268, para. 4.6, 35th supp. B.I.S.D. (1989) 98 at 114.

Charter of Economic Rights and Duties of States, UN GA Res. 3281, 29th Sess. (1974).

Commission v. Denmark (Beverage Containers) Case 302-86, 1988, E.C.R. 4607.

Corfu Channel Case (United Kingdom v. Albania) [1949] I.C.J. Rep. 4.

Declaration of a New International Economic Order, UN GA Res. 3201, 29th Sess. (1974).

EC, Commission. *1992: The Environmental Dimension,* Task Force on Environment and the Internal Market (Bonn: Economica, Verlag, 1990).

———. *Report on U.S. Barriers to Trade and Investment,* (EC, 1993).

EC, *Council Directive 90/313/ECE of 7 June 1990 on freedom of access to information on the environment,* O.J. Legislation (1990) No. L 158/56.

EU, Commission. *European Community, Environmental Legislation* Vol. I *General Policy* (Luxembourg: Office of Official Publications, 1992).

GATT. *Anti-Dumping Code,* 30 June 1967, 6 I.L.M. 920; 11 April 1979, 18 I.L.M. 621.

———. *International Trade 90–91,* Vol. I (Geneva, 1992).

———. *Other Barriers to Trade,* GATT Doc. L/334 & Addendum, para. 13, 3d supp. B.I.S.D. (1955) 222 at 224.

———. *Subsidies: Operation of the Provisions of Article XVI,* GATT Doc. L/1442 & Addendum 1–2, paras. 27–28, 10th supp. B.I.S.D. (1962) 201 at 209.

GATT, Trade and the Environment. *Report on the GATT Symposium on Trade, Environment and Sustainable Development* (Geneva: GATT, 1994).

———. *Sub-Committee on Trade and Environment Begins Work Programme* (Geneva: GATT, 1994).

———. *Work Starts on Environmental Charges, Taxes and Product Requirements.* (Geneva: GATT, 1994).

———. *United States—Restrictions on Imports of Tuna* (16 June 1994) 33 I.L.M. 839 (1994).

In the Matter of Canada's Landing Requirement for Pacific Coast Salmon and Herring (1989), 2 T.C.T. 7162 (Ch. 18 Panel), 1 T.T.R. 237.

In the Matter of Puerto Rico Regulations on the Import, Distribution and Sale of U.H.T. Milk from Quebec, USA-92-1807-02-1992.

International Law Commission *Draft Articles on International Liability,* UN Doc. A/CN.4/428 (1990), Article 11.

Lake Lanoux Arbitration (France v. Spain), (1957)) 12 R.I.A.A. 281, 24 I.L.R. 101.

London Guidelines for the Exchange of Information on Chemicals in International Trade (UNEP GC.15/9 Add./2 Appendix and Supp. 3, as amended by UNEP GC.15/30 *Report of the Governing Council on Its 15th Session,* GAOR, 44th Sess., UN Doc. A/44/25 (1989)). UN GA Res. 1803, 17th Sess. (1962).

OECD, Chairman's report. *Epoc High-Level Session: Environmental Perspectives on Trade–Environment Issues,* 7–8 December 1993.

OECD, Council. *Decision Recommendation of the Council Concerning Provision of Information in Decision-Making Processes Relating to the Prevention of, and Response to, Accidents Involving Hazardous Substances,* OECD Doc. C(88)85.

——. *Recommendation on the Application of the Polluter-Pays Principle to Accidental Pollution.* OECD c(72) 128 (1972); c.(74) 223 (1974) and c(89) 88 (1989), 28 I.L.M. 1320.

OECD. *Economic Instruments for Environmental Protection* (Paris: OECD, 1989).

——. Information Note, *Interim Conceptual Framework for PPM Measures*, COM/TD/ ENV (94) 39, 6–7 April 1994.

——. *Legal Aspects of Transfrontier Pollution* (Paris: OECD, 1977).

——. *The OECD Environment Industry: Situation, Prospects and Government Policies*, OECD/GD (92) 1 (Paris: OECD, 1992).

Principle 19 of the *Rio Declaration* (UNCED), UN Doc. A/Conf. 151/5/Rev. 1 (1992).

Principle 21 of the *Stockholm (UNCHE) Declaration on the Human Environment*, UNGA Res. 2996 (XXVII).

Re Disposable Beer Cans (1989) 1 C.M.L.R. 619.

Report of the ILC to the UN General Assembly, 43d Sess., UN Doc. A/43/10 (1988).

Report of the United Nations Conference on the Human Environment, 16 June 1972, Principle 21, UN Doc. A/Conf. 48/14 and Corr. 1 (1972), 11 I.L.M. 1416.

Rio Declaration on the Environment and Development (UNCED), Principle 1, UN Doc. A/Conf. 151/26 (Vol. I) (1992).

Single European Act, U.K.T.S. 1988 No. 31.

Statute of the International Court of Justice, 26 June 1945, Can. T.S. 1945 No. 7, 59 Stat. 1031, 145 U.K.T.S. 805.

Texaco Overseas Petroleum Co. and California Asiatic Oil Co. v. Libyan Arab Republic, 53 I.L.R. 389, 17 I.L.M. 1.

Thailand—Restrictions on Importation of and Internal Taxes on Cigarettes (U.S. v. Thailand) (1990), GATT Doc. DS 10/R, paras. 74–75, 37th supp. B.I.S.D. (1991) 200 at 223.

Trail Smelter Arbitration (Canada v. United States) (1931–1941), 3 R.I.A.A. 1905, (1939) 33 AJIL at 182, and (1941) 35 AJIL at 684.

Treatment by Germany of Imports of Sardines (Norway v. West Germany) (1952), GATT Doc. G/26, 1st supp. B.I.S.D. (1953) 53.

UN Conference on Environment and Development. *In Our Hands, Earth Summit '92: Relationship Between Environmental Agreements and Instruments Related to Trade and Development*, Research Paper No. 35 (February 1992).

UN GA, Preparatory Committee for the United Nations Conference on Environment and Development. *Internation Cooperation to Accelerate Sustainable Development in Developing Countries, and Related Domestic Policies*, A/Conf. 151/PC/L.71 (31 March 1992).

United States—Imports of Certain Automotive Spring Assemblies (Canada v. U.S.) (1983), GATT Doc. L/5333, para. 56, 30th supp. B.I.S.D. (1984) 107 at 125.

United States—Measures Affecting Alcohol and Malt Beverages (Canada v. U.S.) (1992), GATT Doc. DS 23/R, para. 5.43, 39th supp. B.I.S.D. (1992) 206 at 283.

United States—Prohibition of Imports of Tuna and Tuna Products from Canada (Canada v. U.S.), (1982), GATT Doc. L/5198, para. 4.8, 29th supp. B.I.S.D. (1983) 91 at 108.

United States—Restrictions on Imports of Tuna (Mexico v. United States) (1991), GATT Doc. DS 21/R, 39th supp. B.I.S.D. (1992) 155; 30 I.L.M. (1991).

United States—Section 337 of the Tariff Act of 1930 (European Economic Community v. United States) (1989), GATT Doc. L/6439, para 5.26, 36th supp. B.I.S.D. (1990) 345 at 392–3.

Uruguayan Recourse to Article XXIII (1961), GATT Doc. L/1923, 11th supp. B.I.S.D. (1962) 97.

World Charter for Nature, UNGA Res. No. 37/7 (28 October 1982).

Cases Cited

Canada

Heineman v. Adventure Charcoal Enterprises Ltd., 1 *Canadian Environmental Law News,* No. 3 at 4 (Ontario High Court 1972).

Just v. British Columbia, [1989] 2 S.C.R. 1228.

Kamloops (City of) v. Nielsen, [1984] 2 S.C.R. 2.

Nisga's Tribal Council v. British Columbia (Environmental App. Bd.), 3 C.E.L.R. (N.S.) (B.C.S.C.).

Old Man River Society v. Canada (Minister of Transport), [1992] 1 S.C.R.

R. v. Bata Industries Limited et al. (1992), 7 C.E.L.R. (N.S.) 245 (Ontario Provincial Court).

R. v. City of Sault Ste. Marie (1978), 40 C.C.C. (2d) 353 (Supreme Court of Canada).

Re British Columbia Wildlife Federation and Nu-West Development Corporation (1977), 72 D.L.R. (3d) 381 (B.C.S.C.).

Re Metal Co and MacFarlane (1974), 41 D.L.R. (3d) 161 (Ontario Supreme Court).

Re Pim and Minister of Environment (1979), 23 O.R. (2d) 45 (Ontario Div. Ct.).

Reference Re s.94(2) British Columbia Motor Vehicle Act, [1985] 2 S.C.R. 486.

Stein v. City of Winnipeg (1975), 41 D.L.R. (3d) 223 (Manitoba Court of Appeal).

United States

Block v. Community Nutrition Institute, 467 U.S. 340 (1984).

Brief of *Amici Curiae* Natural Resources Defense Council et al., U.S. Court of Appeals for the District of Columbia Circuit, No. 93-5212, *Public Citizen et al. v. U.S. Trade Representative* (14 August 1993).

Chevron USA Inc. v. Natural Resources Defense Council Inc. 467 U.S. 837 (1984).

Citizens to Preserve Overton Park v. Volpe, 401 U.S. 402 (1971).

Ethyl Corporation v. EPA, 541 F.2d 1 (D.C. Cir. 1976).

International Trade Reporter, 27 May 1992, *Mississippi Poultry Association Inc. v. Madigan,* No. J91-0086[W], DC SMiss 4/23/92.

Other Sources

Annual Program and Budget for the North American Commission for Environmental Cooperation (NACEC) (July 1994).

Arden-Clarke, C. "The General Agreement on Tariffs and Trade, Environmental Protection and Sustainable Development." World Wide Fund for Nature, discussion paper (June 1991).

Audley, John. "Impacts of Trade Agreements on U.S. Environmental Protection and Resource Conservation Efforts." Hearing before the Subcommittee on Environment and Natural Resources of the House Committee on Merchant Marine and Fisheries, 103d Cong. 1st Sess. 23-24 (1993).

Birdsall, Nancy, and David Wheeler. "Openness Reduces Industrial Pollution in Latin America: The Missing Pollution Haven Effect." (Paper presented to the World Bank Symposium on International Trade and the Environment, 21–22 November 1991.)

Blanco, H. Address (Institute of the Americas, 4 March 1994, unpublished).

Bureau of National Affairs. *U.S. Environmental Laws* (Washington, D.C.: Bureau of National Affairs, 1988).

Canadian Environmental Law Association—NAFTA Facts. "NAFTA and the Democratic Process" (Toronto, 1992).

———. "NAFTA and Standards" (Toronto, 1993).

Canadian Nature Federation, Canadian Environmental Law Association, Sierra Club—Canada, Rawson Academy of Aquatic Sciences—Canada, Friends of the Earth—Canada, Cultural Survival—Canada, Pollution Probe—Canada, National Audubon Society, National Wildlife Federation, Community Nutrition Institute, Environmental Defense Fund, Joint News Release. "Binational Statement on Environmental Safeguards That Should Be Included in the North American Free Trade Agreement" (28 May 1992).

Dasgupta, P. S., and K.G. Maler. "The Environment and Emerging Development Issues." (Paper presented to the World Bank Annual Conference on Development Economics, 26–27 April 1990.)

Dean, Judith. "Trade and the Environment: A Survey of the Literature." Background paper, *World Development Report, 1992* (World Bank, April 1991).

Emerson, Peter M., and Elizabeth Wallace Bourbon. "The Border Environment and Free Trade." (Prepared for the North American Institute, 8 November 1991.)

Ferretti, Janine. "Process-Related Trade Measures: Lessons from NAFTA." (Paper presented to the OECD Workshop on Trade and Environment: PPM Issues, 6–7 April 1994.)

Garten, Jeffrey E. "The Changing Face of North America in the Global Economy." (Address before the Americas Society and the Council of the Americas, 17 May 1994, unpublished.)

———. Address (Consejo Profesional de Ciebdas Economicas, 25 March 1994, unpublished).

Gilbreath, Jan, and J. Ben Tonra. *Environment: Unwelcome Guest at the Free Trade Party,* Center for Strategic and International Studies (CSIS). Policy Paper on the Americas, Vol. III (Washington, D.C.: 1992).

Gillespie, C. "An American Perspective on the Summit of the Americas." (Address to the National Round Table on the Environment and the Economy Workshop on Advancing Sustainable Development at the Summit of the Americas, 11 July 1994, unpublished.)

Grossman, G.M., and A.B. Krueger. "Environmental Impacts of the North American Free Trade Agreement." (Paper presented to the Woodrow Wilson School, Princeton University, February 1992, unpublished.)

Hittle, Alex. "The Environmental Implications of the Uruguay Round of GATT." Hearing before the Subcommittee on Economic Policy, Trade and Environment, of the House Committee on Foreign Affairs, 103d Cong., 2d Sess. (1994).

Hudec, Robert, and Daniel Farber. "Distinguishing Environmental Measures from Trade Barriers." (Prepared for Workshop on International Economic Policy, University of Minnesota, 17 November 1992.)

Hudson, Stewart. "Trade, Environment, and the Pursuit of Sustainable Development." (Paper presented to the World Bank Symposium on International Trade and the Environment, 21–22 November 1991.)

Hudson, Stewart, and Rodrigo J. Prudencio. "The North American Commission on Environment and Other Supplemental Environmental Agreements: Part Two of the NAFTA Package" (National Wildlife Federation, 4 February 1993).

Kantor, Mickey. Address (Georgetown University Law Center, 21 January 1994, unpublished).

———. Address (Global Legislators Organization for a Balanced Environment, 28 February 1994, unpublished).

Kirton, John, and Sarah Richardson, eds. *The Halifax Summit, Sustainable Development and Institutional Reform* (Ottawa: National Round Table on the Economy and the Environment, 1995).

Kneese, A.V. "Environmental Stress and Political Conflicts: Salinity in the Colorado River." Discussion Paper QE88-12 (Washington, D.C.: Resources for the Future, 1988).

Low, P., ed. *International Trade and the Environment*, World Bank Discussion Papers, no. 159 (Washington, D.C., 1992).

Low, P., and A. Yeats. "Do 'Dirty' Industries Migrate?" (Discussion paper presented at the Symposium on International Trade and the Environment, 21–22 November 1991.)

McClosky, Michael. Testimony before the Senate Committee on Foreign Relations, 22 March 1991.

McClosky, Michael, and John Audley. "Environmental Concerns Regarding the North American Free Trade Agreement" (Sierra Club, February 1993).

National Audubon Society, Grupo de los Cien Internacional and Centro Mexicano de Derecho Ambiental, Press Release. "Environmental Coalition Files First Petition with NAFTA Commission to Investigate Massive Bird Kill at Silva Reservoir in Guanajuato, Mexico" (7 June 1995).

National Wildlife Federation and Pollution Probe Canada. "Environmental Issues Related to the North American Free Trade Agreement," 7 March 1992.

Natural Resources Defense Council et al. "Review of Environmental Concerns Arising from a North American Free Trade Agreement," 7 April 1992.

Pearson, Charles S., and Robert Repetto. "Reconciling Trade and Environment: The Next Steps." (Paper prepared for the Trade and Environment Committee of the EPA, December 1991.)

Pollution Probe/Sierra Club of Canada, Joint Press Release. "NAFTA Environmental Side Deal: Good Container, Little Content," 14 September 1992.

"Proposed Principles for a Federal/Provincial Agreement Regarding Federal/Provincial Relationships Under NACE." Meeting of the Canadian Council of Ministers of the Environment, 12 May 1993.

Reilly, William. Testimony before the Subcommittee on International Trade of the Senate Committee on Finance, 16 September 1992.

Rentschler, M. "Memo to U.S. Non-Governmental Organizations" (Washington, D.C., 14 March 1994, unpublished).

Report of the Regional Conference at the Ministerial Level on the Follow-up to the Report of the World Commission on Environment and Development in the ECE Region, *Action for a Common Future*, Bergen, Norway, 8–16 May 1990.

Report of the World Commission on Environment and Development. *Our Common Future* (New York: United Nations, 1987).

Reuter Financial Service, Press Release. "NAFTA Commission Asked to Check Mexico Bird Kill" (7 June 1995).

Sierra Club, Press Release. "Administration Mexican Free Trade Proposal Sierra Club Charges a Lack of Assured Environmental Performance Measures" (2 May 1991).

St. Pierre, A. "Impact of Environmental Measures on International Trade," Report 76-91-E (Ottawa: Conference Board of Canada).

USAID. "Environmental Market Conditions and Business Opportunities in Key Latin American Countries," Business Focus Series (October 1992).

U.S. Environmental Protection Agency. "Integrated Environmental Plan for the Mexican–U.S. Border Area: The First Stage" (Washington, D.C.: Environmental Protection Agency, 1992).

Van Grasstek, C. "The Political Economy of Trade and the Environment in the United States Senate." (Paper presented to the World Bank Symposium on International Trade and the Environment, 21–22 November 1991).

Ward, Justin, and S. Jacob Scherr. "Environmental Elements of the NAFTA Package." Testimony of the Natural Resources Defense Council before the Committee on Environment and Public Works, U.S. Senate, 16 March 1993.

Webb, K. "La lutte contre la pollution au Canada: La réglementation des années quatre-vingts." Administrative Law Series, Law Reform Commission of Canada, 1988.

Weekly Compilation of Presidential Documents, 1992.

Williams Commission, *United States Economic Policy in an Interdependent World* (1971) at 777–779.

Winham, Gilbert. "Enforcement of International Environment Measures: The North American Agreement on Environmental Cooperation." (Paper presented to the Conference on Enforcement of International Environmental Agreements, Institute on Global Conflict and Cooperation, 30 September 1993.)

Index

About the Authors

Pierre Marc Johnson is an attorney and a physician by training. He is a professor of law at McGill University and senior counsel with the offices of Guy & Gilbert in Montreal. From 1976 to 1988 he occupied various cabinet posts and was Premier of Quebec in 1985. He is member of various corporate boards and vice-chair of the National Round Table on Environment and the Economy of Canada, as well as chair of its Foreign Policy Committee.

André Beaulieu is an attorney specializing in environmental law who has worked for a number of national and international organizations dealing with governance and the environment. He is currently senior policy analyst in the Office of the Privy Council, Government of Canada.